RAILWAYS

PAST, PRESENT & FUTURE

RAILWAYS

PAST, PRESENT & FUTURE

G Freeman Allen

Foreword by
Sir Peter Parker

William Morrow and Company, Inc.
New York
1982

Endpapers: Locomotive shed at Valladolid, Spain.
Page 1: Union Pacific diesel locomotive at Union Station, Los Angeles.
Pages 2–3 (previous page): Southern Pacific train, headed by a
4–6–2 locomotive, leaving San Francisco in 1952.
Page 7 (overleaf): British Rail's HST 'Inter-City 125'.

Copyright © 1982 by Orbis Publishing Limited

First published in Great Britain in 1982 by
Orbis Publishing Limited

First published in the United States of America in 1982 by
William Morrow and Company, Inc.

ISBN 0-688-00636-1

Printed and bound in Italy

FIRST EDITION
1 2 3 4 5 6 7 8 9 10

CONTENTS

FOREWORD

Geoffrey Freeman Allen brings authority to any study of the evolution of modern railways. Railwaymen can say he has grown up with us, has written about us – sometimes critically, but always fairly – and knows us through and through.

Indeed, he follows his distinguished father Cecil J. Allen, whose writing captivated all those interested in railways and whose lectures were heard by thousands of enthusiasts over a period of more than sixty years. The equally distinguished son brings to *Railways: Past, Present and Future* more than a touch of his father's class and style, coupled with a remarkable depth of knowledge and a dry, crackling wit. What comes right through this compelling book is not only his practical experience of railways here – I would expect that – but also his knowledge of railway operation and management all over the world.

He looks back to the earliest days of railways, going behind the scenes in Czarist Russia, evoking the romantic and dangerous years of the birth of American railroads, and describing the spread of railway systems into China and Japan and across the world. The historical perspective focuses the astonishing achievements of British engineers and entrepreneurs. They made life different literally for much of the world in an age when the tide of technical progress was undeniable, unquestioned and uncomplicated.

The author is as authoritative about what he aptly calls 'The New Age of the Train'. The case for railways is undeniable nowadays: the world is learning to respect anew this transport mode which carries answers to the problems of energy and the environment, and is fundamental to the basic industries and the quality of life in our cities. With the coming of the microchip, I am particularly pleased to see the scope he envisages for electronics in the operation of railways.

When all is told, Geoffrey Freeman Allen wisely sees the modern train in the spectrum of inter-modal transport – as he writes, 'It is also the inter-modal age'.

This is a work of significance and of dedication – a fitting reflection of the dedication of those who work on railways.

SIR PETER PARKER, MVO
Chairman, British Railways Board

THE STEAM RAILWAY IS BORN

For the second time in 150 years railways are offering the only satisfying answer to an urgent economic requirement. In essence, the need which spurred the creation of railways in the early nineteenth century and the demand prompting their 'redis-covery' now is the same: economy in bulk movement. The cost at issue in the nineteenth century was the time and money spent in the road or waterway transport of raw materials to the hungry centres of the burgeoning Industrial Revolution. Today, control of financial costs is even more critical to industry, and the modern railway has new tools to increase its competitiveness on that score. Even more important to the present-day world, however, is the railway's ability to move goods and people in bulk at less cost in energy than any other form of overland transport and with comparable speed and precision.

A glib aphorism of the oil-flush 1950s had it that if the internal combustion engine had been invented ahead of the steam locomotive, no one would have bothered with railways. Steam railways, maybe: but supposing electric traction had antedated steam locomotion? The extra-ordinary rate at which European road hauliers were entrusting their trailers to the railways' 'piggyback' operation for the longer hauls in the 1970s was only one of the more conspicuous indications that there was growing appreciation of the finite character of some primary sources of energy – an appreciation which could well prompt the conception of an electric railway, supposing it did not already exist. By the last quarter of the twentieth century, especially with the perfection of nuclear generating technology, electricity was clearly the most economical method of translating primary energy material into power. And the railway train was the most economical way of using that power for the haulage of goods or people, because, of all transport modes, it was the only one with a fixed path that simplified the continuous supply to it of current from a static generating system. Moreover, the ex-traordinarily rapid development of electric traction practice and of electronics since the middle of the twentieth century had not only enabled trains to use current at full industrial strength straight from national grid systems, but had perfected re-markably compact apparatus to transmute the high-voltage feed into finely controlled power at the wheel rims. It had also evolved, in the electric locomotive with three-phase alternating current motors, a traction unit of unparalleled versatility; a machine of less than 100 tons' weight capable of propelling either a 700 ton passenger train quickly up to 125 mph (200 km/h) or a 2,000 ton freight train at a steady 60 mph (100 km/h).

Such potential could be wasted, how-ever, if it were not continuously applied to haulage of maximum-tonnage trainloads. The railway's cardinal virtue was that the tightly disciplined operation of its reserved highways, properly exploited, enabled it to move masses of people or goods between key points faster, more reliably and with greater economy in energy and manpower than any other medium. It was not a superior medium in any sense for the local collection or delivery of passengers and freight in small lots. The sensible transport policy for the 1980s and beyond was therefore an inter-modal marriage of rail, road, sea and air, harnessing them into systems that smoothly transferred freight or passengers from one to the other in such a way that each component of a door-to-door journey was performed by the most energy-efficient means, yet without pre-judicing overall efficiency or customer convenience. Hence the anxiety of metro-politan authorities the world over to rationalize their public transport, so that low-capacity road vehicles no longer competed with high-capacity radial rail-ways for commuters, but served as their carefully co-ordinated local feeders. Hence, too, the eager embrace of the container by freight shippers, because in that way merchandise could be trunked in bulk, but so easily distributed by the individual box at collection points.

It did not really need an oil crisis or latter-day electric traction expertise to reassert the vital need for railways in the 1970s. If the doom predicted for rail transport in some countries in the years just before the 1973 Arab-Israeli im-broglio had taken place, it would have been largely self-inflicted – the result of late nineteenth-century insensibility to the railway's real purpose, to run trains along routes of bulk traffic flow. When Govern-ments as well as self-interested promoters encouraged the indiscriminate spread of main-line offshoots into countrysides that would forever be purely agricultural, they inevitably drove the railways to deal more and more in vehicle- rather than train-loads. That squandered the inherent economy of the railway. Because, by then, railways were developing the operating disciplines that are now one of their distinctions, it also compelled them to evolve ramified management structures. And it helped to enmesh the railways in intricate regulations that were created to

William Hedley's Puffing Billy *of 1813. This engine was built for the Wylam Colliery tramway and was the first with more than one axle powered.*

The circular railway ('Catch me who can') set up in Euston Square by Richard Trevithick in 1809. This drawing by T. Rowlandson has little authenticity.

control their competition with all other forms of transport, ranging from local parcels carriers to barge lines. The inheritance of a fixed infrastructure and a tightly organized operating method disinclined twentieth-century railway managements from any attempt to break out of this mould; and partisan interests frustrated most Government efforts to reshape railways to the changing needs of a motor transport age.

As a result, to quote British Rail's chairman Sir Peter Parker, 'some twenty years ago the railway the world over appeared to be the incurable victim of a dinosaur syndrome: a huge unwieldy body far removed from its head, its wits seeming quite unable to cope with the nimble, ubiquitous and virile competition on the roads and the soaring speed advantage of modern jet aircraft. Some Governments tried to nourish the beast with investment; most tried to hold it on a subsistence diet, frankly fearful of the political stink that a corpse of this size would generate throughout the countryside if allowed to

expire. But inside the dinosaur was a thinner, tougher, faster beast fighting to get out.'

THE FIRST STEAM LOCOMOTIVES

That beast was essentially a railway once more concentrating on the bulk movement function which over 150 years ago inspired the idea of marrying steam locomotion to a fixed track. Horse haulage of individual coal wagons over a tracked way had been known in Europe since the late sixteenth century, but their use had been confined to carrying loads over short distances between points of origin and places where traditional forms of conveyance, like barge or ship, could take over. With the onset of the Industrial Revolution and increased demand for raw materials and manufactured goods, there was clearly room for new and improved methods of transport. The steam engine had been in use as a water-pumping machine since the beginning of the eighteenth century, but only towards the end of the century did one inventor sense that it could provide the means of hauling large loads in a single movement. He was the burly Cornishman, Richard Trevithick, a man who had established a considerable reputation as a pumping machinery engineer.

Trevithick had already demonstrated one of his first steam carriage essays in London when, late in 1803, he received an order from the Pen-y-Darren ironworks near Merthyr Tydfil, in South Wales, for a stationary steam engine to serve the plant's rolling mill. The ironworks' owner, Samuel Homfray, had been dealing with Trevithick for some years and was convinced of his genius. Not so his neighbours in the iron-founding business. Goaded by one cynic in particular, who was prepared to back his scepticism with a 500-guinea wager, Homfray arranged with Trevithick that the new engine be adapted and wheeled for public trial as a locomotive on the works plateway.

On 13 February 1804 the Pen-y-Darren ironworks thus became the stage for one of rail history's landmarks: the first steam locomotive outing on rails. Within a few hours Homfray was 500 guineas to the good. As a Bristol newspaper described it a few days later, the engine 'was made use of to convey along the tram road 10 tons' weight of bar iron from Pen-y-Darren ironworks to the place where it joins the Glamorganshire canal, upwards of 9 miles [14.5 km] distant; and it is necessary to observe that the weight of the load was soon increased from 10 to 15 tons by about 70 persons riding on the trams, who, drawn thither (as well as many hundreds of others) by invincible curiosity, were eager to ride . . . The engine performed the journey without feeding the boiler or using any water, and will travel with ease at the rate of 5 miles an hour [8 km/h].'

Nothing came of Trevithick's triumph for some years because the flimsy plateway crumbled under the engine's weight. The subsequent development of cast-iron rails with a longitudinal fish-bellied form did not achieve sufficient strength to resist fractures, so for some time the design of a locomotive with enough adhesion weight for load haulage up the often steep grades of the old horse-worked plateways or tramways looked an intractable problem. Would-be builders explored an exotic variety of adhesion aids. One had spikes protruding from the wheel tyres like the petals of a cactus dahlia to dig into the ground, while to his *Mechanical Traveller* of 1813 William Brunton appended an extraordinary contraption of hinged legs with which the machine 'walked' along a towpath between the rails; when its feet managed to avoid sticking in the mud, this oddity actually managed a speed of 3 mph

(5 km/h) on the Newbottle Colliery line in Durham, but its boiler eventually blew up.

The only lasting contribution to future rail development of this period was the combination of locomotive cog wheel and toothed rack rail which John Blenkinsop devised for Matthew Murray's successful locomotives for the Middleton Colliery railway near Leeds, opened on 12 August 1812. The first locomotives built outside England were manufactured on the Blenkinsop model – but unsuccessfully – by the Prussian Mines Administration in 1816, following a visit to Leeds by two representatives of the German concern.

The key to the adhesion problem was turned by William Hedley, superintendent of the Wylam Colliery near Newcastle. It was to apply power to more than one pair of wheels, which Hedley achieved by gearing. In combination with the foreman of his blacksmith's shop, Timothy Hackworth, Hedley proved his point in the so-called *Puffing Billy* of 1813. Originally built as four-wheelers, *Puffing Billy* and *Wylam Dilly* of the same year soon had to be rebuilt as eight-wheelers because of their damage to the track, but in the latter form they were so proficient that *Wylam Dilly* was not retired until 1866.

The cog drive apart, these Wylam engines refined steam-engine technology generally. The credit for that was undoubtedly Hackworth's, which explains why Hedley soon faded from railway history, whereas Hackworth was picked by George Stephenson to be the Stockton & Darlington Railway's resident engineer, eventually managing Stephenson's Newcastle works and becoming one of England's foremost locomotive designers in the burgeoning days of the railway.

GEORGE STEPHENSON AND THE
FIRST PUBLIC RAILWAYS
George Stephenson, born alongside the Wylam tramroad in 1781, was a self-taught engineering prodigy. The second of six children of a colliery fireman, he had already earned himself a better mining job than his father by the time he was seventeen, and at thirty-one he was the enginewright for a whole group of Northumberland collieries centred on Killingworth. By then he was obsessed with the commercial and economic potential of steam locomotion, and absorbed in rectifying the weak points, as he saw them, of the engines so far built.

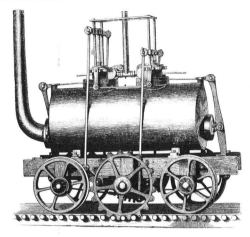

Above: Blenkinsop's engine built for the Middleton Colliery near Leeds in 1811. This was one of the first railways to use steam locomotion successfully.
Below: A Stephenson family group with George (seated) and Robert (right).

Within a year of *Puffing Billy* first blasting hoarsely past his birthplace cottage at Wylam, Stephenson was seeking his employer's consent to build a locomotive of his own. 'I said to my friends', he recalled years later, 'there was no limit to the speed of such an engine, if the works could be made to stand.' The mineowner, Lord Ravensworth, gave him both moral and financial backing and against considerable odds of unskilled help and no practical workshop experience of his own Stephenson had his first Killingworth locomotive, *Blücher*, in steam by the summer of 1814.

Blücher was not much of an advance on its predecessors, but Stephenson's subsequent Killingworth engines were. He discovered the value of exhausting steam through a narrow chimney so as to create a blast that would suck air rapidly over the firegrate and intensify its heat. Like the

earlier practitioners in high-pressure steam Stephenson still thought it advisable to mount the cylinders in the boiler so as to avoid condensation in steam passages, but by putting them on top of the boiler he simplified the mechanical drive to the wheels. And instead of cogs he eventually hit on a method of coupling driving wheels by connecting rods and crank pins which no successor would better, only refine. Within only two or three years of *Blücher*'s debut, and with the coalfields of northern England now interlaced by horse-operated railways, Stephenson was already building engines for other collieries.

Apart from internal works wagonways, a score of railways had been opened or begun up and down Britain by 1820. Most were dedicated to industrial use, but in 1801 Parliament had granted an Act establishing the principle of a public railway to the country's first such enterprise, the Surrey Iron Railway. Horse-operated, this concern's first section ran some 9½ miles (15 km) from the Thames at Wandsworth to the latter-day London suburb of Croydon and, had it not later run out of financial wind, was intended to stretch all the way to the south coast at Portsmouth. While it did not expect or provide for passenger traffic, the Surrey Iron Railway was designed, like the primary means of inland freight transport at the time, the canals, for toll use by any carrier who cared to produce his own vehicles capable of running on its rails. The railway had no wagons of its own.

The 1801 Act laid the foundation for the world's first public locomotive-operated railway. Seeking a more efficient outlet for coal from the inland south Durham pits in the north of England, a company fronted by the Quaker financier, Edward Pease, was eventually persuaded to seek Parliament's assent to a public tramway for 'the conveyance of coal, iron, lime, corn and other commodities from the interior of the county of Durham to the town of Darlington and the town and port of Stockton'. An Act was granted in 1821 and soon afterwards George Stephenson called on Pease to ask for appointment as the project's engineer.

Pease, an astute businessman, was impressed at once – still more so after he had visited Killingworth. Not only was Stephenson appointed the line's engineer at a salary of £300 a year, his advice that the system be built as an iron railway, not the previously planned wooden tramway,

The world's first steam-hauled public passenger train opened the Stockton & Darlington Railway on 27 September 1825.

was adopted and it was agreed, with Parliament's sanction in 1823, that part of the new railway be worked by steam locomotives. Pease and a few others were confident that steam traction would work – so much so that they financed the start of Stephenson's locomotive works at Forth Street, Newcastle upon Tyne in 1823 – but another strong faction of the Stockton & Darlington directors had acute misgivings and insisted that horse power or rope haulage with stationary engine power be retained for some sections of the line.

The railway was ceremonially opened on 27 September 1825. *Locomotion*, one of Stephenson's first two 'improved locomotive engines' for the Stockton & Darlington Railway (S&DR), triumphantly steamed the 21 miles (34 km) from Shildon to Stockton with a load of 69 tons in tow: 6 wagons full of coal and sacks of flour; a covered coach for the directors; 21 wagons fitted with wooden benches and crowded with nearly 600 excited passengers; and at the tail another 6 loaded coal wagons. On the way they reached a speed of 15 mph (24 km/h).

The S&DR was a much severer test of steam traction than any of the colliery lines and Stephenson's first engines were not up to it. Steam's reliability for load haulage

over 20 miles (32 km) and more was not proven until 1827 when Timothy Hackworth – often unjustly overshadowed by Stephenson in accounts of these pioneering days – produced at the Newcastle works he supervised for Stephenson the *Royal George*, first of a line of six-coupled engines which were to characterize S&DR motive power for years to come. Its performance immediately put that of any preceding locomotive in the shade.

But even when steam was at its most fallible in the first two years its potential economy over horse traction was patent. Moreover, horses, although they monopolized the railway's passenger traffic for eight years, were soon overwhelmed by the rapid growth of the line's freight traffic. That was attracted by the obvious thrift of the new transport medium. Within only two months it had cut the delivered coal price in Stockton by a third. Very soon parts of the track had to be doubled and relaid with heavier rail, but more importantly it became clear that the first concept of a public railway, open to anyone's vehicles on payment of a toll, was not sustainable: the owning company must take full control of a disciplined operation. Amongst other things, this was to lead to mandatory fencing of British railway property under the Railway Clauses Act of 1845.

The news of the S&DR which rippled round the Western world was not only of its efficiency but of its profitability. Pease's forecast of a 5 per cent return on capital within a year had been achieved and thereafter dividends went on rising until the rate was as high as 14 per cent by the early 1830s. Thus it was a trip to England to see the S&DR which sent the Quaker Evan Thomas back to Baltimore, Maryland, determined to persuade his fellow businessmen in the city to scrap their plan for a canal to protect their maritime trade from rape by canal-building in New York and Pennsylvania, and to go for a railway instead. Incorporation of the Baltimore & Ohio Railroad – though initially as a horse-powered line – followed on 24 April 1827. In France the first line – 10 miles (16km) long – was opened from the rich coalfield at St Etienne to the Loire river at Andrézieux on 1 October 1828; it was part rope-worked and part horse-operated, although the engineer Marc Séguin was convinced that the S&DR had proved steam as the rail traction of the future. The Germans, surprisingly, were hesitant about railways in the 1820s, but the Austrians had commissioned the opening stage of their first public railway by 1827, as is described in the succeeding chapter.

Back in England the world's first public railway to have its passenger and goods traffic worked entirely by steam was now taking shape. The north-western cities of Liverpool and Manchester had been expanding trade and inhabitants rapidly since the late eighteenth century (after 1790 each more than doubled its population in three decades) and talk of a railway between the two was crystallizing into firm planning by 1821. The area was interlaced by rivers and canals, but although the canal carriers undercut road by 50 per cent they were complacent about their efficiency. They were coining money, too: some canal and river navigation companies were disbursing annual dividends as high as 50 per cent. Small wonder, then, that the Liverpool merchant leading the railway promotion stressed to Parliament the scheme's value as an 'Exposure of the exorbitant and unjust charges of the Water Carriers'.

That was one of the first salvoes in the bitter struggle between railway and canal interests which spanned the early decades of British railway building. Each side fought for allies among that class which had and exercised a great power to simplify, complicate or frustrate entirely the building of new railways – the

landowners whose ground the new lines would skirt or cross. The Liverpool & Manchester scheme was the first to come up against the concerted antagonism of canal men and landowners.

George Stephenson had been appointed the embryonic Liverpool & Manchester Railway's locomotive engineer in 1823. Then, after Parliament had granted the Liverpool & Manchester company an Act, he was made chief engineer of the whole project in 1826. In 1827 his son Robert was ready to take charge of the locomotive building works at Newcastle, so George could concentrate on the civil engineering side of the most formidable railway construction job yet. Once again he had taken on a job for which he had no formal qualification, yet he found ways to lay a firm double-track railway across the bog of Chat Moss which numerous cynics were certain he would find impassable. Other phenomenal engineering achievements for the time were the 70ft (21.3m) deep Olive

A 1975-built replica of George Stephenson's Locomotion, *which hauled the inaugural train on the Stockton & Darlington Railway in 1825.*

Mount cutting excavated from solid stone and the nine-arched viaduct which bore the line over Sankey Valley.

Worried at the continuing unreliability of many steam locomotives – and harried by some of their merchant shareholders who had no faith in steam traction at all – the Liverpool & Manchester Railway (L&MR) directors were racked by last-minute doubts. Should they play safe and go for rope haulage with stationary steam engines spaced out along the line to generate the power? The Stephensons were appalled at this craven indecision and the directors eventually compromised

with a suggestion that builders be invited to submit their machines to competitive trial for a prize of £500 on a specially completed section of track at Rainhill, near Liverpool, in October 1829.

Three contestants showed up: Timothy Hackworth's *Sanspareil*, John Braithwaite's and John Ericsson's *Novelty* (Ericsson was subsequently to revolutionize naval craft with his *Monitor*), and the Stephensons' *Rocket*. *Novelty* actually managed 40mph (64km/h), the *Rocket* only 29½mph (47.5km/h), but for reliability and all-round performance *Rocket* ambled away with the prize. It was the first locomotive to combine the fundamentals which would serve steam rail traction for the rest of its days: separate cylinders driving the wheels via short connecting rods, an arrangement which made much more efficient use of steam; and a boiler with an internal nest of longitudinal fire tubes that was served by an external, water-jacketed firebox, the most capable generator of steam.

The multi-tubular boiler was not the Stephensons' own idea, but a concept of Henry Booth's which Robert translated into hardware. The Frenchman Marc Séguin, who was appointed engineer of the St Etienne-Lyon Railway in 1829, had previously tested a full-size multi-tubular boiler and patented the concept in his own country in December 1827.

Rocket's Rainhill prowess dispelled any doubt among the L&MR directors that their railway should be entirely steam-operated, and four more locomotives of the *Rocket* type were ready for the gala opening

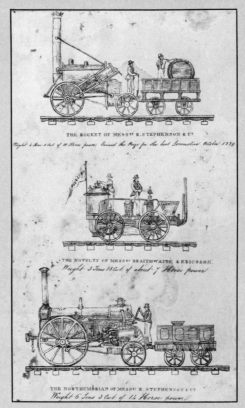

Above: Crane's lithograph of the L&MR, 1830, showing Rocket, Novelty and Northumbrian. *The boiler of the latter shows a significant development in that it was the first with integral smokebox and firebox.*
Above right: Stephenson's famous skew bridge at Rainhill on the L&MR. This is close to today's station.
Below: Braithwaite and Ericsson's Novelty *was one of the locomotives to take part in the famous Rainhill Trials of 1829.*

of the L&MR on 15 September 1830. Despite lashing by thundery rain-squalls, a vast concourse of politicians, nabobs of industry and commerce, high society and working people had gathered for a ceremonial inauguration by the Prime Minister, the Duke of Wellington. The audience even included the great actress Fanny Kemble, probably the first woman to be a self-admitted railway enthusiast, though her fancy for George Stephenson himself, who had taken her riding on his engines, may have had something to do with it. A splendidly embellished coach, crimson-canopied and topped by a ducal coronet, had been built for Wellington, whose train led the cavalcade of specials out of Liverpool's Crown Street station.

For a while only the weather seemed likely to dull a momentous day and the excitement of some 50,000 spectators along the route to Manchester. But no one had thought – who would have dared in those days? – to marshal the nobility and gentry when the inaugural special stopped, as it did at Parkside for the engine to be detached and take water. Most dismounted as they pleased, and on both sides of the train.

Among those who stepped down on the off-side was William Huskisson, a distinguished Tory with whom Wellington was trying to heal a breach that threatened his embattled Government. Stiff-jointed from a chill caught at King George IV's funeral, he lagged behind as everyone else scampered out of the path of *Rocket* when it steamed up the adjoining line after taking water. 'Huskisson!' shouted the Duke, 'do

get to your place! For God's sake get to your place!' But he stumbled, then fell, and *Rocket* ran over his leg. George Stephenson himself commandeered a coach and another locomotive to rush the casualty to Eccles at an average of 35 mph (55 km/h), but Huskisson succumbed to his injuries the same night – the world's first fatality in a train accident on a public railway.

The tragedy had no effect on the L&MR. As early as the end of that same year, 1830, it was showing an operating profit of over £14,000 and the road stagecoaches plying between Liverpool and Manchester had been drained of so many passengers that over half of them had given up.

THE FIRST NORTH AMERICAN RAILWAYS

Meanwhile the first British-built steam locomotives had reached New York in the summer of 1829, one built by the Stephensons at Newcastle, the other three by the firm of Foster, Rastrick at Stourbridge. Track-laying of the pioneer Baltimore & Ohio had only just begun, but the railway concept was already gaining adherents fast. Another two years and nine different lines would be under way in seven states, one of them planned to extend as far as 250 miles (400 km), and twenty more would be seriously projected.

The British imports were not America's first steam locomotives. An inventive New Jersey farmer, Colonel John Stevens, had caught the wind of change from across the Atlantic and begun dabbling in steam at the start of the century. As early as 1803

Stevens had patented his own multi-tubular boiler, though unlike Séguin's and Stephenson's, it was water-tube, not fire-tube. Water-tube boilers were to prove superior to fire-tube in stationary and marine applications because of their aptitude for much higher steam pressures, but they could not stand up to the punishment latter-day railway locomotives handed out to their steam generating plant: no completely successful water-tube boiler locomotive was ever built.

By 1812 Stevens was convinced that railways, not canals, were the overland transport systems of the future. 'I can see nothing to hinder a steam engine from moving at a velocity of 100 miles an hour [160 km/h],' he wrote in a brochure of that year which stupefied most of his business colleagues. Three years later Stevens nevertheless winkled out of his home state America's first railroad charter, authorizing a line from New Brunswick to Trenton. But neither for this nor for a second project

Above: The Dewitt Clinton *was built for the Mowhawk and Hudson Railroad by the West Point Foundry. In 1831 it hauled the first train from Albany to Schenectady – 17 miles – in less than an hour.*
Below right: The Atlantic *went into operation on the B & O in 1832.*

grudgingly endorsed by Pennsylvania in 1823 could Stevens drum up financial backing. He was reduced to building an oval of track round his own Hoboken backyard and there, in 1825, demonstrating the country's first steam locomotive, his crude little single-cylinder carriage of which the driving wheel was a cog engaging a central rack rail.

But already some thinking Americans were doubting the practicality of canals as a medium for the country's westward development. True, the eastern seaboard had just exulted in completion of the Erie Canal and the opening up of a navigable waterway from Buffalo to the Atlantic, and New York had been accumulating fresh wealth every time a new section of the canal was commissioned. The Erie Canal, however, traversed more or less flat country, so that there was no difficulty in maintaining its water level. To follow the trails of the pioneers into the valleys of the Mississippi, Missouri and Ohio, railways would certainly involve crossing the Allegheny Mountains. Everyone in the East already knew the Alleghenies existed; the nagging worry was that even tougher natural obstacles might stand in the way of a lateral communications system in the unexplored country further west.

The Delaware & Hudson (D&H) canal company was already confronting mountain problems in its project to transport coal from north-east Pennsylvania to the Hudson at Rondout, New York. As its chief engineer the D&H eventually appointed, in 1827, a former Erie Canal project manager, John B. Jervis, who determined that the canal must stop short of the anthracite mines: the only sensible way to cover the last, difficult 16 miles (26km) in his view was by railway, part rope-worked in a series of inclined planes and part locomotive-operated. The D&H company was then persuaded to send to England one of Jervis' assistant engineers, the youthful Horatio Allen, not merely to survey the latest steam locomotive practice but actually to buy four engines – a remarkable mandate, seeing that Allen was only twenty-six years old at the time.

So it was that *America*, *Hudson*, *Delaware* and *Stourbridge Lion* were borne into New York harbour in the summer of 1829 and transferred to river packets for the final stage of their voyage to Rondout. On 8 August 1829 it was Allen who opened *Stourbridge Lion*'s regulator to the cheers of spectators and, for the first time in American history, drove a steam locomotive on a public railway. But celebrations were short-lived. In a re-run of earlier English experience the track persistently crumbled under *Stourbridge Lion*. She was soon carted off to store, never to steam again, and none of her three sisters ever turned a wheel on the D&H.

Allen was in no way disillusioned, however. Picked as engineer of the South Carolina Canal & Railroad Co., which the merchants of Charleston had founded in 1828 to arrest the commercial decline of their city, Allen at once grasped that in the planned 136 mile (219km) length of the new railway he had the strongest case yet for steam locomotion. And he won his case. He himself took a hand in the design of the first South Carolina engine, *Best Friend of Charleston*, which was put in hand by a New York marine engineering firm, West Point Foundry, in mid-1830 and shipped to Charleston at the end of October.

The following Christmas Day, 1830, Allen had enough confidence in his machine to write the next important page in American railroad history. Propelling a beflagged flatcar with a cannon strapped to the deck, plus three gunners to fire it in incessant salute, and trailing a string of little four-wheeled coaches wherein some two hundred of Charleston society sat back-slapping each other on their enterprise, *Best Friend* steamed proudly down the first six miles (10km) of track to be completed. America had seen its first public steam-hauled passenger train.

After six months of successful work, sadly, *Best Friend*'s career was rudely interrupted. Irritated by the hiss of steam, a callow fireman tied down her safety valve whereupon – inevitably – the boiler exploded. Incredibly one of the railroad's mechanics painstakingly collected and later reassembled the bits and pieces of the disintegrated locomotive, which eventually resumed a working life under the fitting title of *Phoenix*. Meanwhile, the company sought to reassure its customers by interposing a barrier-wagon loaded with six bales of cotton between locomotive and coaches on all its trains. 'It will protect travellers when the locomotive explodes,' proclaimed the company's public notices with supreme fatalism.

By now the newborn Baltimore & Ohio (B&O) had overcome its reservations about steam power. The B&O had previously been discouraged by no less than Robert Stephenson himself, who had discounted the feasibility of locomotives negotiating a curve of less than 900ft (274m) radius, whereas their terrain had forced the B&O to go as sharp as 400ft (122m). This the B&O patiently explained to a rich New York philanthropist, Peter Cooper, who had urged them to stable their horses and buy steam locomotives. Convinced a horse-worked railway was no match for water transport, Cooper took his put-down as a do-it-yourself challenge.

With an iron-foundry to hand but no practical experience in steam engine construction, and with a good deal of makeshift material (he made his boiler tubes from musket barrels), he put together a little one-ton, vertical-boilered four-wheeler. 'I called it *Tom Thumb*', he recalled years later, 'because it was so insignificant. I didn't intend it for actual service, but only to show the directors that it could be done.'

And so he did. On 28 August 1830 *Tom Thumb* was hitched to a wagon bearing a score of the B&O's hierarchy and – not without a trauma or two – took them 13 miles (21 km) down the track and back, covering a mile in little more than 3¼ minutes at one point. The B&O directors turned about and early in 1831 announced their own 'Rainhill Trial', offering first and second prizes of $4,000 and $3,500 respectively for the most proficient four-wheeled locomotive of not more than 3½ tons, capable of hauling 15 tons at 15 mph (24 km/h) on level track.

The B&O's contest, attracting only five entries and won by the diminutive *York*, brainchild of a Pennsylvania watchmaker named Phineas Davis, elicited nothing as significant for the future of steam locomotive technology as the Liverpool & Manchester's Rainhill Trials did in the Stephensons' *Rocket*. So advanced was English practice, in fact, that many people felt locomotives were best imported from

across the Atlantic. The only snag was that the English were developing the other components of their railways to keep pace with the emerging potential of their locomotives. With track reinforced, they were aligning their routes for pace and designing their next generation of locomotives for speed, whereas for economy in their much less friendly terrain the cash-hungry American railroad companies were laying down much lighter track and going to the limit of sharp curvature to avoid expensive earthworks.

Consequently, when the Mohawk & Hudson Railway in 1831 brought in one of Stephenson's new inside-cylinder four-coupled locomotives of the *Samson* type, it pounded the line's metal-topped wooden rails to pieces. Chief engineer of this 17 mile (27 km) railway from Albany to the Erie Canal at Schenectady, New York State's first, which ran its first passenger train on 9 August 1831, was John B. Jervis. He had also designed the locomotive which headed that inaugural train, the West Point Foundry-built *DeWitt Clinton*. The fiasco of his imported Stephenson engine was now made one pretext for his dismissal by the victors in a boardroom *putsch* on the Mohawk & Hudson.

But theirs was the blunder. In his *Brother Jonathan* of 1832, Jervis came up with the most important improvement yet in American steam locomotive practice – the pivoted leading bogie ahead of the

driving wheel to spread weight and ensure lateral stability on curves (though some historians say that this idea, already conceived in England, had been put to the B&O by Robert Stephenson in 1828). After major engineering achievements in other fields Jervis ended up a shrewd President of the Chicago, Rock Island & Pacific Railroad.

So, at the start of the 1830s the railroad had established a secure foothold in the eastern US. Not without surviving virulent opposition, of course, though a good deal of that was motivated by blind prejudice or even terror of the beast, not commercial judgement or self-interest. There was, for instance, the cleric of Connecticut who persistently warned that one could be driven mad simply by letting one's eyes follow a passing locomotive at speed. Even in academic Boston the promoters of the 26 mile (42 km) Boston & Lowell Railway, which acquired Massachusetts' first railway charter in June 1830, had to deploy the forensic skill of Daniel Webster to counter a widespread rumour that train travel could set off brain damage. But in June 1833 the new medium won the highest possible seal of approval – temporarily speaking, that is – when Andrew Jackson made the first US Presidential rail journey on the B&O. Another nine years elapsed before Queen Victoria first entrusted her person to an English railway.

BALTIMORE & OHIO R.R. "ATLANTIC"

THE WESTERN WORLD'S FIRST MAIN LINES

The Liverpool & Manchester transformed the concept of a railway. Until 1830 only visionaries had clearly seen it as more than a short-haul medium of primary benefit to the mineral extraction industries. For years no one expected its reserved right of way to become so busy that strictly disciplined control would be essential. As late as the original Stockton & Darlington Act it was still thought feasible to permit any landowner on the verge of the line to build his own rail connection to it as he pleased (that proviso was soon amended). As long as the rail speed horizon was not much higher than 15mph (24km/h), it seemed perfectly valid to allow anyone the freedom of the track on payment of a toll – the system used by the waterways.

The Liverpool & Manchester's pace of working, its volume of freight and above all its immediate attraction of a substantial passenger traffic clearly established the railway as a new means of long-distance, inter-city transport with no parallel in existing systems; and not all that many parallels as a gilt-edged investment either,

to judge from the widely published first year's results of the Liverpool & Manchester Railway. With the country just moving in to an upswing of the trade cycle – a very influential factor in each of the really frenetic bouts of nineteenth-century British railway investment – civic authorities, commerce, industry and speculators needed no more inducement to make common cause.

The railway-building boom took time to gather momentun. For one thing the Parliamentary procedures involved in obtaining an Act for the incorporation of a company imposed a restrictive interval of at least two years between the launch of a scheme and its approval. That was generally protracted to three years, chiefly because none of the early projects stood any chance of getting through Parliament at the first attempt. The concerted opposition mobilized by affected land and waterway owners, and in later years by promoters of rival railway schemes, was too powerful. At the start, too, finance was difficult to come by. That pinned even the

Great Western Railway to its starting blocks for a time; a year after it had been promoted in Bristol with the backing of the city's five chief corporate bodies the directors had to tour Wales, the west of England and even Ireland to plead for more money as their expectations in Bristol itself had been 'in great measure disappointed'.

ENGINEERS AND NAVVIES
Just as sobering was appreciation that even the preliminary surveying, let alone the eventual engineering, of some of the lengthy main lines proposed was a much more complex proposition than laying a 30 mile (50 km) line from Liverpool to Manchester, Chat Moss notwithstanding.

Right: A J.C. Bourne lithograph published in 1839 by Ackermann, showing rock blasting at Linslade during construction of the London & Birmingham Railway. Below: First-class coaches on the L&MR. This kind of coach was basically a combination of three stagecoach bodies.

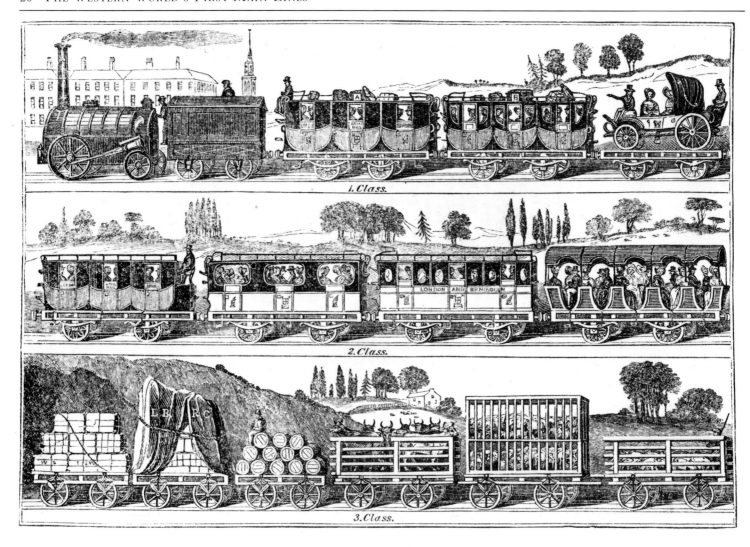

A contemporary print of the L&BR in 1837, showing all manner of conveyances including private carriages on flat cars and freight wagons.

In fixing their line of route the surveyors and engineers now had to contend with landowning opponents on the one hand, and on the other the pressures of every town with commercial interests that the new railway must not pass them by. Even more daunting was their mandate to build for speed, as George Stephenson was voicing reservations about the capability of the steam locomotive; he held that gradients must not exceed 1 in 330 if serious loss of pace uphill was to be avoided. That was the one parameter above all, which sharply distinguished the first British and American railways.

It dictated the prodigiously expensive earthworks of the London & Birmingham Railway (L&BR), begun in 1834 and opened from Euston Square to Birmingham Curzon Street on 17 September 1838. With the less spectacular Grand Junction Railway finished just over a year earlier, the L&BR completed the first main artery of the British trunk rail route system from London to Liverpool. The Stephensons, father and son, were appointed joint engineers of the London & Birmingham, but in 1833, with George's full approval, Robert was made engineer-in-chief (at a salary of £1,500 per annum plus £200 expense allowance). Not yet thirty, Robert was shouldering unquestionably the biggest civil engineering enterprise the country had yet seen. It was the first step in his confirmation as the pre-eminent and most influential of all the early railway engineers. When he died in 1859, the event was marked by a funeral that was almost a state occasion. Silent crowds lined the London route of the cortège, which on its way to his burial-place in Westminster Abbey was granted the rare privilege of passage through Hyde Park, while in his native Northumbria the city of Newcastle shut up shop for the whole day.

Construction of the London & Birmingham was parcelled out to more than a score of contractors. To a contemporary American railroad planner the terrain would have looked friendly enough to get through at ground level most of the way, given reasonable licence to curve and climb, but the Stephenson specification demanded the excavation of long, cavernous cuttings at Tring, Denbigh and Blisworth, and the boring of nine tunnels, of which the two at Watford and Kilsby, near Rugby, were far longer than anyone had previously envisaged. The 2,400 yd (2,195 m) Kilsby tunnel took thirty months to finish and cost three times the original estimate for the job. The traumas of its construction overwhelmed the contractor; panic-stricken when the workings were flooded, he staggered away to his bed and there expired – literally – of shock, obliging Robert Stephenson himself to take over that sector.

The engineering contractor was a child of the new railway age. Except for the canals, Britain had not faced such a programme of heavy public works as the railways were clearly going to offer since the building of the country's great churches in the Middle Ages. George Stephenson, who had a paranoiac streak, especially where civil engineering was concerned, kept all the supervision to himself, but Robert sensibly preferred to delegate.

As the railway-building fever intensified a good many money-grubbing mountebanks got into the contracting game, but the new profession also bred businessmen and managers of men fit to rank with the great railway engineers they served. The prince of contractors, unquestionably, was Thomas Brassey, who cut his teeth on the Grand Junction line from Liverpool to Birmingham and went on to undertake many important commissions abroad as well as at home. In all, Brassey super-intended the construction of 1,700 route-miles (2,750 km) of British railway and another 2,800 miles (4,500 km) elsewhere, as far afield as the Grand Trunk line of Canada; at times he was engaged in three or four countries simultaneously – how he managed it without benefit of telephone or teleprinter is inconceivable.

Brassey's supreme quality was his ability to organize, lead and inspire the devotion of his vagabond labour force – the 'navvies' as they were called, taking the name from the earlier 'inland navigators' who had dug the canals. Many of them were Irish, impelled to England by an upsurge of their home economy which had accelerated the local birthrate and then put employment at a premium. All were hard-drinking, pugnacious hunks of totally uninhibited manhood, used to roughing it on or near site in makeshift shanty towns, where, with their female camp-followers, they would bed down some ten or more pairs to a turf hovel. Paid at piecework rates, each could shift as much as 20 tons of spoil a height of 6 ft (1.8 m) in a day. That put them a cut above the common labourer, who would make little more than half a navvy's daily pay on a farm in the 1830s. But the incentives also made the navvies reckless of safety. Serious injury was common, fatality all too frequent; and though France's Code Napoléon had already enforced employer's liability for staff accidents, pressure for workmen's compensation in England was unavailing until the end of the century.

Nothing, however, diminished the navvies' energy, which staggered other

Bourne's lithograph of Box Tunnel, near Bath, during the construction of the GWR. The broad-gauge track was laid on longitudinal sleepers.

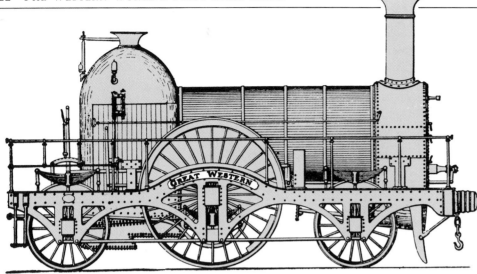

dismantled their scaffolding. The basic structure is still withstanding the 125 mph (200 km/h) London–Bristol and South Wales trains, three each way every hour, of the 1980s.

Brunel's penchant for the unexpected and his natural disinclination to take previous practice for granted were epitomized in his adoption of a 7 ft 0¼ in (2,140 mm) track gauge, instead of the 4 ft 8½ in (1,435 mm) established by Stephenson. Myth has it that Stephenson picked on his odd figure by averaging out the gauges of some specimen wagonways in Northumbria. In fact he was carrying on the 4 ft 8 in (1,422 mm) gauge to which a whole group of north-east England wagonways

Europeans when Brassey took a cadre of his own men to spearhead the labour force he engaged locally for each of his foreign commissions. '*Mon Dieu! Les Anglais, comme ils travaillent!*' a French bystander sighed as he watched Brassey's navvies attacking the earthworks of the Paris-Rouen line. The fact that the visitors were earning much more than the Continental workmen would have had something to do with it, of course. For the forty main years of British railway construction after 1830 an average of 50,000 navvies were continuously employed, but in the peak 'mania' year of 1847 the workforce reached over a quarter of a million.

BRUNEL, THE GWR AND MIXED GAUGE

Most impeccably graded and aligned of the early British trunk rail routes was the Great Western Railway's (GWR) for the greater part of its course from Bristol to London. This was the handiwork of Isambard Kingdom Brunel, the son of a highly reputed immigrant engineer, Marc Brunel, who was in charge of London's Thames Tunnel. The younger Brunel had already made a West Country name as designer of the Clifton Suspension Bridge over the Avon at Bristol when, aged twenty-seven, he successfully applied for the chief engineer's post on the GWR project.

The GWR's progenitors had taken on a man of very different character to the strictly practical Northcountrymen engineering the new railways north of London. Of French ancestry, Brunel combined a brilliant engineering brain with a powerful aesthetic sense and untramelled imagination. He was always a

Above: Daniel Gooch's Great Western *of 1846 was the first engine built entirely at the GWR's workshops at Swindon. Right: The supposed chaos of changing trains in the 1840s when transferring from broad to standard gauge.*

man for the grand gesture, the death-or-glory leap rather than the tentative experiment, so that he was as capable of catastrophic failure – as in his adoption of the 'Atmospheric System' of train propulsion for the South Devon Railway in 1844 – as of triumph.

The unpredictability of Brunel's genius was patent in the design of the Bristol line. Sweeping out of London to Reading (and keeping judicious distance from Royal Windsor and Eton, where some of the College principles not only feared the railway would make London debauchery too convenient for their pupils but even, incongruously, that it would somehow lead to the ousting of English tutors by French governesses and 'mistresses'), Brunel then steered clear of every established town solely to keep his gradient as easy as 1 in 660. But in the more undulating, and, at the approach to Bath, even hilly country west of Swindon easy gradients were impossible without a considerable detour. Thus Brunel dramatically drove Box Tunnel under a ridge on a descent of 1 in 100. To many at the time the indulgence of so steep a gradient on a line to be worked by locomotives, not stationary engines and ropes, seemed highly dangerous. It was not, of course. Nor was Brunel's daring brick-arch bridge over the Thames at Maidenhead, the unprecedented 128 ft (39 m) spans of which were confidently forecast to collapse as soon as the builders

had been built in the late eighteenth century, including the Killingworth system where Stephenson began work (quite likely a 4ft 8in gauge truck was the widest a colliery hand could push on his own). The odd half-inch was added at a later date when flanged wheels came into general use, to provide the necessary clearance between running and inner check rails at switches. Although the reference books still cite 1,435mm, the metric equivalent of 4ft 8½in, as the standard gauge of the majority of the world's railways, British Rail's latter-day vehicle-and-track research has reduced that system's norm slightly to 1,432mm, as a move to limit the tendency of vehicle bogies to lateral oscillation at high speeds.

Brunel insisted that the only way to run fast without prejudice to a locomotive's stability was to build to his much wider gauge. Some other early companies went their own way at first – in Scotland a number adopted varying sizes, while a notorious English example was the initially 5ft (1,524mm) gauge Eastern Counties Railway – but none was of a size to compare with the Great Western. And none persisted so defiantly or so long with a unique gauge as the GWR. As far as locomotive performance was concerned – and once Daniel Gooch was in the saddle at the company's Swindon locomotive works and was building to his own designs, not buying from Stephenson's works – Brunel seemed to have made his point. As early as 1847 Swindon's first product, the 2–2–2 *Great Western*, was reported to have run the 53 miles (85km) from Didcot to London's Paddington terminus at an average of 67mph (108km/h) and in 1847 the GWR was consistently running the morning express over the same stretch at more than a mile (1.6km) a minute.

By then delays and frequent loss or misdirection of goods during tranship-ment at the breaks of gauge between the GWR and its neighbours were infuriating merchants. They had become a national issue on a vital new artery from the Midlands and the north to Wales and the

A viaduct on the London & Greenwich Railway engineered by George Landman in 1836 – the first railway into London.

south-west, where the great Western's protégé, the Bristol and Gloucester, had built to the Brunel gauge but a momentarily lax GWR had then allowed the connecting Birmingham & Gloucester to slip into the Midland Railway's standard-gauge camp. A worried Parliament appointed a Gauge Commission in 1846 to consider imposing uniformity of gauge and making conversion to the selected standard mandatory. Even though Gooch's splendid engines had yet to appear the Commission frankly conceded that 'the public are mainly indebted for the present rate of speed and the increased accommodation of the railway carriages to the genius of Mr Brunel and the liberality of the Great Western Railway Company'. That apart, it damned the broad gauge and all its works, advocating compulsory conversion.

The GWR manned its ramparts in defence of Brunel's dream of extending 'the blessings of the broad gauge' to the north of England and warded off the worst. In part it was saved because the Prime Minister of the day, Sir Robert Peel, fretted that, since Parliament had authorized the GWR's adoption of this idiosyncratic gauge, an enforced conversion might legally be claimed as a charge on public funds. So at the end of the day the Gauge Act of 1846, although it made any further main-line construction except at

4ft 8½in (1,435mm) gauge illegal in Britain (the Irish were allowed to retain the 5ft 3in (1,600mm) gauge with which they had started), not only eschewed immediate conversion of the GWR and its Bristol & Exeter ally but permitted them to carry on with their putative broad-gauge extensions, not excluding a penetration to Birmingham and Wolverhampton. The only safeguard was a proviso that the Board of Trade could compel the GWR to use its own money to lay in a third rail and make its system mixed gauge.

In the following decade the GWR itself saw reason and began of its own volition to make some of its lines mixed gauge. In 1868 it began conclusive conversion to standard gauge, but the last broad-gauge train did not leave Paddington until May 1892, at the conclusion of a masterly operation which converted the whole of the London–Plymouth line and numerous West Country branches in less than a fortnight.

But pursuit of the broad-gauge story has carried us decades ahead of the point at which Brunel entered the narrative. By the start of the 1840s, with public railway construction across the English Channel still in its infancy, the skeleton of Britain's trunk railway network had already been drafted. Much of the finance was coming from the north-west, but the focal point was London. By 1841 the capital had railways operating to Birmingham, Liverpool, Manchester, the East Midlands, Leeds, Southampton and Bristol, and others agreed or under way to East Anglia,

Northumbria and Kent. The first important cross-country railway was opened from Manchester to Leeds in 1841 and Scotland's first railway of significance, the Edinburgh and Glasgow, early the following year. By then the builders were pressing on from north-west England by degrees to the Scottish border.

EXPANSION AND FRAUD
The years 1833 to 1837 were the first of boom periods for railway promotion. The national economy was buoyant and in the light of results from the completed lines the pundits as well as the promoters were promising shareholders some mouth-watering dividends. 'If this undertaking fails in producing the dividend of twenty-two per cent calculated upon in the Report,' proclaimed a shareholder at the first 1836 meeting of the Eastern Counties Railway, 'then I must say human calculations and expectations can no longer be depended upon.'

Given such sanguine faith, raising the wind for almost any scheme had become easy by the mid-1830s, so much so that in 1836–7 alone around 1,000 new route-miles (1,600km) of railway were authorized. The formulation of a valid project was all the simpler because normally Parliament required only 10 per cent of the capital to be raised as a qualification for admission to the legislative process. At the same time the price of shares was dropping fast. From £100 at the launch of the Liverpool & Manchester it had come down to £10 or even less for a stake in some

companies which opened their books in the early 1840s, so that investment in railways was no longer a businessman's preserve. Ordinary people could get in on the ground floor for a very small outlay.

For all too many of the companies floated as railway mania gripped the country the trouble came when the remaining 90 per cent of the capital had to be called up. That was where, for instance, the blind faith in human faculty of the Eastern Counties investor mentioned earlier was shattered. Three years after the company had got its 1836 Act for a 125 mile (203 km) line, the longest authorized up to that date, and had begun construction, it had only managed to garner about 70 per cent of the required capital. Bedevilled as well by feckless management – witness its start on a 5 ft (1,524 mm) gauge, which had to be expensively converted to 4 ft 8½ in (1,435 mm) within a few years – the Eastern Counties Railway had to pause for financial breath in 1843 with only half its route finished. Throughout that decade and the next it was the clown of the railway industry.

Chicanery to starve a company of capital was one of the weapons still available to enemies even when a scheme had survived the long, bitter and frequently unscrupulous forensic battle in and out of Parliament to get its Act. The last resort was physical violence, which here and there ended in some really nasty blood-letting. There was no morality in the formative years of Britain's main-line railways. With Parliament unable either to impose strict accounting practice on the mushrooming companies or to order a rational network development, and the investing public gullible as well as greedy, paradise beckoned the unprincipled speculator. Fraud was rife; and none was for a time more skilful at it than the York draper who, ignorant of the railway business but artful in the ways of men and money-making, had by 1848 seized control of companies worth £30 millions and accounting for more than a quarter of the 5,000 miles (8,000 km) of railway by then open. He was the so-called 'Railway King', George Hudson.

The situation was ripe for a freelance empire-builder and Hudson was made for the role. Starting modestly with a railway from his home base at York to Leeds, by a combination of smooth-talking investors, skimping on staff wages and materials to create a façade of profit, and blackmailing other companies into his net, he had by 1844 created the Midland Railway. Using London & North Western Railway tracks from Derby, he already had access to London. Meanwhile he had hammered into a single force under his control a number of companies squabbling over an extension northward from Darlington and had floated the North British Railway in Scotland, from which enterprise a railway throughout to Edinburgh, bridging Tyne and Tweed on two superb structures by Robert Stephenson, emerged fully operational in 1850.

Eventually Hudson's empire ranged from Bristol to the Tweed, from Cumbria to East Anglia (he was even summoned to mend the hapless Eastern Counties Railway fortunes) and into London. Elected MP for Sunderland, he was welcomed to the Tory front bench in the Commons and lionized by both the *haut monde* and the business community of the capital, who eagerly accepted every invitation to his London house at Albert Gate. But inevitably Hudson had left many seething enemies in his trail, especially the magnates of the North-West whose initiative in new railway finance he had preempted and men like Edmund Denison, whose competing Great Northern Railway scheme for a shorter route from London to York Hudson had contested with every trick in his dubious book. When Hudson's house began to fall, men like these rushed to rub his nose in the brick-dust.

Prime agents in Hudson's fall were those men of the North-West. When Hudson engineered a blatantly self-interested deal with Denison's Great Northern at the expense of his own Midland Railway, they had the backing of a host of fuming Midland shareholders for an enquiry into the company's affairs. That opened up a can of worms which, besides evicting Hudson from the Midland board, precipitated similar enquiries in other sectors of his realm. The extent to which he was found to have fudged the books to lull shareholders, paying them interest out of capital, and to have lined his own pocket by illicit share-dealing and contracting privately with his own companies, was

A photograph taken around 1860/70 showing a train on the GWR running over dual-gauge track. Total conversion to standard gauge was made by 1892.

incredible. The Eastern Counties balance sheet, for instance, revealed a discrepancy of almost £600,000, half of which had gone on a dividend share-out totalling well over twice the accountable profit. Expelled from every railway company chair he occupied and beset by lawsuits, Hudson fled the country in 1855.

No one thereafter dared to emulate Hudson's scale of fraud, but he was only the first of several ruthless moguls who would stop at little else – men like Mark Huish of the London & North Western, James Allport of the Manchester, Sheffield & Lincolnshire and later of the Midland, and John Craven of the London Brighton & South Coast. For, once the major trunk routes had been established, there was the no-man's-land between them to stake out. Years of cunning thrust and counter-thrust were still to come throughout the

The engine house at Camden on the L&BR. During steam days locomotive depots for engine changes were placed at strategic intervals along the tracks.

country as the big companies manoeuvred for the most advantageous frontiers, or stole a march on the enemy by securing running rights over another company's tracks to invade one of his most prized traffic citadels.

The Hudson scandal was only the most egregious of many which burst the railway speculation bubble in the late 1840s. The mania years were 1845–7, the most feverish of them 1846 when a record 815 separate Bills for new railways were laid before Parliament. Many of them never reached formal consideration for one reason or another, but three successive Parliamentary sessions nevertheless sanctioned in all 8,592 route-miles (13,827km) of new railway. The £43.9 millions freshly invested in railway schemes in that peak year of 1846 represented around 10 per cent of the country's annual Gross National Income at the time and swelled the railways' total capital formation to more than £200 millions, five times the gross figure at the start of the decade. Even though some 3,500 miles (5,600km) of

railway endorsed by Parliament in 1845–7 were never built, railway-building was still frenzied enough to absorb an actual expenditure of £130 millions between the start of 1846 and the end of 1849, and – as was remarked earlier – to occupy a construction force of a quarter of a million.

Various economic factors contributed to a national trade balance crisis which triggered the downturn of the railway share market that the enormities of Hudson and others accelerated. A great deal was lost in the collapse of wildly impractical or downright fraudulent schemes, but the halving of railway share prices generally between 1845 and 1850 left scarcely a family in the country unscathed, for the public at large had been betting on railway stocks. How dramatically sentiment changed and established companies retrenched can be gauged from the London Brighton & South Coast's reassurance to its shareholders as early as 1848 that 'there is no large railway company which has so small an extent of works in progress or in prospect'.

RAILWAYS SPREAD TROUGH EUROPE

Meanwhile, in sharp contrast, the first main-line railways on the European mainland had been taking carefully ordered shape. The most intent student of George Stephenson's early activity was Belgium, which had become an independent country for the first time in 1831 and was concerned to make Antwerp competitive with the neighbouring Dutch ports. The newly crowned Belgian King, Leopold of Saxe-Coburg, had immediately impressed on his people their need of an efficient communications system from the Scheldt to the Meuse and the Rhineland, and by 1832 the first proposal for a railway from Antwerp to Liège, envisaging later projection to Cologne, had been tabled. Uniquely and far-sightedly – or so it seemed at the time – the Belgians then decided that the country's railways should be a State-run enterprise from the start and this tenet was embodied in a law of May 1834. George Stephenson was empanelled as consultant and it was locomotives of British design and construction which inaugurated the first 15 mile (24km) stretch of Belgian railway, from Brussels to Malines, on 5 May 1835. The King himself opened the line and decorated the Stephensons, father and son, in the course of the proceedings,

which launched the first steam-locomotive-operated public passenger and freight railway on the European mainland. By 1844 Belgium had both its key trunk routes complete, one north to south from Antwerp to the French border, intersecting at Malines with the other, extending east to west between Ostend and the German frontier via Louvain.

Within a few years the circumstances which had persuaded the Belgians to adopt State control were proving its undoing. The original decision had been largely prompted by fear that the country's ramified waterway system would discourage private investment in railways. Now, because the new railways had to price so keenly to compete effectively with waterborne transport for heavy freight, they were showing a miserable financial return, and the Belgian legislature was increasingly reluctant to sanction extensions. The Government was forced into a mixed railway economy and the grant of concessions to private enterprise, either to build and operate lines independently or else to build and lease to the State railway for operation. Less than a third of the 1,850 mile (3,000 km) network existing by 1870 was State-owned. But from then on paranoiac fears of a takeover by foreign financiers had the Government steadily buying back into the business, a process

The Leipzig–Dresden Railway was the first railway in Saxony in 1837, but the whole route was not finished until 1840. Leipzig station is illustrated below.

culminating in the reorganization of the State railway system as the present-day Belgian National Railways (the SNCB) in 1926.

It was royal enthusiasm, too, which inspired the first German public steam railway, although Ludwig I of Bavaria was not the first German to espouse the new medium. That was Friedrich List. Born at Reitlingen in 1789, List was so outspokenly radical as a young professor in various Württemberg universities that he had to take prudent refuge in the USA in 1825. In Pennsylvania List acquired solid influence as a mine-owner and economist, and also as a supporter of the new railways: in fact he built his own 21 mile (34km) line in the Blue Mountains, which could justifiably be claimed as the first German-built railway. That set him dreaming of railway-building in his homeland; there the German states were closing ranks in the Prussian-led *Zollverein*, or customs union, and List clearly recognized the bonding value to this movement of a comprehensive railway system with Berlin as its hub. He had already confided his vision to Bavaria's Mining Councillor by letter and received an encouraging response, when in 1832 US President Andrew Jackson offered him the post of US Consul in Leipzig and he accepted. The following year, back home, he published his plan, only to have it withered by a blast of scorn, chiefly from academics who advanced objections just as preposterous as their British counterparts had voiced: for instance, one Bavarian savant solemnly warned that the railway would effectively disarm the country by deterring horse-breeding and thus immobilizing the cavalry and artillery.

But the Bavarian professor's monarch ignored him. Emissaries were dispatched to England and on their evidence Ludwig I approved early in 1834 the construction of a 4 mile (6.4 km) railway from Nuremburg to Fürth, which was ceremonially opened on 7 December 1835. Unlike Britain's first all-purpose steam railway, the Ludwigsbahn – which, incidentally, List helped to build – entrusted its passengers to steam from the start, but persisted with horse-powered freight trains until 1862. Robert Stephenson's works were asked to quote for the first locomotive, but were thought far too expensive and the original order went to a German firm at Aalen. But they failed to deliver on time, so it was a Stephenson engine, a scaled-down version of the Liverpool & Manchester *Patentee* type named *Der Adler*, which inaugurated the service. In its first year the Ludwigsbahn, which never became part of the German trunk network, carried 450,000

Above: Der Adler, *the first locomotive on the Ludwigsbahn, was built by Stephenson in 1835. Early locomotive engineers set up their own workshops to supply locomotives not only to the lines which employed them but to others including overseas railways.*
Below: The first locomotive from the famous Borsig works in Germany was built in 1841 for the Berlin–Anhalt Railway.
Below right: Arrival of a train at Deutsch–Wagram on the Kaiser Ferdinand Nordbahn, the first Austrian railway, which opened in 1837.

passengers and generated a return of nearly 50 per cent on its capital investment. Six months elapsed before the railway moved its first freight which, appropriately for a Bavarian enterprise, was two casks of beer.

The Ludwigsbahn's immediate commercial success changed many – but by no means all – minds and the first main lines soon followed. A 5¾ mile (9.25 km) section of the Leipzig–Dresden Railway in Saxony was opened on 24 April 1837, a 16½ mile (26.6 km) line from Berlin to Potsdam on 29 October 1838 and only a month later the first of the old state railways of un-unified Germany, from Brunswick to Wolfenbüttel. At the Berlin–Potsdam opening the Crown Prince, later to become King Friedrich Wilhelm IV of Prussia, was moved to declaim that 'no human arm will ever stop the progress of this car, which will roll through the world'. By 1840 the 75¾ miles (122 km) of the Leipzig–Dresden line, including Germany's first rail tunnel, a 1,683 ft (513 m) bore near Oberau, were finished and further important main lines were under way: Frankfurt/Main to Darmstadt and Heidelberg; Cologne to Aachen; Munich to Augsburg; the Baden State Railway from Mannheim to Heidelberg; and the Berlin–Anhalt Railway from Berlin towards Wittenberg.

The collection of kingdoms and grand-duchies which constituted Germany in those days (so independent of each other that the war between Prussia and Austria fifteen years later would find Württemberg ranged on Austria's side) could already

show 3,725 route-miles (6,000 km) of railway in existence and a great deal more in draft by 1850. The greater part of it was built with infinitely more regard for civil engineering economy and avoidance of bridging and tunnelling than the British main lines – years later, in fact, the Prussian State Railways reckoned to have put down its network for less than 40 per cent the average per-mile cost incurred by British companies. One could now travel throughout by rail from Munich via Nuremberg and Leipzig to Berlin and thence to Hamburg, Stettin, Silesia or the Rhineland. Several of the eight large state railway systems which were amalgamated as a unitary Reichsbahn under the post-World War I Weimar Constitution were already in being; Hanover's was founded in 1842, Baden's and Bavaria's in 1846, and Württemberg's in 1850. Prussia initially rejected the concept of a State undertaking, but changed its mind at the prompting of its military men, who soon grasped the strategic and logistical significance of rail transport. But private enterprise was allowed to co-exist with the State system. A notable example of the former, which was authorized by a Prussian Royal Commission early in 1849 and which survived as an independent concern throughout the twentieth-century Reichsbahn era, was the Lübeck–Büchen Railway; it practically monopolized Hamburg's traffic with Scandinavia. The one tragedy marring this solid progress was the treatment meted out to the prescient List; unacknowledged, unrewarded – ostracized, even – he regressed into miserable poverty and was driven to suicide at Kufstein in November 1846.

Despite the fact that, as history dimly records, a working steam locomotive intended for Silesian mine wagonways had been cobbled together in Berlin in 1815 (it never fulfilled its purpose), the first German railways were largely reliant on imported British locomotives. But one of the great names in German locomotive building, August Borsig, had established his Berlin works by 1837 and was turning out his first engines in 1841 for the Berlin–Anhalt Railway. In the same year two more great concerns, Maffei and Kessler, opened their doors in Munich and Karlsruhe respectively, and Henschel constructed their first locomotive at Kassel in 1848. By the end of the decade some of the bigger states had also set up their own locomotive plants.

CENTRAL EUROPE AND RUSSIA

Central Europe had its equivalent of England's Surrey Iron Railway in a narrow-gauge (1,106 mm/3 ft 7½ in), horse- or bullock-worked railway open to the public on a toll-paying basis, which was completed from Budejovice, in what was then Bohemia but is now Czechoslovakia, to Linz in Austria in September 1827. It is the most convincing claimant to the title of mainland Europe's first public railway and it earned fresh distinction in 1854 when, following its admission of passengers (in 1832) and subsequent extension, it became the first European narrow-gauge public railway to operate steam traction.

The Central European railway age proper, however, dawned with the late 1837 opening of the first stage of a railway northward from Vienna across the Danube to Floridsdorf and Deutsch-Wagram. Its genesis was the far-sighted proposal of a Vienna University professor, Franz Riepl. Impressed by the dramatic achievement of Stephenson's *Rocket* and the instant commercial success of the Liverpool & Manchester Railway, Riepl powerfully advocated an immense network of railways radiating from Vienna to Trieste, to Milan and to the borders of the Ukraine as a means to check the fissiparous tendencies of the Austro-Hungarian empire. The Emperor Francis I determinedly rejected the concept, but his successor, the weak Ferdinand I, was easily persuaded by the all-powerful Prince Metternich to con-

sider a proposal for an initial 280-mile (450 km) line from Vienna to the neighbourhood of what is now Krakow, in Poland. The proposal came from Salomon de Rothschild, the banker, whom Riepl astutely enlisted to his cause and who was to become one of the dominant figures in subsequent Austrian railway expansion. No doubt the Emperor was the more easily persuaded when Rothschild couched his request for a railway-building concession in the most obsequious terms – from the 'most loyal and humble bank' to the 'Most Excellent and Most Puissant Emperor! Most Gracious Emperor and Lord!' – and added the final flourish of a suggestion to name the new railway after the Emperor himself, the Kaiser Ferdinand Nordbahn. Here again, British locomotives were imported to open the first stage of the new railway. The Austrians were careful to conduct on-the-spot studies of British and American practice before they contracted Robert Stephenson's firm for their first machines – a 2–2–2 and a pair of improved *Planet* 2–2–0s – but early in the 1840s the Austrians were already laying the foundations of their own ultimately world-reputed industry.

Few British-built locomotives can have had a more unusual initiation than one of three supplied for Russia's first railway exercise: a mid-winter journey by sled from the Baltic coast to St Petersburg, with attendants fending off marauding wolves on the way, followed, before steaming for

service, by the solemn ritual of the Russian Orthodox Church baptism with bell, book, candle (a hundred of them), dashes of sanctified water (for engine crew as well as locomotive), choir and a splendid array of priestly acolytes. This first Russian railway really went nowhere. The Austrian engineer Von Gerstner, pioneer of the Budejovice–Linz narrow-gauge line just mentioned, had been allowed by Czar Nicholas I to prove his case for authority to build major Russian railways by constructing an experimental 6 ft (1,829 mm) gauge line at just 30 miles (50 km) from the capital, St Petersburg, via the Czar's summer palace to a species of Xanadu, with ballrooms and buffets, that had been set up for the recreation of St Petersburgers at Pavlovsk. Von Gerstner's line was inaugurated by a ceremonial train to the Czar's residence, Tsarskoye Selo (after which the railway was named), on 30 October 1837 and finished to Pavlovsk the following summer.

Von Gerstner had predicted an annual passenger traffic of 800,000 and he was all but vindicated in the line's very first year of full operation, 1839. Encouraged, the Czar approved construction of a 4 ft 8½ in (1,435 mm) gauge railway from Warsaw to Vienna, which was begun in 1839 and, after faltering for lack of money in 1842, was completed in 1848. But even though Russia's quickening steps into a capitalist economy were throwing into stark relief the high cost and dismal speed of its existing transportation – frequently confined to waterways in winter, when the wretched roads degenerated to a morass that defeated pack animals and carts – some powerful reactionaries in the Czar's administration remained committed opponents of the railway. The Tsarskoye Selo line they dismissed contemptuously as the 'Czar's toy'.

The Czar, however, was not to be denied. In 1841 he ordered a commission to make a feasibility study of a St Petersburg–Moscow railway and sent engineers to investigate American railway practice. Their findings added up to an unarguable case and the formidable project got under way in 1843 under American tutelage (although the Czar was determined on Russian control of the operation from the start, one of his first requirements being that the American advisers set up a St Petersburg locomotive works). A vast horde of serfs, more than 50,000 of them at times, were flogged – all too often literally – into completing the 406 mile (653 km) line by 1851. Several thousand are said to have died in the process, many of them killed off by recurrent typhoid epidemics. Just over a century later a Soviet poet paid them feeling tribute in this verse:

> The way is straight, the embankment narrow
> Telegraph poles, rail, bridges.
> And everywhere on both sides are Russian bones –
> Vanechka, do you know how many?
> Brothers, you remember our reward,
> Fated to be strewn in the earth!
> Do you still remember kindly us poor ones,
> Or have you long forgotten?

The St Petersburg–Moscow Railway established what is still the Russian

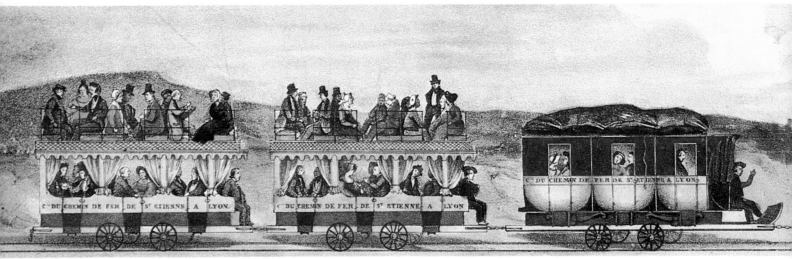

nach H. Hei

Above: The ceremonial departure of the first train from Nuremberg to Fürth, the Ludwigsbahn, on 7 December 1835, hauled by Stephenson's Der Adler. *Here passenger trains were steam-hauled from the start, but freight continued to be pulled by horses for some years.*

Left and below: This early French line, opened between Lyon and St Etienne in 1829, was partly horse-operated, although its engineer Marc Séguin was a firm believer in steam power. In 1827 he had patented in France the idea of multi-tubular boilers (first used on the Rocket).

standard track gauge of 5 ft (1,524 mm). Folklore has it that the Russians had paranoiac visions of enemies free-wheeling into their country had they adopted 4 ft 8½ in, but the truth is prosaic. As yet there was no ground for certainty that the Stephenson gauge would be standardized internationally; that being so the Russians had acted on the advice of their chief American technical adviser, the soldier and engineer Major George Washington Whistler, who recommended 5 ft rather than the 6 ft (1,829 mm) of the Tsarskoye Selo line, which the majority of the Czar's

Russian railway experts were counselling.

The Czar viewed his huge enterprise from end to end shortly after it had borne its first passenger train throughout on 1 November 1851. His insistence on minute personal inspection of detail along the way was partly responsible for protracting the journey to just under twenty-two hours, but another factor was the misplaced zeal of a railway official who thought to smooth the Imperial progress through his sector by greasing the rails. After the Czar's death in 1855, his son honoured his father's initiative by naming the railway the

The Gare du Nord, Paris, in 1847. The large Nord network was absorbed into the State system in the 1930s.

Nikolaev, but in present-day Soviet Russia it is called the October Railway, the premier electrified trunk route of the country, already operating the USSR's fastest passenger trains and at the time of writing struggling to make its tracks fit for the 125 mph (200 km/h) train-sets built for for them in 1977.

FRANCE, HOLLAND AND ITALY

On the other side of Europe France was a slow railway starter, displaying only 350 route-miles (563 km) of railway by 1842. Over much of the country there was little inducement to improve transportation because the economy was still predominantly agricultural and the road system efficient. Radicals were urging industrialization and the railways to go with it, but their advocacy germinated the issue of State versus private enterprise sponsorship, which was debated interminably in and out of the National Assembly. Private promoters were granted only a handful of concessions for lines that clearly had strategic point should a national system be developed – Paris to Rouen and Le Havre, for instance – and the Government did not feel it had the political backing to take over others it rejected.

Expectedly, the opening of the first public passenger railway changed the climate. Its shrewd promoters, the banking brothers Emile and Isaac Pereire, foresaw that the most effective way of swinging national opinion behind the railway concept would be to evangelize Paris by a practical demonstration. Given the franchise, on 24 August 1837 they opened a 13 mile (21 km) line, only steam-worked in part in the beginning, from stations in the capital at Pont de l'Europe and Rue Saint-Lazare to Le Pecq, across the river from Saint-Germain. Straight-away Parisians flocked to the trains, which ran every hour from seven in the morning to ten at night.

But the ownership issue was not dead. Continuing argument was fuelled by the inadequate capitalization of the first private companies. After the Paris–Orléans company had come to financial grief in 1840 and been rescued only by a Government guarantee of dividends, which gave it the strength to return to the capital market, the Assembly accepted that without State involvement an efficient, ordered railway system would never develop. In its Railway Law of 1842 the Assembly laid the foundations of a planned trunk route network centred on Paris which would spare twentieth-century French administrations all the route rationalization dilemmas that their British counterparts in the automobile age were to inherit from the cut-throat, uncontrolled promotion of competing main lines.

In France the railway companies' spheres of influence were not left to their managers to resolve, belligerently or any other way: they were delineated by the State. For the price of these sensible constraints, the companies had their trackbed, its earthworks and engineering structures built for them with State and local authority finance; all they had to do was lay the track, erect the buildings, provide the rolling stock, then man and run the railway. The 1842 Law's concept of part-State ownership of the track is reflected in the continuing provision for Government underwriting of about a third of present-day French Railways track maintenance costs. Another important clause of the 1842 law entitled the State to repurchase the new railways entire in the future.

The French went on to consolidate the lasting benefits of a strategically planned main-line network by having the new railways built with the same handsome disregard of civil engineering costs as Stephenson had insisted upon for the London & Birmingham. Taken as a group, the trunk routes of French Railways today remain the most ideally aligned for sustained speed of any in Europe, nowhere near as prone to undulation or curvature as those of British Rail; nor are they as frequently intersected by junctions, partly because the bulk of French commercial life radiates from Paris but also because the mid-nineteenth-century discipline obviated so much of the speculative cross-country building which occurred in British development. As a result, when French Railways rapidly electrified the main lines after the Second World War, they were soon able to build up and hold a higher average, end-to-end, express train speed than the rest of the Continent.

British contractors and navvies were active in the early years of French railway construction. So were British locomotive builders; the country's own industry did not take significant shape or breed distinctive designers until 1850. By 1848 some 1,250 route-miles (2,000 km) of railway had been laid (as against 3,750 [6,050 km] in Britain and 3,100 [5,000 km] in Germany), but then progress was checked by the 1848 Revolution, which fixed the railways as one of its targets – and did them substantial physical violence in places – because of their employment of premium-wage foreign contractors, engineers and workers. The companies lost business and once more found cash hard to obtain; some sold out to bigger systems, others had to hand over to the State.

Under Napoleon III's Second Empire, which ennobled technology but discouraged dissent, the merger process was sagely encouraged, with such success that the seventy-seven companies, large and small, existing at the start of the decade had come down to six by 1858. They were the Nord, which had originated in 1842 and which plied from Paris to Calais, the border of Belgium and Lille; the Est from Paris to the German frontier, which had

developed from the Strasbourg Railway; the Paris–Orléans, which by now had reached Bordeaux; the Midi, so far confined to south-western France between Bordeaux, Toulouse and the Spanish border, and yet to attain Paris; the Ouest, from Paris to Brittany and Normandy (in which, incidentally, the English London & South Western Railway had a financial interest); and the Paris–Lyon–Méditerranée, from Paris to Marseille. Largest of the sextet was the last, better known as the PLM, whose writ was ultimately to extend to Algeria; and the most profitable the Nord, whose passenger routes were highly rewarding and whose freight business encompassed the rich coalfields of Northern France.

All were granted ninety-nine year leases of their tracks under conventions signed with the Ministry of Works, to which were annexed *Cahiers des Charges* laying down a long series of meticulous specifications as to the running of the rail service and the types of passenger eligible for reduced fare. Echoes of these are detectable in the statutory prescriptions for today's French Railways, although, admittedly, there is no echo of the 1857 ordinance that locomotives, besides being of the latest model, must 'consume their own smoke'; but one does find a resonance of another 1857 requirement, that convicts and their attendant *gendarmerie* be accepted on any

Part of the Turin to Genoa line in the Appennine Mountains, between the tunnels of Villavecchia and Graverina.

train (though in prison vans built at State expense), in the 1978 issue of a special decree relieving French Railways' new 160 mph (260 km/h) Paris–Lyon TGV line of the obligation to carry prisoners.

The creation of railways in Holland was naturally inhibited by the country's superlative waterway system, which in turn posed a unique problem when the first railways were engineered. A railway from Amsterdam to Rotterdam was promoted in 1837, but the sponsors coaxed money out of sceptical Dutch investors until the King himself guaranteed them dividends. For unfathomable reasons, since the ultimate aim was a railway system to connect with that fast developing in Germany, the appointed engineer, F. W. Conrad, was allowed to start on an esoteric 6 ft 4½ in (1,943 mm) gauge; subsequently the Government had to underwrite conversion to 4 ft 8½ in. Employing British-built locomotives of Stephenson pattern, the railway opened its first section of 10½ miles (17 km) from Amsterdam to Haarlem in September 1839.

When Conrad had progressed a further 30 miles (50 km) to The Hague he had already had to cross 58 waterways and cope with a bridging problem unknown to his fellow pioneers in Europe, as the flatness of the terrain always brought him to the water's edge far below the necessary height to clear shipping. Even if it had not been operationally absurd to switchback over the canals and rivers in one sharp hump over another, the boggy ground on the verges ruled out the idea. Instead Conrad enterprisingly resorted to swing bridges of his own design. The waterways had another marked influence on the early Dutch railways; not until a line right across the country had been forged did the operators think it worth making a serious bid for freight business.

To round off early European history one must record that the first railway in what is now Italy, but was then a number of different states, was opened in the south in 1839. The old dual Kingdom of the Two Sicilies granted Armand Bayard de la Vingtrie, a French engineer, a concession to construct a network of railways radiating from Naples to Salerno, Avellino, Caserta and Capua, and a British-built locomotive named *Bayard* inaugurated the first completed stretch, from Naples to neighbouring Portici, on 3 October 1839. Thereafter the system was steadily extended. But the unsettled

condition of the Italian peninsula hampered the spread of main-line railways until the second half of the century. All that the map had to show by 1848 besides a knot of lines around Naples was: the Leopoldina Railway from Leghorn and Pisa to Florence; the Sardinian kingdom's first step in its creation of a State railway from Turin to Genoa via Alessandria and the Giovi pass; and the extremities of the Lombard-Venetian Railway (first proposed in 1837 but thereafter repeatedly checked by sacrifice to Austria's military effort), which had struggled from Padua and Vicenza to Venice, and in the west from Milan as far as Treviglio.

Only three other European countries had realized their first railways before 1850. The makings of the Hungarian Central main line from Budapest to Vienna had emerged in 21 miles (34km) of track from Budapest to Vác by 1846 and in the following year Switzerland opened its account with a 15 mile (24km) line from Baden to Zurich. The Iberian peninsula welcomed its first railway, 17 miles (27km) of track from Barcelona to Mataró, in 1848.

RAPID EXPANSION IN NORTH AMERICA

Meanwhile railroad-building in America had been accumulating the momentum which peaked so spectacularly in the 1850s, when the Americans were laying down as much new track as the rest of the world combined. A route-mileage of 2,800 (4,500 km) had already expanded to 9,000 (14,500 km) by 1850, but in the ensuing decade it would soar to 30,000 (48,300 km). The concerted opposition of cranks, canal owners, stagecoach operators and turnpike companies had taken time to whittle down, particularly as it was frequently backed by state legislatures, who could be prevailed upon to hobble the early railways in favour of the already entrenched transportation interests. That was one reason why the first American railways were often more passenger than freight carriers. The Utica & Schenectady, for instance, was specifically debarred by New York from freight movement under its original charter of 1833 and the restriction was not lifted until 1844. It was imposed at the behest of the Erie Canal company, which also had any railways running parallel to its course mulcted of state taxes no less than its own. The Utica & Schenectady even had to buy out a rival turnpike company before New York would disgorge its 1833 charter.

Commerce had grasped the value of railroads well before the 1830s had faded, however. For freight transport the train was not as cheap as the canals (though it was infinitely more economical than the country's deteriorating turnpikes), but it had the cardinal virtue of all-weather reliability: ice could jam the canals for four months or even more every winter and in summer water levels could be difficult to maintain. Moreover, a railroad could project a branch right up to a manufacturer's or shipping agent's doorstep. As for passenger travel, while the cream of the great paddle-wheel packets on the Hudson and Mississippi rivers could pace the early trains, they could not trace as straight a course on their meandering waterways as the new railways.

So from the 1829–31 germination of the Delaware & Hudson, the Baltimore & Ohio, the South Carolina Canal & Rail Road Co. and the Mohawk & Hudson (earliest constituent of the New York Central to come), new railways reached inland in a flowering all the way down eastern America from Canada to the Gulf of Mexico. Virginia and Pennsylvania had their first lines operational in 1832, North Carolina followed in 1833, Kentucky and Massachusetts in 1834, Rhode Island and the District of Columbia in 1835, Michigan, Maine, Florida, Quebec and what was later to become West Virginia in 1836, Mississippi and Georgia in 1837, Illinois, Indiana, New Hampshire and Connecticut in 1838.

The pioneer Quebec railway, however, did not trigger an immediate spread of track in Canada. Sponsored by a group of Montreal businessmen and worked with a Stephenson-built locomotive from Britain, the 14¼ mile (23km) Champlain & St Lawrence Railroad was a portage, or land-link, in an otherwise all-water route between Montreal and New York, running from Laprairie on the St Lawrence River to St Johns on the Richelieu River; for many years it did not function in winter, when the lakes and rivers were frozen over and shipping was immobilized. The only other Canadian railway to take shape before 1850 was not commissioned until 1847, when the stagecoach route around Lachine Rapids was replaced by a railway between Montreal and Lachine. Both railways were subsequently absorbed in the Grand Trunk Railway, which was formed in 1852 and in due course became a major constituent of Canadian National.

The Americans took far longer than the Europeans to arrive at a standard gauge. As late as 1860 almost half the country's by then ramified railway system was not to 4ft 8½in gauge. The South had followed the 5ft (1,524mm) example of the pioneer South Carolina line, but not exclusively; Louisiana and Arkansas had started on 5ft 6in (1,676mm), while North Carolina had gone wholly, and Virginia partly, for the standard Stephenson gauge. In New York the Mohawk & Hudson had built to 4ft 9in (1,448mm), but in New Jersey next door the Camden & Amboy had selected 4ft 10in (1,473mm), and that was adopted not

only for succeeding railway projects in New Jersey but also for Ohio's lines and some in Indiana. Most railways north of the Potomac fixed on the Stephenson gauge, but there were yet more mavericks to reckon with. The New York & Erie (later the Erie), which finally reached Dunkirk on Lake Erie from the Hudson River near New York City in 1851, was 6 ft (1,829 mm) and there were two 5 ft 6 in systems: one was the first line across the border into Canada, begun in 1846 from Portland, Maine, to Montreal, which diplomatically titled itself the Atlantic & St Lawrence on the US side and the St Lawrence &

Atlantic on the Canadian side of the 49th Parallel, and the other the portentously named European & North American, which was promoted in 1850 as a component of a rail-sea route to Europe via Maine, New Brunswick and ship to Ireland from Nova Scotia (exhausted by two decades of halting effort to complete the line, the company went bankrupt in the 1870s). Finally, although the tentacles of railway groping west in the Mississippi were mostly 4 ft 8½ in, Missouri obstinately elected to make every line out of St Louis 5 ft 6 in. It would take a Civil War to impose, amongst other things, gauge

The opening of the first railway line in Italy, between Naples and Portici, by the King of Naples in 1839.

unification and logical uniformities of practice on the incoherent, inefficient and all-too-often unsafe railway system that was developing so haphazardly at the mid-point of the century.

In less critical particulars some distinctive American railroad characteristics had certainly been established at that juncture. At last railroad builders had accepted that iron rails were a *sine qua non*. The pioneers had shunned them because the iron, chiefly imported from England, was so costly; they had tried to make do with 'strap' track – strips of iron fastened to wooden longitudinals – but that was prone to work loose, then curl up and erupt dangerously through the floor of a passing vehicle.

The pattern of the American iron road was set by Robert L. Stevens, son of the Hoboken steam pathfinder Colonel John Stevens. As president of the early New Jersey railroad, the Camden & Amboy, the younger Stevens sailed for England late in 1830 to buy iron rails and passed his Atlantic voyage by whittling out of wood a flat-bottomed rail shape and a hook-headed spike to pin it to the cross-tie, or sleeper, for which he placed orders on arrival. That way he would at least save his railroad the expense of the chairs into which, as described in the previous chapter, the round base of the English rail had to be bedded as a sleeper mounting. Stevens' orginal intention was to employ stone blocks as ties, plug their centres with wood and spike the rails to the wood, but when his English rails arrived the quarries let him down on deliveries, so he had to order a recourse to wooden ties – temporarily, as he thought. Very soon, however, it was patent that a wooden-tie track, apart from being cheaper, was more resilient, more durable and more conduc-ive to good vehicle riding. Although within three years the Boston & Providence was being built from scratch with flat-bottomed iron rails on wooden ties, some companies were extraordinarily slow to recognize the clear practical and economic superiority of what became the standard American track structure; even in 1848 the first railway to extend west of Chicago, the Galena & Chicago Union, was putting down strap track.

In parenthesis one might add that although Continental European railways also standardized flat-bottomed rail, Brit-ish railways clung to their traditional bullhead rail cross-section and chaired track until well into the twentieth century. First to disturb a rooted British conviction that their prescription was somehow safer and stronger was an enlightened civil engineer of the mid-1930s, W.K. Wallace, who was employed by the London Midland & Scottish (LMS). His experi-

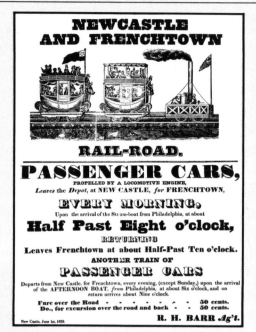

Above: An American railroad poster of 1833, setting out train times and fares between New Castle and Frenchtown.
Below right: The John Bull, *built by Robert Stephenson in 1831, was fitted with an early type of cow-catcher.*
Above right: The archetypal American locomotive of the early transcontinental period with headlamp, bell and pilot (cow-catcher). These four-wheeled coupled locomotives were to become the standard type for passenger services.

ments were followed by the London & North Eastern, and it and the LMS were the only two railways of the British 'Big Four' to go very far in flat-bottomed track-laying before the Second World War. Not until the start of 1949 did the newly nationalized British Railways decide at last to standardize flat-bottomed track.

No one obliged the foundling American railroads to fence their track and few of them, scurrying to lay their routes as cheaply as they could, had either the time or the cash to undertake it as a social benefit. Town streets as well as country roads were crossed – or even threaded for a distance – on the level, proliferating the innumerable grade crossings which would be the bane of twentieth-century North American railroads. Livestock as well as people could roam the tracks as they

pleased, but whereas many mainland European railways were laying the fencing onus on the farmers by legislating heavy penalties for anyone allowing his cattle to trespass on the railway, the Americans held the railways culpable for any harm they did to wandering animals. As one Kentucky judge thundered to a loudly applauding jury: 'The railroads must learn that he who kills his neighbour's ox, his ass, or his shoat, shall pay back twentyfold.'

Hence that historic American locomot-ive appendage, the cow-catcher, or pilot, ahead of the leading wheels. One early device of the kind caught its trespasser all too securely. The Philadelphia & Reading slung across the front of one of its engines a crossbar from which projected long rods, the idea being, hopefully, that any errant animal would be caught and imprisoned between any two of them until the train could be halted and the beast levered out to freedom. Alas, the contraption's first encounter was with a massive bull for which it was not made to measure; its rods lanced the animal so deeply that another locomotive had to be called up to rope-haul the gory carcass free. The gently tapered, prow-fronted pilot which treated vagrants more gently and came into general use was contrived by the master mechanic of the Camden & Amboy (C&A), Isaac Dripps, in 1833, at roughly the same time as the Philadelphia & Reading's ill-starred in-vention, and was fitted to the C&A's Stephenson-built *John Bull.*

The same considerations that gave rise to the cow-catcher also sired the traditional American locomotive headlight and bell. Horatio Allen had run the first nocturnal train in 1831 simply to prove the practice feasible, warning of its coming by having the engine propel a flatcar on which blazed a bonfire of fircones bedded in sand. But for the next ten years the lack of any commercial requirement for night run-ning, given the short end-to-end distances of the early lines and uneasiness at their safety and reliability even in daylight, dissuaded anyone from night running save in an emergency; then the journey would be done at a crawl by a train festooned in lanterns.

It was in 1841 that the Boston & Worcester first set about night freight

whistle, both for safety and also to limit the play of whistles in the towns and cities, which their railroads penetrated more intimately than England's. As time went on American enginemen, captivated by the variations of pitch possible by playing on the whistle valve, coaxed their shop foremen into making cluster, multi-tone whistles. These were always supposed to sound as a single chord, or chime, but many enginemen quickly learned how to control the steam supply to each whistle cup independently and thus to voice a recognizable tune or declaim some other distinctive aural signature. To jump ahead in time, the whole English-speaking world has been made aware of one immortal American whistle artist since an April night in 1900, when John Luther 'Casey' Jones, Illinois Central's cavalier of the footplate, perished as his 'Cannonball Express' careered into a freight train that had strayed into his headlong path. As the deathless ballad later written by one of his colleagues has it, everyone 'knew by the whistle's moan that the man at the throttle was Casey Jones'. As much his trademark as the 2–8–0 No. 638 assigned to him for seven years was the whippoorwill bird cry he played so perfectly on its whistle.

In 1850, on the threshold of its decade of huge growth, the American railroad system already covered three times the mileage of the country's canals. Three-fifths of the network were still concentrated in the eleven eastern states, but the westward drive across the continent had begun in earnest.

operation as a deliberate policy, to avoid daytime delay of passenger trains, and soon set a fashion for massive reflector-backed oil lamps ahead of locomotive chimneys. Nature's imitation of artefact confounded at least one engineer in the early days; careering out of a curve, a notorious driver of the New York & Erie is reported to have grabbed terror-stricken for his reversing lever and slammed on his brakes to avoid head-on impact with the rising moon. Very quickly the huge headlamp casings inspired some re-markable decorative artistry; hand-painted embellishments ranged all the way from elaborate filigree to beautifully

executed Grecian ladies at their lyres, damsels with parasols and ancient build-ings. The oil-lamps gave way to electric headlights fed by steam-powered gener-ators in the last quarter of the century.

As for the bell, it had been the warning device of the first English locomotives. But there it had been discarded after a Manchester firm, Sharp Roberts & Co., in early 1835 devised the now familiar cup whistle to exploit the boiler's head of steam. The first American locomotive bell probably dates from 1834, the first American locomotive whistle from 1837. The Americans deemed it prudent to retain and develop the bell as well as the

GROWTH OF THE RAILWAYS IN EUROPE

Just as the railways began in Europe, so it is that the first mature national networks are to be found in Europe. A mere fifty years after the first steam railway line was opened in 1825 the railway was already established as the main transport system for the continent.

The impetus for this growth was provided by industrialization. Although the movement of people was always significant (252 million passengers travelled on Britain's railways in 1865), the great driving force was freight transport. The strength of this factor is shown by the Netherlands where the railway could not compete successfully for goods traffic with the much cheaper canals, and as a result the country has only 1,791 route-miles (2,892 km) today.

Another factor in the pattern of growth was political. In 1825 Germany and Italy were collections of different states. This diversification hindered the growth of

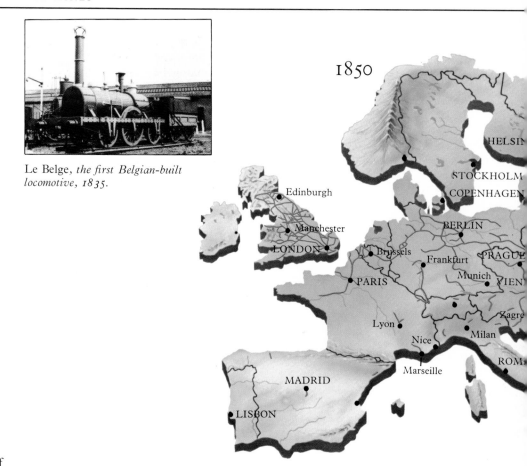

Le Belge, *the first Belgian-built locomotive, 1835.*

1850

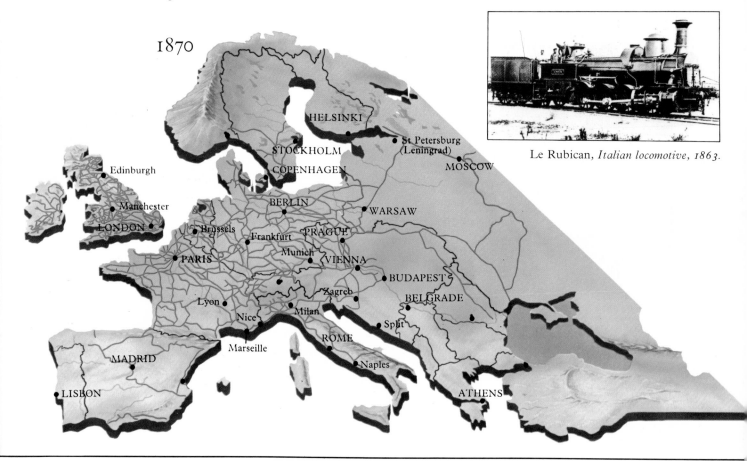

Le Rubican, *Italian locomotive, 1863.*

1870

Italian railways, for the first line was opened in 1837 but there was no co-ordination of the system until unification of the country in 1861. Germany, on the other hand, enjoyed rapid growth as the individual states saw it as being in their interest to encourage railway building. Consequently Germany had about 3,000 route-miles (4,800 km) in 1850.

Another factor of importance was the lucrativeness of the railway and the degree of government support and intervention. Even during economic depression private railways were attractive to investors throughout the nineteenth century. This fostered growth, but also, when unchecked, produced wasteful competition and uneven coverage. In 1914 Russia had the largest system in Europe, but it was run by 38 private and State-owned lines with little co-ordination between them and a patchy national network. In France on the other hand, the Government intervened to control railway growth as early as 1842 and when private lines proliferated in the 1850s and 1860s the Government encouraged departments and communes to build their own lines so as to ensure a nationwide service.

The networks of most European countries reached their maximum extent in the years either side of World War I. Greater competition from the roads coupled with the Depression of the 1930s turned railways into loss-makers. Line-cutting followed in the 1960s and 1970s – Great Britain had as many as 15,000 route-miles (24,000 km) as early as 1880, but has only 11,188 miles (18,005 km) today, France around 24,500 miles (37,450 km) in 1913 (without Alsace and Lorraine) and 21,452 miles (35,527 km) today (with them), and Belgium about 3,100 miles (5,000 km) in 1913 and 2,686 miles (4,326 km) today.

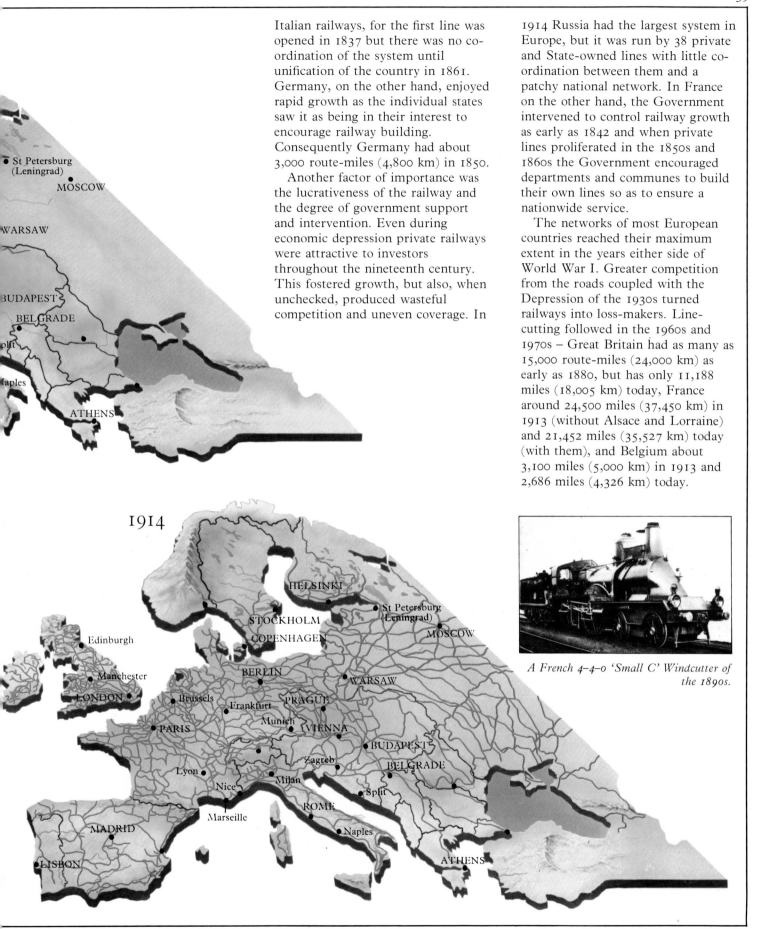

A French 4–4–0 'Small C' Windcutter of the 1890s.

1914

EARLY LOCOMOTIVES AND TRAIN TRAVEL

The Stephensons' *Rocket* established the fundamentals of steam locomotive technique, but it was Robert Stephenson's subsequent 2–2–0 *Planet* of October 1830 for the Liverpool & Manchester Railway which perfected a layout standardized by most British railways for the rest of the nineteenth century. In *Planet* the two cylinders were arranged horizontally within the frames below the smokebox, to which they were attached, so that their exhaust had a shorter and more effective route to the blastpipe; and the drive was direct to the double-cranked rear axle. *Planet* proved markedly more powerful than any of its predecessors, partly because the design laid 25 per cent more adhesion weight on the driving axle, partly because of the superior thermal efficiency achieved by juxtaposing smokebox and cylinders, which protected the latter from cooling, thus reducing steam condensation.

To satisfy a Liverpool & Manchester demand for more power Stephenson soon enhanced adhesion by producing a coupled-wheel 0–4–0 version of *Planet*, his *Samson*. Both types were so proficient that Stephenson's own works could not cope with the demand, chiefly from the rapidly burgeoning railways of his own country but also from the first eager promoters overseas. Apart from licensing another firm originated by Matthew Murray, the builder of Blenkinsop's engines, to construct to his designs, Stephenson in 1831 also financed a new locomotive manufacturer in Newcastle, R. & W. Hawthorn (which ultimately merged with the Robert Stephenson works over a century later, in 1937) and in 1833 he established a Lancashire works near Warrington that was later known worldwide as Vulcan Foundry.

Stephenson's next major design, the *Patentee*, as well as exerting a major influence on British practice, had global success. In it Stephenson answered the clamour for more power by enlarging

Right: In the late 1840s Alexander Allan evolved a series of small but effective outside-cylinder 2–2–2s and 2–4–0s. Highland Railway No. 32 Cluny *was a good-looking development of this type.*
Below: Stephenson's Planet, *a 2–2–0 with inside cylinders built for the L&MR in 1830. Layouts using inside cylinders were standardized by most British railways for the rest of the century.*

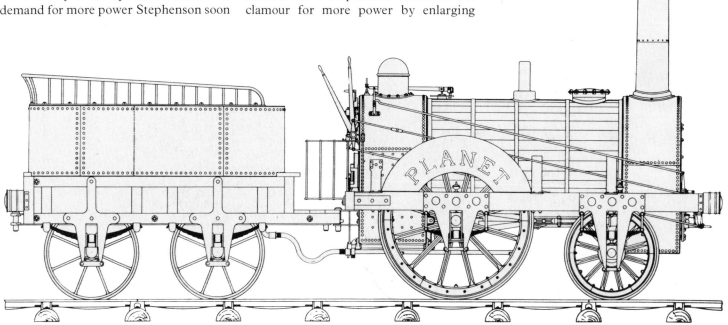

boiler and firebox, of which the latter needed support by an additional axle; that was made idle, with smaller-diameter wheels, and at the same time the leading idle axle was reduced to similar dimensions, creating the 2–2–2. Throughout the mid-nineteenth century the 2–2–2 arrangement was by far the most commonly employed by British railways. One firm alone outshopped more than 600 with varied sizes of driving wheel and cylinder.

That was the concern, first set up in Manchester in 1833 and later transferred to Glasgow, where it assumed the title of Sharp Stewart, which was the Stephenson factories' keenest competitor both at home and abroad. In France, especially, the early railways were characterized by studs of 'Sharpies', as the distinctive Sharp Stewart 2–2–2s with their neatly symmetrical outline were always tagged in Britain and frequently overseas.

The final pre-1850 European development of the basic six-wheeled engine was the 0–6–0, with all wheels coupled. Robert Stephenson's first essay in this format had emerged in 1826, but the real precursor of the standard British freight engine throughout the latter nineteenth century was *Atlas*, constructed by Stephenson for the Leicester & Swannington in 1834.

Before the 1830s had set, several locomotive engineers in Europe were grasping the potential gain in thermal efficiency if steam were allowed to do more of its work by expansion. That needed a device to interpose lead time between the respective actions of piston valve and piston, so as to cut off the admission of steam to the cylinder before the piston completed its stroke. For the remainder of the stroke the steam already applied would exert its pressure by expansion. A French engineer on the Paris–Versailles (Right Bank) railway, Benoît Paul Emile Clapeyron, was the first to obtain practical results, in 1840. Perforce working with a cut-off fixed at 70 per cent of the stroke, he immediately gained a 40–50 per cent increase of load-haulage power and a halving of fuel consumption. The next step, obviously, was to contrive a gear linked to the piston rod but capable of independent contrapuntal variation, so that the percentage of cut-off could be altered by the driver to suit differing load

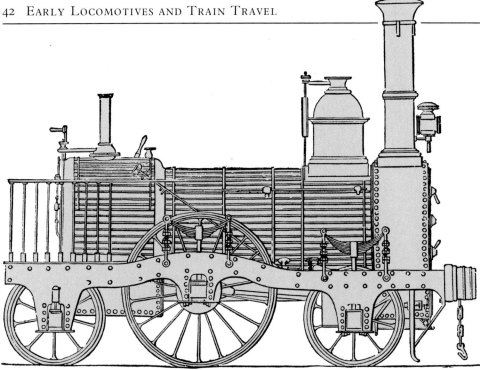

and route situations. Here again Robert Stephenson was first in the field with a practical apparatus, his so-called link motion, which was first seen on a locomotive in 1842. Other valve gears were devised in the subsequent careeer of the steam locomotive, of which two demand mention: the gear perfected in the mid-1840s by the young foreman mechanic of the Belgian State Railways workshops, Egide Walschaerts, which was probably the most widely used in world steam traction history; and that of Abner D. Baker, which he invented in 1903 and patented for rail locomotive use in late 1911, after which it was standardized by the majority of North American builders.

In the 1830s Stephenson's only significant competitor as a locomotive designer was Edward Bury, the traction chief of the London & Birmingham Railway. One characteristic of the Bury locomotive was its cylindrical firebox with hemispherical crown, a feature that appealed to early American builders because of its simpler maintenance and adjunct of a boiler layout which was more tolerant of uneven track. The Bury firebox, widely nicknamed the 'haystack' or 'haycock' by virtue of its shape, was a hallmark of the first-generation US steam locomotives.

The first and ultimately the greatest American locomotive works proper, which turned out more than 80,000 engines in its steam age span of 118 years, was founded in 1832 by a Philadelphian, Matthias W.

Baldwin, who had despaired of turning a profit from his original profession, watchmaking, and opened a machine-shop. For that he designed and built a successful stationary steam plant, the reliable reputation of which was soon the gossip of the city's business world. It excited a local museum owner, Benjamin Franklin Peale, with visions of a miniature indoor railway to ferry passengers about his premises and Baldwin was invited to produce the locomotive: this, with little else for a manual but English press cuttings reporting on the Liverpool & Manchester's Rainhill Trial contestants, Baldwin successfully did. The upshot was a commission from the newly chartered Philadelphia, Germantown & Norristown Railroad for a copy of a full-scale Stephenson *Planet*-type locomotive; and in another achievement – remarkable since he was working without the advanced power tools of contemporary English locomotive foundries – Baldwin fulfilled that commission with his *Old Ironsides* in November 1832. By mid-decade Baldwin had evolved a 4–2–0 design so impressive that he had orders adding up to forty engines a year to employ a labour force of over 300.

Another significant American pioneer was William Norris, who had been taken on as plant foreman by a West Point graduate, Colonel Stephen H. Long, when the latter founded another Philadelphia concern, the American Steam Carriage

Company, in 1828. Long eventually took Norris into partnership, but the firm produced no effective locomotives until Norris had the reins and in 1836 turned out *George Washington*, the progenitor of a long line of Norris 4–2–0s, for the Philadelphia & Columbia.

A key feature of the Norris 4–2–0 was the siting of the single driving axle just ahead of the firebox, which markedly increased its adhesion weight. That above all enabled *George Washington* to stagger the whole railroad fraternity by hauling 14 tons up a 1-in-14 slope where the Philadelphia & Columbia had previously thought anything but power-operated rope haulage of trains inconceivable. The feat earned Norris engines respect throughout Europe. In England they were bought by the Birmingham & Gloucester for its 1-in-37¾ Lickey Incline, but it was in South Germany and especially in Austria, where locomotive builders were grappling with the same constraints of grade and curvature as the Americans, that the Norris influence was paramount in the late 1830s and 1840s. So much so that Norris, rashly ignoring local advice, set up his own Vienna works in the mid-1840s; but, as he had been warned, it failed because local Austrian builders could turn out far cheaper facsimiles of the Norris engine, which was a considerably simpler piece of engineering than anything then emanating from Britain. The Norris concept was eventually undone by its instability at the gathering speeds of railways and by the adoption of higher boiler pressure, to which the 'haycock' firebox boiler was ill-suited.

The mounting American demand for rail freight soon outstripped the tractive effort of a single driving axle, but when a second driving axle was added the stability problems set up by the uneven, serpentine track were exacerbated. The first to appreciate that a degree of guidance could be achieved by preceding the driving wheels with more idle axles was the engineer of the Philadelphia, Germantown & Norristown, Henry R. Campbell, who created America's first 4–4–0 in 1837. His thinking was flawed, however. His objective was implicit in the wording of the patent he took out, yet he unimaginatively made a fixed assembly of his leading wheels, and sought lateral play by stripping the leading driving wheels of their flanges. The engine was little less susceptible to derailment than its forerunners.

It was yet another Philadelphia partnership, Eastwick and Harrison, which conceived the equalizing beam and shaped the first successful American 4–4–0 with a species of pivoted bogie. Built for the Philadelphia & Reading (P&R) in late 1839, the engine was gratefully named *Gowan & Marx* in salute of English bankers who had rescued a cash-starved P&R extension project from the wastepaper basket. *Gowan & Marx* was assigned to the P&R's inaugural train on 5 December 1839 and confronted a load of no less than 368 tons, forty times its own weight – 80 small vehicles bulging with 60 passengers, 1,635 barrels of flour, $73\frac{1}{4}$ tons of iron blooms, 6 tons of coal and 2 hogsheads of whisky. Though it failed *en route* and had to be helped home, it had done enough to compel respect; soon it was recording regular performances the fame of which rippled around the world. When the tidings reached Russia, in fact, Eastwick and Harrison were immediately invited by Czar Nicholas I to found his St Petersburg–Moscow Railway works at Aleksandrovsk, whereupon the Americans closed their Philadelphia plant and set sail.

Above, far left: A further development of the inside-cylindered locomotive, a Sharp Stewart standard passenger engine of 1837.
Above: A typical Bury 2–2–0 outside the L&BR's Camden freight depot in 1840.
Below: The Batavia, *a 4–2–0 built in the mid-1830s by Baldwin, perhaps America's greatest locomotive manufacturer.*

In Russia the expatriates carved themselves another niche in traction history by sireing amongst the Czar's first 200 engines the world's first 2–6–0s, a wheel arrangement soon dubbed 'Mogul' around the railway globe because of its provenance. As for the 4–4–0, that became the 'American'; ideally suited to mixed traffic haulage, given an undemanding speed requirement, and indulgent of America's generally mediocre nineteenth-century track, it dominated the continent's motive power until the last quarter of the century, when it steadily yielded freight work to custom-built multi-wheeled types.

COMPETITION BETWEEN THE GAUGES

Back in Europe the English 'Battle of the Gauges' was profoundly influencing design. The broad-gauge locomotive's debut on the Great Western was unpromising, since Brunel had bought haphazardly from a number of builders on little more than their undertaking to come up with a product that would slake his thirst for high speed at a low piston rate. Consequently when the twenty-one-year-old Stephenson works graduate Daniel Gooch, a passionate believer in broad gauge's potential, won Brunel's appointment as GWR Locomotive Super-

intendent, he was surrounded by monstrosities. Surveying ludicrous freaks in which driving wheels of 8 ft (2,438 mm) or even 10 ft (3,048 mm) diameter dwarfed puny boilers and cylinders, Gooch confided to his diary deep misgivings that 'they would have enough to do to drive themselves along the road'.

He was right. Slaving night and day and simultaneously training his own workshop force, Gooch modified some of Brunel's hasty purchases into reasonable load-haulers, but this exacting baptism convinced him that no more locomotives must be ordered without the backing of his own detailed specification. He was the first traction chief of a British railway to take over full command of its locomotive design and, following the establishment of the Swindon works in early 1846, to commit the greater part of GWR locomotive construction to the railway's own workshops. This move would in time be copied by most of the major British companies and distinguish their motive power policy from custom elsewhere.

The first product of Swindon and the first machine with Gooch's stamp on every essential of its drawings was the 2–2–2 *Great Western*, built in a mere thirteen weeks at the opening of 1846. Within two months *Great Western* had joined the

locomotive immortals and revealed a previously unimagined rail speed horizon by averaging almost 60 mph (100 km/h) with a 100 ton train over the 77.3 miles (124.4 km) from Swindon to Paddington, then running non-stop from London to Exeter via Bristol, 194 miles (312.2 km), at a mean of 55½ mph (89.3 km/h). *Great Western*, too, had massive 8 ft driving wheels, but Gooch made sure they were served by a large boiler and firebox and appropriate cylinders, achieving overall a machine eminently suited to high speed with light trains over Brunel's superlatively aligned broad-gauge route from Bristol to London.

Standard-gauge operators were desperate to match Gooch's engines' pace, but obsessed with worry that the closer wheel-spacing of their engines diminished stability. Alleviation of that fear by lowering the locomotive's centre of gravity was one stimulus to development of a longer boiler. The other was the obvious thermal inefficiency of a short-boiler barrel, spectacularly demonstrated by the red-hot smoke-boxes and flame spurting from the charred chimneys of Stephenson *Planets* and *Patentees* when their drivers were spurring them hard.

More productive use of the fire's heat by lengthening of boiler tubes was the prime objective of Robert Stephenson's long-boiler design, patented in June 1841. In that he was eminently successful, but in the traditional Stephenson short-wheelbase 2–2–2 format the new boiler, with its clumsy overhanging firebox at the rear, compounded the stability problem. A rash of derailments with the first English examples precipitated a Government investigation which damned the long-boiler 2–2–2 as unsafe above 45 mph (70 km/h). The solution was to redraft the concept as an 0–6–0, in which guise the first examples were delivered to the York & Midland Railway in 1843 and proved much more acceptable, not least because they answered mounting clamour for a special-purpose heavy freight locomotive. Stephenson long-boiler 0–6–0s were a particular asset in colliery and docklands, where their short wheelbases were comfortable on the incessant tight curves of industrial layouts; that made them welcome above all in the north of England, where the North Eastern Railway was still ordering fresh batches up to 1875. Most British railways, however, opted for a longer-wheelbase 0–6–0.

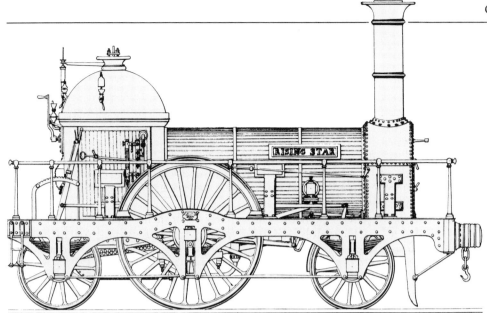

Above: A broad-gauge 2–2–2, the Rising Star *was built by Robert Stephenson for the GWR in 1841, before the advent of Gooch-designed locomotives from GWR's Swindon works.*
Below left: Henry R. Campbell's original 4–4–0 of 1836 presaged the most popular wheel arrangement of the century. Sadly the locomotive itself was unstable.
Below: A Stephenson long-boiler 2–2–2 locomotive, built in France in 1847 for the Paris-to-Strasbourg Railway.

Its aptitude for sharp curvature made the Stephenson long-boiler design vastly more popular on the European mainland, where the great majority of routes had been inexpensively engineered and there was yet none of Britain's craving for speed. Here the 2–2–2 arrangement was soon discarded for a 2–4–0 layout with outside cylinders that became an extremely serviceable mixed traffic machine, widely employed by French and German railways, but the 2–4–0's success was eclipsed

by that of the 0–6–0 version. First customer for the latter, in 1845, was the Paris & Orléans, but its real vogue dates from the Nord Railway's development of an outside-cylinder variant and, soon afterwards in 1854–5, the whole-hearted embrace of this concept by the Bourbonnais Railroad, which was later absorbed by the PLM: hence the 'Bourbonnais' nickname for the 1,054 outside-cylinder long-boiler 0–6–0s eventually acquired for French railways and frequently applied to their prodigious kin which were built throughout Europe.

The long-boiler idea was specifically exploited for speed on the standard gauge by a man who polished his skills as assistant to Gooch at Swindon and then went his own way in keen competition with Gooch and the broad gauge – Thomas Russell Crampton. In early 1842 Crampton patented a long-boiler layout with large-diameter driving axles at the rear of the firebox and only carrying wheels beneath the boiler, thereby achieving a lower centre of gravity and avoiding any unbalanced overhang of superstructure. It was an ingenious arrangement, but contrived by recourse to such dubious expedients as an oval boiler cross-section and a projection of the lower part of the firebox beneath the driving axle.

WHEEL NOTATION: STEAM

The descriptive number given with a type of steam locomotive refers to the number of its wheels. Most steam locomotives have a combination of driving wheels (shown in the diagram in red) and bogie or trailing wheels (shown in blue). The first figure of the three-figure combination gives the number of bogie wheels at the front of the locomotive, the next the number of driving wheels and the last the number of trailing wheels. A

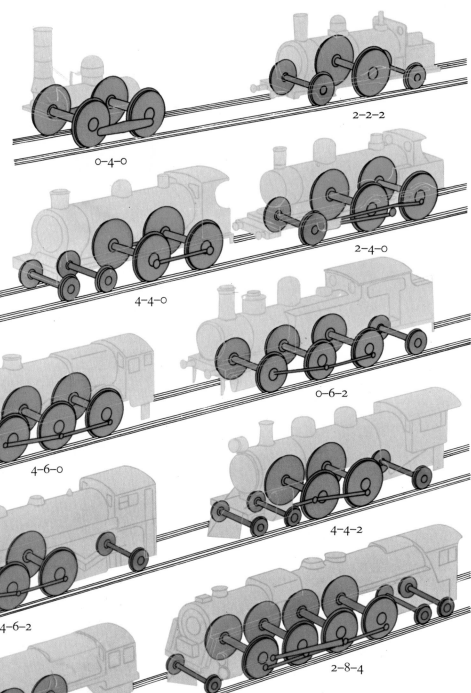

2-2-2

0-4-0

2-4-0

4-4-0

0-6-0

0-6-2

4-6-0

4-4-2

4-6-2

2-8-4

2-10-0

suffix 'T' if added to the notation denotes a tank engine.

On the Continent the number of axles is counted, instead of the number of wheels, giving figures exactly half those of their British and American counterparts. Thus a steam engine with four bogie wheels, six driving wheels and four trailing wheels is known in Europe as a 2-3-2.

Above: A typical Baldwin 4–4–0 showing the decorative embellishments provided in the early days of railroading.
Below: A French 'Crampton' on the Est Railway in the 1880s. The long-boiler idea was exploited by Thomas Crampton in his layout of 1842 using large driving wheels at the rear of the firebox.

The first 'Crampton', the 6–2–0 *Liverpool* of 1848 for the London & North Western Railway (LNWR), was certainly a rock-solid rider and fleet enough to challenge Gooch's best – it was alleged to have touched 78 mph (125.5 km/h) on one early run – but it pounded the track to pieces. It was scrapped in 1858 and the South Eastern alone of British railways was persuaded to buy a batch of 'Cramptons'. The French, on the other hand, took enthusiastically to the Crampton principle and with minor modifications the Nord, Est and PLM all had classes closely derived from the *Liverpool* constructed under licence in France. Once the driving-wheels had been suitably balance-weighted to counteract and equalize the crank thrusts, derailments were obviated and track damage mitigated, enabling the Nord in particular to exploit the 'Cramptons'' speed, accelerate its Paris–Channel Coast and Cologne/Brussels expresses and wear the crown of mainland Europe's fastest railway for many years. Indeed, such was its stature that for countless Frenchmen to take the express was '*prendre le Crampton*'.

In Germany the Prussian Eastern, Hanover State, Bavarian Palatinate, Baden State and Hessian Railroads all acquired 'Cramptons', but the only other European system to run them in quantity was the Zeeland of Denmark. In America a few were tried by the Pennsylvania and by the Camden & Amboy in 1848–9 – the Camden & Amboy's 6–2–0s, with their gargantuan chimneys perched on a boiler looking pencil-slim by comparison, were surely the most grotesquely shaped engines of the decade – but they were very imperfect adaptations of the Crampton concept and an operational fiasco.

EARLY PASSENGER FACILITIES

On both sides of the Atlantic the pioneer passenger coach builders let logic dictate the shape of their first vehicles. Better the devil you know, so why not reassure apprehensive citizens steeling themselves to risk the unknown by cocooning them in the kind of bodywork they already knew and trusted, that of the stagecoach? But then it was realized, given the diminished

friction of wheel on rail, that horses could cope with a bigger, weightier vehicle on rails than the average road coach. That inspired the styling of the first rail coach bodies as a terrace of three stagecoach bodies on a single four-wheel wagon frame. Which, of course, was also the genesis of the railway coach compartment. Many of these early coaches were individually named.

Fine, so far as premium-fare paying passengers were concerned; but not for humbler folk who, for a reduced charge, were at first allowed to ride on the roof with the richly accoutred brakeman, the predecessor of the railway guard, as they had with the team of the stagecoaches. That had been perilous enough on a rutted road, but it was soon downright lethal on a 30mph (50km/h) train speeding under bridges, and never mind the misery of exposure to the locomotive's exhaust and malign weather. Even the brakeman was ultimately forced inside the train (though until 1901 Queen Victoria insisted that a minion do purgatorial sentry duty at the rear of the locomotive tender when she travelled by royal train, in case she should wish an imperious command for more prudent speed to be conveyed to the engine-crew). That left only the luggage on the roof; some British railways were still carrying that way as late as the 1860s.

It took a long time for any European railway to concede ordinary passengers decent accommodation. In the 1830s they were tolerated by and large as an inescapable evil and consigned to little better than open wagons, often innocent of seats and with their only concession to protection from the weather a honeycomb

Right: Abingdon Road on the GWR about 1840. Railways at this period were not carefully segregated from their surroundings, and existing buildings were often used as shelters or 'booking offices'.
Below: The Stockton & Darlington 'Experiment' coach of 1825. The first passenger coaches were a form of stagecoach or personal carriage such as were used on the roads.
Bottom: An American bogie coach, photographed in the 1880s.

of drainholes in the floor to save the wretched occupants shivering ankle-deep in water during a deluge. The makings of an intermediate second-class developed when some of these open cars were given a verandah roof. Second-class compartment coaches did not emerge until about 1837, which was also the year when mails between London and the North-West were first entrusted to rail, the Liverpool & Manchester taking them over from road at Birmingham. A year later a Post Office man, John Ramsay, devised the essentials of the long-lived British railway apparatus whereby speeding mail trains could pouch mailbags suspended from lineside standards *en route*; the system was briefly copied by the Prussian State Railways and the Nord of France, but not elsewhere.

Trainboard lavatories were inconceivable before 1850 (it would have been a solecism to broach such a subject). No matter that in 1836 the Cumberland Valley Railroad in Pennsylvania was already operating between Harrisburg and Chambersburg a crude dormitory car with three tiers of berths down the side of the body – the bunks, with self-service bedding that was only spasmodically laundered, were contested for on a first-come, first-served basis – and in England the London & Birmingham had in 1838 evolved a 'bed-carriage', in which a trestle

could be inserted between facing seats and a cushion placed upon it to complete a couch. Where bodily needs were concerned, both ingestion and excretion had to wait until the next of the train's frequent stops. In time many stations built up a high reputation for their restaurants and luncheon baskets.

America progressed to general use of bogie carriages well before European railways. The fixed-wheel four- or six-wheeler rode solidly enough on the generally well-laid-out lines of Europe, but its rigid wheelbase and light weight were as ill at ease on the curves and corrugations of early American track as the British locomotive imports. The American switch to longer, bogie cars was inspired by another of those improbable individuals whom the railway concept stimulated to inventive genius, a New Jersey farmer named Ross Winans.

Winans' first contribution to rail technology was the integral wheel-and-axle assembly, which he then applied to a swivelling bogie or, as Americans have termed it ever since, 'truck'. In 1831 he put two bogies beneath a car more than twice as long as anything in contemporary use and this vehicle, the Baltimore & Ohio *Columbia*, set the style for all future American railroad passenger car-building, with its open verandahs at each end and its saloon layout with central gangway as opposed to the compartment format already established in Europe.

Winans subsequently accepted an invitation from Czar Nicholas I to set up a car-building plant at Aleksandrovsk. There he created the most splendidly appointed passenger vehicles yet seen on rails before he returned home, bequeathing management of the Russian enterprise to two of his sons. Back in America Winans turned to locomotive design and manufacture, vying with Baldwin to evolve the country's first successful six- or eight-coupled machine. Baldwin got there first with an 0–8–0 for the Georgia Railroad in 1842, but Winans, who established his own Baltimore workshops in 1844, made the more lasting mark on American locomotive history with the first Baltimore & Ohio 'camelback' 0–8–0s of 1848, so-called because the driving cab was mounted saddle-fashion on top of the long boiler, ahead of the firebox.

As mid-century approached the miserable lot of the ordinary European rail passenger was becoming a critical issue, above all in Britain. There the new transport mode, besides superseding stagecoaches, was stimulating a new travel market so vigorously that by 1850 the annual total of rail passengers would reach 80 million. The impact of railways on national life was epitomized by the 1851 Great Exhibition portraying the country's industrial achievement, which was staged in London within Paxton's phenomenal Crystal Palace. Baited by a massive programme of excursion trains, working men from provincial cities like Leeds and Manchester flocked to the capital on cheap return fares of only five shillings, making journeys previously unthinkable by stage-coach, which would have cost thirty-five shillings for the single journey each way and that for nothing better than a perch on its roof.

But it was still possible for an inquest to record that one wretched passenger 'died of cold and exposure whilst travelling in a second-class carriage of the Great Western Railway'. As for his inferiors, the GWR was not even prepared to dignify them as 'passengers' in its official terminology. Third-class ticket-holders were not admitted to passenger trains proper but consigned to night goods trains, where they huddled on planks laid as crude seats across ordinary wagons; that meant, of course, that third-class travellers boarded their trains in the goods depot, not the passenger station. When one of these mixed trains ran into a landslip in Sonning Cutting, near Reading, in the small hours of Christmas Eve 1841 and was derailed, the eight people who died did not succumb to vehicle damage but to broken necks when their overturning wagon threw them out. Some railways refused to carry third-class passengers at all.

In 1844 the Gladstone government was roused to enact that 'each company be required to run over their line on each weekday at least one train conveying third-class passengers in carriages provided with seats and protected from the weather, at a speed of not less than 12 miles an hour, including stoppages, and at a fare not exceeding one penny a mile for adults, children under twelve half-price and under three free, 56lb of luggage to be allowed without charge.' For some years all that meant on many railways was the supersession of open wagons by what were little better than cattle-wagons, dimly illuminated by a single pot-lamp burning a pungent vegetable oil (the standard form of vehicle lighting in all classes of accommodation from the late 1830s); the passengers could only view the passing scene by standing to peer through meagre shutters – or, on a few benevolent lines, poky windows – high up the van walls.

The First Railway Stations
The British pioneers set the fashion for the world's first railway stations just as they

The L&BR train shed at Euston Square in 1837, with open third-class carriages in the background.

had in the locomotive design field. Like their stagecoach antecedents, the early passenger railways frequently appointed convenient inns to shelter intending passengers and sell them rail tickets – the term 'booking office', in fact, is an echo of the old stagecoach practice of ticket issue from a tear-off book. Before long, however, the characteristics of the railway demanded custom-built premises to combine passenger handling with operating business.

Here and there railways adapted existing buildings as station offices, but for the most part the companies built new. At first, for economy and what was also imagined to be operational simplicity, every railway adopted the single-platform layout, with the platform track bisected by crossovers connecting with an adjoining

through line so that each half was reserved for trains going in one direction. Two of the earliest city stations, Crown Street in Liverpool and Mount Clare in Baltimore, were patterned thus; so, elsewhere, were Malines (1835), St Petersburg (1837), Potsdam (1838), Vienna and Amsterdam (1839).

The last single-platform station of any consequence was Newcastle, built in 1855. It was already something of a dinosaur at its completion, as the intensification of train services and the lengthening of trains had outstripped the capacity of other single-platform layouts. Derby had had to co-opt some of the carriage storage tracks under its overall train-shed (that was also a feature conceived from the start at Liverpool Crown Street) for passenger loading and put up with passengers

stumbling over intervening tracks to get to them. Throughout most of the world, where railways were content with low platforms (or none at all), passengers were allowed to roam the station layout to and from their trains for a century and more, but the British soon made the footbridge essential station furniture, as multi-platform layouts came into vogue. The first British station to be built with separate platforms for each direction of travel was London's original Euston of 1838, but before long that arrangement was soon confined to through stations. At the start of the 1840s terminals were adopting the 'head' format, in which the platforms' inner ends were joined by a cross-section fronted by the station's main buildings – David Mocatta's Brighton station of 1841 was an early instance.

As late as 1850–52 a few terminals were still laid out like the 1838 Euston, such as the original King's Cross in London and Gare Montparnasse in Paris. Quaintest of them all was Pötsch's 1844 station at Leipzig, where the train-shed was fronted by a huge classic arcade, through which the four tracks projected to converge on a turntable in the forecourt and rivet public interest with a daily show of engine manoeuvres. But by then it was clear that the 'head' layout was the one to elaborate for termini in the face of a steadily expanding train service. It was the French who unveiled the model, first in the initial Paris Gare du Nord of 1847 but much more grandly in the Paris Gare de l'Est of 1847–52, acclaimed for decades afterwards as the world's finest station both aesthetically and operationally. Key feature of the French concept was the frontal building's spacious concourse through which passengers could move freely to and from any of a number of parallel platforms without hampering train operating business. *La salle des pas perdus* they called it, romantically if enigmatically, and still do at every French station large or small.

The first European station buildings were conceived simply to fulfil a basic function as an assembly and ticket-issuing point for passengers. But as the railways rapidly built up status and business not only did their operational accommodation enlarge: the bigger stations attracted adjuncts of hotels, restaurants and bars. For the resultant complexes of public service buildings and, as it were, industrial plant – i.e., the train operating area – there were neither architectural nor stylistic

precedents, and the railways had to proceed empirically. Hence the eclecticism of nineteenth-century stations. The French at least imposed a logical unity on their structures by integrating the design of buildings and train-shed, but in Britain the train-sheds of the bigger stations were left mostly to the railway's engineers while the frontage was entrusted to prestigious architects of the day.

To inculcate in the public an impression of the railway as the modern counterpart of the old city gateway to the outside world managements generally encouraged their architects to the monumental. Most celebrated manifestation of this syndrome, of course, was Philip Hardwick's colossal Doric Arch at the approach to Euston, which was the wonder of London when it was first erected, drawing omnibus-loads of wide-eyed sightseers every day. But to a number of respected critics the railways were overplaying flamboyance at the expense of developing operational convenience. 'A piece of Brobdignaggian absurdity', snorted Pugin at the Euston Arch, adding that it 'must have cost the company a sum which would have built a first-rate station, replete with convenience, and which would have been really grand from its simplicity.' Ruskin, too, called the 'decoration of the railroad station' one of the 'strange and evil tendencies of the present day'.

No such extravagance marked the early American stations; all available capital had

Cannon Street station, London, which like Charing Cross station was and still is a terminus for trains to the Kent coast and London's south-east suburbia.

been absorbed in tracklaying, bridge and tunnel construction. To a greater extent than in Europe existing buildings were appropriated or neighbouring taverns designated as shelter for waiting passengers. Quite often trains were advertised simply as departing from the 'vicinity of' a known street intersection. Such stations as were built were styled in the local idiom and distinguishable from their neighbours only by belfries (to signify an impending train movement) and clock-towers. Nearly all were of wood, with the forseeable pyrotechnic consequences in more than one town.

More imposing and solid stations of the European city pattern, and initially apeing European styles, began to develop in the country's first railroad hub, Boston, in the later 1830s. At last, in 1849, America's first significant city terminal was completed by the New Haven Railroad on Boston's Union Street, a splendid edifice with a 300 ft-long frontage in predominantly Italian style, but with Moorish touches about its two extraordinarily ornate flanking towers, and unprecedentedly opulent public rooms. Their users would have to wait two more decades, however, before comparable comfort could be found on American trains.

RAILROAD BOOM IN THE AMERICAS

In rail history the opening years of the nineteenth century's second half were dominated by the dynamic expansion of the American railroad system. Its motivation was nationwide appreciation, at last, that the new transport medium was not an ancillary of the waterways but one of pivotal importance to the country's social and economic development in its own right.

THE NEW LINES OF THE OLD NORTH-WEST

Up to the midpoint of the century a few local enterprises had already been launched essentially to connect adjacent towns and cities, such as New York and Philadelphia. But for most railroad promoters the primary objective was a lateral link between eastern seaboard centres and the waterborne transport of the Middle West, on the Great Lakes and on the Ohio, Mississippi and Missouri. These great rivers, their navigable tributaries and associated canals were still regarded as the natural north-south highways. The railway's virtue was its ability to cut through the high ground separating the river valleys from each other and the ports and commerce in the east.

That was why Chicago was uninterested in railways until the late 1840s. A charter for a railway from the city westward to lead mines at Galena had been granted in 1836, but the project had been shelved for lack of any support from the city fathers. Who needed a railway in a city ensconced on the shore of Lake Michigan and with a network of plank wagonways adequately serving its quayside? At last, in 1846, an affluent real estate broker who became the city's first mayor, William Butler Ogden, espoused the scheme, shrugged off the obstructionist attitudes of his civic colleagues and sold the idea to the farmers of the plains. Opened in October 1848, the Galena & Chicago Union thrived immediately on wheat loads from the prairies. Within little more than a decade it was to burgeon into the powerful Chicago & North Western.

The success of Ogden's company, at a time when there was barely 100 miles (160 km) of track in the whole State of Illinois, awoke the old North-West to the crucial role the railway could play in opening up the territory commercially by making its products available to widespread US markets without intolerable transportation costs. The train was to be the making of the great US grainlands, not least in its encouragement of farming on a commercial scale.

Part of the hectic 1850s expansion in this area multiplied links between the farmlands and the eastern seaboard, influencing two-way trade in produce from the agricultural upper Mississippi valley and new farm machinery from the factories of the East, but just as significant was emergence of the first important north-south trunk railways. Outstanding among these enterprises was the Illinois Central, of which the 705 mile (1,135 km) route from Chicago the length of Illinois to its southernmost tip at Cairo was laid in the incredibly short space of five years, between 1851 and 1856. It was the longest main line in the world at the time.

It was also by far the costliest railroad yet built in America and would never have been undertaken at that early date but for

The great event in American railroading history was the completion of the first transcontinental route on 10 May 1869. A final, golden spike was driven to celebrate the occasion.

ILLINOIS CENTRAL RAILROAD COMPANY

OFFER FOR SALE

ONE MILLION ACRES OF SUPERIOR FARMING LANDS,

IN FARMS OF

40, 80 & 160 acres and upwards at from $8 to $12 per acre.

THESE LANDS ARE

NOT SURPASSED BY ANY IN THE WORLD.

THEY LIE ALONG

THE WHOLE LINE OF THE CENTRAL ILLINOIS RAILROAD,

For Sale on LONG CREDIT, SHORT CREDIT and for CASH, they are situated near TOWNS, VILLAGES, SCHOOLS and CHURCHES.

An advertisement for the sale of land underlines the ability of railroads like the Illinois Central to raise large sums of money from land deals.

land grants, a financial aid that spurred so much of the subsequent railroad extension to the Far West. The idea was the brainchild of a visionary young attorney, Stephen A. Douglas, who was appointed US Senator for Illinois in 1847. At that time the Federal Government was having scant success in selling off the land west of Ohio which it mostly owned since the nation's formation. Since modern transportation had elsewhere proved the key to commercial development, why not, thought Douglas, present some of the land to the individual state administrations on condition that they exploit the gift to create an integrated, state-owned transport system? That would vastly enhance the value of the land and magnetize new settlers.

Despite support in the Lower House of Congress from Abraham Lincoln, then a Representative, Douglas' first move for his principle was voted down, but he won through in 1850. To his disgust his original theory of state control went by the board; instead of scheming a co-ordinated rail and canal system, Illinois simply handed its grant of just over $2\frac{1}{2}$ million acres (1 million hectares) to the Illinois Central, which promptly mortgaged most of the land for

nearly eight times the figure per acre at which the Federal Government had been finding few takers. But with the $17 million realized the Illinois Central was soon at work on its railway.

For 'land grant' read 'land grab', according to some later historians. That is hardly warranted, because the Federal Government was careful to attach conditions which some hold have more than recouped the price of the gift, never mind how one quantifies the added value which new railroads unquestionably generated. For instance, lines built with benefit of land grant were for ever after required to hand over 7 per cent of their gross earnings, which all but doubled the taxes the normal route paid in the ensuing century; they were compelled to carry troops and war materials at half-rate; and at a later date they were subjected to a 20 per cent discount on the usual scale for carriage of US mails.

Following the Illinois Central precedent (to be accurate, one should note that the Mobile & Ohio in Alabama and Mississippi shared with it the distinction of receiving the first grants under the Bill of 1850), some 20 million acres (8 million hectares) of land were disbursed during the 1850s alone. These grants were the making of the big 'Granger' railroads (so-called because they ranged from Chicago over the grain-growing states extending northwards from Kansas, Missouri and

Illinois to the Canadian border): the Chicago & North Western; the Chicago, Milwaukee & St Paul; the Chicago, Rock Island & Pacific; and the Chicago, Burlington & Quincy. But the hand-outs following the Civil War, especially to promote completion of the transcontinental routes, were vastly bigger. At the end of the day US railroads had benefited in all by the gift of nearly 250,000 sq. miles (650,000 sq. km) of land, an area bigger than that of France.

For the Granger railroads the land grants stoked a fire of ambition lit when the 1848 discovery of gold at Sutter's Mill, in California, sent the 'Forty-niners' scurrying across the continent after the news had percolated to the East Coast the following year. On their way the 'Forty-niners' created growing townships which were tempting bait for railway development now that promoters had grasped there was more to the future of trains than service of waterway transport. The explosive growth which resulted was remarkable. By 1855 both Galena & Chicago (the embryonic Chicago & North Western) and Chicago Burlington & Quincy, which had been born as no more than a 13 mile (21 km) local line west of Chicago at its opening in late 1850, were at the Mississippi; and the following year the Rock Island was across it on the first Mississippi rail bridge. By 1854, too, Chicago had through rail connection with St Louis to the south-west when the Rock Island joined tracks at Joliet, Illinois, with the railroad heading up from east St Louis that was later known as the Chicago & Alton.

A significant feature of the Granger roads' expansion was the companies' rapid accretion of financial strength. The railroads which had generated the radial drive from the region's economic centre, Chicago, quickly made such good money that bankers readily extended them credit. That gave them the resources to accelerate their advance by buying out local schemes or weaker concerns along their line of route and reducing the amount of new track necessary to attain their objectives in the west and south-west. The same process marked the natural race of the eastern seaboard companies to tap this rich-looking railroad activity in America's old North-West. But these were only the first tentative steps towards sensible integration of a national rail system that was otherwise developing in an inefficiently fragmented fashion, with no common agreement on gauge and very tenuous arrangements for inter-company movement of freight even where common gauges adjoined.

On the eve of the Civil War the American railroad map had been transformed within just ten years. The focus of development had moved sharply north-westward from the eastern seaboard and nearly a third of the country's 30,000 and more route-miles (48,300km) of railway interlaced the five states of the old North-West; Illinois, which had begun the 1850s with only 111 miles (179km) of line, had suddenly jumped to second place in the table of states with 2,790 miles (4,490km), beaten only by Ohio with 2,946 (4,741km). Chicago, all but rail-less in 1850, was by 1860 the hub of eleven different railroads, with three routes to the Atlantic coast, one

reaching beyond St Louis for a new goal of New Orleans, one to the Missouri and three more stretching out beyond the Mississippi for Iowa. The 'Windy City' was on its way to its eventual dais as the busiest railway centre in the world, served in its later prime by as many as twenty-two different main-line railroads, six main-line passenger terminals and a clutch of railways whose sole business was the interchange of freight vehicles between the main-line systems.

CIVIL WAR AND THE TRANSCONTINENTALS

The American Civil War erupted in the spring of 1861. It was the first war waged with the logistical support of railways and, moreover, its outcome was strongly influenced by the way the railways had

developed in the previous decade. The tremendous growth of east-west rail links between the North-Eastern states and the upper Mississippi and Ohio Valleys contrasted sharply with the sparse railway map of the eleven states in the Confederacy, which together aggregated only 9,000 route-miles (14,500km), or less than a third of the country's total. Not only that, but in quality and quantity of equipment the Southern railroads were eclipsed by those of the North and Middle West, which made the economic and military resources of Mid-Western states available

The rapid development of railways in the old North-West was particularly reflected in the expansion of the Illinois Central, here seeking to proclaim the global advantages of its services.

to the Union cause to a degree inconceivable had the crunch come a decade earlier. The entire railway system in the South fielded no more locomotives than the Erie and the Pennsylvania Railroads combined and it was desperately short of the means to build locomotives, rolling stock and track. Worse still, it was deserted by a good many of its staff, for Southerners had a congenital distaste for things mechanical and had recruited a good many Yankees to run their railways.

The epic 1862 affair of the *General* is well known: a Confederate 4–4–0 locomotive, the *General*, was hijacked deep in Southern territory near Chattanooga by a daring party of Union scouts under Capt. James J. Andrews and run north with the aim of ripping up track and bridges *en route* so as to disable a vital Confederate Army supply line. But it was pursued, until the last stick of wood in its tender was exhausted, by some doughty Confederate railwaymen on the *Texas*. They were undaunted by every desperate ploy of the Union band to halt them – rails torn up, a wagon sent rolling back to plough into the *Texas*, another set alight on a wooden bridge, and so on. But the railways played out a much more vital if less romantic role in moving men and

munitions – whole armies, in fact; in the autumn of 1863, to cite one instance, thirty trains aggregating 600 vehicles ferried 25,000 men and their entire equipment the 1,200 or so miles (1,900 km) from the Potomac to Tennessee for the relief of the Union force in Chattanooga.

Many railroads behind both lines grew financially fat out of their war work. None more so than the Louisville & Nashville (L&N), which was right in the cockpit of the struggle and made a killing from both sides; L&N gross revenue soared 500 per cent during the war, though the takings were heavily offset by the fierce scorching

Above: A Federal camp at City Point, Virginia, set up around the railroad tracks. The American Civil War saw the first military use of railways.
Below: The exploits of the General, *a Western & Atlantic Railroad 4–4–0, during the Civil War inspired Buster Keaton's 1927 film of the same name.*
Above right: Results of the destruction of railroads during the Civil War, at Richmond, Virginia, in 1865.
Below right: The Union Pacific Railroad demonstrates the toughness of its Devil's Gate Bridge during the construction of the first transcontinental.

its infrastructure suffered in battle and especially from the Confederate Armies when they retired defeated from Atlanta. Even the Illinois Central managed a 10 per cent dividend in 1865, despite the reduced rates paid for its heavy traffic in men, horses, guns and wounded under the conditions of its land grant. The railways on both sides were severely hammered during the Civil War, but those of the Confederacy were ravaged by far the worse, particularly in the final months when Sherman's army was methodically ripping up the rails and gutting almost every vehicle and depot in its path through Georgia and the Carolinas.

California's first railway, the Sacramento Valley, had opened a 21 mile (34km) line early in 1856 and its young engineer from the East, Theodore Judah, was soon fired with ambition to drive a line inland across the Sierras, but it took him five years to drum up enough support to form a company, the Central Pacific of California, for his objective. At that juncture, in the spring of 1861, Abraham Lincoln had just been inaugurated President and the Republicans had come to power confronting a threatened break-up of the nation. Now it was vital to bind east and west securely; and with no Southerners in Congress rational plotting of a central route across the continent was that much simpler. In July 1862, once they had got essential war measures out of the way, Congress passed and Lincoln signed a Bill authorizing with benefit of loans and land grants both the Central Pacific, to run east from Sacramento, and the Union Pacific,

to run westward from the Missouri River at Omaha, Nebraska; the two were to converge in the vicinity of Nevada and Utah.

Both projects were under way by the end of 1863, but on the Union Pacific (UP) mismanagement and inexperience got the job off to a slow start. In its first two years the UP had only a beggarly 40 miles (65km) of finished track to show. Meanwhile the Central Pacific was forging over the Sierra Nevada mountains and threatening to advance beyond the Great Salt Lake into the UP's assigned territory. In early 1866 a rattled UP management brought in a couple of Ohio contractors,

the Casement brothers, who before the Civil War had established a Brassey-like reputation for leadership, man management and logistical acumen in the building of several Mid-Western lines. They transformed the UP work force.

It was a job that had to mix military discipline with business management and the inspiration of labour by exhortation and incentives. The men generally worked with rifles in reach, alert for the whine and thud of arrows from prowling Cheyenne or Sioux, and a good many vehicles in the work train had ceiling racks bristling with spare weaponry. From time to time the whole force would have to retreat inside the train and defend it like a fortress.

In sharp contrast to the meagre output of 1864–5, 305 miles (491km) of UP track were laid in 1866, 240 miles (386km) in 1867 and 425 miles (684km) in 1868. Now it was an unashamed race with the Central Pacific. As the two fingers of track edged towards each other in the spring of 1869, the Casements coaxed their men into laying over $7\frac{1}{2}$ miles (12km) in a single day. The UP's exuberant vice-president, T.C. Durant, a doctor turned machiavellian stock manipulator who was given to making any event in the UP's progress the pretext for a public relations jamboree, loudly bet $10,000 that the Casements' feat was unbeatable. Only a few days before the meet of the two lines the Central Pacific trounced him by laying over 10 miles (16km) in one day.

On 10 May 1869 special trains ferried the hierarchy of both railways to Promontory Point, Utah, in a wild valley north of the Great Salt Lake, where the meeting of two lines and completion of the first transcontinental route was solemnized by the driving of a ceremonial last spike made of pure gold. In all some 1,750 route-miles (2,820 km) of track had been put down in four years. Other transcontinentals were soon under way and four more were complete by the 1890s: the Northern Pacific from Minnesota to Seattle in 1883; the Santa Fe, which by 1899 was a 7,000 mile (11,300 km) network ranging from Chicago to the Gulf and the Pacific, with a 2,577 mile (4,147 km) route from Chicago to San Francisco; the Great Northern, also from Minnesota to the Pacific at Seattle in 1893; and finally the Southern Pacific between Southern California and, eventually, New Orleans.

OPERATING THE NEW RAILWAYS

In their race to build, American railroads had been paying considerably less attention to disciplined operation, compatibility with each other and durability of their components than the Europeans. Until the 1850s the railroads were operated solely by timetable, which prescribed at what loops or points of siding refuge, and when, opposing trains on the single line should meet; and, according to a very broad classification of train types, which had priority. It was a valid system so long as trains ran to time; but whenever they were late there was no way of improvising a variation – the whole service had to be put back. Trains could kick their heels for hours on end, waiting for a drastically delayed train to turn up at its prescribed meeting place. That was rectified after the advent of Morse's electric telegraph in 1844 and an Erie operating man's realization, six years later, that with its use one could verify the whereabouts of a train defaulting on its meet and discover whether the timetable could be safely varied. Thus was born train despatching: the continuous control of traffic over a delineated sector by a central despatcher, issuing to drivers paper orders specifying where they were to make their meets according to his latest information by telegraph about other trains in the area.

But reliance on timetable, time intervals between succeeding trains and obedience to despatcher's orders still left a great deal to crossed-fingers dependence on human discipline where safety was concerned. As railroads grew more speed-hungry, so did their engine-crews' obliviousness to risk. It took some pretty gruesome wrecks before the majority of railroads accepted that block signalling on roughly the British pattern was inescapable, even though it did nothing for their dividends.

A powerful disincentive to disciplined working in the early days was the total lack of systematized clock-setting in the country. Each locality worked by sun-time, so that Chicago's clocks, for instance, would be 31 minutes behind Pittsburgh's, 19 minutes ahead of St Paul's and 33 minutes ahead of Omaha's. A single state could be functioning on up to forty different local times, but by basing their operation on the clocks at their major terminals the railroads had managed to cut their time variations nationwide to fifty-four by mid-century. It was an inter-railroad convention which eventually put forward the four-zone clock scheme – Eastern, Central, Mountain and Pacific – that was adopted for the nation as a whole in 1883, despite the bitter objection of many that they would rather live by God's time than that of the railroad barons.

Gauge variance was one of the most urgent problems at the conclusion of the Civil War. Its extent, ramified by an

Above and left: Two posters advertising railroads with transcontinental routes. The first (left) opened in 1869 on the joining of the Union Pacific line from the east with the Central Pacific from the west, while the Northern Pacific (above) began its service in 1883.
Above right: An early American transcontinental train is greeted by Chinese coolies (used in large numbers on construction work) as it steams through a series of snow sheds. These were to keep tracks clear of avalanching snow.

outbreak of narrow-gauge construction in the mountain states of the West, has already been described in Chapter Two; at the start of the 1860s nearly half the national system was not of standard 4ft 8½in (1,435mm) width. Lincoln himself had wanted to make the first transcontinental to the 5ft (1,524mm) gauge favoured by many in California at the time, but thankfully he acceded to eastern railroad pressure for 4ft 8½in. Construction of the Union Pacific that way at last persuaded the non-standard lines they had better conform. But the changeover was a slow business. The broad-gauge Erie held out until 1882 and the South – which went blindly on building over 4,000 new route-miles (6,440km) of 5ft gauge between 1865 and 1880 – finally followed suit in 1886.

The demands of the Civil War traffic had inculcated a much more healthy respect for strong track and engineering works. Iron rail was being universally employed for new construction by the 1860s and within two more decades steel rails, steadily increasing in weight, were in common use.

From the start of the century's second half, too, railroads were building substantial metal bridges, not the accumulation of trestles that cheaply satisfied most of them in the early days because good timber surrounded their routes and trains were light; if the waterway's current was too strong or it was too wide for such a flimsy structure, then the majority had previously terminated their railway at its banks and decanted passengers and freight on to ferries. One should add that the trestle principle was not discarded: trestle structures in metalwork became commonplace, up to sizes such as that of Canadian Pacific's Lethbridge Viaduct in Alberta, a mile (1.6km) long and 314ft (96m) high.

'LAW! WHAT DO I CARE ABOUT LAW?'
Feverish expansion of the American railroad system resumed after the Civil War, the additions climbing steadily from a rate of about 3,500 new route-miles (5,600km) annually in the late 1860s to 5,700 (9,200km) in the first decade of the twentieth century, with only one dip between 1890 and 1900, when a fresh financial panic cut the figure to around 3,000 (4,800km). It was the age of the great railway builders – of men like the Canadian-born James J. Hill who built the Great Northern, was closely involved in the birth of the Canadian Pacific and eventually gathered the Northern Pacific and the 8,000 mile (12,900km) Chicago, Burlington & Quincy into his empire; and Edward H. Harriman, who won control of the Union Pacific, which had been perennially debilitated by financial problems after its completion, rebuilt it as a sturdy, modern track the whole way from Omaha to the Salt Lake at Ogden, and then did the same with the Southern Pacific main line.

But the second half of the century was the period, too, of corruption and intrigue, as the now big – and largely very profitable – business of railways created its millionaire barons and laid such tempting bait for mountebank contractors and stock manipulators. Pre-eminent among the barons was Commodore Cornelius Vanderbilt (or Van Derbilt, as he himself pretentiously spelled it), who had already accumulated a multi-million-dollar fortune from steamboat operation on the Hudson river, Long Island Sound and the high seas before the Civil War. At sixty-eight, taxed by the states of the Union with duplicity in the use of his ships during the war, and anyway sceptical about the future of American shipping, he bought his way into the New York railroad scene. Within five years he had control of the New York Central (NYC), created in 1853 from an amalgam of twelve small New York State systems. The Commodore died in 1877, but he had brought his eldest son, William H., into the business, under whom the boundaries of the Vanderbilt rail empire were rolled further and further out until at the turn of the century New York Central route-mileage had exceeded 10,000 (16,100 km) and its trains roamed the whole North-East, from New York to Boston (over the leased Boston & Albany), Buffalo, Cleveland, Chicago, Indianapolis and St Louis and Cincinnati.

Historians now doubt the substance of the table-thumping demand so often attributed to Vanderbilt senior – 'Law! What do I care about law? Hain't I got the power?' – but it plausibly summarizes the philosophy of this domineering old Napoleon, who certainly had to retreat and regroup on occasion, but never once submitted to a Waterloo. Though he had a fortune of some $105 millions to hand on to his son, it had to be conceded that he ran his railroad efficiently and kept its stockholders content with solid dividends, even

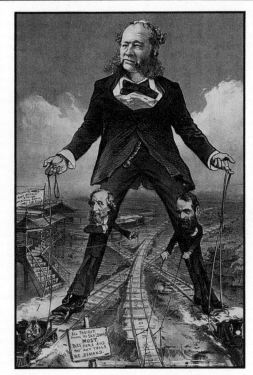

though – like that of a good many railroads at the time – the NYC capital structure had been heavily inflated.

The rogues of the Eastern railroad scene were Daniel Drew, James Fisk and Jay Gould. Drew, a one-time cattle drover, was the archetypal financial mugger. To him there was no such thing as immorality in business dealing (or scarcely any such thing: from time to time he fretted about the after-life and hedged his position by contributions to religious institutions). Other speculators were there to be fleeced. Drew, too, had been a power in the steamboat business, but had left that to play the New York Stock Exchange. When the first of the East's trunk lines, the Erie Railroad, was taking shape at mid-century he scented a killing, manoeuvred himself

on to its board of directors (easily enough done, as the financially embarrassed company was happy to sell anyone with money a place) and bided his time. It came in 1856 when the Erie needed money in a hurry and Drew offered it on loan in exchange for a mortgage on Erie equipment and the post of Erie Treasurer. Drew never became Erie President – he didn't need to; as it couldn't repay his loan unless he said so, the railroad was effectively his.

The high summer of Drew's Erie malfeasance was the years 1864–72, when he had attracted to his side Fisk, a former peddler and circus ticket-seller from Vermont, and Gould, the most astute stock manipulator of the three, a Wall Street broker born in Roxbury, New York. In that period the Erie's book value was trebled (and the trio's fortunes made), without any tangible enhancement of its worth or injection of new money, solely by poker playing with Erie stock on Wall Street.

At the height of the action they even trapped Commodore Vanderbilt. The Drew-Vanderbilt war of 1867–8 for control of the Erie was an incredible imbroglio of stock juggling, confidence trickery, injunction and counter-injunction, of setting the courts of one state against those of another, of exploitation of state lines to escape the validity of unfriendly writs, and of efforts to corrupt pliable state legislatures. The skirmishes ended in Vanderbilt's one really serious defeat, teaching him, he growled, that 'it never pays to kick a skunk'. But at the end of the day Drew, too, was ousted by Gould, who became President of a ruined Erie, which paid no dividend for the next seventy years. Fisk was gunned down in a quarrel over his mistress in 1872 and the same year Gould was ejected from the Erie,

largely at the instigation of its English stockholders.

Gould, however, moved on to his masterstroke in the West. Buying himself into control of the Union Pacific in 1878, he upped the price of its stock by payment of quite unwarranted dividends, then sold off his own holdings at immense profit. The money was spent on buying rival but financially distressed routes from Cheyenne, Wyoming, to Denver (the Denver Pacific) and Denver to Kansas City (the Kansas Pacific), then launching a rate war and threatening to build westward and run the UP into the ground. Gould's fellow directors on the UP needed little prodding to take the point. In 1880 they accepted a merger on the basis of a share exchange, a transaction from

Above left: A cartoon of the time illustrating the huge power which was wielded by the railroad magnates during the building of their empires.
Left: Even in 1880 the standard form of the American 4–4–0 was little changed. Many thousands had been built by such manufacturers as Baldwin and supplied almost from stock.
Above: An excellent example of a typical American timber trestle bridge with a mixed goods/passenger train. Although the photo was almost certainly taken in the 1880s, the locomotive pre-dates it by about twenty years.

which Gould netted yet more millions of dollars. A complicated character who in his private life was widely respected for his charity, Gould died of tuberculosis in late 1892. The shares of every railroad in which he was involved responded, as they say, in sympathy – with a prompt and substantial rise.

The American species of railroad tycoon expired with Gould. By the end of the century its environment had been so soundly sanitated by progressive Government regulation that there was precious little dirty ground left to feed on. It was the viciousness of the internecine railroad warfare which provoked Government action, especially a bitter contest between the New York Central and Pennsylvania in the early 1880s, when each embarked on plans for a number of new or extended lines which closely paralleled the other's main routes.

One might think customers would have revelled in the benefits of rate-cutting. Not so. For one thing, the keenest rate-cutting generally betrayed the most feckless railroads: a company teetering on the brink of bankruptcy and unable to pay interest to its creditors could afford what a well-managed concern could not. For another, some customers were more equal than others when it came to rate-cutting: big concerns – like, for instance, John D. Rockefeller's Standard Oil – were not only conceded discounts on the basic rate

but a kickback from the above-average rates some other customers were conned into paying. Finally, railroad users got more and more irritated at the frequent, unpredictable fluctuations of rate when railroads were locked in battle; some shippers alleged that they were being quoted up to fifty different rates in a single twelve-month period.

First to clip the rapacious railroads' wings were the farmers of the Mid-West. Enraged by the discriminatory, 'what-the-traffic-will-bear' charging of railroads which they had largely financed into being in the first place (sometimes by mortgaging their own land), they united to persuade several Mid-Western states into quite draconian regulation of railroad freight rates in the early 1870s. The railroads fought these so-called Granger laws up to the Supreme Court but made little headway until a case of 1886, when the Supreme Court held that the Wabash Railroad was exempted from the constraints in the case of goods crossing state lines. That made Federal intervention inevitable.

Early the following year the Interstate Commerce Commission (ICC), the bane of mid-twentieth-century American railroading, was established. Initially the ICC was mandated chiefly to set and enforce maximum freight and passenger rates, and to eradicate under-the-counter rebates, kickbacks and all the other nefarious practices of the buccaneering companies. But in time its powers were extended step by step until by 1920 they covered almost every facet of railroading, from prescription of accounting method and authority over service withdrawals to the fixing of speed limits.

Finally, the railroads roused their own workers to concerted action. The first railroad labour unions were formed in the 1860s, but more for social objectives than economic purpose, as their title of 'brotherhoods' suggests. Then, in 1877, the railroads attempted to cut wages even though they were disgorging massive dividends to their stockholders. A strike by Baltimore & Ohio enginemen soon spread throughout the eastern states and westward to Chicago and St Louis. Riots erupted as first state militia, then Federal troops were mobilized to protect railroad property. By the time it was all over 100 had been killed and 500 wounded. From then on the brotherhoods steadily solidified.

GROWTH OF THE RAILWAYS IN NORTH AMERICA

The first train in the USA ran in 1829 and prompted an immediate rush of railway building. By 1850 9,000 route-miles (14,500 km) had been laid, mainly along the eastern seaboard. The next decade saw a further 21,000 miles (33,800 km) added as activity shifted to the booming Mid-West; in the same decade Chicago was transformed by the railway from a town of 29,000 inhabitants to a city with 109,000. Construction rapidly spread south and west, the first transcontinental line being finished in 1869 when engineers from the Union Pacific and Central Pacific shook hands in Utah.

Despite having its first line in 1836, Canada enjoyed much slower growth. In 1850 route-mileage stood at only 100 miles (160 km), but the construction of the Grand Trunk Railway added 800 miles (1,300 km) by 1860, and the agricultural potential of the prairies stimulated westward expansion. The Canadian Pacific completed Canada's first transcontinental route in 1885. Further opening up of the interior and west pushed the network up from 10,200 route-miles (17,100 km) in 1886 to 30,000 miles (48,300 km) in 1914.

The USA's railways reached their maximum extent in 1916 when the total length of routes stood at 249,433 miles (399,342 km). By 1979 this figure had declined to 184,500 miles (295,000 km). Canada reached 41,630 miles (66,650 km) in 1933, a figure increased to 46,000 miles (74,000 km) in 1973 by the opening of new lines to exploit resources in the north of the country.

The South Carolina, *a double-ended locomotive built by Horatio Allen for the South Carolina Canal & Railroad Company, 1832.*

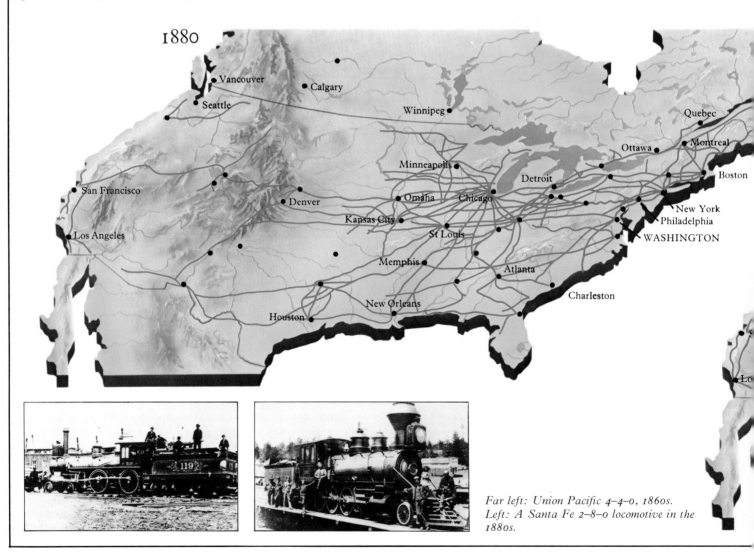

1880

Far left: Union Pacific 4–4–0, 1860s.
Left: A Santa Fe 2–8–0 locomotive in the 1880s.

1850

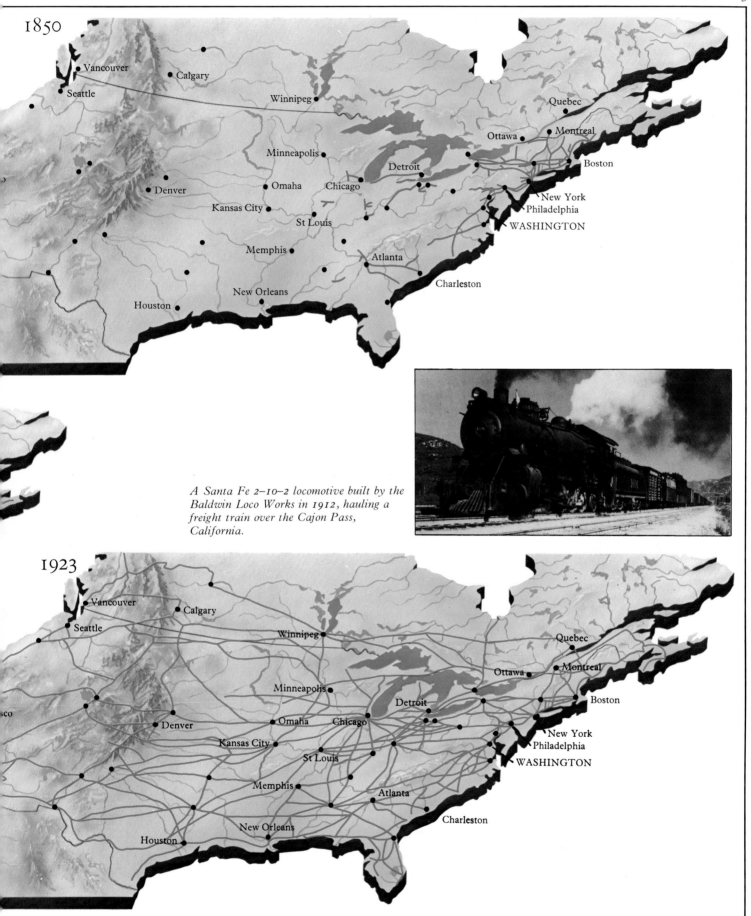

A Santa Fe 2–10–2 locomotive built by the
Baldwin Loco Works in 1912, hauling a
freight train over the Cajon Pass,
California.

1923

The first Canadian transcontinental route was built by the Canadian Pacific between 1881 and 1885. This photo was taken in the Rockies in about 1893.

WESTWARDS ACROSS CANADA

In neighbouring Canada railways did not become a force until the second half of the nineteenth century. With US route-mileage already topping 10,000 (16,100 km) at the start of the 1850s, Canada's sum of track was less than 100 (160 km). In the less friendly climate to the north inland settlement was nothing like so rapid as in the USA and the much sparser population was clustered about the coastlines or along the navigable waterways.

Canada's first trunk route was the Grand Trunk Railway, which started as a line from Montreal to Portland, Maine in 1853 and by 1860 stretched over 800 miles (1,300 km) westward through Toronto to the Michigan border at Port Huron and eastward through Quebec to Rivière du Loup, lower down the St Lawrence river. The Grand Trunk's capital was British, attracted by the Canadian Provincial Government's Guarantee Act of 1849 which ensured a 6 per cent return on half the construction costs of any railway of not less than 70 miles (110 km) in length. Unhappily, a provision added to the Act in 1851 also stipulated 5 ft 6 in (1,676 mm) gauge, to which practically all new Canadian railway was built until 1873, when the Grand Trunk, by then a system of over 2,000 miles (3,200 km), undertook a costly conversion to standard gauge.

Railways appeared in the Maritime Provinces of New Brunswick and Nova Scotia in the 1850s, but incentive to develop them had been dampened by the 1842 agreement over the north-eastern US boundary with Canada, concluded by US Secretary of State Daniel Webster and British plenipotentiary Lord Ashburton. Ceding most of Maine to the Americans had driven a thick wedge of US territory up the coast and ruled out beeline connection between the Maritimes and Quebec. Formation of the Dominion of Canada from Ontario, Quebec, Manitoba, New Brunswick and Nova Scotia in 1867, however, obliged the newly established Dominion Government to link all its components by rail and the Intercolonial Railway, financed under Imperial guarantee, was founded for the purpose in 1867 and finished in the summer of 1876. The Webster-Ashburton treaty drove the Intercolonial route on to a parallel course with the St Lawrence estuary, exposing it to severe waterborne competition and lossmaking operation from the start; but it was a political and strategic necessity – one of the first instances, probably, of deliberate Government upkeep of a railway as a social service.

Meanwhile, discovery of the agricultural potential of the great Canadian plain ranging a thousand miles (1,600 km) from the Great Lakes to the Rocky Mountains had been attracting a stampede of people and money to the north-west. The rich prospect was equally enticing to many American politicians and picaresque entrepreneurs; among the latter was the Philadelphia banker Jay Cooke who was sponsoring the Northern Pacific transcontinental just across the border in the USA. It was therefore vital for the Dominion to confederate the isolated west coast colony of British Columbia, which it did in 1871 on the basis of an undertaking to build a railway across Canada within a decade. The trouble was that the topographically most appealing route lay partly within the American states of Michigan, Wisconsin and Minnesota. Ambition in some US quarters to annex at least part of the territory between Manitoba and British Columbia had been foiled through acquisition of the latter by the Canadian Government from the Hudson's Bay Company in 1871, but there would be rich pickings yet from a railway that had to use US states as a corridor. The door to Jay Cooke was opened still wider by the Dominion Government's lack of resources for transcontinental construction, given its commitment to the Intercolonial Railway.

Fairly scabrous wheeling and dealing characterized the opening chapter of Canadian transcontinental history. It was abruptly concluded by the autumn of 1873 collapse of Jay Cooke's bank (precipitating a US Stock Market crash) and an immediate political furore in Canada, known as the Pacific Scandal, which forced the Government's resignation. Construction was tentatively begun in 1875, but it was 1881 before the last ripple of the Pacific Scandal had subsided, and the Canadian Pacific was incorporated under legislation which not only bestowed on it a huge grant of land and a $25 million subsidy but an undertaking to build about 700 miles (1,100 km) of route as public works. Building then began in earnest along a formidably difficult course but one that was wholly Canadian.

For its part the company had guaranteed to finish the railway in ten years. Incredibly, with construction armies working inwards from each end it was done in less than half the time, by early November 1885 (scheduled transcontinental operation did not start until the summer of 1886, however). The crossing of southern Ontario, then little more than a chaos of crenelated mountains, swamps and forests, was almost as taxing as the crossing of the Rockies and the even more daunting Selkirk Mountains. Around the rockbound northern shore of Lake Superior the route had to be hewn through solid rock – then came the swampland, into which the trackbed sank time and time again before it was stabilized. These 200 miles or so (320 km) absorbed 12,000 men, 2,000 teams of horses and twelve ships for four years, yet some 700 miles (1,100 km) in the prairies were finished in only fifteen months. In the Rockies the line was carried up to a summit of 5,329 ft (1,624 m) in Kicking Horse Pass, the so-called 'Great Divide', and to another peak of 4,300 ft (1,310 m) and the Selkirks, at Rogers Pass.

One of these summits soon had to be bypassed. Despite 4½ miles (7 km) of snow-shed protection – a very expensive insurance in itself, because the shelters had to be patrolled day and night against an engine exhaust's spark or, in summer, frequent forest fires setting their timberwork alight – the Rogers Pass line was far too vulnerable to blockage by snow and avalanches. In 1916 it had to be obviated by the 5 mile (8 km) Connaught Tunnel driven to the south-east of the pass under Mount Sir Donald. As for Kicking Horse Pass, the problem there was the 7½ miles (12 km) of 1 in 22.7–28.6 gradient, the steepest ever operated by adhesion on a main line, which the builders had indulged to avoid a great deal of costly tunnelling in the descent of the steep Yoho Valley defile from the summit to Field. Enginemen and operators alike abominated the notorious 'Big Hill'. To lift 710 tons, the maximum train weight per-mitted, to the top demanded the very vocal effort of four engines, two up front and two at the rear. The speed limit coming down was a rigid 6 mph (10 km/h) and at intervals a train's brakesmen had to jump down and run along it to make sure no wheels were sliding or brakes overheating. Every two miles there were safety spurs at which trains had to halt for inspection. Even so, disastrous runaways were frequent. Eventually, in 1909, the 'Big Hill', too, was eliminated by the boring of two spiral tunnels on an easier gradient (but still as steep as 1 in 45).

The dynamic expansion of Canadian railways did not get its momentum until the Canadian Pacific had opened up the prairies to settlement. From 1886 to the outbreak of the First World War the country's rail route-mileage tripled to just on 30,000 (48,300 km) as the Canadian Pacific and Grand Trunk consolidated and extended their empires in the east by acquisition or purchase of existing companies, and as a third major railway took the stage. This was the Canadian Northern, a late 1890s agglomeration of several small lines to east and west of the Great Lakes which soon began such a rapid sweep to east and west through acquisition or new construction – far too precipitate for the depth of its purse, in fact – that by 1915 it was operating a 9,000 mile (14,500 km) system stretching from Montreal to Vancouver.

The never well-heeled Grand Trunk desperately needed to be in the transcontinental business if it was ever to get securely into the black. The Dominion Government tried in the early 1900s to associate it with Mann and Mackenzie, the thrusting entrepreneurs of the Canadian Northern, but failed. So, in 1903 the Government endorsed a third transcontinental route. It would itself build, for subsequent leasing to the Grand Trunk, a National Transcontinental Railway on strictly controlled grades from New Brunswick via Quebec to Winnipeg which would be easier to operate than the often steeply inclined Intercolonial; and it would authorize private construction of a Grand Trunk Pacific Railway onwards from Winnipeg via Edmonton to a Pacific port at Prince Rupert. In sum the two lines would complete a railway of 3,453 miles (5,557 km).

The northerly route plotted for the National Transcontinental through the backwoods of Quebec and northern Ontario posed its builders fiercesome difficulty. The only habitation in this wild country was the few lonely outposts of the fur-trading companies. There were few trails, let alone any roads, through the vast

Three locomotives are needed to drag a train of only eight wooden cars up the original gradient of Kicking Horse Pass in the Rockies.

The only Route via
NIAGARA FALLS & SUSPENSION BRIDGE

An 1876 advertisement for the Canadian GWR route, which crossed Niagara Falls on the world's first metal suspension bridge.

primeval swamps and dense forests, which were relieved only by the clefts of tumultuous rivers. None of it had been reliably mapped. So treacherous was the ground that in summer the line of route was only approachable by the often hazardous rivers; movement at least was much easier in the depth of winter, when a thick carpet of snow firmed up the swamps and ice armour-plated the angry rivers, but then all too many of the construction workers were maimed by frostbite or incapacitated by snow-blindness in the viciously low temperatures.

Nevertheless the whole route was finished by the end of 1914, apart from a superb twin-cantilever bridge over the St Lawrence near Quebec, a 3,240 ft (990 m) long facsimile of Britain's Forth Bridge but with a record 1,800 ft (550 m) long centre span, which was not ready until December 1915. The Grand Trunk Pacific and the Canadian Northern survey-

ors approached the Rocky Mountains simultaneously and both parties tramped the range from end to end before each concluded that the only sensible passage was the lowest of the mountains' defiles, the 3,700 ft (1,130 m) Yellowhead Pass. At last sense prevailed: rather than extravagantly building its own line, the Canadian Northern sought running rights over the Grand Trunk Pacific line through the pass, beyond which it went its own way to Vancouver, which it reached in the autumn of 1915.

Sadly, the First World War staunched the influx of immigrants and westward spread of settlers on which both new transcontinentals had been relying, penning capital within the long-settled territories. The Canadian Northern subsided into bankruptcy and the Grand Trunk had to pass up its lease of the National Transcontinental, which was handed over to the former Intercolonial Railway, by now amalgamated with some other Federally owned lines as Canadian Government Railways. Concerned to sustain its war effort, the Dominion Govern-

ment dared not let the Canadian Northern go to the wall, so a Royal Commission was appointed to investigate the country's seriously deteriorating railway situation.

At the Commission's recommendation the Government took over the Canadian Northern in 1917. Next year the accumulating Government rail enterprise was reconstituted as Canadian National Railways, into whose maw a financially castrated Grand Trunk Pacific fell in 1920 and finally, after protracted negotiation, the Grand Trunk itself in 1923 (though to observe the legal and diplomatic proprieties the Grand Trunk title survived on some of the company's lines penetrating US territory).

Through all this upheaval the private enterprise of the Canadian Pacific stood firm, fortified above all by its 1887 diversification into deep-sea shipping at the instigation of its astute General Manager William C. Horne, who later became President and Chairman of the Canadian Pacific Board. For a major shipowner the First World War was something of a licence to print money.

BRITISH CONSTRUCTION IN SOUTH AMERICA

South America might conceivably have been the birthplace of the world's first public steam railway had the sub-continent not become ungulfed in the struggles which led to the creation of its independent states in 1825. The progenitor would have been Richard Trevithick, who arrived in Peru in 1816 to instal some of his Cornish pumping engines in local mines and was soon sketching a 9-mile (14.5 km) railway from the country's capital, Lima, to its port of Callao. But the wars doused his scheme and once they were over European bankers were reluctant to invest in any of the new South American countries until the latter had demonstrably achieved a measure of financial and political stability. Trevithick's Peruvian railway was not built until 1851, and then closely followed in 1852 by the first railways in Brazil and Chile.

American engineers were dominant in the earliest days of South American railway building, but before long the major financial and construction effort was British, especially in Argentina. The four major railway companies – the Buenos Aires Great Southern, Central Argentine, Buenos Aires Pacific and Buenos Aires Western – as well as a clutch of smaller concerns were British enterprises and remained in British ownership until the Peron regime appropriated them in 1948. Until then they were the richest of captive markets for the British locomotive and railway equipment supply industry; in signalling and other facets of operating practice, too, these British-owned railways closely followed the home style.

South American railways never established a common front on gauge. Brazil selected 5 ft 3 in (1,600 mm) for the start of what was to become the main-line network in the country's central area, but a few years later Argentine started the first section of the subsequent Buenos Aires Western Railway on 5 ft 6 in (1,676 mm) – solely because that happened to be the gauge of two Crimean War-surplus locomotives originally built for India which the Argentinians secured at a knockdown price to launch their project. Within two more years Chile had begun its State Railway system on the Argentine gauge. Some other countries, such as Mexico and Venezuela, have built to standard gauge, but a large part of the South American system is of various narrow gauges.

The highest railways in the world are South American – not surprisingly when one recollects that La Paz, principal city of land-locked Bolivia, is itself just over 12,000 ft (3,660 m) above sea level, in fact nearly 1,000 ft (300 m) higher than the summit of Switzerland's most striking mountain railway in the Bernese Oberland snows at Jungfraujoch. The railways of Bolivia and Peru attain no fewer than thirteen summits in excess of 14,000 ft (4,300 m), in every case by simple adhesion working, up to an astonishing peak of 15,848 ft (4,830 m) at La Cima, on the Peruvian Central branch in the heart of the Andes between Ticlio and Morococha.

The long chain of the Andes mountains had to be surmounted once its foothills and the land beyond were found to be rich in copper, nitrates, tin and other valuable minerals. The first trans-Andean railway to be completed, after it had been taken over by British interests in 1888 following a chain of crippling vicissitudes that included a Chilean-Bolivian war, was the Antofagasta (Chile) and Bolivia Railway. Begun from the Pacific port of Antofagasta in 1873, it reached Uyuni, on the Bolivian side of the mountains, in 1892 and was extended to La Paz by 1908. How soon inland the Andes surge upward can be gauged from the fact that within 225 miles (360 km) of its start at sea level on the Pacific the railway had to be lifted to a height of 12,976 ft (3,995 m), at Ascotán in Chile; but thereafter it did not drop below the 12,000 ft (3,600 m) contour for more than 500 miles (800 km) – at this equatorial

latitude, of course, snow is not a problem even at 12,000 ft. Although built originally to 2 ft 6 in (762 mm) gauge – it was converted to metre (3 ft 3½ in) gauge in 1928 – this line was built with such generous clearances that even on so narrow a track its international trains could run with sleeping cars, lounges and diners of near-standard-gauge roominess. Subsequent extensions allowed these expresses to run beyond Bolivia into Argentina and there connect with Argentine State Railways.

Another highly spectacular rail link between Argentina and Chile was forged in 1908 – again, ultimately, with British finance – with completion of the metre-gauge Transandine Railway from a junction with the 5 ft 6 in (1,676 mm) gauge Buenos Aires & Pacific in the far west of Argentina at Mendoza, over the 10,450 ft (3,185 m) Cumbre Pass to Valparaiso. Supreme among the South American mountain climbers, however, is the Peruvian Central line from Callao, on the Pacific coast, to the country's inland wheatfields at 10,000–11,000 ft (3,000–3,300 m) around Huancayo. That had to be lifted nearly 12,900 ft (4,000 m) in 118 miles (190 km) to its 15,694 ft (4,784 m) summit under the Andean roof in Galera Tunnel – the equivalent of a 1-in-48½ gradient the whole way. Small wonder its passenger trains came equipped with oxygen cylinders.

Opening a bridge in 1890 on one of the great trans-Andean lines, the F.C. Lima–Oroya, later the Central of Peru.

CONSOLIDATION IN EUROPE, GROWTH IN THE EAST

In Europe at least the issue of track gauge was resolved as railways expanded in the second half of the nineteenth century. The Russians persisted with their 5ft gauge (1,524mm) – shared today with Finnish State Railways (VR), since Finland was part of the Russian Empire when its first railway was erected from Helsinki to Hämeenlinna in 1862. The rest of Scandinavia opted for the Stephenson gauge when they opened their railway accounts in the 1850s, though there was an interlude when the Norwegians tried to switch to 3ft 6in (1,067mm) gauge to cut the high costs of construction in their often unfriendly terrain.

Apart from Russia – and, of course, the countless minor railways of many countries built to a narrow gauge for economy in difficult or sparsely populated terrain – Europe's only other iconoclasts were the Iberians: Spain's 5ft 6in (1,676mm) example in its first lines, from Madrid to Alicante and to Barcelona in 1858 and 1860 respectively, had to be followed by its Portuguese neighbour for its main lines to avoid overland isolation. But Portugal could not afford such an expensive gauge in its mountainous north, where all but the coastal main line remains metre gauge (3ft 3½in) to this day and inconveniently includes part of Oporto's commuter system. Elsewhere the main-line gauge was stabilized at 1,440mm, the nearest equivalent – about 4ft 8¼in – to Stephenson's parameter. After the First World War most railways revised that to a nominal 1,435mm, but in Europe today one encounters slight variations which are yet sufficient to affect the riding of vehicles on international transits. On West Germany's DB, for instance, the gauge tolerance is 1,430–34mm, but on France's SNCF 1,435–40mm.

COMPETITION FOR ROUTES IN BRITAIN

Several of the bigger countries were exercised by the question of State control of this vital, rapidly growing industry for the rest of the century. But not to any significant extent in Britain. There at the outset of the second half of the century companies still feuded fiercely for exclusive sovereignty of a territory and recklessly duplicated routes as a result. The final instance of this came as late as the 1890s, when, with the East Midlands and the North-West already adequately served from London by two and three main-line services respectively, the last of the empire-builders, Sir Edward Watkin, drove his Great Central extension to London, partly with the grandiose vision of linking his provincial Manchester Sheffield & Lincolnshire Railway with mainland Europe via other railways in the South-East of which he was Chairman and via a Channel Tunnel (Watkin was engrossed in the company trying to get that project off the ground, too).

Most passengers living on the parallel trunk routes had little to complain about. These, naturally, were the lines where rivals spared little expense to court the

market with high-quality service. It was the internecine competition stimulating the drive for speed and better passenger equipment that in the last quarter of the century had Britain's railways outdistancing those on the European mainland, and more significantly so where the second-class trunk-route passenger was concerned; there was no external or foreign stimulus. The trouble was that the money lavished on crack service over these prime routes too often left little change for the rest of the system, and where companies were chronically short of cash – as they were particularly in the country's south-eastern corner – the public could get a squalid travelling deal on lines immune from other rail competition.

Once the strong men had basically established their spheres of influence, however, the major companies – not without some prodding from the Government – started to recognize the benefits of collaboration: such as allowing another concern running powers over their lines to reach its objective rather than battling to keep it out by a rate war or by bribing neighbours to make obstructive alliances against the intruder. There were a few more skirmishes on the less well-defined frontiers of the principal empires, but otherwise the country's main-line network was essentially complete and stabilized by the 1870s.

Four companies, London Chatham & Dover, South Eastern, London Brighton & South Coast, and London & South Western, partitioned the south-eastern quarter south of the Thames (though the first two were one of the most outstanding cases of overlapping territory and wasteful duplication of facilities). The London & South Western had penetrated Devon, but in general the Great Western ruled the radii from London to the Far West and Wales, and was alongside the London & North Western in the West Midlands. The London & North Western writ ran from the capital through the Midlands to the North-West and, in association with the

The Bristol express on the Great Western Railway. One of Britain's oldest trunk route networks, the GWR extended north-west to Chester and Birkenhead via Birmingham, and south-west to Bristol, Exeter, Plymouth and Penzance.

Caledonian Railway beyond Carlisle, to Scotland. The other main route from London to Scotland via the industrial West Riding of Yorkshire and the North-East was a partnership of the Great Northern as far as Yorkshire, the North Eastern to the Scottish border and the North British beyond. To the east of this, covering agricultural East Anglia from London, ran the Great Eastern.

Between East and West Coast routes to Scotland, overlapping them in many places, stretched the most remarkable empire of them all – Hudson's Midland Railway, which had not only reached as far west as the port of Bristol but had an outpost in South Wales. By 1876 it had created – at great expense, by lifting its Settle and Carlisle line over the Pennines

via England's highest main-line summit, the 1,167ft (356m) Ais Gill crest – a third Anglo-Scottish main line in conjunction with the Glasgow & South Western and North British beyond Carlisle. By through coach workings it also had footholds ranging from England's south and south-west coastal resorts to East Anglia, the North-East and Perth, Dundee and Aberdeen in Scotland. It was the only one of the big companies with a London terminus which was not based on London. Its nerve centre was in the Midlands at Derby, situated at the convergence of its trunk routes and on the threshold of the great East Midlands coalfield, which from the railway's inception to its eventual dissolution in 1923 generated the greater part of its income.

SOCIAL EFFECTS OF TRAIN TRAVEL

By mid-century railways had already transformed the face of Britain. They did not ignite the Industrial Revolution as they did in some other countries, since in Britain the revolution was already stirring when the pioneers were mastering the basic principles of the steam engine. There it was the catalyst of steam and track from which the concept of a railway emerged. Its effect in subsequent years was not only to accelerate the revolution but to give it new dimensions.

Canals were not so quickly crushed as horse-drawn freight carriers and passenger stagecoaches on the roads, but the speed as well as the bulk haulage capability of the railway snapped the shackles off industrial development. The distance of a

Above: A busy London terminus (here probably Cannon Street) was a good place to advertise. The date is 1874, but the locomotives appear to be of earlier origin. Left: Arrival of a train at the Nord-West station in Vienna, painted by Carl Karger in 1875. The Nord-West was one of seven termini in Vienna before 1914.

coalfield or an industrial plant from the nearest coast or waterway was no longer an overriding consideration (before the 1860s were out London was getting more of its coal by rail than by sea); nor, with the ease and low cost of travel for the skilled working class, was the immediate local availability of a labour pool. A worker could be persuaded to re-locate for good prospects now that the train made it simple for him to keep periodic touch with his family until they could join him. Largely thanks to the railway, too, there was a Penny Post. As early as 1838 the first Travelling Post Office, or TPO, had been introduced between London and Liverpool; this was a mail van equipped to pick up and set down mailbags at lineside apparatus, as well as sort their contents, while its train was on the move.

The application of the steam engine to industrial processes had begun to magnetize the population into factory towns. The coming of railways added such impetus that by mid-century Britain was the first country with more than half its population urbanized. The effect was naturally most marked in the areas where railways had chiefly proliferated – around London, South Wales, the Midlands, the North-East, Clydeside in Scotland and the major ports – to satisfy the demand for cheap bulk transport of raw materials. And so the trend continued for the rest of the century. From 1850 to 1890 the proportion of town-dwellers rose to 72 per cent, the number of towns in England and Wales with more than 20,000 inhabitants from 63 to 185, and their share of the population from 35 to 54 per cent. About 70 of these towns, moreover, did not exist in the previous century, except in some cases for their names which they borrowed from nearby villages. The railways themselves created one or two of those close-packed huddles of chimneys, factories and terraced housing. Most notable of these were Swindon, where the Great Western established its own iron and steelworks as well as sprawling locomotive and rolling stock manufacturing plant, and Crewe, a hamlet of 200 souls in 1840 but a borough with 42,000 population by the turn of the century.

Just as striking was the railways' stimulation of pleasure travel. The 1851 Great Exhibition of the wonders of the new industrial age staged within Paxton's Crystal Palace in London's Hyde Park could never have drawn the six million visitors it attracted from every corner of the country during its six months' currency had it not been for the railways. They not only provided the mechanical means to ferry people *en masse* from the provinces to the capital but brought the

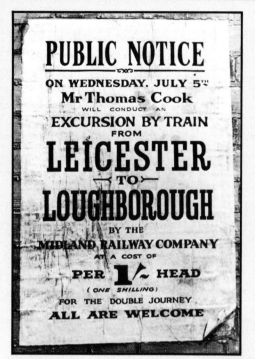

PUBLIC NOTICE

ON WEDNESDAY. JULY 5TH

Mr Thomas Cook

WILL CONDUCT AN

EXCURSION BY TRAIN

FROM

LEICESTER

TO

LOUGHBOROUGH

BY THE

MIDLAND RAILWAY COMPANY

AT A COST OF

PER 1/- HEAD

(ONE SHILLING)

FOR THE DOUBLE JOURNEY

ALL ARE WELCOME

trip within the scope of almost any town-dweller's pocket by offering return excursion fares from the industrial north no higher than the day-wage of a craftsman or the equivalent of two days' pay for a labourer. As early as 1841 Thomas Cook was prompted by the overcrowding of scheduled trains to sponsor the first chartered excursion train – an 11 mile (18 km) return trip for a thousand temperance reformers from the East

Midlands town of Leicester to Loughborough and back, with tea and (decorous) dancing thrown in for an inclusive price of a shilling per person. Benevolent employers soon seized the idea as an annual bonanza for their workforce and by the mid-1840s a commentator was rhapsodizing on 'the degree in which railways are everywhere contributing to the recreation and health of all classes, by removing them in the intervals of labour from the confinement of streets and lanes to the fresh air and verdure of the country'.

In its encouragement of optional travel, which had already helped to record 80 million rail passenger journeys a year by 1850 and contributed to the trebling of the total within the two ensuing decades, the railway spawned new holiday resorts as well as industrial towns. On the South Coast, Brighton's population doubled between the railway's arrival in 1840 and the end of the century; in one summer week of 1859 trains decanted more visitors in the place than the total of its residents. At first it was chiefly the middle class who exploited the railway to encroach on the formerly upper-class preserves of the inland spas and the coast. But just as they provoked the leisured rich to prospect for new enclaves of their own kind in the Lake District or Scotland, and very soon to shun their own country and make for the exclusive spas of mainland Europe, so the middle-class in turn had its nose put out of

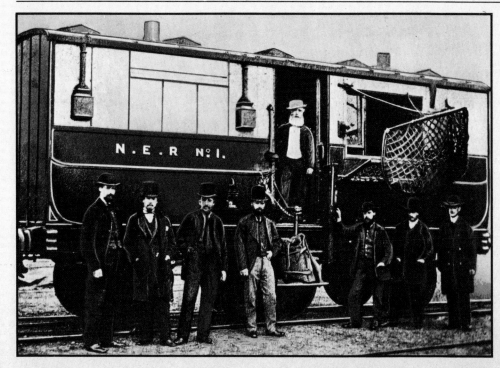

Above left: As can be seen by this poster, Thomas Cook, the pioneer of railborne excursions, set up his stall as early as 5 July 1841.
Above: The Travelling Post Office. A special van, like this North Eastern Railway coach, was equipped to pick up mailbags (above right) from the side of the line while on the move.
Below: The restored Stirling single-driver locomotive No. 1 of the Great Northern Railway with a replica train. The Great Northern along with the North Eastern and North British railways formed the East Coast alliance to Scotland.

joint by insurgent hordes of the working-class.

These trends were the making, amongst other things, of Thomas Cook. After his first venture Cook had continued in the business of sponsoring inland excursion trains, but his name was not eternally impressed on the world travel scene until the mid-1850s. Then he once more grasped the implications of rail travel trends at home and organized his first 'Grand Tour' of Continental cities by rail. Within another decade he was attracting a middle-class clientele which, soon courted by his imitators as well, grew with such

rapidity that just before the outbreak of the First World War three-quarters of a million of Cook's countrymen were vacationing abroad every year.

In the last quarter of the nineteenth century the railways set off the final shock wave of a similar class explosion to create the sprawling suburbia of the great British cities. By the 1860s the higher echelons of the middle class had already realized that they could decamp to virgin green pastures 10–15 miles (16–24km) from the city centre and still be little more than half-an-hour's journey time from their office or their bank. But the lower classes stayed

Left: The arrival of a workmen's 'penny' train at Victoria station, London, in 1865. Although Gladstone's Act of 1844 had required all railways to run trains with proper seating, protection from the weather and fares of not more than one penny per mile, third class, conditions were still primitive.
Right: Stockport viaduct about 1850. Urban squalor went hand in hand with the growth of railways and industry.
Below: The Brighton terminus on the London, Brighton & South Coast Railway in 1862. The size of the station at this early date emphasizes the large amount of traffic carried.

put; to live on the doorstep of one's workplace was still ingrained. Nor were the railways yet giving them much incentive; they were still too preoccupied with establishing a main-line network to pay much attention to purely urban railways, but with that more or less stabilized by 1870 they were ready to seize the new chance for growth, patent in the overcrowded cities and their choking horse-drawn traffic.

As might be expected, the effect of creating an urban railway system and with it the commuter was most marked in London. In 1867 the capital housed only $3\frac{1}{4}$ million people and its territory radiated no more than about 4 miles (6.4km) from a nuclear point on the Thames at Charing Cross. In those days the main-line railway terminals were only just within the city's perimeter. But by the turn of the century the city's land area had been enlarged by

ten times as much and its population had doubled.

The railways not only built new suburban lines and stations but accelerated the residential exodus from the centre by making a bargain of their use. The Great Eastern Railway, for instance, packed north-east London with new suburbs by putting on a phenomenally intensive local train service and backing it with absurdly low fares for workmen, and half-rate fares

even for clerks commuting to and from their offices. Until then a town like Edmonton had been a gracious knot of large houses nobly set in ample grounds, almost all with their ancillary coach houses and stables. Those that survived were now submerged in an endless honeycomb of terraced housing.

Simultaneously the railways were dangling before the affluent, whose inner suburbs were being overrun, inducements to emigrate to the outer suburbs, where they would be valuable commuter business. With an eye to the longer term the London & North Western Railway tried to shape the tone – and purse – of its residential clientele in the outer north-west suburbs of the capital by offering an eleven-year free pass to anyone taking up a house at Harrow of more than a specified value; in the case of two towns further out still the premium was enhanced to twenty-one years' free travel. At the end of the century London's railways were moving more passengers every day than the city's horse-drawn buses and trams together. By then the electric railway had become a practicality, as will be described in Chapter Ten 'Enter Electric Railways', and the range of commuting and suburbia was extended still further.

THE UNIFICATION OF GERMANY

In 1850 Germany was in third place in the world league table of rail route-mileage in use, with 3,778 (6,080 km) to Britain's 6,658 (10,715 km) and America's 9,072 (14,600 km). France was lagging with 1,972 (3,174 km) and of the rest only Belgium had more than 500 (800 km). Spain had agonized for so long over a choice of gauge (it finally determined on something broader than Stephenson's, despite a personal visit from the ageing George himself) that its first railway was well over a decade from draft to realization, and thus had only that line's $17\frac{1}{2}$ miles (28 km) to show. Switzerland had a mere 16 miles (26 km). And Africa, Asia and Australasia had yet to see a train.

In Germany the impact of railways on population and industrialization was much the same as in Britain, although it took place something like two decades later, the zenith of German railway expansion coming between 1850 and 1870 when the country's route-mileage more than trebled to around 12,000 (19,300 km). Typical of the effect was the growth of Berlin; in 1845 its occupants barely numbered 300,000, but by 1885 the total was over $1\frac{1}{4}$ million.

The German railways had a powerful influence on their country in another

respect – the unification of the country. At the start, as recorded in Chapter Two, the German states were not of one mind on the issue of public control of railway construction and operation. Smaller states such as Württemberg, Brunswick and Oldenburg plumped for this policy almost exclusively, but many of the bigger were for allowing private capital free rein. That was true above all of Prussia, also of Saxony. The Prussian railway entrepreneurs, however, were more sensible than some of their buccaneering British counterparts. Recognizing that the new medium promised much more profit from co-operation to exploit its increasing economy over distance than from beggar-my-neighbour competition, ten of the seventeen Prussian companies had by 1846 formed a Union of Prussian Railways to harmonize tariffs and operating practice, and to facilitate inter-working of traffic.

A year more and the association had been enlarged to welcome the railways of other states and to become the Union of German Railway Administrations. As one German commentator put it, thereby 'the frontiers of the races and the states lost their disruptive power, rivalries were forgotten and the Germans discovered the pleasure of getting to know one another'.

Prussia changed tack in the wake of the 1848 Revolution, when it decided to build the great Prussian Eastern Railway from Frankfurt-am-Oder, south-east of Berlin, across Danzig and to Königsberg (spanning territory now wholly Polish apart from its eastern extremity, where Königsberg has become the USSR city of Kalingrad). This was undertaken as a State enterprise to mollify the radicals by a show of concern for the poorer areas of the kingdom and to create jobs; it had little prospect of making money. That did not worry Prince Otto von Bismarck, who had come on to the Prussian political stage on the eve of the 1848 uprisings, though the pretext for discounting profitability was anathema to his oligarchic philosophy. He was now arguing tirelessly for the absorption in one nationalized system, not merely of Prussian railways but of all German main-line railways, partly because of belief in the corporate organization of industry, partly because of his dedication to the political unification of the German states, and partly because he and the Prussian General Staff had grasped the potential value of railways to a war machine. This last factor conduced to a number of railway extensions towards and along frontiers in the years preceding the Franco-Prussian war of 1870–71.

Besides that the Prussians had carefully thought out the adaptation of the railway as a weapon of war. In 1869 the General Staff had set up its own railway department and had military timetables drafted against possible mobilization. A military railway was built near Berlin and there engineer battalions were trained both to destroy and rehabilitate.

These preparations were thoroughly vindicated in the Franco-Prussian war. The railways' conveyance of 384,000 men and their equipment to the front within thirteen days and the speed with which reserves were thrust into the line overwhelmed the French. Equally significant was the rapidity with which the engineers made wrecked French track serviceable as the Prussian spearheads forged into France.

Even so, Bismarck did not have it all his own way so far as the railways were concerned when he was enthroned as Chancellor of the new German Reich. 'The State is entitled to the immediate supervision of the railways', ran a preamble to the provisional 1875 draft of a Railways Act, but Saxony, Württemberg and above all Bavaria refused to submit to Prussian hegemony. Bavaria's resistance went as far as taking over some of its private companies to forestall any backdoor Prussian Government ploys aimed at buying control. For the time being Bismarck had to be content with a vigorous nationalization drive in Prussia itself, where the State-owned railway mileage jumped from 3,921 (6,310 km) to 13,106 (21,092 km) between 1879 and 1885 while that of the private companies simultaneously dropped from 8,463 (13,620 km) to 1,548 (2,491 km), and with a series of

Above left: The military style of Prussian railway officials is well illustrated in this 1900 portrait of a Koblenz stationmaster. Above: A Forquenot 2–6–0 of the Paris–Orléans railway. Above right: The Wyler viaduct near Hospenthal on the metre-gauge Furka-Oberalp Railway, which runs close to the Rhône glacier. This is one important Swiss route which has never been nationalized.

compacts binding all German railways to common practice in such areas as signalling systems and construction and equipment standards.

Inexorably, however, Prussia did come to dominate the greater part of the pre-First World War German railway system, either by agreement or by annexation. The Imperial Railway Office which Bismarck managed to establish to coordinate the policies and practice of the German network as a whole was an annexe of the Prussian State Railway headquarters in Berlin. Prussian influence was patent in the method of most German railways, not least in the military bearing, discipline and extreme deference to rank of German railwaymen – characteristics still evident to a degree in the immaculately uniformed operating staff of modern Deutsche Bundesbahn stations and trains. By the outbreak of the First World War just over 24,000 (38,600 km) of a total of 36,500 (58,750 km) route-miles was Prussian State. The Bavarian State, next down the list, operated only some 5,200 route-miles

(8,700 km) and the third biggest, the Saxon State just over 2,000 (3,200 km). Private railways totalled about 2,900 route-miles (4,700 km).

Between 1870 and 1914 the German railways were arguably the most enterprising and best equipped in Europe. In that time they increased their network well over threefold, but their stock of locomotives, passenger cars and goods vehicles sixfold, their goods tonnage eightfold and their passenger traffic volume a phenomenal sixteenfold to over 1.8 million journeys a year. Only one state, Württemberg, had trouble in achieving a minimum 3 per cent return on the massive capital employed. The rest contrived 4 per cent or better – Prussia a consistent 6 to 7 per cent – for ironically, the state railways, Prussia particularly, yielded no points to private enterprise for hard-nosed dedication to maximization of profit. And the state governments blessed them for it, since those profits were the equivalent of taxes raised without need of making a case before the state legislature. But in the main commercial and population corridors, at least, the public was getting good service for its money. Even before the First World War Berlin and Hamburg were linked by eleven passenger trains each way daily.

THE GROWING ROLE OF THE STATE

The Franco-Prussian war left many scars on French railways. They were blamed for the French defeat – although their incoherent performance by comparison with the German machine's precision was the fault primarily of military mismanagement – and as a result the nationalization issue was revived. Over the whole system a good deal of scheduled maintenance and renewal had been allowed to lapse, and the Est Railway had been battered in the front line. Moreover, it had been truncated by the German annexation of Alsace-Lorraine. Bismarck made the sector of the Est he appropriated a separate system, the Imperial Railways, and had it methodically converted to German practice – so methodically, in fact, that when the territory was restored to France after the Second World War, French Railways found it most practicable to segregate the Alsace-Lorraine railways from the rest of its Est Region. Apart from anything else the Germans had changed the lines' operation from French left-hand to German right-hand running practice;

after they regained control French Railways had to erect some costly flying junctions to facilitate through running on the trunk routes linking the disputed area with the rest of France.

The war also aggravated the financial difficulties into which several secondary railways, particularly in western France, had slumped and a number fell into the clutches of a Belgian banker, Simon Philippart. Then in 1877 Philippart's financial empire fell apart and the railways he controlled were threatened with closure. The French Government intervened, bought out the luckless shareholders at a knockdown price and grouped its acquisitions in 1878 as the Etat Railway. For the rest of the century the Etat's only link with the capital was a nondescript train it ran daily from Bordeaux to Paris to exercise running powers it had secured over the neighbouring Ouest Railway. But the Ouest was slowly sinking into a quagmire of inefficiency and financial instability which made it a national butt. In 1908 it was absorbed by the Etat, which thereafter all but monopolized western France, its rule undermined chiefly by the intruding Paris–Orléans route from Nantes to Quiberon, Quimper and Brest; that was eventually rationalized by an exchange of lines between the two systems in 1933.

The Etat's creation signalled a boom in secondary railway-building which all but doubled French railway mileage between 1878 and the century's close. Instigator of

this French railway mania was Charles Louis de Saulces de Freycinet, sometime mining engineer and Midi Railway traffic manager, who then gained rapid stature in public life through his flair for organization. Leon Gambetta had fully exploited this in the Franco-Prussian war, during which Freycinet was chief of the military cabinet. In 1876 Freycinet entered the French Senate and within a year he had been handed the Ministry of Public Works, from which there emanated in 1879 the Freycinet Plan – almost as momentous in its different way for France's railways as was Beeching's for Britain's railways just over eighty years later.

Freycinet envisaged gradual nationalization of French railways and a vast programme of new building to create a so-called 'third network'. To take the second of these objectives first, Freycinet persuaded the French legislature to ordain construction of standard-gauge lines to or through every town of Prefecture or Sub-Prefecture status throughout the country. The aim was never achieved so far as the Sub-Prefectures were concerned, but enough new trackage had been laid down by 1914 to surfeit rural France with rail transport. Freycinet had hung on the neck of the country a lace of pebbles that would grow into a chain of millstones when depression and road transport combined to make a farce of the economics of these bucolic branches in the 1930s.

The first steps towards the eventual nationalization of 1 January 1938 were

taken by strengthening the State's financial interest in the railways, which had been embodied in agreements in 1859 between the Government and the companies. Under conventions signed in 1883 the railways became effectively tenants of State-owned fixed assets.

The railways agreed to build and operate lines that were initially bound to be unremunerative and to assume the financial responsibility for the running of these as well as the rest of their systems in exchange, first, for State guarantees to meet their interest charges and cover shareholders' dividends at roughly the levels of 1883, and, second, for the State's undertaking to reimburse the railways annually for capital investment in new lines. Under the second heading there was more money to be had if double track was required for a route where receipts did not reach a predetermined rate per mile, and extra cash, too, for a railway laid down to serve the Government's strategic requirements. Advances under the first heading were repayable, plus 4 per cent interest, out of any profits which, if they exceeded what was needed to cover both repayments and dividends at the guaranteed level, were to be split two-thirds to the State and one-third to the railway company. It was still the case, of course, that no new railway could be laid without State approval (nor, for that matter, could any railway invest in new rolling stock without Government endorsement). Thus the State gained

strategic control of the railways, though the companies were left the initiative to make a success of the day-to-day working of their lines.

Apart from the decline of the Ouest Railway which ended in its 1908 absorption by the Etat, mentioned earlier, these arrangements proved very serviceable. Up to the First World War the Nord had never had to dun the State for its guarantee money; by 1914 the Paris–Lyon–Méditerranée and the Est had repaid all their advances; and the Paris–Orléans, except in 1910 when it was debilitated by flood calamities, was gradually clearing its debts. The Sud did wobble rather precariously from year to year between repayments and appeals for guarantee coverage, but only the Ouest was unfailingly knocking on the Treasury door year in and year out, until its demise. One reason for this stability was that while their development was not as spectacular as that of the American, German and British railways in the last quarter of the nineteenth century, French railways were developing a solid base of technical quality and operating efficiency. That was evident from their operating ratio – that is, the relation of their running costs to revenue – which at the start of the twentieth century was among the lowest in Western Europe; in 1906, for instance, it was down to a very creditable 53 per cent.

Four other European countries had made the bulk of their railways a State concern before the First World War. The Danish Government had gone into the railway business with a line from Aarhus to Randers in Jutland, finished in 1862, and from then on acquired existing private railways alongside its own new construction until it established the Danish State Railways (DSB) in 1885.

The first Swiss railway running the $14\frac{1}{2}$ miles (23 km) from Zurich to Baden – officially the Swiss Northern but unofficially the *Spanisch-Brödli-Bahn* or 'Spanish Bun Railway', because it obtained the *Hausfrauen* of Zurich speedier delivery of a confection that was a Baden speciality – was inaugurated on 9 August 1847, but it was a commercial failure. Interest in the medium lapsed until 1849, when the Federal Assembly invited Robert Stephenson to plan a network that would serve the country's defence as well as its commerce. His 400 mile (645 km) network, which stuck to the valleys and eschewed all Alpine crossings, was

eventually laid out in full, and a great deal more besides. The country's first Federal Constitution of 1848 had authorized the Confederation to undertake railways amongst its public works, but at first the National Council opted to allow the various Cantons to grant concessions to private enterprise. Before 1860, when nationalization became a talking-point, some voluntary amalgamation – voluntary, that is, except that it was pressed by many foreign shareholders in the small companies – had already grouped the main-line railways into three major concerns, the North Eastern, the Central and the United Swiss Railways, which

Left: A French double-decker painted by Detti in 1885.
Right: This Swiss 2–6–0 used to work the Old Hauenstein line from Basle to Bern, which was built by the ubiquitous British contractor Brassey in 1858.

were concentrated chiefly in the German-speaking area of the country; to this trio were added in 1871 the Gotthard and in 1890 the Jura-Simplon, the enterprises which resulted in the great Swiss transalpine tunnel routes described in the next chapter.

The North Eastern was presided over by Dr Alfred Escher, who was a buccaneer almost as unprincipled as the privateers of early British history. It was his single-minded pursuit of his own or his shareholders' interests at the expense of national need which primarily decided the Federal Government to buy out all the main private companies as soon as their

terms of concession allowed, As Swiss tradition dictated, the issue was put to popular referendum and approved by a 68 per cent majority in 1898. Nationalization was not then and has never since been total. Today it excludes from the Swiss Federal Railway system four important standard-gauge companies, the Bern–Lötschberg–Simplon, Bodensee–Toggenburg, Bern–Neuchâtel and Südostbahn, as well as over a hundred others, many of them built since 1898, including such vital life-lines in the high mountain areas as the metre-gauge Rhaetian Railway with 225 electrified route-miles (362 km), the Furka-Oberlap and the Visp-Zermatt.

Following the unification and establishment of the new Kingdom of Italy in 1862 the Government looked to railways to integrate the country. The companies were tempted with an offer to refund their construction costs as soon as new lines were open and reacted so eagerly that within four years every principal city was interconnected, except those in the impoverished South where ironically Italian railways had been born. By 1867, furthermore, the international route over the Brenner pass into Austria was open. The Government also took a first step to nationalization by ordering an 1865 grouping into four companies, which

twenty years later were restructured as three. But all the economies of scale failed to generate cash sufficient to keep the railways in good order and their staff reasonably paid. In Italy railways were never a blue chip business. Desperate to rebut mounting criticism of the railways' poor service and decaying assets, the Government of the day made the major railways a Government department as the Ferrovie dello Stato (FS), or Italian State Railways, in 1905. Final additions in 1906 launched the FS with a route-mileage of 8,007 (12,886km).

In route-mileage the third largest State railway system in Europe by the end of the nineteenth century was the Kaiserlich-Königlich Staatsbahn, or KK Staatsbahn, of the Austro-Hungarian Empire, exceeded in route-mileage only by the Russian and Imperial German networks. The Imperial Government in Vienna had intended in the early 1840s to be the prime mover in railway construction, but it was so weakened financially on a national basis as well as exhausted by the cost of its first major enterprise – the crossing of the Semmering Pass in the projection of a trunk route from Vienna to Trieste (see next chapter) – that in the 1850s it handed over most of the State lines then existing to private enterprise and left them to develop a national network until the 1880s. Most of the capital was French, with the Rothschild banking concern dominant.

Following Rothschild's astute naming of his first railway the Kaiser Ferdinand Nordbahn after the then Emperor, most of these Austro-Hungarian railways were grandly titled in honour of the Imperial hierarchy. Another Rothschild project, the Vienna–Salzburg main line laid in 1856–60, was the Kaiserin Elisabeth Bahn; the line opened from Vienna through Bohemia to Prague and Pilsen in 1870 was tagged the Kaiser Franz Josef Bahn, after the Emperor who succeeded the weak-kneed Ferdinand when he abdicated in the wake of the 1848 revolution, which seriously threatened to fissure the Empire and spurred the Government to trunk-railway building in the hope of binding the provinces to the centre; and the Kronprinz Rudolf Bahn, finished from St Valentin south through the mountains to Selzthal in 1872, commemorated the heir-apparent who eventually committed suicide in 1889.

When the State changed tack in the 1880s and exercised a right to absorb the

private companies in the KK Staatsbahn, two successfully resisted the embrace. One was the Nord-West, opened in 1872, which led from Vienna northward into Moravia and was the route to Dresden and Berlin. Amongst Vienna's seven termini pre-1914, the Nord-West was perhaps the most elegant, with matching arrival and departure buildings on each side, each embodying special areas for travellers from the Imperial court, who had the luxury of an enclosed garden in which to await the departure of their trains. The Nord-West held out only until 1908, but the greatest of all the Austro-Hungarian private systems, the Südbahn, did not give up until First World War damage and loss of so much trunk-route mileage in the subsequent dismemberment of the Empire forced it, almost bankrupt, to surrender the Austrian, Yugoslav and

Top: Brindisi station in the late 1860s. At one time Brindisi was the shipping point for Indian mail from London. Above: Rome's Termini station in 1869. Note the typical European brakeman's lookout at the rear of the coaches.

Italian sectors of its network to the national systems of those countries in 1923, and the Hungarian rump to that country's railway administration in 1932.

The Südbahn's mid-century beginnings with the grandiose title of 'The United South Austrian, Lombardian and Central Italian Railway' are a reminder of the extent of the old Austro-Hungarian Empire. Even after Lombardy and Venetia had been ceded to the new Italy in 1858 and 1867 respectively, it still covered almost all present-day Yugoslavia, Hungary, Czechoslovakia and Galicia that is now partly

Polish and partly Soviet Russian. The Südbahn, which was split in two unconnected sectors, ran from Trieste to Vienna and Budapest in the east, and from what is now the Italian Tirol over the Brenner Pass to Innsbruck and the Bavarian border at Kufstein in the west.

To encroach briefly on the twentieth century before we survey the first railway development in the far eastern world, the effect of the post-First World War dismantling of the Austro-Hungarian Empire on its railways tends to be forgotten. At the outbreak of war the KK Staatsbahn system totalled some 28,750 route-miles (46,250 km). Not only did the victors strip away as much as 72 per cent of it, but the greater part of its rolling stock. As late as 1920 Vienna was dealing, in all its stations, with fewer than ten expresses a day – and those were only a ramshackle assembly of the miserable residue of coaching stock left to the luckless Austrian railways. It was 1925 before the Allies eventually completed a fully fair restitution of equipment. But the vast problems of rationalizing the railway system to suit the new Austria's contracted size and national economy are even yet short of complete resolution.

INDIA: THE BEST PLANNED SYSTEM IN ASIA

The railway's potential in India, most alluring of all Britain's overseas possessions with its thriving agriculture and industry, beckoned entrepreneurs as soon as the railway mania had a grip on the home country. But India's commercial development was still vested in the by then effete East India Company, which was quite apathetic about railways. So was the Governor-General of the early 1840s, Lord Ellenborough, who dismissed the vision of a sub-continent interlaced by railways as 'moonshine'. Numerous schemes were floated and some concessions granted, but not an inch of track was operational by 1850. The collapse of the British railway stock market made the outlook still bleaker, and the more far-sighted of the prospective pioneers realized that no major scheme would get off the ground without an infusion of official finance and backing. One of those was the Londoner John Chapman, who put forward such a closely argued case for a railway across the western half of the peninsula, to link with another project in the east and connect Bombay with Calcutta, that the East India Company Directors grudgingly unbuttoned their purse.

Chapman's Great Indian Peninsular Railway (GIP) and the East Indian Railway starting from Calcutta, on the opposite side of the country, were both authorized in 1848. That year, however, was historically even more significant for its New Year's Day inauguration of the Governor-General who more than anyone else fathered Indian railway expansion, Lord Dalhousie.

Dalhousie arrived in India a keen railway advocate – and better still, an informed one, for earlier in his career he had served in Britain's Board of Trade during the formative years of railways. The railway portfolio was one of the first laid on his desk by the East India Company, and after due consideration of it he offered them his historic Dalhousie Minute, sometimes honoured as the 'Indian Railway Magna Carta'. It recommended immediate construction of an extensive trunk network reaching inland from the main ports to interconnect in the interior, and the stimulation of the investment from London to build it by a Government guarantee of a dividend not lower than 5 per cent, any excess of that figure to be shared between private enterprise and the Government. The main provisos were that the Government should retain the right to take over a railway after twenty-five years of operation if it wished; that the Government alone should ordain the routes (naturally, military and internal policing requirements were in mind here); and that the railways must be built to standards prescribed by the Government.

The Dalhousie Minute was accepted as policy in 1854, though one vital standard – that of gauge – was not officially promulgated until 1856. The surveyors of the early GIP route had actually gone into the field with that railway's gauge undecided, but eventually it was fixed at 5 ft 6 in (1,676 mm) and this was endorsed by the Government for all the planned lines.

Thanks to Dalhousie India acquired both the most rationally planned railway system of nineteenth-century Asia and equally the most soundly constructed, though in this last respect Dalhousie set perhaps too high a standard. Civil engineering costs were so high – partly because of the finicky attention to detail of a horde of self-important and not always professionally competent Government inspectors – that by the end of the 1860s the first railways were losing vast sums of money, which were out of all proportion to the very substantial increase in India's trade and revenue which they were generating. With areas off the routes of the early trunk lines clamouring for rail service, the Government decided to take on railway construction itself.

By now the light railway concept was taking shape and in 1871 the Indian Government's railway office dispatched a

A derailment in India in 1870. Railways here began life badly, with little private money available, until the Government took over responsibility.

The reversing station at Poona Ghat on the Bhor Ghat Railway. The zig-zag system is still used in some mountainous areas, such as the Peruvian Andes.

consulting engineer, Guilford Molesworth, to study and report on the newborn narrow-gauge line serving some slate quarries in Britain's North Wales, the Festiniog Railway. Molesworth returned firmly persuaded that the civil engineering economy of such a railway was not worth the subsequent harassments of a break of gauge. But his passionate advocacy was wasted. Without waiting to hear it, the Government had already decided irrevocably to build metre-gauge (3 ft 3½ in) secondary lines. Later still, lines of 2 ft (610mm) and 2 ft 6 in (762mm) gauge were authorized to remote hill stations. The Government was little more successful than private enterprise in curbing construction costs and in a very short time it opted out, leaving the field once more to private companies. Whatever it did save was microscopic compared with the heavy cost in time and money incurred by Indian commerce for decades to come through break-of-gauge transhipment.

Robert Stephenson was appointed consulting engineer of the Great Indian Peninsular Railway – the first in the subcontinent to open a section for business, with 24 miles (39km) from Bombay to Thana in April 1853 – and he fulfilled the job until his death in 1859. This was a remarkable association because whereas Stephenson had been so obsessed with

taming gradients to what he imagined were the limitations of the steam locomotive when he laid out the London & Birmingham Railway in Britain, the GIP's Resident Engineer, James J. Berkley, was eventually able to indulge long stretches of 1 in 37. In only twenty years steam locomotive technology had already made their operation practicable. Berkley could only attack boldly in any event, for after he had taken his line across the swamp surrounding Bombay he confronted the daunting barrier of the Western Ghat mountains, with their deep valleys and high escarpments that looked almost unscaleable by a railway. But scale them he did, by dint of an ingenious technique that overcame the lack of any ledges or plateaus wide enough to allow gain of height by curvature; the line was carried up the face of the mountain in a near-vertical zig-zag, with a reversing station in each angle of the pattern. The only flaw in the concept was that Berkley could not foresee the extent to which rail traction power would develop and the length to which trains would grow. In time his reversing stations could not accommodate intact trains and the nuisance of having to break up formations, work them over the Ghats in sections, then reassemble them on the other side became so intolerable that the high cost of carving and tunnelling a direct line through the mountains had to be accepted. The last of the Ghat zig-zag inclines was eliminated in 1918. The zig-zag technique, incidentally, was also adopted in 1869 by the builders of the

original New South Wales main line out of Sydney to overcome the steep western escarpment of the Blue Mountains.

With the East Indian Railway pushing rapidly inland from Calcutta the two lines met to inaugurate coast-to-coast rail communication on 8 March 1870. By then total Indian railway route-mileage was closing on 5,000 (8,000 km). The Government was now hard put to it to sustain financial inducements to investors either substantial enough to obtain the continuing expansion it wanted, or on the other hand framed so that the Government pocketed a decent share of the return if the company was successful, yet was not saddled with ruinous obligations if it struggled. Nevertheless, by 1893 India was operating 18,000 route-miles (29,000km) of railway and by 1913 35,000 (56,300km), vastly more per square-mile of territory than Africa or Australia.

AUSTRALIA'S TANGLE OF GAUGES
News of the Liverpool & Manchester Railway's triumphant 1830 opening in England fired some Australians in New South Wales with railway-building ambition almost as soon as they heard it, but it needed the British type of railway mania to arouse sufficiently widespread interest in action. Not until January 1846 did a public meeting in Sydney vote to look into the 'expediency and practicability of establishing Railways in the Colony' and inspire surveys which led to the formation of the Sydney Railway Company in October 1849. Almost simultaneously there were stirrings in Victoria and South Australia.

The early days of Australian railways were very chequered. From the start the colony administrations had to bale the companies out, partly because construction was delayed by the distractions of the gold rush, but mostly because railway construction in Australia was a fairly uninviting proposition. The early settlements hugged the coast, and mountains barred the way into the then little-known and hence questionably remunerative hinterland. But since the country lacked navigable rivers the need for railways became more and more emphatic, so that as in time one company after another began to stagger financially and its construction work to stutter, the various governments, who were themselves stretched for funds, had no choice but to take over the railways.

GROWTH OF THE RAILWAYS IN AUSTRALIA AND NEW ZEALAND

Australia's 27,000 route-miles (43,000 km) include only one transcontinental line; most lines link the coastal cities or open up one particular stretch of the interior. In the fifty years from 1870, 1,000 route-miles (1,600 km) were expanded to 23,000 (37,100 km). In contrast, New Zealand's last main line was not opened until 1945. Its present-day network of 2,900 miles (4,610 km) includes lines built in the 1950s to exploit the forests of North Island, but it nevertheless represents a decline from the peak figure of 3,535 miles (5,660 km) in 1953, due to the closure of several unprofitable branch lines.

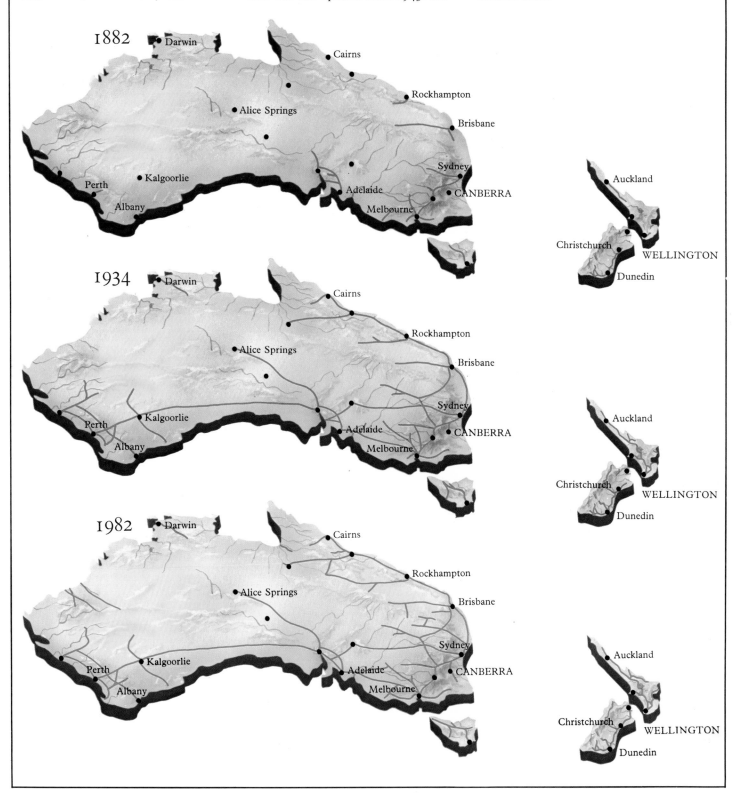

Nowhere else was there a more disastrous disagreement over gauge. At the start it looked as though the three pioneer states were of one mind on 5ft 3in (1,600mm). William Gladstone, who was the British Colonial Secretary at the time, had urged adoption of the Stephenson standard gauge, but an Irishman, Shields, who had been appointed engineer to the New South Wales project, insisted on the gauge of his native country and Victoria and South Australia were content to follow suit. Unfortunately Shields reacted to a salary cut in the first wave of economies to keep the troubled project afloat by walking out. His Scots successor, James Wallace, vehemently insisted on the Stephenson gauge and got his way. To compound the inconsistencies, the later-comers, Queensland and Western Australia, both adopted 3ft 6in (1,067mm) gauge for economy in their less populous territories. A century elapsed before Australia was at last driven to mitigate some of the tedious transhipments involved in transcontinental journeys.

The harassed Sydney Railway took five years to get its first 14 miles (22.5km) of track operative. They were thus beaten to the post by Adelaide, whose citizens were too impatient to wait for steam power. South Australia's first 7 mile (11km) line from Goolwa to the Murray River mouth at Port Elliot was opened as a horse tramway on 18 May 1854 – and that, officially, was Australia's first railway.

The first steam railway, the 2½ miles (4km) of the Melbourne & Hobsons Bay Railway from Flinders Street, Melbourne, to Port Melbourne was

Victoria's. All Melbourne downed tools on 12 September 1854 to attend its flamboyant opening. Craft in the bay were decked in bunting and two warships added the thunder of a gun salute to the huzzahs of the huge crowd as the inaugural train bearing the Governor, his lady and favoured guests steamed proudly on to the Port Melbourne jetty. The celebration lunch tables laid out in the engine shed must have groaned from a greater weight of bottles than food, as there was a crescendo of toasting from 'three times three' for the gracious Queen to a 'nine times nine' for the ladies, before the guests rose unsteadily at a quarter past four to take train back to the city. With everyone safely aboard the driver opened the throttle. But the engine had been

Top: An Australian train of the 1860s – similar to the first to operate in New South Wales between Sydney and Parramatta. Above: Tarcoon station, New South Wales, at the turn of the century.

stopped with its pistons at dead centre point in the cylinders and it would not budge. Male passengers dismounted, thinking to solve the problem by lightening the load, then the womenfolk and finally even His Excellency, patently vexed, had to be prevailed upon to detrain. All was in vain, though, until a score of dutiful Victorian police ripped off their jackets and heaved the locomotive out of its embarrassing immobility.

The wretched engine was a last-minute substitute. It had been hurriedly built by local firms in ten weeks because locomotives ordered from Robert Stephenson's works in England were not going to be delivered on schedule. Very soon it was breaking down so frequently that the company had to abandon service until the following Christmas Day, when the first two Stephenson engines were at last available.

The financial frailty of so many early Australian railway enterprises curbed construction to barely 1,000 route-miles (1,600 km) up to 1870. Queensland did not have its first steam railway until 1865, Western Australia its first until 1879. But railways had emerged at the start of the vital period of Australian immigration, which saw the country's population soar from around 400,000 in 1850 to over 3¼ million by the end of the 1880s. By 1870 the clamour to open up the land was vociferous and the golden age of Australian railway-building began. At the turn of the century the network had reached a total of more than 12,000 route-miles (19,300 km); by 1921 it was over 23,000 (37,100 km).

Until this century Western Australia had no rail connection whatever with the rest of the country, from which it was separated by a vast expanse of desert. Only when the six Australian territories had been federated into a Commonwealth in 1901 was there the resource to undertake one of the most formidable rail construction jobs in rail history, which was begun in the autumn of 1912 under the aegis of the newly formed Commonwealth Railways and finished in October 1917. Practically the entire 1,051 miles (1,691 km) of standard 4 ft 8½ in (1,435 mm) gauge line from Port Augusta, in South Australia, to Kalgoorlie in Western Australia had to be projected through desperately arid and totally uninhabited country devoid of any natural running water, and where temperatures veered from sub-zero Fahrenheit in winter to over 120°F (50°C) in high summer. At its midpoint the route crossed the lunar-like Nullarbor Plain – or 'Plain of No Trees', quite barren of any feature or vegetation – where the surveyors plotted what is still the longest stretch of continuous straight track in the world, 297 miles (478 km) of it (some accounts have it, perhaps apocryphally, that the distance would have been greater still if the surveyors were not being paid on a rate that gave them more for designing curves).

The first locomotive in China. Foreign enterprise was heavily involved in Chinese railways from the start, making them a target in later revolutionary times.

A transcontinental journey still entailed break-of-gauge transhipment, of course. That was not eliminated until late 1969, after a Western Australian decision to build a standard 1,435 mm gauge line so as to move ore in 9,000 ton trains from deposits west of Kalgoorlie to a coastal steelworks complex south of Perth fired determination to tackle the nuisance head-on. In a series of very expensive operations 216 miles (348 km) of South Australian 5 ft 3 in (1,600 mm) gauge main line were reduced to standard gauge and a great deal of New South Wales track was rebuilt or fettled up to higher standard to complete a continuous 1,435 mm line the whole way from Perth to Sydney. Now that 2,462 mile (3,962 km) journey can be made undisturbed over 2¾ days of travel in supreme air-conditioned luxury by the 'Indian Pacific', one of the lamentably few trains to maintain the great transcontinental train tradition of a rolling hotel.

New Zealand had the sense to grapple with the gauge controversy before it got out of hand. The islands' first steam railway, a 4¼ mile (6.8 km) stretch of the Lyttleton & Christchurch opened on 1 December 1863, copied the Australian 5 ft 3 in (1,600 mm), but elsewhere promoters were toying with both standard and 3 ft 6 in (1,067 mm). Fortunately the colonial Government stepped in at the end of the 1860s, primarily to take control of railway planning and construction (though some private enterprise building was conceded in the 1880s), and fixed on the 3 ft 6 in gauge. All lines already in existence, which used other gauges, were converted to 3 ft 6 in gauge by 1877.

JAPAN AND CHINA

By the last quarter of the nineteenth century only the Far East remained virgin territory for British railway-building enterprise. While it was under the feudal, xenophobic rule of the samurai, Japan was as hostile to foreign industrial technology, investment and culture as present-day Iran, but the attitude changed completely with the restoration of the Emperor's power in 1867. Suddenly Japan was hungry for Western aid and advice on modernization, and the new Government readily accepted the view of the British Minister Plenipotentiary, Sir Harry Parks, that they needed railways as a priority. They also needed the money to build them, though, and some dissent rumbled when the Government opened the door to the West so wide as to admit foreign money on loan. That way, nevertheless, the first 19 mile (31 km) line from Tokyo to Yokohama was built by British engineers and opened in September 1872, closely followed by lines from Kyoto to Osaka in 1873 and Kobe to Osaka in 1874. All were on the 3 ft 6 in (1,067 mm) gauge, which became the standard of the Japanese Imperial State Railways (reshaped as the Japanese National Railways, a public corporation, in 1948).

The 1872 inauguration of Japanese railways was made the stage for a public manifestation of the new Japanese order. Astonishingly the Emperor Mutsuhito

GROWTH OF THE RAILWAYS IN JAPAN

No railway was built in Japan until the Meiji Restoration of 1868 ended the long policy of excluding foreigners from the country. Such was the fervour then for modernization that the first line followed only four years later, a 19 mile (31 km) track from Tokyo to Yokohama. The earliest lines were owned by the Government, but private construction – especially of local railways – was not slow in developing. There were as many as thirty-nine companies operating in 1905, but nationalization of the major companies in 1906 and 1907 placed most of the network in Government hands, although many private lines still exist today.

The problems in constructing any railway network have been compounded in Japan's case by its geography. The central area of the islands is mountainous, restricting the population to three large coastal plains. By 1912 the high standards of engineering already attained had enabled Japanese engineers to connect the main cities in a network of 5,600 route-miles (9,000 km). By 1980 this figure had grown to 13,000 miles (21,000 km), including 664 miles (1,061 km) of existing Shinkansen, with two further Shinkansen lines under construction. Political pressures have prevented the cuts in mileage introduced by most West European railways in recent years, with the result that the present network includes many unprofitable branch lines.

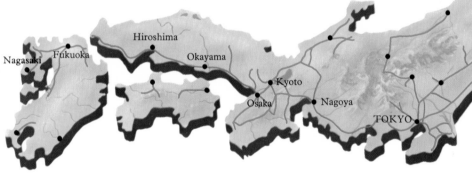

himself, in his full regalia, made an unprecedented appearance before a celebratory crowd that included foreigners, and rode the first train from Tokyo to Yokohama behind a 2–4–0 constructed by England's Vulcan Foundry. After the dutiful rituals at Yokohama the chair occupied by the Mikado was said to have been kissed, then ripped into souvenir fragments by a frantic throng of his subjects.

Between 1881 and 1891, a period which saw completion of what was to become by 1950 the country's most heavily trafficked trunk route, the 374 mile (602 km) Tokaido from Tokyo to Kobe, State and private railway building were pursued in parallel, but in 1891 the Government took control of main-line planning and construction so as to ensure evolution of an orderly network. The 1891 legislation authorized the Government to buy up private lines crucial to its scheme and seventeen were nationalized between 1906 and 1907.

However, private enterprise was left scope to build feeder and local lines, hence the existence in present-day Japan of a considerable number of very important and sizeable private railways, such as the Kinki Nippon, which deploys some 1,500 electric railcars over a 367 mile (591 km) network.

Until the twentieth century British influence was patent in both the equipment and the style of Japan's railways. All the early locomotives came from British firms such as Dubs and Neilson of Glasgow, Sharp Stewart of Manchester (who also constructed much of the rolling stock) and Kitson of Leeds. That was largely attributable to the consulting presence of an Englishman named William M. Smith, an engineer who was a prime mover in the design of Britain's most successful compound locomotives. Apart from the look of the trains, the high platforms and buildings of early Japanese stations were recognizably English in style.

China was no less suspicious of foreigners and their inventions than the Japanese. Eventually a British firm, Jardine Matheson, winkled its way in by trickery. It won consent to build a road from Shanghai to Woosung, on the Huangpu River, laid the foundations, then suddenly produced rails and rolling stock to run over them. The locals, surprisingly, were quite enraptured when the Woosung Railway began operation on 30 June 1876, but sadly a train soon hit and killed a coolie and the service had to be stopped forthwith. Eventually the Chinese Government agreed to buy the railway, but in instalments, and until they stumped up the final payment the English builders at least extracted some return from their assets by converting the thoroughfare to a road.

Right: Although the American Commodore Perry demonstrated this miniature railway at Yokohama in 1854, the British eventually built the first line in Japan in 1872.

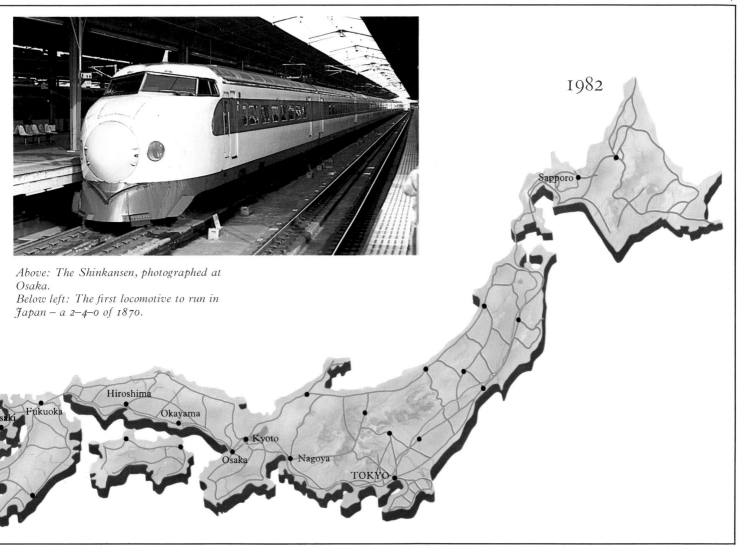

1982

Above: The Shinkansen, photographed at Osaka.
Below left: The first locomotive to run in Japan – a 2–4–0 of 1870.

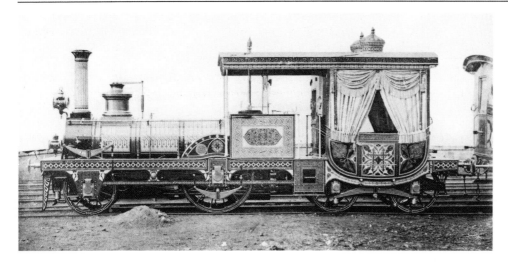

Built by Robert Stephenson in 1862, the 'Khedive's Special' was used by the Viceroy of Egypt to move his court between his Montaza summer palace and Alexandria.

When they did take possession, with traditional reverence for the dead the Chinese not only shipped the rails and rolling stock to Formosa, where they were left to rust away on a beach, but even demolished the road, topping off their penance to the luckless coolie by erecting a small temple to the Queen of Heaven on the site of the Shanghai station.

There was little significant railway construction in China until the country's defeat by Japan in 1895, which opened eyes to the strategic worth of rail transport. What followed had a powerful influence on the troubled history of the country and its Communist culmination, for much of the railway system was built either for Government operation with foreign money or else as a foreign enterprise under the system of concessions. Not only European but American money was heavily involved, and so were the resources of Tsarist Russia in the construction of the Chinese Eastern Railway which continued the Trans-Siberian into Manchuria. Popular agitation for nationalization of the railways and the ousting of all foreign involvement in their finance, control and forward planning was a mainspring of the revolution which established the republic and ultimately Mao-Tse-Tung's Communist regime. The railways were thus front-line targets through each phase of the country's turmoil. The resultant damage, misuse and neglect is a prime reason for the huge backlog of development which China's present-day regime is so concerned to overtake.

RHODES' VISION:
THE CAPE TO CAIRO

British influence was paramount in the conception of Africa's first railway. With the Suez Canal still in the future, overland travel through Egypt was a pivotal link in the route from Britain to India; at one time the P&O Steamship company maintained a stock of 3,000 camels to hump mails, stores and baggage from Alexandria to the Gulf of Suez while passengers bumped across the desert from one ship to another in abysmally uncomfortable horse-drawn carriages. In 1851 Khedive Abbas I, concerned to nourish this traffic, commissioned Robert Stephenson to engineer and build a 120 mile (193 km) railway from Alexandria to Cairo, which was finished in 1856 and extended to Suez in 1858. The Suez extension lost point after the canal's completion in 1868, but gradual projection of the railway up the Nile valley to Luxor, reached in 1898, and eventually to Aswan, created an appealing alternative to the Nile steamers. In the first two or three decades of this century it captivated countless Anglo-American tourists affluent enough to make the 'Grand Tour' and the Egyptian State Railways regaled them not only with night trains of Wagon-Lits sleepers but also by day with the 'Sunshine Pullman', formed of cars that almost precisely reproduced the British model of the period except for their gleaming white overall livery.

Railway-building in the colonies of various European powers in North, Central and South Africa was initiated by the opening of a short line from Durban (then Port Natal) to its harbour in 1860. But it was leisurely and entirely self-contained within each territory, directed primarily at simplifying the exploitation of local

mineral resources, until the discovery of gold and then, at the end of the 1860s, of the diamond fields around Kimberley. As late as 1870 South Africa could only show 69 miles (111 km) of railway, all but six of them (10 km) in the Cape Colony. Four years earlier the Senators of the Cape had been firmly resisting railway expansion on the grounds that it would 'put out of employment the bullock drivers of the Colony – a most meritorious class of men – and would also hasten the transit of wool to the shipping port: a facility in no way required, as it gets there fast enough'. That attitude helped persuade the Cape Government to expropriate the existing railways in 1872, make itself responsible for construction to develop the colony and simultaneously to standardize a gauge of 3ft 6in (1,067mm), which entailed conversion of some trackage previously laid to standard 4ft 8½in gauge. Natal followed suit under all three headings in 1877.

A railway projected northward from Cape Town was already approaching Kimberley in 1880 when Cecil Rhodes became a member of the Cape legislature. Popular history credits Rhodes with his celebrated vision of a Cape-to-Cairo railway purely in terms of through travel, but his business acumen was too sensitive for such tunnel-vision romanticism. He had internal trade clearly in his sights as the main target. A century later, with the new nations of black Africa intent on Pan-African economic and social union, fulfilment of Rhodes' real ambition has become a priority of the Union of African Railways. It has drafted an ideal 10,000-mile (16,100km) master plan of new railways to achieve the objective.

The 'Cape-to-Cairo' tag of Rhodes' scheme – most likely first coined by an engineer discussing African railway projects in an English magazine of 1889 – was part-cause of its frustration, because of its empire-building connotation. A distinguished British journalist, W.T. Stead, once observed astutely that the line would have built itself bit by bit if no one had tumbled to its potential until the last link was finished and the first astounded passengers found themselves on a train travelling all the way from the Cape to the Mediterranean.

Rhodes' railway did not even reach Bulawayo without traumas. He had planned to skirt the two unfriendly Boer republics north of the Cape on their western edge, but changed course when gold was discovered in the Transvaal in 1886. At that the Boers enlisted Dutch finance to project a railway eastward to the Portuguese East African coast at Lourenço Marques, while at the same time Transvaal's President Kruger strove to block Rhodes' incursion into his territory. But the Boer money ran out and the Rhodes railway was first into Pretoria by two and a half years. In time, with the evolution of Johannesburg as the nerve centre of the gold-mining industry, that city not only displaced Pretoria as Transvaal's commercial centre but assumed such national significance that it became the operational hub of South African Railways.

Rhodes had had to coax money from the Cape Government to maintain his winning constructional pace to Pretoria and his funds were again in poor state when he reached Bulawayo. Despairing of adequate money from London he even went to Berlin to seek help from an interested Kaiser, but in the event the British South Africa Company and various Rhodesian mining concerns agreed to top up his reserves. He died two years before the railway reached the Victoria Falls in the summer of 1904. The following year it was across the Zambesi on one of the world's most majestic civil engineering structures, the 650 ft (198 m) Victoria Falls bridge with a centre arch span of 500 ft (152 m) soaring 420 ft (128 m) above the boiling river. In a phenomenal feat of construction this was erected in only nineteen weeks from assemblies prefabricated by the Cleveland Bridge & Engineering Company of Darlington, England, and by only twenty-five skilled men imported from England to supervise a hundred native labourers. Beyond the falls, Broken Hill in Rhodesia, about 2,000 miles (3,200 km) from Cape Town, was attained in 1906, but the great project got no further beyond that point than the Congo. The authorities of Egypt and the Sudan could envisage no return from a connection that would remotely justify its high engineering cost and rebuffed every approach from the Rhodesian successors to the Rhodes heritage.

In modern times political change and the creation of new independent countries has split the Cape-to-Cairo route between several administrations. Only as far as Mafeking is it part of South African Railways, which was created in 1910 from the railways of the Cape, Natal and the former Boer Orange River and Transvaal republics.

The inscription on this first train from Salisbury to Umtali underlines the Rhodesian belief in Cape-to-Cairo schemes, although the opening of this relatively short line would hardly seem to warrant such optimism.

EUROPE'S CIVIL ENGINEERING MASTERWORKS

Most of the memorable tunnelling and bridgework in the first fifty years or so of railways was British, since the early British main-line builders were more concerned to design for future speed than their European and American counterparts and hence less inclined to bend and grade their routes around topographical obstacles. Would that they had been as far-sighted where the potential size of rail vehicles and the development of track to withstand heavier rolling stock was concerned.

Instead they put up fixed structures with clearances which are now the most restrictive of any standard-gauge national network in the world, and with every passing decade enlargement has become more prohibitively expensive. Only on the main routes of the former Great Western Railway is there some latitude, because Brunel built to accommodate his broad-gauge equipment. Elsewhere the British loading gauge permits only 12ft 11in (3.95m) height and 9ft (2.75m) vehicle width, compared with the standard 10ft 2in (3.1m) width and 14ft 9in (4.5m) height of the so-called Berne loading gauge, standardized in mainland Europe, the 10ft 10in (3.3m) width and 16ft 2in (4.9m) height of North America, and – most generous of all – the 11ft 2in (3.4m) width and 17ft 4in (5.3m) height of the USSR railways.

SPANNING THE RIVERS OF BRITAIN AND FRANCE

Circumstances forced Robert Stephenson and Brunel to undertake metal bridgework on a scale previously inconceivable. When Stephenson was appointed engineer of the Chester & Holyhead Railway in 1845 he confronted Admiralty insistence that the narrow Menai Strait separating the mainland from the Isle of Anglesey, on which the port of Holyhead lies, be kept free of impediment to shipping. The Lords of the Admiralty would countenance the erection of stone piers at only one point in midstream, on the small Britannia rock. With reinforced concrete as yet unknown the stipulation ruled out a multi-span masonry structure of the kind hitherto used for the longer bridgework, and suspension bridges had thus far proved vulnerable to the weight of a train.

After exhaustive calculation and experiment with a one-sixth scale model Stephenson concluded that the requisite strength for a span of over 400ft (122m) length was obtainable from a box tube of iron. The point was proved in a bridge of 423ft (129m) span to carry the railway at low height over the river estuary at Conway, on the shore of the North Wales mainland, but the Menai Strait enterprise was far more formidable. It entailed prefabricating two main spans each 460ft (140m) long and of over 1,500 tons weight apiece on land, then floating them out into the stream on pontoons and finally hoisting them intact into position 130ft (40m) above water between the piers of the bridge. But it was done and the double-track Britannia Bridge was ready for rail traffic in October 1850. Stephenson was commissioned to design a bridge on similar principles, with a single-line tube 6,588ft (2,008m) long in twenty-five sections resting on twenty-four stone piers, to achieve the first rail crossing of the St Lawrence river at Montreal.

A few years after Stephenson's Britannia Bridge achievement Brunel came up

Weissen viaduct on the narrow-gauge Rhaetian railway in Switzerland. The transalpine routes have inspired many great feats of railway engineering.

against a similarly constricting Admiralty stipulation when he was projecting his broad-gauge railway from Plymouth, across the Tamar estuary at Saltash and into the extreme south-western county of Cornwall. Here again huge ironwork spans – but in this case an elliptically shaped hybrid of tubular and suspension construction principles – had to be assembled on shore and lifted into place. In May 1859 the Prince Consort formally opened the bridge, which ever since has borne his name – the Royal Albert Bridge.

In the ensuing age of metalwork and steel bridges the name of a Frenchman best-known in another context, Eiffel, figures in the credits for some of Europe's most impressive railway structures. He designed the graceful bridge with a centre span of 528 ft (161 m) which was completed over the Douro river at Oporto in 1877 and which is still a lynch-pin of Portuguese Railways' principal Oporto–Lisbon trunk route; its main contemporary drawback is that it is single-track, which makes it a severe operational handicap and in consequence of which it is likely, after some years of deliberating the expense, to be replaced by a new bridge in the 1980s. In 1881 Eiffel also built one of France's most spectacular nineteenth-century bridges, the Garabit Viaduct on the secondary line from Marvejols to Neussargues in the Auvergne; 1,850 ft (564 m) long in total, its central span soars over the Truyère river 400 ft (122 m) up. That height was exceeded by Fades Viaduct in Languedoc-Roussillon, built in 1905, the central 473 ft (144 m) long span of which swings the track 435 ft (133 m) above the river in the Sioule valley below; until the 1976 completion of Yugoslavia's new Belgrade-Bar line and its 495 ft (151 m) high Mala Rijeka Bridge the Fades Viaduct was the highest above ground level on any railway in the world.

The last great European railway bridge of the nineteenth century was Britain's Forth Bridge, the opening of which in March 1890 completed a direct route from Edinburgh to the north-eastern Scottish city of Aberdeen. The other waterway in the path of this route, the Tay estuary at Dundee, had been successfully bridged at the second attempt three years earlier. The first bridge, 11,653 ft (3,552 m) long, had no sooner been ceremonially opened by Queen Victoria and its designer, Thomas Bouch, knighted for creating the longest bridge in the world, than in the following winter, on 28 December 1878, a savage gale

blew down its central spans and cascaded the train at that moment crossing them into the water, killing the train crew and all seventy-three passengers. An enquiry blamed both faulty calculation of stress tolerance and deficiencies of workmanship. Rebuilt, the bridge survives in good order, one of the last major structures in wrought iron, but the disgraced Bouch did not move on to design the Forth Bridge as he expected before the Tay Bridge catastrophe. That assignment was passed over to Benjamin Baker and Sir John Fowler, who decided that the best way to minimize central supports and keep the waterway navigable was to adopt the historic cantilever principle (it dated from

Top: Stephenson's Britannia Bridge over the Menai Straits links Anglesey with the mainland. Completed in 1850, the bridge was built of prefabricated iron box tubes, held in position by the piers.
Above: Brunel's Royal Albert Bridge, built over the Tamar at Saltash for the GWR, was opened by the Prince Consort in 1859. It is still a single line bridge today.
Top right: The Garabit Viaduct on the secondary line from Marvejols to Neussargues in the Auvergne, built by Eiffel in 1881.
Above right: The rebuilt Tay Bridge in LNER days. The first bridge collapsed during a storm on 28 December 1878, and its piles can be seen alongside.

at least the late seventeenth century, when Indian travellers came upon a wooden cantilever bridge in the Himalayas). The Edinburgh–Dundee–Aberdeen route was the North British Railway's, but the Forth Bridge project was so massive that it had to be financed by a consortium of that company and the three others whose through traffic would benefit from it – the Great Northern, North Eastern and Midland. Together they had to put up £3 millions.

Altogether 54,000 tons of steel and 6½ million rivets went to the making of the six great cantilevers of the Forth Bridge and their approach viaducts, the whole edifice extending 8,298 ft (2,529 m). The canti-

levers themselves added up to a length of almost exactly a mile (1.6 km), the two main spans they created each measuring 1,710 ft (521 m) long, and the peak of each cantilever tower rose 361 ft (110 m) above the water. The railway itself crossed 156 ft (47.5 m) above the Firth of Forth. The structure took just over seven years to complete and at the peak of the constructional activity, in the autumn of 1888, it engaged a work-force of over 4,500 men. The job was pretty expensive in human life: accidents were frequent, the vast majority being the consequence of individual workmen's recklessness, no fewer than fifty-six of whom lost their lives before the bridge was finished.

THE SEMMERING PASS LINE

It was the creation of the European mainland's transalpine main lines, of course, which evoked the great sustained feats of civil engineering. The Austrians were the first to venture into the mountains. Within only a year of commissioning the country's first railway in 1837, the General Engineer Director of the Imperial Army, Archduke Johann, was not only pressing the Government to build a steam railway along the country's vital north-south trade axis, but had despatched four of his own officers to prospect for a possible route over the Semmering Pass, the mountain funnel for traffic from Vienna to Styria and Carinthia, in the south of the country, and to the then all-important port of Trieste.

Access to the Semmering Pass from the Vienna side entailed a rise of about 1,900 ft (580 m) in little more than 6 miles' (10 km) progress from Gloggnitz. In the contemporary state of the locomotive art, the British pioneers – the recognized fount of wisdom on railway practicalities – did not dream of tackling such a proposition with pure adhesion. Their recommendation was that the pass be scaled by a series of level sections linked by rope-worked inclines.

Initial indecision on the part of the Austrian civil authorities encouraged private enterprise to step in, but when one of their protagonists showed an inclination to bypass the traction problem by deviating a railway from Vienna on a longer route through Hungary the Government stepped smartly off the sidelines. It was not about to let the main north-south trade axis shift to its neigbours' territory. In 1841 an Imperial proclamation foreshadowed a railway from Vienna to Trieste and Milan; and in the same year, with the bankruptcy of two private railways aggravating concern for the new medium in its strategic role, the State took powers to build and operate all key routes deemed critical to the national interest. That made the Semmering Railway a State project – though, as related in the previous chapter, in the next decade the Government handed it over to private enterprise.

The vital move in the preliminaries was the despatch of Karl Ritter von Ghega across the Atlantic to study early American railroad practice. Von Ghega was a Venetian doctor of mechanical engineering with long experience of road-bulding in the Alps who had graduated to railway

(19 km/h) with 83 tons in tow, and that in drizzling rain, with which he unashamedly and forgivably mingled some exultant tears.

The competitors in the trials proper had to conform to a maximum axle-loading of 6¼ tons, be comfortable on curves of 200 yds (183 m) radius and be capable of sustaining a minimum of 7 mph (11 km/h) up 4.7 miles (7.6 km) of continuous 1 in 40 with a trailing load of 125 tons; they must also run satisfactorily downhill at 19 mph (30 km/h) and be able to stop within 160 yds (146 m) on a 1-in-40 downgrade. Each engine was

construction on the Kaiser Ferdinand Nordbahn in 1836. Five years later he was appointed chief engineer of the Vienna-Trieste project. What he saw of the railways' advance into the Allegheny Mountains during his tour of thirty American systems convinced von Ghega that steam traction could surmount the Semmering Pass. Just how, however, neither he nor the Government was clear. So, while von Ghega's supreme confidence encouraged the Government to build the new railway south of the pass from Mürzzuschlag towards Graz and Trieste, the critical mountain section was in suspended animation for several years, which were naturally open season for all manner of fanciful theorists on the best technique to adopt for the attack on the Semmering itself. At one time even the Atmospheric System looked to be in serious contention.

In 1848 the Government ordered the Semmering Pass section to be put in hand as an adhesion-worked line on von Ghega's original, circuitous alignment. This was something of a desperate move, born of the 1848 political crisis and anxiety to relieve mounting unemployment in Vienna, and over the next year or two the Government was pilloried for its recklessness. Certainly no railway project since Britain's Liverpool & Manchester had fired such bitter nationwide controversy. Jeremiahs gloomed loudly that a national humiliation was in store. This was understandable; construction had been started without any practical proof of a steam locomotive's

Above: Göltzschtal Viaduct near Plauen in Germany – one of the more grandiose achievements of nineteenth-century railway engineering.
Right: As impressive today as when it opened in 1890, the massive Firth of Forth Bridge was the last great European railway bridge of the nineteenth century.

ability to work by pure adhesion the 14.3 miles (23 km) of stiff 1-in-40 gradients, much of them sharply curved, which von Ghega was forced to adopt to gain the required height in the short distances from the valleys to the pass. Even the Minister of Public Works who authorized the project, as von Ghega disclosed some years later, was soon persuaded by the sceptics that he would never see the Semmering Pass conquered by simple adhesion locomotives.

But von Ghega confounded the faint-hearted. The Austrian Government took up a suggestion floated by a Stuttgart railway journal that a replica of the Liverpool & Manchester's Rainhill Trials be staged to find a suitable locomotive, and as soon as enough track had been laid from Gloggnitz into the mountains, in July 1851, four contenders were put through their paces over an 8 mile (13 km) stretch between Payerbach and Abfaltersbach. The official trial day must have been rather anti-climactic for von Ghega, since he had organized a private, highly emotional triumph a little earlier. Borrowing the Südbahn engine *Save* he had climbed the gradients at a minimum of 12 mph

required to make at least a dozen test runs. Three of the contenders met the specifications and were bought for the Semmering line. Two of them, Günther's Vienna-built *Wiener Neustadt* and John Cockerill's *Seraing*, the latter constructed at the works of its name, pioneered in different ways a double-engine arrangement that in later years was to be refined and exploited with immense success worldwide in a variety of articulated locomotive guises, from the Meyer and Fairlie double-ended format to Beyer-Garratts, Mallet compounds and the last articulated giants in the USA.

In regular use none of the accepted trio was convincing, however, and with time in hand before the Semmering line's completion the Austrian authorities cast about for something better. They found it in a design named after its patentee, Wilhelm Engerth, in which a very short tender was supported on a longer two- or three-axle frame which projected forward beneath the engine's cab and firebox. At first the leading axle of the rear frame was cog-driven from the rear driving axle of the engine's pair, but the cogs wore out too quickly and this arrangement was discarded. In a November 1853 Semmering test the Engerth engine so outclassed a rival derived from Norris practice that French and Swiss railways hurried to adopt the Engerth model for their hilly lines. Besides seventy-six built for the Austrian railway, 110 were ordered by Swiss railways and a considerable number by the French, especially the Nord Railway. In time, however, the penalties of a permanently coupled engine-and-tender layout came to outweigh the benefits of exploiting the tender to enhance adhesion weight; maintenance costs escalated and

re-railing an Engerth engine when it left the track was a tricky business because it was so difficult to unhitch the tender. Most were ultimately rebuilt with a separate tender; the Semmering engines, built as self-contained 0–6–4s, were converted to orthodox 0–8–0 tender engines.

The Semmering line was finished in October 1853 after six years of work. The engineering work was superb and an extraordinary feat considering the comparatively primitive tools available at the time – the fifteen tunnels, for instance, had to be hewn without benefit of pneumatic drills. The sixteen viaducts were amongst the most graceful of the age, especially the Kalte Rinne, with its two tiers of stone arches. But the human toll during the building of the line had been appalling. Von Ghega's organizing genius did not run to provision for sanitation in the shanty towns set up in the hills for his labour force. Cholera and typhus struck time and again with such virulence that scarcely anyone escaped a bout at one time or another and some 700 died before the line was complete. Emperor Franz Josef ceremonially inaugurated the Semmering line, Europe's pioneer mountain main line, in October 1853, in no way disconcerted by a final contretemps at Gloggnitz when the chimney of his inaugural train's engine struck the station roof, disintegrated, and the carriages were filled with smoke.

THE MONT CENIS TUNNEL

Meanwhile every fresh advance of railways in Central Europe had been heightening consciousness of the great Alpine massif itself – above all in Italy, of course, where the railways were as yet totally isolated from the rest of the continent. The Vienna–Trieste line did not make connection with the Lombardy–Venetian at Udine until 1860, two years after von Ghega's next major Austrian project, the Inn Valley line, had reached Innsbruck; by the spring of 1859 a railway had been driven north from the plain at Verona up the Trento valley to Bolzano and construction of the Brenner Pass link, technically the least taxing of all the transalpine routes to build, could begin. By then a far more formidable transalpine undertaking was making its first painful progress.

Well before the unification of their country the Italians had begun serious contemplation of a tunnel under the Mont Cenis Pass from Piedmont to Savoy. At the time, the early 1840s, both territories were Italian domain. The 1848 war between Piedmont and Austria interrupted the planning, but at the end of August 1857 the preliminaries were finished and King Victor Emmanuel II of Sardinia, as he then was, formally inaugurated the project. Two years later the French took over Savoy, but were well content to have the

tunnel and agreed to pay a share of its costs (as the job progressed the Italians became short of cash and in the final stages the French had to pay their instalments in advance to keep the funds liquid).

At this distance in time it is hard to appreciate the daring of the undertaking, which a good deal of European opinion sternly condemned as a far more lunatic folly than the Semmering project. One London newspaper warned of unimaginable terrors to follow from this sacrilegious intrusion into the 'bosom of the mighty fortress'. Other sceptics were convinced that the two work-forces boring towards each other from each portal would veer off course and each forge on hopelessly to the other side of the mountains; in the event they were just 1 ft 11½ in (60 cm) off target vertically and 1 ft 4 in (40 cm) horizontally when the meet was made. The most vivid reflection of the enterprise's audacity, probably, is the original expectation that it would take twenty-five years to finish.

Even that estimate sounded euphorically optimistic when each army of some 2,000 men could only manage to advance 45 ft (14 m) a month for the first three years. But all they had were picks and shovels. The turning-point was perfection by one of the tunnel's chief engineers, Germain Sommeiller, of the pneumatic drill; when that was put into the tunnellers' hands in

November 1860 progress immediately quickened to around 250 ft (76 m) a month.

Sommeiller, a Savoyard who opted for Piedmontese nationality when France acquired Savoy, had been appointed one of the tunnel's three chief engineers partly because of his promising work on compressed-air drilling equipment. But with his colleagues, the Italians Sebastiano Grandis and Severino Grattoni, he had already won great kudos for the successful engineering of the steeply graded line out of Genoa through the Giovi Pass of the Ligurian Appennine Mountains towards Turin. For a time its 4¼ miles (7 km) of 1 in 28½ and 2 miles (3 km) of 1 in 33 to the summit tunnel were considered in-superable except by cable haulage – Robert Stephenson, passing through Genoa in 1850, was eagerly corralled for advice, took one look and would only vouchsafe that he was glad it was not his problem. Eventually, stimulated by von Ghega's Semmering triumph, the three local men found that by coupling two

Above left: Vitznau station, Switzerland, in 1880. A rack-and-pinion railway, the Vitznau–Rigi employed locomotives with upright boilers for its first ten years.
Above right: Using the third-rail system, Fell locomotives operated over the Mont Cenis Pass for three years before the tunnel was built under the pass.
Below: Pneumatic drills speeded up work in the Mont Cenis Tunnel.

engines back-to-back to form an 0–4–4–0, manned by a single driver, the gradients could be conquered by simple adhesion. With these *Mastodonti dei Giovi* ('Giovi Elephants'), as they were nick-named, the line was successfully opened to traffic shortly after the Semmering inauguration, on 6 December 1853.

To return to the Mont Cenis, the tunnelling could not keep pace with

mounting impatience for better Franco-Italian communication. That prompted the English railway engineer John Bar-raclough Fell to build a narrow-gauge (3 ft 7 in/1,092 mm) railway *over* the pass. Completed in 1867, it ran from St Michel du Maurienne, 2,330 ft (710 m) up in France, to Susa, 1,625 ft (495 m) up in Italy, tracing a zig-zag route of 48½ miles (78 km) along a one-time military road built by Napoleon I and reaching a summit of 6,680 ft (2,036 m), which entailed protection by avalanche shelters in notoriously vulnerable stretches at the highest altitudes. The gradient was as severe as 1 in 12½ and to negotiate it Fell employed a method adapted from earlier systems of Vignoles and Ericsson, but nowadays invariably associated with his own name – a centre third rail to provide additional adhesion for an extra locomot-ive wheel uphill, but which could also be gripped by a braking device on the descent. The Fell third-rail system found several applications around the world, longest-lived of which were the spectacular Rimutaka incline in New Zealand and the still extant Snaefell tramway in the Isle of Man.

Travel by Fell's Mont Cenis railway was a laborious business. The 48½ mile (78 km) trip took six hours, but it did bring Turin within twenty-eight hours' rail travel time of Paris overall and for three years its business included the all-important Indian mail from London for shipment from Brindisi. Opened to regular traffic on 15 June 1868 it was closed soon after the main-line tunnel was opened on 17 September 1871 and subsequently dismantled; most of its roadbed has since been appropriated for the French *Route Nationale* leading from Paris to Turin.

The original double-track tunnel, fractionally less than 8 miles (13 km) long, was actually finished in just over thirteen years, for the parties working from each end had broken through to each other on Christmas Day 1870. A few years later trouble with landslips at the French entrance compelled an extension, finished in 1881, but in September 1944 the retreating Germans collapsed nearly half of it when they simultaneously mined the mountainside above and detonated a trainload of explosives within the tunnel. A combined force of French and South African Army engineers uncovered the original 1871 entrance and attempted to recommission the tunnel as a single-line bore, but were defeated by fresh landslides. A new double-line entrance had to be built and after fifteen months of work the tunnel was reopened at a new total length of 8 miles 868 yds (13,668 m) on 14 August 1946. Since it superseded the old coach road over the pass as well as the Fell railway when it was opened, the tunnel has been loosely

The first Simplon tunnel was opened on 17 May 1906 after many traumas and almost eight years of work.

dubbed the Mont Cenis, but its alignment is beneath the 8,323 ft (2,537 m) Col de Fréjus and it is properly the Fréjus Tunnel – the Col de Mont Cenis lies about 17 miles (27 km) north-east of the railway.

THROUGH THE ALPS AGAIN
AND AGAIN

Completion of the Mont Cenis Tunnel was the first positive action on a rail passage of the Swiss Alps, which had been mooted within a year of the 1847 opening of Switzerland's first line, the Zurich–Baden 'Spanish Bun Railway'. The Swiss actually embarked on a mountain tunnelling project before the Mont Cenis was under way, but through the Jura Mountains on their western border, to project a railway from Basle to what is now a vital crossroads of the Swiss Federal rail network, Olten, and thence to Bern. The ubiquitous British contractor, Brassey, was engaged to build the railway and its Old Hauenstein Tunnel of just over 1½ miles' length (2,495 m), which took the five years from 1853 to 1858 to bore. Right at the start the Swiss were made grimly aware of the hazards of digging deep into their mountains; sixty-three workmen were killed when one tunnelling shaft collapsed in May 1857. The tunnel was superseded when the Swiss Federal, electrifying after the First World War, concluded that the moment was ripe to bypass the 1-in-38 gradients of the Brassey route by constructing a lower-level railway through a longer tunnel, the lower Hauenstein of just over 5 miles (8,134 m).

So far as transalpine aspirations were concerned, by the late 1860s political change reinforced the stimulus of the Mont Cenis achievement. Italy was unified and Bismarck had begun to shape the German Reich by creation of the North German Bund; both were now urging action on Switzerland, where the Cantonal administrations were at cross-purposes on the financing of a tunnel. The French, naturally, were anxious to abort any move which would undermine a promising monopoly of international traffic via the Mont Cenis route, but their opposition was soon drastically muted by defeat in the Franco-Prussian War. So, following a month-long Bern conference of delegates from Switzerland, Italy, North Germany, Baden and Württemberg in September 1869 at which the Gotthard Pass was confirmed as the sensible route to Italy, the Gotthard Railway company was formed at Lucerne on 1 November 1871.

Because of the acrimonious dissension between the Swiss Cantons on how the railway should be built and their lack of adequate cash to meet the prospective bill, finance had to be sought from the governments involved. The Italians paid promptly (they in fact contributed by far the biggest share of State money), the Germans and especially the Swiss less eagerly. Within eight years they all had to increase their contributions substantially, for the first building estimates turned out to be far too low and the company gradually slumped into a financial quagmire. Even with the new infusion of cash it was only rescued by some drastic economies, including postponement of some of the route's proposed link lines within Switzerland, realignment with a steeper ruling grade of 1 in 37 and initial construction as single instead of double track. But prudently the formation was built with a provision for double track; within a very short time of the line's opening the great weight of traffic compelled doubling of lengthy sections of the route, including the Gotthard Tunnel itself, but not until 1968 was the last single-track bottleneck – on the Melide causeway across Lake Lugano – enlarged.

One could justifiably expend a whole chapter on the spectacular engineering of the entire Gotthard route from Lucerne to the Italian frontier at Chiasso, with its 101 striking bridges and the sets of spiral tunnels by which it rapidly gains vertical height where mountain valley floors shelve

abruptly. But there is room only to record that the 9 miles 562 yds (15 km) long Gotthard Tunnel, wherein the railway reaches its 3,786 ft (1,590 m) summit, was finished in just over eight years thanks in part to the experience gained with the Mont Cenis. The triumphant engineer was a Geneva tunnelling specialist, Louis Favre, but his reward had to be celestial since he succumbed to a heart attack during a visit to the tunnelling front-line in the summer of 1879.

The mainly Italian workforce was indomitable. Around 2,500 were employed throughout the job and a creditably large number saw it right through, undaunted by the death of 177 and the prostration of over 400 more by injury or serious illness. Main causes of the casualty list were the fierce rock pressure around the underground workings, the constricted working space (the Gotthard was built without benefit of a parallel work tunnel for incoming supplies and outgoing spoil, unlike many later great tunnels) and the high temperatures at the tunnelling

faces, which the water-powered air-pumping system never adequately mitigated. The converging tunnellers met on 28 February 1880 and on 23 December 1881 the first locomotive steamed beneath the pass from Göschenen to Airolo. One should add that the Gotthard was only one of eighty tunnels from Lucerne to Chiasso, together making a total length of 28½ miles (46 km), in the 140½ miles (226 km) journey.

The next transalpine tunnel to be finished was the Arlberg, just outside Swiss territory. Austria, Hungary and Rumania were soon hankering for a rail link with Switzerland and France, and a line through the mountains to Lake Constance had been canvassed as early as 1847, but for over two decades prospective investors were rebuffed. At last, in 1871, the railway planning authorities evinced some interest, but they took nine years more to persuade themselves that the return on the outlay on the Vorarlberg Railway would be rewarding. Centrepiece of the route was the double-track Arlberg Tunnel, 6 miles 639 yds (10.25 km) long

A modern express passes Gurtnellen on the Gotthard route, which remains one of the most spectacular pieces of railway engineering in the Alps.

and at the line's 4,300 ft (1,311 m) summit, which was begun in the summer of 1880 and completed on 19 November 1883. The remainder of the Arlberg route from Bregenz and Buchs to Innsbruck was frugally built as single track, to the inconvenience of the present-day Austrian Federal Railways, for whom the route is a busy and prestigious east-west thoroughfare but who can only find the resources to double short stretches at a time. They have the same problem on the Tauern route, which is described later in this chapter.

Within a few years of the first airing of a Gotthard route over the Alps western Switzerland was seeking a more accessible route of its own into Italy. From 1857 onwards some thirty different schemes were dismissed partly because of daunting physical and material costs, partly because the various railway companies whose lines converged on the obvious route, beneath the Simplon Pass, had no cohesion. At last, after the Gotthard's completion had redoubled pressure for a Simplon link, all the approach lines were finally amalgamated in the Jura-Simplon Railway. In 1893 its plan for a base tunnel of some 12½ miles (20km) length between Brigue, on the Swiss side of the pass, and Iselle in Italy, was agreed; two years later Swiss and Italian governments agreed the methods of construction, subsidy and operation and in August 1898 the project was begun by the Hamburg firm of Brandt & Brandau.

The Germans were the first to employ the pilot bore technique. Alongside the main single-track tunnel they drove a parallel, smaller bore (which would later be enlarged to full single-track parameters) and interconnected the two at approximately 660ft (200m) intervals by lateral galleries. The pilot tunnel was for the removal of excavated rock, drainage of any inflow of water from subterranean streams and – perhaps most important of all – to help ventilate the working faces. Benefiting from a new and more efficient model of drill, the 4,000 tunnellers advanced so rapidly that for a time it looked as though the target date of November 1903 for an underground meet of the two bores would be handsomely beaten. But gradually euphoria evaporated.

First the temperature at the working faces, thought unlikely to exceed about

The meeting of the two bores of the Lötschberg Tunnel on 31 March 1911.

35°C (95°F), climbed remorselessly beyond that level the deeper the drillers penetrated the massif. Four miles (6.4km) in from the north portal it had reached 45°C (113°F), but near the midpoint, at 5¼ miles (8.5km), the thermometer was touching an unbearable 53°C (127°F). The powerful ventilating fans made so little impression on the heat that they had finally to pump ice-cold water into the tunnel and keep it spraying continuously over the bore and the working faces before the workers could resume. Then the men driving from the Italian side hit a zone where the pressure of the rock was so intense that it splintered and smashed the strongest baulks of timber and even bent substantial steel reinforcements out of shape. Several times the supports could not contain the pressure and workings caved in. More than once, too, the job was brought to a standstill when the boring suddenly tapped a vicious hot spring coursing through fissures in the rock. The water irrupted into the workings so fiercely that at one stage both pilot bore and main tunnel had to serve as sewers to get rid of a cascade of some 15,000 gallons (70,000 litres) a minute. After all that it was sixteen months behind the planned timetable when the two bores of the main single-track tunnel met on 24 February 1905. A panoplied opening in the presence of the Swiss President and King Victor Emmanuel III of Italy followed on 17 May 1906.

Within a very short time Simplon route traffic was overtaxing the single track, but the German contractors were not prepared

to enlarge the pilot tunnel on the terms provided for in their original contract. They were prudent. It turned out to be a nine years' job for the Swiss Government, which, in view of the New Year's Day 1902 creation of the nationalized Swiss Federal Railways and the consequent absorption of the Simplon line in its network, had decided to make enlargement of the pilot tunnel a State enterprise. Completed in December 1921, the second Simplon tunnel, at 12 miles 559 yards (19.82km), is slightly longer than the first, which ran out at 12 miles 537 yards (19.80km).

Three more major transalpine tunnels were needed to tidy up the international network in the heart of Europe in the early years of the twentieth century. After thirty years of mulling over various schemes for a second north-south route to Trieste and of indecision over the route, the Austrians finally plumped at the turn of the century for a link between Salzburg and Carinthia via the Tauern Pass, and beyond that a route through the Karawanken mountains into what is now Yugoslavia. The Tauern line was to diverge from the Innsbruck-Wörgl-Salzburg main line at Schwarzach St Veit, take the Gastein valley up to the Tauern Pass, then drop down the Mallnitz and Möll valleys to Villach; there it would connect with the Karawanken line from the Carinthian provincial capital of Klagenfurt to what is now Jesenice in Yugoslavia but was then the Austro-Hungarian town of Assling. Both projects were begun in 1901 and the whole network, including the 5 mile 551 yard (8.55km) Tauern and almost 5 mile (7.98km) Karawanken tunnels, was complete by midsummer 1909.

Switzerland's third great Alpine tunnel, the Lötschberg, was bored in this century. Bern, the Swiss capital, had been hankering for direct access to an Alpine passage to the south since the late 1850s and a variety of routes had been canvassed and rejected before the Lötschberg Pass route was accepted in 1899. The Canton of Bern took over the project and in a 1902 referendum won the approval of its electors to finance 25 per cent of its estimated cost. The Federal Government also agreed to put up some money, but the rest of the capital was largely French, attracted by the significance of the route to international traffic from and to northern France, and was enough to allow constitution of the Bern–Lötschberg–Simplon Railway in July 1906. It was to be the first

Alpine main line that was electrified from the outset.

The Lötschberg Tunnel was begun in March 1906 before the approach routes from Spiez up the Kander Valley or, on the other side, up from the Rhone valley at Brigue existed. Lugging the supplies by fiercely graded temporary railways up the mountain gorges of the Kander and Lonza to the 4,000 ft (1,220 m) altitude of the tunnelling site was arduous enough, but in the opening months of the year the supply trains were harassed by the heavy avalanches for which the Lonza gorge is notorious. In the second avalanche season the entire construction camp at the southern portal was overwhelmed on a February night of 1908 and twelve were killed. Time and again the tunnel entrance was submerged by snow as much as 80 ft (24 m) deep. Substantial avalanche protection works had to be erected on the slopes above the tunnel and when the line was finished avalanche shelters had to be extended all along its traversal of the precipitous east wall of the Lonza valley.

The worst catastrophe, however, occurred within the tunnel. The engineers were convinced they were tunnelling deep enough below any mountain valley floor to be sure of confronting nothing but solid rock. They were terribly wrong. About 1¾ miles (2.8 km) in from the northern entrance in the early morning of 24 July 1908 a routine explosion of a charge broke into a totally unexpected fissure of phenomenal depth, piercing 600 ft (183 m) down through the rock from the little, mountain-hemmed basin of the Gasterntal above. The rupture instantaneously released a vast mass of water and glacial detritus which had accumulated in the fissure. It poured into the tunnel, crushing all but one of the twenty-six Italian workers at the face, ripping away their tunnelling equipment and eventually filling almost a mile of the completed northern bore. After months of deliberation the engineers decided that their only option was to wall off the ruined area (the eventual masonry seal was 33 ft [10 m] thick) and re-bore around it well to the east. This trauma apart, the tunnellers also had to surmount the same hot rock and underground stream hazards as their Simplon predecessors, though not on so alarming a scale, before the two bores met on 31 March 1911. The 9 miles 140 yds (14.61 km) Lötschberg Tunnel was opened to traffic on 15 July 1913, by which

date its spectacular approach routes had also been laid.

Approaching from the north the narrow Kander valley floor climbs 1,275 ft (389 m) in only 5 miles (8 km) and, like the Gotthard, the Lötschberg line has to spiral in and out of the mountain-sides to gain height quickly enough without recourse to a gradient steeper than 1 in 37. The line's 4,076 ft (1,240 m) summit is in the Lötschberg tunnel. Then, when it emerges from the Lonza gorge on the south side, the railway is perched 1,500 ft (457 m) up the north wall of the Rhone valley, to which it

One of the many dramatic moments on the Lötschberg line – a tunnel leading straight onto a viaduct over a deep ravine.

gradually descends on a steady 1 in 37 marked by a thrilling succession of tunnels through mountain outcrops and graceful viaducts over deep clefts. Apart from the Lötschberg Tunnel, nearly all this, from Spiez on the Lake of Thun right through to Brigue, was built as single track with passing loops, but addition of a second track throughout will be completed, with the aid of Federal money, in the 1980s.

LOCOMOTIVE DEVELOPMENT FROM 1850 TO 1900

At the opening of the second half of the nineteenth century locomotive design had broadly stabilized in three schools. In America, as an earlier chapter has outlined, the 4–4–0 wheel arrangement had come into such widespread vogue as to earn for evermore the tag of the 'American' type. Europe, on the other hand, had settled for a three-axle arrangement, though British railways were applying to it different principles from those prevalent on the European mainland.

Steel had yet to come. Therefore, sceptical about the strength of constructional materials then available, British builders preferred to build double-framed locomotives with inside cylinders driving the leading coupled axle. The most common wheel arrangements were the 2–2–2 and 2–4–0, supplemented by 0–4–2s for secondary work and – in increasing numbers – by 0–6–0s for freight. In contrast, mainland Europeans were building chiefly outside-cylinder locomotives with single inside frames. Both in Britain and Continental Europe there were hybrids, however. For instance, William Buddicom's French locomotives mounted outside cylinders between the plate frames in which the driving axles were located, while the axleboxes of the leading pair of idle wheels were fixed in outer plate frames. In Britain David Joy's *Jenny Lind* 2–2–2s embodied inside axleboxes for the driving wheels but outside boxes for the fore and aft idle axles, a layout that enhanced stability at speed.

DESIGNING FOR GREATER SPEED

By the mid-1850s the tentacles of new railway on the European mainland were starting to intertwine and create routes of a length which called for a grade of passenger train service that did not stop at every station. The 'express' or 'courier'

train had come into being; and with it the glimmer of more comfortable accommodation to mollify passengers making longer and longer journeys and naturally demanding better travelling conditions. As yet there was not the pressure for speed that the existence of so many rival routes, the outcome of uncontrolled network

Below left: A GWR 4–2–2 built in 1850, the Lord of the Isles *was one of Gooch's most successful broad-gauge locomotives. Below:* Lady of the Lake – *an LNWR 2–2–2 of 1862. Rebuilt, these engines were still in use at the turn of the century.*

expansion, was generating in Britain. By 1875 the average speed of British express trains had progressed to 41.5 mph (67 km/h), but on the European mainland the pace was 8–10 mph (13–16 km/h) slower. Moreover, a far higher proportion of Britain's trains qualified as expresses; at that date French timetables, for instance, were showing only a sixth of Britain's daily express train mileage and for an average speed overall of only 32.8 mph (52.8 km/h). Yet locomotive engineers on both sides of the English Channel were confronting demands for more power as improved coaching stock inflated train weights.

In the third quarter of the century the major railways of mainland Europe found the 2–4–0 the most satisfying arrangement for front-rank passenger duty. The outstanding French example of this type was a design with 6 ft 7¾ in (2,026 mm) driving wheels by the chief engineer of the Paris–Orléans Railway, Victor Forquenot. He found that a 2–2–2 lacked the adhesion to tackle increasing loads on the 1-in-60 to 1-in-100 grades of his main lines as they clambered over the ridges between Brive and Toulouse and Limoges and Agen, where the railway cuts across the delightful valleys which funnel the rivers

down from the Massif Central to the Atlantic coast. The only flaw in these engines, deriving from an unusual suspension system, was that they were hard riders; that was cured in 1873 when Forquenot started to convert them to 2–4–2s (some were subsequently rebuilt as two-cylinder compound 4–4–2s). The design was also adopted by the PLM and Etat Railways and some of its examples survived well into the twentieth century.

For some time the north German railroads, which were easily graded and comparatively free of sharp curvature, were happy with the 2–2–2s which August Borsig – founder of one of the twentieth century's pre-eminent steam locomotive manufacturing plants – began building in the 1840s. But by the early 1870s these so-called 'Borsig Spinners' had to be supplanted by 2–4–0s as the Berlin–Cologne expresses lengthened to ten six-wheeled coaches and schedules stipulated start-to-stop average speeds of 45 mph (70 km/h) over short stretches in the Ruhr. These Borsig and Hartmann 2–4–0s were distinctive for a remarkably long, pencil-slim boiler that necessitated what was for the times an unusually lengthy wheelbase, tolerable because of the easy curvature on north German routes. The essentials of the design were adopted for one of the two standard types (the other was an 0–6–0) which, at the Prussians' instigation, German companies agreed in the mid-1870s should be mass-produced for the country's railways. That was the first-ever instance of a calculated, forward-looking standardization of design for a collection of railways (although, as will have been clear from earlier passages in this book, a number of types had been subsequently taken up by railways other than those on which the engines had made their debut).

Europeans did not really take to the leading two-axle bogie – or truck – of carrying wheels until the 1870s. Of course, Gooch had built 4–2–2s for Britain's Great Western Railway as early as 1847, but on these engines the two closely spaced leading axles were located in main frame-mounted axleboxes. Not until the 1860s was the design of the leading bogie perfected. The early centrally pinned bogies of American 4–4–0s soon proved vulnerable to derailment as train speeds increased, because the rigidly fixed central pivots were prone to stick on curves, and to have allowed the pivot unrestricted lateral

play would have nullified the essential purpose of the bogie, which was to steer the locomotive into a curve. But Levi Bissel in the USA and, more importantly, William Adams in Britain eventually devised methods of suspension and attachment which permitted the leading bogie the required degree of lateral movement, yet kept it strictly in check.

Until the 1870s the British express passenger locomotive scene had been dominated by the Great Western's broad-gauge single-drivers. Only a few of the standard-gauge 2–4–0s, notably Kirtley's Midland type and Fletcher's burly 901 class for the North Eastern Railway, could

Above: The famous Stirling singles – 4–2–2s with huge 8ft driving wheels – were designed by Patrick Stirling for the GNR in 1870 and headed East Coast expresses for many years. This engine (left) is seen with a later inside-cylinder single (centre). Below: An outside-cylinder 4–4–0 designed for the LSWR by William Adams, another late nineteenth-century trend-setter in express locomotive development. Above right: A Midland Railway inside-cylinder 4–2–2 designed by Samuel Johnson in the mid-1880s. The use of sanding apparatus to improve adhesion in poor weather conditions had ensured the continuing success of single-drivers.

match them for pace and hauling prowess. The first man to dim the Great Western's locomotive lustre was Patrick Stirling of the Great Northern.

In 1870 Stirling produced the forerunner of his celebrated 4–2–2s with huge driving wheels of 8 ft (2,438 mm) diameter. Stirling was one of the by this time diminishing school of British designers who believed that a single pair of very large driving wheels was a prerequisite for a high-speed locomotive. His determination on speed also persuaded him to adopt the newly perfected leading bogie. To keep the centre line of the boiler low for stability's sake he had to adopt outside cylinders, as with such big driving wheels the latter's centres would be too high for inside valve motion between the frames; and tests with an outside-cylinder 2–2–2 borrowed from the Great Eastern had warned him that an engine of that wheel arrangement tended to lurch alarmingly if it were pushed up to any speed. In those days, moreover, the track was nothing like as firm as it was to become in the twentieth century. The wrought-iron rails were comparatively lightweight and the packing of ballast between the sleepers could be perfunctory, to say the least. A leading bogie, in Stirling's view, was essential 'because it gradually laid down the road so that the driving wheels laid hold of it'.

In these two particulars – employment of a leading bogie and outside cylinders – Stirling was one of two trend-setters in late nineteenth-century British express

passenger locomotive development. The other was William Adams, who opened his career on the North London Railway, where his initial leading bogie development was done on some 4–4–0 tanks, and moved via the Great Eastern to the London & South Western Railway, where he made his most significant mark on British rail history with a fine series of outside-cylinder 4–4–0s.

To the British public of the 1870s and 1880s the Stirling 8 ft single epitomized modern railway power. Almost until the end of the century it was first choice for the Great Northern's principal East Coast Route expresses, which at the time were among the fastest trains in the world. And unlike most British railways at the time, which for the most part – possibly influenced by Queen Victoria's abhorrence of unseemly speed on the railway – visited ponderous rebukes on enginemen caught exceeding a 60 mph (100 km/h) average and were reputed to have concealed inspectors about their territory to monitor the pace of every passing express, the Great Northern made no bones about its predilection for speed. A Stirling single – though one of his inside-cylinder 2–2–2s, not a 4–2–2 – was credibly reported to have touched 86 mph (138.4 km/h). During the 1888 Race to the North, which is dealt with more fully in the next chapter, these 4–2–2s were consistently working the East Coast train

from London Kings Cross to Grantham, where engines were changed, and from there to York, a distance of 188.2 miles (302.9 km), at an average speed start-to-stop of just over 55 mph (90 km/h).

Because it needed less power to move itself than a coupled engine of comparable size, and hence had more of its output available for train haulage, the single-driver was an admirable tool for express passenger duty in favourable conditions. But it was prone to lose its feet in any environment militating against good adhesion – it could easily be sapped of power in a sudden rainstorm, for instance; hence it was generally spurned by mainland European railways. That handicap was mitigated by a Midland Railway engineer's invention of sanding apparatus, whereby a driver could blast sand onto the rails ahead of the driving wheels (at first with compressed air as the power, but later by steam). As a result the Midland Railway's locomotive chief Samuel Johnson unexpectedly reverted to a series of inside-cylinder 4–2–2s in the mid-1880s. Classes of 4–4–0 were constructed concurrently, however, and although the elegant 4–2–2s were timed up to maximum speeds of 90 mph (145 km/h) the coupled engines gratified the operators

more because of their all-weather dependability. The Great Western, the Great Northern and the Midland were the only serious single-driver protagonists in the final years of the century. The one major British railway to persevere with series after series of 2–4–0s as express passenger engines right up to the 1890s was the London & North Western, under its engineering chiefs John Ramsbottom and then Francis William Webb.

MULTI-WHEELED ENGINES
These major exceptions apart, the trend in the final quarter of the century was to 4–4–0s, in most cases with inside cylinders. This was the phase in which another distinction between British and mainland European locomotive practice

Above left: A GER 'Claud Hamilton' class 4–4–0, taking water at Cambridge in 1902, exhibits the clean lines so typical of British express design.
Above: Two 0–6–0 tank engines (a Prussian T3 and a Swiss E3/3) cross the Beisenbach viaduct in W. Germany.
Left: A Midland Railway 2–4–0, designed by Kirtley. These were one of the few early types to challenge the pace of the GWR's single-drivers. No. 158 now belongs to the National Railway Museum.

became marked and stayed that way, that of external outline. Late nineteenth-century British express passenger engine designers established a national hallmark, not so much in their concern for symmetry, in which they were not unique, as in their dedication to continuity of line and avoidance of excrescent detail. Not until the 1940s and Oliver Bulleid's idiosyncratic designs for the Southern Railway, then the final standard steam types of the 1950s for the nationalized British Railways, did preoccupation with weight-saving and accessibility of working parts for maintenance outweigh devotion to a gracefully curved and splashered running-plate and a determination not to break a clean boiler line by draping it with exterior piping or auxiliary apparatus. Designers elsewhere grew more and more insouciant about festooning their boilers with unpatterned plumbing. In the twentieth century, too, running plates rose higher and higher up the boiler side to leave gaping daylight between boiler and driving-wheel tops for convenience of access by depot staff.

The evolution of steam power capable of working Austria's pioneer mountain line over the Semmering Pass, described in the preceding chapter, was the first step in development of a European heavy freight engine. In the early 1850s France's Nord Railway was finding the coal traffic it had generated beyond the capability of 0–6–0s. The six-coupled, tender-supported Engerth type devised for the Semmering project looked a promising substitute, but like the Austrians the French soon found the cog drive to the rear wheels beneath the tender too frail and when that was disconnected the Engerth engine's adhesion was too debilitated for the job. Instead, the Schneider Works in Le Creusot designed and built in 1855 France's first authentic eight-coupled engine. Like the Engerth engine, it was tender-supported to take some of the weight of a big firebox overhanging the rear driving axle, so that it was in effect an 0–8–4 tank engine, but there was no attempt to interlink the driving and trailing axles. These machines were triumphantly successful on the Nord, where they contentedly tackled forty-wagon trains of some 450 gross tons, but a batch built for the Est constantly left the rails on that system's sharper curves and less well-maintained track; that difficulty was solved by separating engine and tender and the long-lived French eight-coupled freight engine was born.

By far the most influential 0–8–0 design, however, was the Wien Raab conceived for the Vienna and Raab Railway in 1855 by John Haswell, one of the Englishmen – and among the most

A French 'Mammoth' 0–6–0 locomotive heads a local train on the Nord Railway near Crépy-en-Valois in the 1880s.

eminent of them – who decided to fructify their talent in early railway development outside their own country. The Vienna and Raab Railway was to be built with decidedly light track and Haswell's Vienna works was handed a locomotive specification ordaining an axle-load that did not exceed 9 tons. Haswell's answer was to take the well-known 'Bourbonnais' 0–6–0 layout as a basis, extend it slightly to allow an extra driving axle, then adopt a diminutive driving-wheel diameter of 3 ft 10 in (1,168 mm), space the axles as closely as possible to keep the total wheelbase short, and finally to devise an axlebox arrangement which would allow the rear driving axle a modest degree of lateral play for comfortable negotiation of curves. This final concern for the engine's behaviour on the flimsy track quickly proved superfluous and was soon discarded.

In its prototype and subsequently more powerful models the basic Haswell 0–8–0 was not only acquired by many Austrian companies, which by the first decade of the twentieth century had over 450 in use, but by North Italian railways to the tune of over 300, by the Midi, Paris–Orléans and Etat Railways of France and the Norte Railway of Spain in a version built in France at Le Creusot, and in Germany, Hungary (where it became a standard class from the 1870s onwards) and even Russia in series manufactured in Germany by Kessler of Karlsruhe. The Germans did not take to the 0–8–0 until comparatively

late, in the early 1890s, when the Prussian State embarked upon a series; until then use of the wheel arrangement was confined to one or two companies with severely graded routes.

These mainland European engines were outside-cylinder, but needless to say when British railways at length adopted the 0–8–0 arrangement around the turn of the century they preferred an inside-cylinder layout. The first British eight-coupled engines had been built much earlier, in the 1860s, for Indian Railways. The principal customer of that decade was the Great Indian Peninsular Railway, seeking power to cope with the formidable inclines of the Ghat 'zig-zags' described in Chapter Five.

TANK ENGINES AND DOUBLE-ENDED LOCOMOTIVES

The Ghat inclines had opened their account with pairs of little 0–4–0 engines coupled back to back. They then acquired in 1862 some very singular-looking engines from Britain – self-contained 4–6–0s in which most of the boiler was cloaked by a semi-circular saddle-tank that protruded in a cowl well forward of the smokebox front. From 1866 onwards, however, these engines were succeeded by a large fleet of more orthodox-looking 0–8–0 saddle-tanks designed by James Kitson and constructed by two other major British locomotive builders, Neilson and Vulcan Foundry, as well as Kitson. Some similar engines were constructed by Sharp Stewart for the standard-gauge Mauritius Railways.

The self-contained tank engine in its eventually accepted European configur-

ation, with either side or boiler-saddling water tanks ahead of the driving cab and a fuel bunker to the rear, was an admirable concept for short-distance duty entailing frequent reversal such as urban passenger train haulage or yard shunting, but it never attracted many adherents in the USA. However, the interest of more than one American engineer was kindled by the early essays in double-ended engines born both of European railways' first attacks on the mountain passes and of attempts to secure a high power for light weight per driving axle that would satisfy engineers of the railways being driven as economically as possible through the undeveloped countries of the world.

The man who particularly caught the world's eye on this score was the locomotive superintendent of Ireland's Londonderry & Coleraine Railway, Robert Fairlie. A fervent propagandist for the economic potential of the narrow-gauge, light railway in the undeveloped world, Fairlie perfected and in 1864 patented a double-ended locomotive design that would support his case. The first models were actually built for British standard-gauge railways – in 1865 for the Neath & Brecon and in the following year for the Anglesey Central – but the one which brought engineers hotfoot from mainland European countries all the way from Norway down to Spain, from Russia and from South America, to see it put through its paces was *Little Wonder*. This Fairlie eagerly designed in response to a request from James Spooner, engineer of the newborn 1 ft 11½ in (597 mm) gauge, slate-carrying Festiniog Railway in the mountain area of Wales. Delivered in September 1869, *Little Wonder* showed itself capable early the following year of lifting trains of seventy-two wagons, grossing 180 tons up a 1-in-85 gradient.

In essence the Fairlie concept mounted two boilers firebox to firebox on one common main frame. Each boiler steamed a separate set of wheels, cylinders and motion, but these were arranged as independent bogie assemblies pivoted beneath their respective boilers to allow negotiation of curvature beyond the compass of the same length of locomotive with an orthodox fixed driving-wheelbase. In the earliest Fairlie models each boiler had its own firebox, but that was soon superseded by a single firebox linking the two boilers and fired from the side. One should add that some Fairlie engines were built as single-boilered tank engines, with the driving wheel assembly as free to rotate about its axis as the trailing bogie beneath the rear coal bunker.

Fairlie was an energetic and often extravagantly euphoric propagandist for his invention and for the virtues of the narrow gauge. Within five years of its impressive 1870 première on the Festiniog his febrile advocacy had already sold the Fairlie principle to the extent of eighty-four locomotives, chiefly to Mexico and to the Peruvian builders of trans-Andean railways. Mexico's final Fairlie imports of 1911 were 138 ton, oil-fired 0–6–0 + 0–6–0s which pursued an exacting career on a railway that struck uphill from the Atlantic port of Vera Cruz to the country's inland plateau on an unyielding 1 in 40 for 22 miles (35.4 km) on end. Fairlie engines also opened the first railways of Queensland and the first 3 ft 6 in (1,067 mm) line of New Zealand, from Dunedin to Port Chalmers, and they were widely employed in India, but the Russians were the only Europeans to acquire them in quantity.

The first American to be captivated by the Fairlie system was William Mason, a prosperous Massachusetts textile machinery manufacturer who was a passionate locomotive enthusiast and evaporated most of his company's profits in his hobby. The USA looked a promising market, for by the last quarter of the century narrow

gauge was very much in vogue in the remoter areas of the country and by 1900 over 700 so-called 'slim-gauge' systems were operative. Scarcely any state of the Union was without one, but they predominated in the west, with Colorado the leader in route-mileage.

Mason's prototype – which he labelled the 'Fairlie-Mason' type – was standard-gauge, however. Named *Janus* after the mythological two-faced deity, it was tested without enthusiasm by a couple of Massachusetts railroads and eventually acquired by the Lehigh Valley as a freight train banker (locomotive that assists from the rear) up a 1-in-60 gradient east of Wilkes-Barre, in Pennsylvania. But *Janus*, constructed in 1871, was consigned to scrap metal within six years. One indictment against it was the meagre fuel capacity of its bunkers, but the *coup de grâce* for the Fairlie concept in the USA was enginemen's reluctance to master the twin-engine controls and their powerfully voiced antipathy to its unusual firing layout.

Mason had more luck with his second double-ended creation, the so-called 'Mason Bogie' of 1876. It was a variant of the single-boiler Fairlie layout with boiler, cab and tender on one rigid frame surmounting a swivelling cylinder-and-driving wheel assembly and a trailing bogie. For a time 'Mason Bogies' were quite fashionable and examples were

procured by railroads in all parts of the USA, but the boom was ephemeral.

The prototype 'Mason Bogie' had been promoted as the ideal power for the emergent urban commuter railways of North America. But the man who conquered that market was Matthias N. Forney, a largely self-taught engineer who had graduated from an apprenticeship with Ross Winans at Baltimore to a design post in the Illinois Central Railroad's Chicago offices. Forney felt that the European tank engine layout, with the water tanks above the driving wheels, had the disadvantage of reducing adhesion weight and diminishing tractive effort as the water was consumed. Consequently he followed Mason's ideas to the extent of assembling boiler, cab and tender as one unit, the tender mounted over a trailing bogie so that that alone would be affected by the variation in load as fuel was consumed, but he fixed the driving assembly firmly to the engine bed and adopted flangeless driving wheels to avoid trouble on curves.

Forney patented his layout in 1866, but for some years the railroads' reaction was apathetic. Disconsolate, he took to railway journalism and as the associate editor of a

A unique design – Fairlie's double-ended locomotive, Snake, *at Auckland, New Zealand, in 1874. A Fairlie engine opened the first 3 ft 6 in line in New Zealand.*

contemporary technical magazine preached fervent sermons on the critical need to create urban mass transportation systems. He was gradually fanning interest when in 1872 providence set it aflame by visiting a catastrophic plague of distemper on the horse-power of the country's street tramways. The cavalier treatment of the wretched animals, which were dying off in thousands, suddenly became a national issue. That focused admiring attention on the first steam-powered elevated railway which New York had just inaugurated between Battery and Central Park and a scurry to extend the system had over 300 Forney engines chattering about the city's rooftops before the decade was out.

The most common Forney wheel arrangement was an 0–4–4 – outside-cylindered of course – with the boiler prodigiously overhanging the front driving wheels by a whole smokebox length. The cab, fully glazed on all sides with windows reaching down to almost half the depth of its structure, was so roomy that it looked as though it could have done equally satisfactory duty as the bodywork of a tycoon's cabriolet. In time various users modified the wheel arrangement to their own taste; there were, for instance, 2–4–4, 0–6–4 and 0–4–6 Forneys, the last so as to indulge a bigger bunker and extend the engine's range of action. Until electrification Forneys were the mainstays

of the 'Elevateds' which several American cities hastened to build, and at the peak of the 'Elevated' boom no fewer than seven major American locomotive works had Forney assembly lines. No other single steam locomotive design was so instrumental in revolutionizing urban transport.

The US railroads' other pressing concern by the 1860s was increased power

Above: A Santa Fe Railroad 2–8–0. Although the tender seems laden with coal, the locomotive still retains its spark-arresting smoke stack for wood burning.
Above right: A typical Forney 0–4–4 tank on the New York 'Elevated' in the 1870s.
Below: Commuter trains at Randolph Street station, Chicago, in 1895. Chicago was the 'railroad centre' of the USA.

for their rapidly rising freight tonnage. America saw its first 0–12–0, no less, as early as 1863. This was a one-off monstrosity that prefigured a range of multi-wheeled heavy freight engines with driving wheels of such small diameter that their connecting rods almost brushed the ground at the bottom of each strike – hence their generic branding as 'cabbage-cutters'. The 50 ton 0–12–0, America's heaviest locomotive by far up to that time, was a 'camelback' built purely as a banking engine for the Philadelphia & Reading by its engineer James Millholland.

Much more significant for the future of American freight power was the work of Alexander Mitchell, master mechanic of the Lehigh Valley's Mahanoy Division. Matthias Baldwin at first ridiculed Mitchell's design of a straightforward 2–8–0 tender engine as totally impracticable, but was eventually manoeuvred into building one in 1866. That was the year of the Lehigh Valley's absorption of some of its small feeder companies, so the new machine was commemoratively christened *Consolidation*, which became the universal nickname of 2–8–0s for the rest of the steam era.

Baldwin's scepticism was confounded from the day *Consolidation* went into service and promptly walked away with a 100 wagon train of 300 gross tons on a 1-in-66 gradient. That emboldened Mitchell to

A Baltimore and Ohio 'camelback'. The 'camelback' arrangement of the cab on top of the boiler was followed by John Wootten in his 'Mother Hubbards'.

step straight up to the 2–10–0, a pair of which were built in 1867 and which immediately outclassed the 2–8–0 for hauling strength; but they were too prone to leap the track, especially when reversing, and Mitchell had to convert them to 2–8–2s. These were not the engines which earned the 2–8–2 arrangement the nickname of 'Mikado'; that tag originated with a batch built by Baldwin in 1897 for the Nippon Railway of Japan, which Baldwin quite fallaciously claimed to be the first 2–8–2 tender engines in the world.

Apart from the railroads hauling coal from the Allegheny Mountains, companies in the western USA were also clamouring for greater power to lift their trains over the Rocky Mountains. The market for the 2–8–0 was insatiable and it quickly became a standard type, practically monopolizing American freight traffic until the First World War. Altogether a staggering total of 22,900 were built. Some western railroads attempted to surpass it for size and power in the later decades of the century, but the age of the really massive North American locomotive did not open until the early years of the twentieth century. And not until then did European railways even take up the 2–8–0 in earnest.

BRAKE SYSTEMS: FROM BLOCKS TO AIR

Conclusion of the development history of the nineteenth-century express passenger locomotive needs prefacing with a reminder that continuous train braking was not generally adopted until the final decades. Until 1870 few railways used anything but mechanically operated vehicle brakes of one sort or another. On passenger trains the brake-van was literally that – a vehicle manned by a brakesman who, on a coded whistle signal from the engine-driver, would feverishly tug at a lever or a handwheel that activated the van's brake-blocks. A train's brake-vans were the only supplement to the locomotive's braking power, except on a few railways – the Highland and Lancashire & Yorkshire were British examples – which experimented with a system linking mechanical brakes on all vehicles to a control on the locomotive via a revolving shaft that was connected between coaches by universal-joint couplings.

Modern electric traction has brought into play dynamic braking – the exploitation during deceleration of the traction motors as dynamos, which oppose momentum and generate current that is either dissipated through resistances or fed back into the supply current wires. Furthermore, the high-speed rolling stock of European railways is equipped nowadays with electro-magnetic track brakes. But both this and dynamic braking are used only as supplements to the compressed air

brakes devised by an American inventor, George Westinghouse, way back in 1868. The stimulus to his idea was the use of compressed air drills in the boring of the Mont Cenis Tunnel. Latter-day technology has refined the methods of air-brake control, making it much quicker-acting, but the basic Westinghouse principle is unchanged: the maintenance of air pressure in a continuous pipe extending the length of the train to hold the brakes off and the release of the air to apply them. Almost all the world's major railways eventually standardized the air brake, but as a result of some empire-building chicanery only a few British companies took it up when, following an appalling 1889 accident at Armagh in Ireland, legislation at length compelled the recalcitrant railways to spend the money on continuous brakes. Most British railways were inveigled by the London & North Western into standardizing the less efficient vacuum brake; thereby they fashioned a huge millstone for the neck of the nationalized British Railways when it set determined course for high speed in the 1960s and had to embark on a costly change-over to air brakes.

THE SUPREMACY OF THE COMPOUND LOCOMOTIVE

The progression of American express passenger locomotive layout from the classic 4–4–0 to the 4–4–2 is indirectly traceable to an 1877 idea of John Wootten, general manager of the Philadelphia & Reading and previously the railroad's superintendent of motive power. Large fireboxes had been a characteristic of American locomotives because they needed a sizable grate for good combustion of the anthracite fuel in common use. But, providing the anthracite was of good quality, the size could be obtained satisfactorily by lengthening the box, though that entailed mounting the cab on the boiler as Ross Winans had done in his pioneering 'camelbacks'. What struck Wootten was that with a wide as well as a long firegrate in a box of special design he could burn the immense quantities of dust – or culm – which were an otherwise virtually useless waste product of the anthracite manufacturing industry, for an enormous saving in his railroad's fuel bills. He was right.

The only snag was that without small trailing wheels there was little room left at the rear of a Wootten firebox engine to locate a driving cab. Wootten sent one of his first wide-firebox engines to a Paris exhibition in 1878, but it was precluded from demonstration on French tracks because its traditionally sited cab was too wide to clear lineside structures. It was the French who recommended reversion to a boiler-mounted cab and thus a new generation of 'camelbacks', or 'Mother Hubbards' as they were also known, took shape.

A large number of Wootten 'Mother Hubbards' were built in a variety of wheel arrangements for both passenger and freight assignments, but chiefly for the anthracite-hauling railroads in northern Pennsylvania and southern New York State. They were anathema to most of their crews, especially to the fireman, who had to work on his own at the front of the tender, skimpily protected from the weather and exhaust by a rudimentary shelter fixed to the rear of the firebox, and doing his best to aim his shovelfuls at the right spot in the huge firegrate (so huge that it had two fire-holes) from the front of a tender whose bucketing rarely synchronized with that of the locomotive. Eventually, in 1918, the Interstate Commerce Commission banned any further building of 'Mother Hubbards' on safety grounds, though a few 4–6–0s survived on local trains of the Central of New Jersey until as late as 1954. By the date of the ICC's edict the advantages of a wide firebox as an aid to steaming had long since become patent, using coal just as much as anthracite, but by no means were all subsequent wide fireboxes of the Wootten type. All it needed

was small trailing wheels to support the firebox and the cab could be conventionally shaped, arranged and located.

In 1885 the Philadelphia & Reading bought up a narrow-gauge railway to Atlantic City, rebuilt it as a standard-gauge double track on a good alignment, and set about converting what was previously a coastal hamlet into an enticingly convenient resort for the citizenry of Philadelphia, less than 60 miles away. One had to take ferry across the Delaware River to reach the railway's terminal on the east bank at Camden, but by 1890 the trains were taking only an even hour for the $55\frac{1}{2}$ miles (89.3km) thence to Atlantic City. Not unnaturally business was booming, the trains had to be lengthened and the existing 4–4–0s lacked the breath to keep time. Bigger-boilered engines were essential and the answer sensibly evolved with the Baldwin works was a 4–4–2. The initial product of 1894 was a narrow-firebox machine, but its performance was so pleasing that the Philadelphia & Reading was soon back in Baldwin's office seeking a more powerful version capable of cutting the schedule to fifty minutes with a six-car train.

These second two machines were perhaps the most celebrated 'Mother Hubbards' of all – Vauclain compounds with driving wheel diameter increased by just over a foot compared with their predecessor to a high-stepping 7ft 0¼in (2,134mm). Day after day they improved on the exacting new Camden–Atlantic City schedule, recording start-to-stop averages as high as 73.6mph (118.4km/h)

with a six-car train of 183 tons on the crack 'Seashore Flyer'. They naturally took the title of 'Atlantic' from their destination; and so has every 4–4–2 since. One was even claimed to have touched 106mph (171km/h), but solid supporting evidence is lacking. What is certain is that the 'Seashore Flyer' was the world's fastest regular train at the turn of the century.

Energetically publicized by the Philadelphia & Reading management and agreeably reported at length in the press, these feats naturally goaded the Pennsylvania Railroad, which was strongly contending for the Atlantic City traffic. It too acquired some 'Mother Hubbard' 4–4–2s in 1899, the Class E1, but within years it switched to the first of a brilliant series of orthodox Atlantics. In their final manifestation, the Class E6 constructed from 1914 onwards, these engines were treated the same as the Pennsylvania's subsequent 4–6–2s and were assigned almost interchangeably with the bigger engines to massive expresses of twelve to sixteen all-steel cars which they would haul unchanged for 750 miles (1,210km) from New York to Fort Wayne, Indiana.

Before describing the Atlantic's advent in Europe, the compound locomotive concept, noted in the evolution of the Philadelphia & Reading Atlantics, needs explanation. Since the pioneering days locomotive engineers had been venturing steadily higher boiler pressures with every

A 'Mother Hubbard' 4–4–0 of the Philadelphia and Reading Railroad standing on a turntable.

After his three-cylinder compounds, Webb developed this four-cylinder compound 4–4–0 for the LNWR in 1897, but it turned out to be unsuccessful.

improvement in materials and technology. From Stephenson's *Rocket* values had progressed from 50 lb/sq. in (3.5 kg/sq. cm) pressure to 100 lb/sq. in (7 kg/sq. cm) in Gooch's *Great Western* of 1846; by the 1890s 180 lb/sq. in was common and 200 lb/sq. in was in sight. The benefit of higher pressure was calorific economy, because the steam did more work in the cylinder for a given coal consumption figure. But the reverse of the coin was loss of steam through condensation in the cylinders, because the higher pressure widened the difference between the steam's temperature at admission to the cylinder and at its expulsion to the exhaust. In the 1860s marine engineers had found a way to mitigate that disadvantage by prolonging the steam expansion process – applying the steam first to a high-pressure cylinder, then passing it on for further expansion in a bigger, low-pressure cylinder before it was exhausted.

It was a Swiss, Anatole Mallet, who in 1874 patented the first practical application of this technique to the steam

locomotive. The previous year the world's first compound-expansion – as opposed to simple-expansion – steam locomotives had been built to Mallet's designs by Schneider of Le Creusot: three little 0–4–2 tanks which went into service on the Bayonne-Biarritz Railway. Straightaway they cut fuel costs by about 25 per cent. These first attempts were two-cylinder compounds, which because of the valve layout were impossible to start from rest with compound expansion of the steam; a device was necessary to enable them to be moved off as simple-expansion machines, then switched to compound expansion after a few driving-wheel revolutions.

Two engineers who immediately fastened on to the compound technique were August von Borries, the locomotive superintendent of Germany's Hanover State Railroads, and Francis Webb, his counterpart on Britain's London & North Western Railway. Whereas von Borries developed the outside two-cylinder compound layout with conspicuous success, Webb, constrained by the British loading gauge, went for a three-cylinder system so that he could mount a single, big low-pressure cylinder between the frames and two high-pressure cylinders outside.

In his initial express engines Webb divided the drive. The inside low-pressure cylinder powered the leading driving axle, the outside high-pressure cylinders the rear, and the two axles were not coupled. Thus the LNWR 'Experiment' class of 1882 looked like 2–4–0s but were technically 2–2–2–0s, and the bigger 'Greater Britain' type of 1891 – by which time the LNWR was the only major British railway which had not moved up to 4–4–0s – were ostensibly 2–4–2s but actually 2–2–2–2s. One of the latter, *Queen Empress*, was proudly shipped to the USA for display at the 1893 Chicago World's Fair along with some of the latest LNWR coaches and the whole equipage was later demonstrated on the Lake Shore & Michigan Railroad.

Despite this hopeful intimation of immortality none of Webb's various three-cylinder compound designs – including over one hundred of the 0–8–0 freight engines which from 1892 onwards he was the first British engineer to build in quantity – was thoroughly successful, even though a few put up performances that earned them an honourable niche in British history. Best remembered is the 2–2–2–0 No. 1304 *Jeanie Deans*, which day in and day out, from January 1891 right through to August 1899, worked the midday Euston–Glasgow express each way between the London terminus and Crewe, except for legitimate time off to undergo routine overhauls at Crewe.

Few other engineers produced three-cylinder compounds. The only fully successful versions of this layout were a class of 2–6–0s built from 1896 for the Jura-Simplon and Federal Railways of Switzerland, some of which survived to end their career on Dutch railways in the 1940s; and best known of all, probably, the Midland Railway 4–4–0s which evolved from a 1901 design of that company's locomotive chief Samuel Johnson and a North Eastern Railway colleague, Walker Smith. They eventually multiplied to a total of 245 engines after final batches had been built by the London Midland & Scottish Railway following the latter's absorption of the Midland in the 1923 'Big Four' Grouping of British companies. The last Midland compound 4–4–0 did not disappear from the British scene until 1961.

Like Mallet, von Borries started with compound designs for light secondary work, but graduated to bigger things when their economy became clear. In 1875, two years after the emergence of Mallet's first compound tanks, von Borries was appointed locomotive superintendent of the Prussian State Railways and under his guidance that system rapidly acquired some 6,000 compound locomotives. In the later 1890s and for most of the twentieth century's first decade Prussian passenger trains were virtually monopolized by over 2,000 von Borries two-cylinder compound 4–4–0s, roughly half of them the express passenger Class S3 type with 6ft 6in (1,981mm) driving wheels, the remainder the Class P4 with 5ft 9in (1,753mm) driving wheels, each derived from the same basic design and both premiered in 1893.

That same year of 1893 brought to the fore, also with a passenger 4–4–0 design, another great European practitioner of two-cylinder compounding and one of the outstanding men of European locomotive engineering in general – Karl Gölsdorf of the Austrian State Railways. Gölsdorf's first compound 4–4–0 was particularly significant because in it he achieved a powerful locomotive capable of a smooth-riding 80mph (130km/h) on track that was decidedly less substantial than that of the British, French or German trunk railways. He did it chiefly by dint of a very long-wheelbase bogie which reduced the weight on the driving axles and permitted him a bigger boiler than that of the Prussian 4–4–0s.

Just before the turn of the century, in 1897, Gölsdorf laid the foundations for mainland Europe's twentieth-century heavy freight locomotives with the continent's first fully successful 2–8–0s, again two-cylinder compounds, which he designed to haul both passenger and freight trains over the Arlberg route's fearsome gradients. The Germans had built some 2–8–0s a few years earlier, but in performance they were no advance on existing 0–8–0s. Gölsdorf's engine, which exploited the possibilities of the wheel arrangement much more competently and embodied new ideas for the

A Gölsdorf two-cylinder compound 4–4–0 of the Imperial Royal Austrian State Railways. This locomotive was fitted with a Schmidt superheater.

comfortable negotiation of curvature by multi-wheeled engines, eclipsed the effort of any previous eight-coupled locomotive in Europe by keeping a 700 ton train on the move at a steady 13.7mph (22 km/h) up a 1-in-100 gradient. The Gölsdorf 2-8-0 became Austria's most numerous class and after the First World War many were acquired by the Czech and Russian railways. Still more widely dispersed throughout Europe after 1918, because numbers were appropriated as post-war reparations, was the equally successful 0-10-0 which Gölsdorf evolved in 1900.

Most prolific of all the compound variants were the four-cylinder engines. In one guise this concept inspired the ultimate mammoths of North American steam power, the great articulated locomotives.

Mallet had very early visualized the potential of his compound system in double-ended engines such as the Fairlies, but instead he patented in 1884 a configuration of a single-boilered machine mounted on two sets of driving wheels, the rearmost driven by the high-pressure cylinders and rigidly fixed to the main frame, the foremost powered by the low-pressure cylinders and free to swivel like a leading bogie. Gölsdorf's proof of eight- and ten-coupled practicality even around the curves of comparatively light track dimmed European enthusiasm for standard-gauge Mallet compound articulateds, but a considerable number were procured by Russian railways and especially by the Hungarian State Railways, where track conditions imposed stringent axle-load limits (the Hungarians built more standard-gauge Mallet compounds than anyone else in Europe). Other countries to try them included France, Germany, Switzerland and Spain.

The epochal year in Mallet compound history was 1904 and the locale the 1904 World's Fair in St Louis, USA. There the Baltimore & Ohio Railroad exhibited No. 2400, an 0-6-0+0-6-0 Mallet compound tender engine it had commissioned from the American Locomotive Co., or ALCO as it was much better known in the twentieth century, which engrossed every railroad visitor (though this particular pioneer suffered from instability and was soon rusticated from its intended assignment in the Allegheny Mountains). With an engine of that size and power, assuming it could be made to hold the track, the nuisance of having to divide the heaviest

freight trains for negotiation of the steeper mountain grades would be at an end. What followed is matter for Chapter 11, 'The Zenith of Steam'.

Back in Europe, meanwhile, the other family of four-cylinder compounds had reached perfection following the pioneering work of Gaston du Bousquet, chief engineer of France's Nord Railway, and Alfred de Glehn, technical director of the Alsace Locomotive Works, with whom de Bousquet developed his designs. The de Glehn system was not the only four-cylinder arrangement. The Russians, East Europeans and one American firm, Brooks, favoured what was called a tandem compound layout with all four cylinders in line and exerting a common drive, while Samuel Vauclain of America's Baldwin works opted for superimposition of high and low-pressure cylinders on each side of the locomotive, with a separate piston from each cylinder to one common crosshead per pair; that was the arrangement in the Philadelphia & Reading's fleet-footed Atlantics discussed earlier in the chapter. In England Webb was finally driven by his three-cylinder compounds' shortcomings to try 4-4-0s – the LNWR's first – with four cylinders in 1897. But he had no more luck. He did not follow precisely what was to prove the most efficient and by far the longest-lived layout for high-speed passenger locomotives, de Glehn's system of rearward outside high-pressure cylinders driving a rearward axle and forward-placed inside low-pressure cylinders powering the leading axle, but with all

Above: A French Nord Railway de Glehn 4-4-2 compound of 1904. These very successful machines worked the Paris–Calais expresses for many years. Below right: A big-boilered, superheated Ivatt Atlantic on the LNER.

driving axles coupled. Another virtue of the de Glehn system was the driver's facility for independent control of steam supply to high and low pressure cylinders as best suited changing route and running situations.

With its first de Glehn compound 4-4-0s of 1891 the Nord opened a long lead over other French railways for speed. The time of the fastest train between Paris and Calais came down with a run from 4 hours 33 minutes to 3 hours 41 minutes between 1892 and 1896, which meant an overall average speed of 50mph (80km/h) including intermediate stops, while the 'Nord Express' was scheduled to average just over 55mph (90km/h) between Paris and St Quentin. The rest of the world was immediately impressed. Prussians bought some for trial and were sufficiently admiring to require von Borries to produce a modified version; the success of his resultant Class S5 4-4-0s in fact inspired further four-cylinder compound development in Germany – the only school which seriously competed with the de Glehn precepts in the early twentieth century. A few other railways acquired de Glehn 4-4-0s, but the de Glehn compound type which saw widest use throughout most of Europe was moulded in 1894 when the

Baden State Railway had the Alsace works build some 5 ft 3 in (1,600 mm) driving wheel 4–6–0s for its severely graded Black Forest line.

Nevertheless the du Bousquet/de Glehn masterpiece was the 1900 enlargement of the Nord 4–4–0 into the classic Nord 4–4–2. To cope with the heavier trains of more luxurious stock which affluent society was demanding in its late nineteenth century urge to travel, the Germans and the British had introduced the 4–4–2 to Europe almost simultaneously, though the Germans were the first by a whisker to optimize the wheel arrangement's potential for a wide firebox in the Palatinate Railroad's inside-cylinder Class P3 engines of 1898. In England Ivatt's first Atlantic of 1898 for the Great Northern was a narrow-firebox design; his much better-known big-boiler Atlantics with wide fireboxes, engines of great free-steaming pace and often phenomenal power for their size, did not emerge until 1902.

The Nord had the first two de Glehn Atlantics built for trial in 1900 and they immediately exceeded their specification by sailing up the 1-in-200 bank to Survilliers, on the Paris–Calais route, at 60 mph (100 km/h), not with the 200 tons load stipulated but with 285 tons. Three were imported by the English Great Western for study and won so much acclaim that several railways were prompted to build Atlantics as a hedged bet against the viability of the newly emergent 4–6–0 arrangement for express passenger duty; but only one company, the London Brighton & South Coast, sensibly followed the Great Northern's Ivatt in adoption of a wide-firebox design and only the Great

Central and the North Eastern essayed any compound Atlantics. Surprisingly, fewer than 100 de Glehn Atlantics were built for French railways – the Paris–Orléans and the PLM were other users besides the Nord – but the Prussians had seventy-nine, the Egyptians ten and just over a score were exported to the Bengal and Nagpur and Eastern Bengal Railways of India, where the Atlantic wheel arrangement – in simple-expansion two-cylinder form, with narrow firebox – had probably its greatest vogue.

The Prussian State's ultimate wide-firebox Atlantics, the four-cylinder von Borries compound Class S9, of which ninety-nine were constructed in 1907–10, was with little doubt Europe's most powerful 4–4–2, consistently deputed to haul trains of more than 500 tons non-stop over the 159 miles (255 km) between Berlin and Hanover. But in their final form none surpassed the French de Glehn Atlantics or Ivatt's big-boilered Great Northern 4–4–2s for fleetness of foot.

The critical factor in their ultimate prowess was superheated steam, the last great contribution to steam locomotive development of the nineteenth century. It had been recognized by an Alsatian named Hirn in the 1850s that superheating of steam before it was admitted to cylinders could substantially reduce condensation

losses and either effect fuel and water consumption economy or enhance power. The limitations of existing lubricants forestalled successful development at mid-century and it was almost 1900 before a German engineer, Wilhelm Schmidt of Kassel, could perfect and patent a practical superheating device for a locomotive. First applied to two German 4–4–0s, a Class S3 and a Class P4, in 1898, superheating is basically achieved by passing the generated steam through a large number of small tubes encased within the main, enlarged flues of the locomotive boiler before it is admitted to the cylinders. Different methods of superheating were contrived after Schmidt's pioneering, but the principle is the same.

After they had been superheated from 1910 onwards, the Nord's de Glehn Atlantics happily sustained mile-a-minute schedules with 350-ton trains between Paris and Aulnoye. The Nord was still allocating them to crack trains of medium weight, such as the Paris–Brussels–Antwerp 'Oiseau Bleu' Pullman, well into the 1930s. And until the early 1930s, too, the superheated Ivatt Atlantics were confidently entrusted to the London & North Eastern Railway's prestigious and tightly timed Pullman trains operating between London and the West Riding of Yorkshire.

THE DAWN OF PASSENGER COMFORT AND SPEED

Generally speaking, only rank or wealth elicited much attention to the comfort of rail travel from the major railways of Europe and America or their car-builders until at least the 1860s. For many managements the rationale of that, no doubt, was that, if the flower of society and commerce could be enticed to set an example of regular rail travel, then a mass travel response could be taken for granted.

Thus the directors of Britain's Great Western Railway must have hoisted several extra glasses at one of the bibulous lunches to which railway boards were accustomed in those days, when they learned that Prince Albert of Saxe-Coburg-Gotha proposed to take their train from London to pursue his courtship of the young Queen Victoria at Windsor Castle. From that it could only be a short step to getting the royal seal itself upon train travel, particularly as the GWR's new Bristol main line passed within sight of the royal windows at Windsor. So at their own expense they built a saloon 'handsomely arranged with hanging sofas of carved wood in the rich style of Louis XIV . . . and fitted up with rich crimson and white silk and exquisitely executed paintings', to quote a contemporary description, humbly advised her Majesty of its availability and impatiently awaited the royal pleasure.

The royal saloon's first regal occupant was actually King Frederick William IV of Prussia, for whom it was attached to a scheduled public train when the German monarch travelled to Windsor for the Prince of Wales' christening in January 1842. Another six months elapsed before the royal household suddenly passed word one Saturday afternoon that the Queen was minded to ride to London by train at midday the following Monday, 13 June 1842. No railway up to that date can have gone through a more anxious weekend of mobilization, but both planning and execution of the world's first train to be operated exclusively for a royal party were practically flawless.

Some were aghast that the royal household should have allowed the Queen to expose herself to perils that were very far from unimaginable, and which had just had the French Government peremptorily bar their sovereign from train travel. Only a month earlier, on 8 May 1842, a royal function at Versailles had ended in the world's first catastrophic train accident in terms of human life. The lead engine of a double-headed train returning many of the Versailles guests to Paris had fractured an axle and overturned, whereupon the second engine jack-knifed on the first and showered its fire over the frail wooden coaches which splintered against its tender. Locked in their carriages for some unrecorded motive of security, fifty-seven of the wretched occupants perished as flames engulfed the wreckage.

Queen Victoria, however, was very soon using other railways for her travel as well as patronizing the GWR to the greatest extent possible for her Windsor–London journeys. Before mid-century her example had emboldened most of the mainland European royals to entrust themselves to railways. Some of them indulged their fancy in royal saloons a great deal more elaborate than Britain's railways at first turned out for Queen Victoria.

As early as 1845, for instance, Emperor Ferdinand I of Austria had his State

A royal saloon built for Queen Victoria by the LNWR in 1869. It was fitted with oil lamps at the express wish of the Queen and later with electric lamps.

Railways construct for him an American-style bogie coach with an armchair-furnished state saloon, a two-berth bedroom, a retiring room with *chaises-longues*, a room for the equerries, and even – something yet unthought-of in vehicles for commoners' use – a small ante-room housing a decently veiled commode. Over the next twenty years the potentates of the world's railway-owning countries vied with each other in their pursuit of opulence and flamboyance.

One of the most extraordinary creations was a saloon built in 1859 by the French financiers of Italy's early Pio Latina Railway for the last Pope to exercise temporal as well as spiritual authority, Pius IX. Not only was its interior throne room sumptuously furnished and curtained in white velvet, but its exterior moulded to create above the throne an imposing papal dome supported by an extraordinary confection in carved wood or papier mâché

of sculpted pillars portraying Faith, Hope and Charity. Nothing so rococo distinguished the exterior of the royal train personally styled in the 1860s by the Bavarian eccentric, Ludwig II. But inside Ludwig's train there was extravagance and fantasy that outdid even that of the Pio Latina's papal offering. No need to describe it in detail – to note that the lavatory seats were soothingly encased in cushioning of pure swansdown is enough to convey the character of the rest.

Private coaches were not the exclusive prerogative of the royals, however. One had to be a Bismarck to be given one, as the Count was by the confederation of privately owned German railways, but only affluent to acquire one. In Europe the private coach was chiefly the perquisite of upper echelons of the British peerage, the princes of the Central European states (whom the German railway staff manuals of the period obsequiously graded as

Höchste und Allerhöchste Herrschaft – 'Highest and All-Highest Personages') and the great of industry and finance, such as the Krupp and Rothschild families. Europe's private coaches, however, were as a Brooklyn tenement to a Manhattan penthouse compared with the ultimate, post-Pullman flowering of the American private or business car, of which more shortly.

In Europe private coaches do not seem to have proliferated on the mainland in the later years of the nineteenth century to quite the extent they did in Britain, where by the end of the 1870s practically every railway of significance had accumulated a stock of family saloons for hire. Every night the Scottish expresses from London would have their regular fare-paying formations swollen by one or two of these saloons, of which the usual layout was a roomy first-class saloon with two arm-chairs for the parents, two bench settees for the rest of the family, and flanking this at one end a room with lavatory, at the other a second-class compartment for the family retainers. Not that the saloons were confined to family expeditions. Race-going parties were frequent customers, so were paternalist employers, who would lease them for annual staff outings.

At least one railway, the Great Eastern, also indulged its first-class smoking clientele with separate saloon coaches. It was 1868 before Parliament made it mandatory for all British railways – unless exempted for special reasons, as London's Metropolitan was – to provide at least one smoking vehicle in every train consisting of more than one vehicle of each class. Until then many railways took a puritan line on the vice (as they did, too, on the European mainland for much of the nineteenth century), though their concern was far

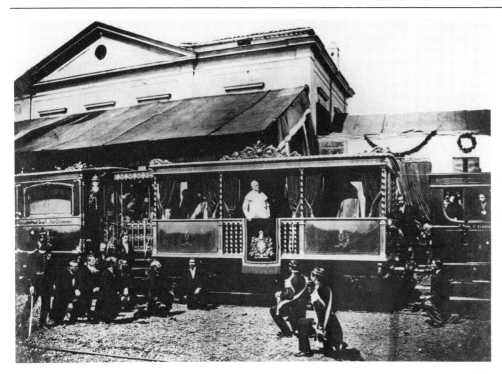

particularly brisk demand at English station bookstalls in mid-century.

Even in the later 1850s and 1860s long-distance trains were still subject to so many intermediate stops – of as much as thirty and forty minutes at bigger stations – that thrifty railway companies saw no need to squander potential revenue-earning space in their coaches on lavatories, though the pressure on station conveniences did eventually drive some Continental systems to insert small lavatories in the luggage vans that fronted or tailed their trains. These major station stops were likewise the only chance for those who had taken no food on their journey to grab some refreshment. Several refreshment and dining rooms on both sides of the English Channel gained a high repute not only for their catering but for the dexterity with which they served and fed a throng of famished passengers before the station bell clanged warning of an imminent re-start.

more for the well-being of their carriages than that of the passengers.

GEORGE PULLMAN INTRODUCES THE HOTEL ON WHEELS

The Americans, as an earlier chapter described, found the European rigid-wheelbase passenger coach format too unyielding for their early track and were the first to develop bogie cars as standard accommodation. A few American-style cars with open verandah ends were operative in Central Europe by 1870, but the preponderant pattern both on the mainland and in Britain at that date was still the four- or six-wheeler, devoid both of lavatories and of corridor connection to allow free movement along a train in motion, and primitively lit and heated. Candles were among the wares in

Above left: The arrival of Queen Victoria at Gosport on the occasion of the French King Louis Philippe's visit to England in 1844.
Left: The exterior of Queen Victoria's coach built in 1869. Queen Victoria was one of the world's first monarchs to travel regularly by rail.
Top: Pope Pius IX in the papal train in Italy during the 1860s. The Vatican had its own small railway system.
Right: A French scene of the 1890s. Before the general advent of through-train steam heating, footwarmers were often necessary.

By the 1870s, though, the most delectable of refreshment room collations was regarded as no compensation for the other harassments and discomforts of train travel. As the fingers of main line in North America and Europe stretched further and intertwined, establishing lengthier through runs, the tedium of so many stops *en route* became more insupportable, and confinement to one's seat more unbearably muscle-cramping – especially overnight. In the lowest class of accommodation, moreover, that seat would still be wood. Even in second-class some British railways were only just steeling themselves to apply modest upholstery to the seating; usually thin, it was generally carried only a little way up the seatback.

From the late 1830s one or two American railroads had made some shift to mitigate the penance of night travel by a crude arrangement of tiered bunks after the cheapest shipboard fashion, but a sleeping car proper did not emerge until September 1859. It was the enterprise of a one-time bookkeeper and cabinet-maker, a twenty-eight-year-old from New York State named George Mortimer Pullman who had gravitated to contracting, a profession entailing extensive travel. What Pullman experienced in that travel con-

vinced him that almost all his fellow-travellers would happily pay for some facsimile of terra firma hotel accommodation and service on rail.

Early in 1859 Pullman put draft ideas to the Chicago Alton & St Louis Railroad, which provided him with two of its day cars for experiment. These Pullman adapted as day-night convertible vehicles, deploying his skills as a cabinet-maker to refurbish them with cherrywood panelling and dividing the interiors into what was to become the classic 'Pullman section' arrangement. Matching bays or 'sections' on each side of the car flanked a central vestibule. At the lower level the plush upholstered seats had backs which could be lowered to form a base for mattresses; above them was a line of bed-bases raised flush with the ceiling during the day but lowered by ropes and pulleys to about window-frame height for night travel, when each pair of upper and lower berths could be curtained off from its neighbours (lateral wood partitions separating each section came later, but the curtain sufficed to secure privacy on the vestibule side of the berths until the twentieth-century age

Top: The Pioneer *of 1864 was Pullman's first specially built sleeping car.*
Above: An early Pullman railroad car with three-tier bunks, about 1859.
Left: An advertisement of 1879 for the Chicago, Rock Island and Pacific, boasting the addition of Palace Dining Cars to all its express trains.
Above right: Night scene with passenger trains at an American railroad junction. Currier and Ives lithograph of 1876.

of exclusive room accommodation for sleeping-car passengers). For each berth there was a mattress and one blanket; one 'section' was reserved for storage of this equipment during the day. The floor was innocent of carpet, the only illumination was by candle and sanitary provision was confined to one wash-basin, at which one's toilet was open to full view from the rest of the car. There was one other innovation. In the primitive 'bunk' cars of other railroads passengers had to fend entirely for themselves, unless they could prevail upon the train's conductor to save them the struggle to grab bedding and make up their bunk for them. Pullman persuaded the

railroad to let him man his experimental cars with his own conductor, supernumerary to the train staff proper.

How unused Americans were to civilities on their night rail journeys is apparent from the Pullman conductor's complaint, after the inaugural public run of one of Pullman's cars from Bloomington, Illinois, to Chicago on 1 September 1859, that it needed a good deal of sternness to dissuade the first customers from getting into bed with their boots on. But enough of them warmed to the concept for Pullman to sink all his capital into the recruitment of a small corps of craftsmen and set about building a much more ambitious prototype, ten times as costly as his first conversions. The result, the celebrated *Pioneer* of 1864, was unbelievably exotic for the times, with an internal finish of polished black walnut, elaborate chandeliers for the candles, pure linen bedding and marble washstands – altogether a blatant incitement to unimaginable nocturnal vice, some warned. As for technicalities, the crucial distinction of *Pioneer* was that it was a foot (30 cm) wider and no less than $2\frac{1}{2}$ ft (27 cm) higher than

any railroad car previously seen on US railroads, primarily to allow Pullman to discard his first pattern of upper berth for one that was hinged and folded against the bodyside above the window – the arrangement, of course, which was standard from then on.

For a while it looked as though there would be no 'then on'. Practically unanimous that Pullmans anyway were a ludicrous extravagance, the railroads were not going to dip into their own pockets so as to modify lineside structures which might foul *Pioneer*'s unprecedented girth, but within months a *volte face* was forced upon them when the State of Illinois requested that *Pioneer* be part of the funeral train of the assassinated President Lincoln on 2 May 1865. The Chicago & Alton had hastily to make its tracks fit to comply. Not long after that General Grant sought use of the car for a trip from Detroit to Galena, his home town, and more railroads were constrained to follow suit.

The Chicago & Alton was quickly encouraged by public response to become Pullman's eager client, though some companies were harder to convert. The

cracking of the Michigan Central was a turning-point. Sceptical that passengers would be prepared to pay Pullman's supplementary charge for use of his cars, it eventually accepted Pullman's challenge to put the issue to practical proof by running its own 'bunk' cars alongside Pullman sleepers. In a matter of days the Michigan Central was red-facedly withdrawing its near-empty 'bunk' cars and doing its best to mollify patrons bitter at being crowded out of the Pullmans.

By 1867 Pullman's sleeper fleet, either wholly owned by himself or operated in partnership with railroads, was forty-eight cars strong and railroad interest had become explosive. That year, besides forming the Pullman Palace Car Company, he took the first step in broadening the scope of Pullmans by introducing on the Great Western Railway of Canada his first so-called 'hotel car', the *President* – an orthodox Pullman sleeper except that one end of the car incorporated a small kitchen from which meals, such as steak and potatoes for 60 cents or a plate of sugar-cured ham for 40 cents, could be served to passengers at tables set up in their sections.

From that Pullman progressed in 1868 to his first full-length dining car, named *Delmonico* after the celebrated Swiss-born restaurateur of New York, which went into service on the Chicago & Alton.

The fast-growing business outstripped Pullman's capacity to manufacture in his own plant more than a handful of his fleet. Acquisition in 1870 of a big, specialized car-building works at Detroit still failed to keep pace with demand and in 1880 Pullman had finally to establish the town which bears his name on the southern fringe of Chicago, an integrated complex of manufacturing plant and residential development for the workers which was the USA's first comprehensively planned industrial community.

Pullman never had a monopoly of the US dining-car business. Several railroads elected to develop their own train catering, some to just as widely reputed effect as Pullman, such as Santa Fe through its Harvey House. That was the concern born of the initiative of a London-born mail clerk christened Frederick Henry Harvey but imperishably known as Fred Harvey. His claim to posterity's tribute is twofold. In 1862 he helped a Missouri postmaster to realize the latter's scheme for a mobile railway postal sorting car, the direct genesis of the Railway Post Office business once so healthy a contributor to the revenue of the US passenger trains but now surrendered to the airlines. Harvey is better known, however, for the chain of eating houses he founded along Santa Fe

routes in meal-stop days, establishments which subsequently took on the responsibility for Santa Fe train catering.

Nor did Pullman monopolize the supplementary-fare day and night car market until 1927. For a number of years certain railroads – the Chicago, Milwaukee & St Paul, the Great Northern and New Haven were cases in point – opted to run their own sleeping cars, but the principal rivals were entrepreneurs like Pullman himself. Best known of them was Webster Wagner, a New York politician and inventor whose car business was a protégé of Commodore Vanderbilt and who consequently had a dominant foothold in the eastern US railroad market. At the close of the century the Wagner Palace Car Company's fleet was 700-strong. But during his lifetime, which was ended by a heart attack after a traumatic industrial dispute at his own works in 1894, Pullman had been sedulously buying out his competitors and that process was completed by his successors.

BARBERS, BRANDY AND MARBLE BATHTUBS

As the century entered its last quarter, with through rail travel possible the whole way from New England to the Pacific coast, the famed North American luxury train was rapidly taking shape. Passengers would have to wait until the early 1880s to have the coal or wood stoves replaced by through-train steam heating piped from the locomotive and until almost the end of

Above left: Life in a Palace Car of the Union Pacific Railroad in 1879.
Above: Pullman's invention of the closed vestibule in 1887 permitted a safe and weather-proof passage between vehicles and encouraged the development of 'feature' cars such as dining, parlour and sleeping cars.
Above right: The bridal suite, Gladiolus, on the 'Pennsylvania Limited', built by Pullman in 1898.
Above far right: An observation car with an open verandah at the rear, built for the 'Twentieth Century Limited' in 1898.
Right: Handbill of 1877 advertising Pullman's hotel cars.

that decade for the first electric lighting to supersede gas or kerosene coach lighting, the first successors of plain candlepower. But already – provided you were prepared to negotiate the perilous and exposed step from one car-end verandah to another over the couplers – you could leave your berth to find diversion elsewhere in the train, including a hairdressing and shaving saloon; a club car where men could relax with the tobacco and drink they were for long debarred from consuming anywhere else in the train; a richly draped, ornately panelled and armchair-furnished parlour car with quite possibly a library and a vintage American organ; and a diner whose menus were already challenging the cards of any good restaurant for length.

The same went for the fare in Pullman's 'hotel cars'. Travelling on one of those

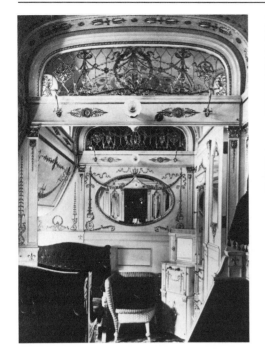

drinking alcohol in other public cars, the club car excepted, did not evaporate until the 1933 repeal of the country-wide Prohibition enacted in 1919; by the 1930s so many of the womenfolk whom the smoking ban had sought to protect were themselves addicts that the male preserve of the club car had lost all point and from then on it went steadily out of fashion.

Long-distance rail travel got a fresh fillip in 1887 from Pullman's perfection of his patent, fully-enclosed, concertina-like connection to link the vestibules of adjoining cars and dispense with the traditional open verandahs. This, naturally, made the train more appealing to the gentler sex. The first train to feature it was the New York–Chicago 'Pennsylvania Limited'.

The suffix 'Limited' indicates that by 1887 the all-Pullman train was a fact of American railroad life, as well as trains that combined segregated Pullman cars with ordinary stock for coach-class passengers, the only other category of rail travel in the American canon. Naturally, if the Pullman segment of a mixed train included the diner, that as well as the Pullman club and parlour cars was forbidden territory for the basic coach-class farepayer. As the late Lucius Beebe put it, the advent of the Pullman had 'put to rest the notion that Americans were members of a classless society, and, from the very beginning, social and economic barriers were erected to separate all travellers into the categories to which a just God has assigned them'.

The turn-of-the-century American 'Limited' trains came as close to emulating the first-class amenities of the transatlantic liner in its prime as human ingenuity could devise within a rail vehicle's bodywork. Besides the classic 'section' accommodation a train like the re-equipped 'Pennsylvania Limited' of 1898 offered handsome staterooms, private bedrooms and even a bridal suite sumptuously finished in white woodwork, leaded glass, gilt and metal ornamentation, and heavy velvet drapery. In the sleeper lavatories one stood on tiled floors or paused between operations on a wicker chair to contemplate the rooms' finely polished woodwork reflected in bevelled mirrors. There were full bathrooms for each sex as well as a hair-dressing saloon. While the womenfolk relaxed in the saloon of the rear-end observation car, an innovation that was just coming into fashion, a husband could be dealing with correspondence in the adjoining writing room, where a train stenographer was always on call. Or he could be unwinding in the smokeroom section of the buffet-lounge car, thumbing through the latest newspapers and magazines always to hand on the tables, sitting in on a poker game (cards and other game-packs were standard smokeroom equipment) or waiting for the next batch of Wall Street prices, telegraphed to main stations along the train's route, to be handed aboard in typescript at the next stop. What the stock market was doing might hurt, but any wounds would be assuaged by a Lucullan

between New York and Chicago via the Pennsylvania you would be invited to take your pick from an incredible range of chicken, ham, chops, steaks, snipe, quail, golden plover, blue-winged teal, oysters and clams, in most cases offered in varying styles, and each one priced at no more than about half-a-dollar a plate. You could, of course, drink with your meal; and the wine list would be finely headed by champagne and tailed by brandy. The restriction on

TRAIN DE LUXE

Jadis, quand une jolie femme, grande dame ou bourgeoise, voyageait en chaise de poste en compagnie d'un mari vieux barbon, la route était propice aux amoureuses aventures. Un galant cavalier, comme par hasard, se trouvait faire même trajet et parcourir mêmes étapes aux mêmes heures. Il dépassait la berline, se laissait rejoindre, récoltait chaque fois un regard, obtenait un sourire aux relais, dérobait un baiser ou mieux encore à l'hôtellerie, tandis que le grison était plongé dans la lecture du dernier numéro du Mercure.

Aujourd'hui... il n'y a de changé que le décor, le véhicule, les costumes des personnages et le titre de la gazette.

dinner in the diner, digestion soothed by its heavy embossed leather chairs and elegant decor freshened by festoons of greenery from wall-suspended potted plants. On some trains the meal was prefaced by the presentation to each lady diner of a corsage of flowers.

All this was staffed on a matching hotel scale by a finely drilled retinue of Pullman conductor, porters, chefs, waiters, valets, ladies' maids and barber, primed to deal courteously with every conceivable circumstance or passenger eccentricity by their voluminous and incredibly pedantic staff instruction manuals. That the customarily negro Pullman porter symbolized customer service in the USA for decades and that Pullman staff in general were perennially head-hunted by hostelries on terra ferma (even by the White House) is adequate testimony to Pullman achievements in this area. The Wagner company was just as meticulous.

With the railroads looming so large by the end of the century not only in everyday American life but also in the industrial and

financial spectrum, it followed that ownership of a private Pullman became the most conspicuous status symbol of the day. Ownership of more than one – and the financier Jay Gould had a train of four, so did Henry E. Huntington – was the really valid mark of a tycoon. The appeal of the private railroad car was the stronger because for a great deal less money than the price-tag of an Old Master or a noble pile on Boston's Beacon Hill one could fashion a miniature mobile palace that would excite just as much reverence for one's wealth. Most private cars adopted the same basic layout of a capacious dining room, a master bedroom with adjoining bathroom for the owner, three or four lesser rooms for his guests, a kitchen and quarters for a crew of at least two, who were the equivalent of chef and butler, but within that framework the richer purchasers indulged a breathtaking variety of conceits. Marble bathtubs, gold plumbing ('the only thing that's economical in our car – it saves polishing, you know' one magnate's wife is said to have boasted), solid gold and silver

Above: According to the French caption, luxury trains in the early twentieth century were eminently suited to amorous adventures, especially while the ageing husband was buried behind a newspaper. Above right: Conditions in a third-class carriage in Brittany were clearly not so conducive to such activities, even if the young lady did not look so much like a 'wax doll in an ethnographic exhibition'.

dinner services, pipe organs, period furniture, rare paintings and ceiling murals executed by specially commissioned international artists, even air-conditioning long before it had been entertained for rail vehicles in public use: all these were unremarkably commonplace features of the American private car by the 1890s and the early 1900s.

The temptation to dwell on North America's imaginative exploitation of the luxury rail travel potential is irresistible, but one must emphasize that space in a Pullman or a 'Limited' cost more than the basic fare and, moreover, that at the end of

LIGNE D'INTÉRÊT LOCAL

Là-bas, au fond du Finistère. La Compagnie y enverra dans trente ans de nouveaux wagons, ceux qui étaient neufs il y a dix ans. C'est le sort ordinaire du matériel qui vieillit : aujourd'hui Paris-Le Havre, demain Morlaix-Roscoff.

Le voyageur de première classe a le sommeil exigeant ; il lui faut quatre places pour s'étendre, une couverture, un oreiller ; il est énervé, agité. En troisième, sans tant de manières, on dort paisiblement, cinq par banquette : l'artilleur sur l'épaule du lignard, le Breton en habits de fête sur l'épaule de l'artilleur. Tout le monde penche à droite parce que la voie vient de tourner à gauche ; à la prochaine courbe en sens opposé toutes les têtes dodelineront à gauche et l'infanterie pèsera à son tour sur l'artillerie. Il n'y a que la belle fille de Morgat ou d'Audierne qui ne bougera pas. Elle restera droite et raide, ne regardant rien mais les yeux grand ouverts, coiffée serré, parée de rubans, semblable à ces poupées de cire qui figurent, vêtues de costumes nationaux, aux expositions ethnographiques.

the nineteenth century it was far from being a ubiquitous option. As one jaundiced Englishman wrote in 1897 on his return from an American tour:

> The unhappy traveller who has been deluded into the belief that his long journey from the Atlantic to the Pacific seaboard will embrace [Pullman] class of travelling throughout its entire length has made a grievous mistake. Certainly the specious advertisements of some companies would lead him to suppose this. But he will find that he is conveyed to Chicago at a ruinous fare; and before he has got used to his barber's shop, library and stenographer, will find that he has to change to a train in which one car will form his home night and day for several days, and which he will learn to curse before he reaches his destination.
>
> The seats by day are hard and the backs are too low to afford any support to the head; the berths by night are short and stuffy . . . Dining cars are by no means universal and

even on the long-distance trains the traveller will probably have to gulp down badly cooked meals in wayside stations at inconvenient hours. As an instance, I may state that on the 'Oregon Express' from San Francisco, California, to Portland, Oregon, breakfast is served at about 9 am and dinner at Ashland at about 4 pm, these being the only meals the traveller gets during the day. There are, moreover, only two lavatories on the car – one for ladies and one for gentlemen. The discomfort when crossing the Rockies on a winter's morning of waiting one's turn, while still ten from the coveted washing-basin, can be better imagined than described. The inconvenience caused to English ladies [used to an adequacy of ladies-only compartments in their own home trains] by the fact that no part of the car save the lavatory alluded to is reserved for them is very great. American ladies cannot be so particular . . .

Mind you, this supercilious critic would have been on a flimsy platform if the railways of his own continent had not

generally awoken around 1870 to their long-distance passengers' demand for more creature comfort and embarked on quite rapid development of amenity and equipment. It was the early 1880s before any railway in his own country of Britain broke away from the compartment format for ordinary day coaches and built the first side-corridor vehicle, a Great Northern Railway six-wheeler. On the European mainland, however, the Hessische-Ludwigs Railway of Germany had inaugurated the *Durchgehende Zug* – 'D-train', a term still employed to categorize an ordinary, non-supplementary-fare express on today's German railways – by ordering that country's first side-corridor vehicles in 1873. Admittedly, the Austrians took to the concept more readily than the rest of Germany, where it was the 1890s before bogie, side-corridor coaches were used in express passenger trains to any extent. By then, of course, the side-corridor format had gained immense point through perfection of inter-coach vestibule connections.

The fashionable 'Boston & Mt Desert Limited' of 1887 included a four-door baggage car, a Pullman dining car (with staff) and three Pullman parlour cars, all with early vestibule connections.

SLEEP COMES TO EUROPE

From the London & Birmingham of the late 1830s onwards various European railways had dabbled with schemes of overnight accommodation, most of them rather makeshift ways of converting day seating into a night-time bed. By the 1860s, however, Europe had a few purpose-built overnight vehicles to show. Quaintest of them without doubt was a semi-double-decker conceived by the American engineer Winans for the Nicolai Railway of Russia, wherein two-bunk compartments and a crude closet at each end of the vehicle were linked by side-corridor with a pair of day saloons superimposed on each other in the centre of the body and interlinked by a cramped spiral staircase. More forward-looking by far was an Austrian design anticipating American practice of nearly a century later by ranging two lines of single-bunk rooms athwart a centre corridor. The special night coaches run by the Hanoverian State Railway in its Berlin–Cologne 'Courier' trains, on the other hand, vulgarly packed three-tiered bunks into each of their small compartments.

One discouragement to sleeping-car development was the reluctance of railway administrations and their governments to entertain the idea of international through trains. The very first, inaugurated from Basle in Switzerland to Rotterdam in Holland in 1863, was only achieved after an alliance of the major European banking houses had reinforced diplomatic pressure

with an offer of capital investment cash to the railways concerned. Thus when a twenty-three-year-old Belgian engineer named Georges Nagelmackers, son of a rich Belgian banking family, was sent off to America in 1868 by his parents as penance for an indiscreet *amour*, he was astounded not only by the quality of Pullman sleepers but by the freedom with which they crossed railway boundaries on through transits. Europeans would jump at – and happily pay for – such transcontinental service, he was convinced.

European railway administrations were not so easily persuaded when Nagelmackers eagerly approached them with draft plans on his return home early in 1870. Nor was there rapturous public response when Nagelmackers got his first tiny four-wheelers, internally structured like Pullman's initial Chicago & Alton conversions, into Ostend–Cologne operation in 1873. Fiasco looked inevitable when Nagelmackers ran out of cash, but at the critical juncture he fell in with a crafty ex-US Army engineer, Colonel William d'Alton Mann, who had astutely patented every piece of equipment he had designed in his military career and was seeking to re-invest the proceeds in rail sleeping cars. Sanguine at any prospect of competing with Pullman on his home ground, Mann tried to sell his designs to British railways but had been rebuffed.

The partnership was near perfect. Mann had the money and intelligent design know-how; Nagelmackers was the shrewd marketing brain. The new company's vehicles, branded 'Mann Boudoir Sleeping Cars', ignored Pullman format and prefigured some essentials of future European sleeping-car design. The berths

were in compartments with the forerunner of the side-corridor, although in these first cars that space was used to adjoin each compartment with its own washroom and lavatory. Like the first British sleeping car of 1873, a six-wheeler built by the North British Railway for the East Coast Route's Anglo-Scottish trade, the pioneer Mann six-wheeler included a spartan compartment for the principal occupants' servants.

The future of the international sleeping-car service was sealed during 1873, partly by Nagelmackers' breakthrough to contracts with previously obdurate French railways, but perhaps most of all by the old ploy of playing the royal card. Mann coaxed the Prince of Wales, King Edward VII to be, into employing a 'boudoir car' for a trip through Berlin to the Russian border *en route* to St Petersburg. That roused a furore of high society interest which, coupled with the French contracts, broke open the door to Nagelmackers' priority objective – a through Paris–Vienna service. His certainty of immediate commercial triumph was vindicated; within a year he had pocketed agreements with several railways and was operating forty sleepers. In 1876 he bought out Mann and registered in Brussels his own *Compagnie Internationale des Wagons-Lits et des Grands Express Européens*, more concisely known to European rail-users ever since as the 'Wagons-Lits Company'.

An essential step to realization of the *Grand Express* component of the organization's title, naturally, was ability to feed passengers throughout their journey, and feed them well. Nagelmackers was just beaten to the post for the première of European train dining. Britain's Great Northern Railway installed the first regular restaurant car in its London King's Cross–Leeds service on 26 September 1879, whereas it was 1880 when the Wagons-Lits company started experiments with a converted third-class six-wheeler between Weimar and Bebra, attaching it to a Berlin–Frankfurt/Main express with the co-operation of the Berlin–Anhalt and Thuringian Railways. At first the car was supplied with ready-cooked meals, but the difficulty of keeping them hot before service soon compelled Nagelmackers to convert an accompanying six-wheeler into a kitchen. In that same year of 1880, significantly, the Wagons-Lits company turned out its first sleeper with inter-car communication, though as yet it was across an open platform: it was the creation of on-train catering as much as anything else which persuaded European railways to move into vestibuled corridor stock with increasing rapidity as the century faded, especially after the Great Eastern Railway set a precedent in 1891 by providing separate dining accommodation for all classes of passenger.

On-train dining was not instantly popular. The reserved British sniffed at taking a meal when the train stopped in full view of the common people on station platforms and for some time many preferred to tuck into hampers in the seclusion of their compartments. One or two British railways, notably the North Eastern, refused to sacrifice the known profits of their station dining rooms for the speculative return on dining cars and held out against the innovation until the turn of the century. German station restaurateurs were still more loth to see a Belgian company decimate their business with its new-fangled cars. Their outcry deprived Nagelmackers' company of the monopolistic grip of domestic as well as international train catering it eventually secured in countries such as France and Italy. Half-a-dozen German companies won the catering concessions for the internal services of their country, paving the way for the emergence in 1916 of Mitropa – the usual contraction of *Mitteleuropäische Schlafwagen und Speisewagen AG*.

All Wagons-Lits interests in the Reich were sequestrated by the Kaiser's Government in 1915 and the following year Mitropa was established by consortium of German and Austro-Hungarian railways and banks to operate both sleeping and restaurant cars. After the war the Wagons-Lits company failed to manoeuvre Mitropa out of business and had to swallow an agreement which conceded Mitropa some international rights in exchange for Wagons-Lits' freedom to resume its international transits through Germany. In essentials that pact also governed post-Second World War relations between the Wagons-Lits concern and Mitropa's successor, the *Deutsche Schlafwagen und Spiesewagen Gesellschaft*, or DSG.

When the century faded over 500 Wagons-Lits diners and sleepers had a firm foothold on a 90,000 mile (145,000 km) tracery of European routes stretching from the English Channel coast to Russia, the borders of Turkey and southern Italy, and were conveying two million passengers a year. They would have reached Spain and Portugal as well if Nagelmackers had been able that early to devise a way of changing the bogies beneath his cars at the frontier break of gauge, but that did not materialize until the post-Second World War innovation of the overnight Paris–Madrid 'Puerta del Sol'.

The European *train de luxe* was born on 5 June 1883 in the legendary 'Orient Express', after the Paris–Vienna success had made railway administrations amenable to Nagelmackers' next objective: to operate trains composed exclusively of his sleeping and dining cars, except for accompanying luggage vans. At the start the through journey to Constantinople entailed two transfers to water transport *en route*, but by 1884 the train could get as far as the Turkish border. In 1883, too, the Wagons-Lits company began to tap the British travel market with a through service from Calais to the French Riviera and Rome. Once in Italy, Nagelmackers rapidly expanded his bridgehead by a progressive takeover of Pullman concessions (of Pullman's foray into Europe, more in a moment). Early in the 1890s the first Calais–Rome service was supplemented by the 'P&O Express', a Calais–Brindisi landbridge for British travellers to India by the Peninsular & Oriental Shipping Co.'s vessels plying to and from the Italian port, and in November 1897 the Calais–Paris–Rome route was finally ennobled by inauguration of the 'Rome Express'.

The most fascinating Wagons-Lits achievement of the late nineteenth century was Nagelmackers' success in crumbling Czarist Russia's resistance to any improved access to its country from the west. The 1898 outcome of that was first the grandest, undoubtedly, of all pre-First World War European trains, the St Petersburg–Vienna–Nice–Cannes; and second the 'Trans-Siberian Express', which started in December 1899 over the half of the line by then finished from Moscow but which by 1903 was making a nine-day journey from Moscow right through to Kharbin in Manchuria. Stoicism enough is implied by the

Nagelmackers (seated) and Mann (standing) in front of the 'Mann Boudoir Sleeping Car' of 1873. Nagelmackers went on to form Wagons-Lits in 1876.

COMPARTMENT BY DAY

COMPARTMENT BY NIGHT

CORRIDOR AT NIGHT

WASH BASINS

THE BIRTH OF LUXURY TRAVEL

The passenger train has never been merely a means of getting from one place to another. Even today the train offers one indisputable advantage over its rivals – comfort. Although the poor had to make what they could of travel, for the wealthy – and not so wealthy – long-distance trains became in the late nineteenth century hotels on wheels. They were places where people could relax by day, sleep well by night, enjoy good food and be treated as well on their journey as they would expect to be at their destination.

Royalty and the grand had their magnificent private coaches from the time they first accepted trains as a suitable means of transport, but the public luxury service began in 1865 when the Chicago & Alton took on George Pullman's *Pioneer*. With long

journeys making overnight travel a commonplace in the United States, and with increasing affluence giving large numbers of people the means to afford the services offered, luxury trains burgeoned, and by the first decade of this century the traveller going a long distance along any major route in the USA could expect to go in style.

Public luxury travel did not begin in Europe in earnest until later, when the 'Orient Express' ran its first journey in 1883. As one that crossed international frontiers, it was to become the most romantic of all trains. That first train was modest in length only: its three passenger coaches were designed with grandeur in mind. Two accommodation cars, each with three double compartments for four people each and two single for two people each, served as ordinary coaches by day, and at night the seats converted into beds. The

seats were made of leather embossed with gold patterning, the walls were of teak and mahogany inlaid with marquetry. At night the beds were made with silk sheets, and an attendant was constantly at hand. After the coaches came a dining car with at opposite ends a ladies' drawing room and gentlemen's smoking room and library. The drawing room contained an arm-chair and chaise-longue in petit-point embroidery and was decorated with tapestries. The dining car was even more elaborate, with carved wood, metal flowers and brightly coloured paintings. Although food was bought *en route*, a refrigerator, a great rarity, was kept to ensure freshness. So plentiful was the fare that passengers could expect to spend three hours over dinner and a separate four-wheeled *fourgon*, or covered truck, was needed to store the food, wine, champagne, port, brandy, and

KITCHEN

DINING CAR

SMOKING ROOM

FOOD AND DRINK FOURGON

liqueurs as well as the passengers' luggage. A similar but larger *fourgon* at the front of the train carried mail.

This attention to fine eating was to be a hallmark of the great trains. Many American railroads at the turn of the century established a $1 dinner, which could be of as many as seven courses. The 'California Limited', for example, offered a menu which included clams, consommé, red snapper, chicken cutlet Marchale, salad, ice cream and cheese. And when the 'Super Chief' began running between Chicago and Los Angeles in May 1936 its *à la carte* menu included caviare, salmon and asparagus, and a choice of champagnes between Veuve Cliquot, Bollinger and Dom Perignon Cuvée.

Excellent food was not the only luxury provided. A large number of staff catered to passengers' needs. Any of the great trains – the 'Train Bleu', the 'Orient Express', the 'Trans-Siberian', the 'St Petersburg-Vienna-Nice-Cannes Express', the 'Twentieth Century Limited', the 'Broadway Limited' – provided valet service, library, bar service, and a lounge car or observation car. The 'Trans-Siberian Express' of 1900 also had a chapel car, gymnasium and music room. Barber's shops were common on American trains, with the 75 mph (120 km/h) speeds necessitating the employment of highly skilled men. Santa Fe's 'De Luxe' which ran between Chicago and Los Angeles from 1911 to 1917 outdid them all, giving its sixty passengers brass beds, an air-conditioned dining car, a manicurist, librarian, daily papers and periodicals in addition to all the above.

The grandest train of them all was never actually built. Hitler dreamed of a 3m (10ft) gauge monster running across Europe with banqueting rooms and vast salons. Plans were made and research actually started.

Today only South Africa's 'Blue Train' has survived the collapse in demand for leisurely but elegant comfort. It provides three-roomed suites with lounge, bedroom and bathroom, constant bar and valet service, individually controlled air-conditioning and entertainment channels, a lounge car and a sumptuous dining car. But, although the 'Blue Train', which dates from 1939, is the only such train to have run in continuous service, the day of luxury travel is not yet over. Despite the demise of the original in 1977, a 'Nostalgic Orient Express' appeared in 1981 running from Zurich to Istanbul and a new Venice-Simplon express started running in 1982 from London to Venice. Both trains consist of the original rolling stock of the 1920s, fully reconditioned, and offer all the comfort and service of the trains at their heyday.

scheduled duration of the journey, but that was often prolonged because the Trans-Siberian railway was of single and none-too-substantial track, derailments or rail fractures frequent, and the operators' skill in unravelling the ensuing traffic jams decidedly underdeveloped. Nevertheless the 'Trans-Siberian Express' did healthy business as an overland route to Chinese cities (the Wagons-Lits company backed its assiduous promotion of the service by building its own hotel in Peking) until the Russian revolution put paid to Wagons-Lits' activity anywhere in that country.

Nagelmackers was just as preoccupied as Pullman with the attainment of expensive elegance in the finish and equipment of his cars and with the deportment of his car staff. He needed to be, for on the St Petersburg–Nice–Cannes train especially the occupants would be mostly the flower of Russian and Central European nobility and *haut monde*, many of them trailed by their own valets and maidservants. Passengers would don full evening dress for dinner as a matter of social routine. Except in jewelled accessories one cannot believe that any of them outshone the Wagons-Lits train conductors of those days, who were gorgeously arrayed in crimson tailcoats with gold-coloured lanyards, frilled shirts embellished with lace cuffs, blue knee breeches, white silk stockings and pumps with silver buckles.

PULLMAN IN EUROPE

The instrument of Pullman's incursion into Europe was James Allport, manager of Britain's Midland Railway from 1853. To his enduring credit, Allport's initial concern in the improvement of his passenger services had been for the third-class travellers, who were not only condemned to ride in cramped, wooden-seated compartments only half-partitioned from each other, but debarred from the fastest and most convenient services. It took him twenty-five years to grind down the conservatism of his railway board and others. At last, in 1875, he could set the British railway scene in a ferment by abolishing the Midland's three-class structure. As fast as new construction allowed, the wooden-seated cells-on-wheels were scrapped; second-class disappeared from the Midland rubrics; the former upholstered second-class seating was regraded as third-class, to which the better trains were to be opened; and a year

later the Midland reinforced its challenge to the British railway establishment – already enraged enough at the Midland's initiative – by putting on the track the first of its handsomely contoured and furnished dual-class twelve-wheeled bogie coaches with clerestory roofs. At that date they were oil-lit, offered passengers no heating except footwarmers, and lacked lavatories and inter-coach vestibule connections, but they were still advanced enough on previous British accommodation to be epochal in the development of the British express train.

At the same time, however, Allport was trying Pullmans on his up-market clientele. In 1872 he too had travelled about the USA, where Pullman's enterprise impressed him more than that of Nagelmackers and Colonel Mann, and on his return he prevailed upon his directors and shareholders to import for trial some 'knocked-down' cars of American build at Pullman's Detroit works. Assembled at the Midland's Derby works these vehicles were mostly convertible sleepers generally conforming to Pullman's early American 'section' layout, but they included Pullman's first parlour cars, day vehicles furnished with fully rotatable and even partly reclining armchairs; it was the British reaction to these last which encouraged Pullman to introduce his first US parlour cars in 1875.

The first public Pullman train, mixing sleepers and parlour cars from America with some Pullman-style day cars built by the Midland itself, was inaugurated from

Above: The elegant dining car of a train de luxe in 1912, with the superbly dressed Wagons-Lits staff looking more like footmen than waiters. This was the heyday of the luxury train.
Above right: The interior of Midland Railway's Pullman day car, which was fitted with fully rotatable and partly reclining arm chairs.
Right: Midland Railway Pullman car No. 18. The first public Pullman train in Britain mixed sleepers and parlour cars from America with some Pullman-style day cars built by the Midland Railway itself. Its first trip was from London to Bradford on 1 June 1874.

London St Pancras to Bradford on 1 June 1874. Not since the British dawn of steam railways can one of the country's trains have embodied so many 'firsts' as this one. As yet it meant stepping between typical Pullman car-end verandahs – and the Midland discouraged the practice until the enclosed Pullman vestibule was devised – but to walk the length of the train was at last possible. First- and third-class passengers alike had access to lavatories, previously standard amenities only of family saloons. It was the first British train to be decently heated, through radiators fed from a Baker coke-fired boiler in each car (the Baker heater was by then in widespread US use). And it was almost, but not quite, the first train lit by gas instead of by foul-smelling oil-lamps.

Pullman sleepers served alongside the railways' own growing stock of sleeping

Pacific Railway, which in 1912 had some Pullman-type saloons built in Vienna and Prague to form, with Wagons-Lits restaurant cars, a comfortable through train to Vienna for tourists disembarking from its steamships at Trieste.

FASTER AND FASTER

In Europe and America express train speed as well as comfort was advancing fast when the nineteenth century came to its close. In Britain acceleration was ignited by the Midland's 1875 admission of its upgraded third-class traffic to all trains, with which it coupled a reduction of first-class fares to second-class level. Since the Midland concurrently had the country's third Anglo-Scottish route on the way with its construction of the Settle–Carlisle line over the Pennines, the East and West Coast companies responded with schedule-cutting – the economy-minded London & North Western on the West Coast with great reluctance, it should be said; when it did steel itself in 1883 to a ten-minute cut of the day London–Glasgow train's schedule the time was saved entirely at the expense of the wretched passengers' digestion, since they had their lunch-stop at Preston trimmed from thirty to twenty minutes.

But on the East Coast the Great Northern, as remarked in an earlier chapter, was thirsting for speed. By 1880 it was unarguably the world's fastest railway, working to start-to-stop shedule averages of 54mph (87km/h) with its London–Leeds and London–Manchester expresses in competition with the Midland and London & North Western. On a nine-hour overall schedule from London King's Cross the East Coast day train was already an hour or more faster than the rivals' services, which because Edinburgh was not their main Scottish target conveyed third- as well as first- and second-class traffic. Suddenly, in November 1887, the East Coast consortium announced that it was following the Midland precept: the crack 10 a.m. King's Cross–Edinburgh would henceforward carry third-class passengers. In face of superior East Coast speed the West Coast companies could see almost all their third-class Anglo-Scottish traffic going the way so much of the superior-grade business had gone. Not even the penny-pinchers of the London & North Western could stomach that.

The starting-pistol had been fired for the extraordinary Races to the North of

cars until well into the twentieth century, but not in Pullman ownership – the Midland had taken its cars over from Pullman in 1888. They did not play a continuous role in British railways as the parlour cars did. Following an abortive experiment at the start of the 1880s, the London Brighton & South Coast Railway solidly established the British supplementary-fare all-Pullman day train in 1888 between London and Brighton, at first as a Sundays-only service but from November 1908 as a daily first class-only operation. As the 'Southern Belle' this became one of Europe's best-known luxury services and initiated a line of day Pullman trains which were front-runners among the express trains of several British routes, until the nationalized British Railways drive for economical regular-interval operation with standard train-sets

progressively eliminated all but one survivor in the 1960s and 1970s.

England and, as mentioned earlier, Italy were Pullman's only European footholds in his lifetime. But after his death and that of Nagelmackers the Wagons-Lits company under the chairmanship of the British financier Davison Dalziel (later Lord Dalziel) acquired the British Pullman Palace Car Co. from Pullman's trustees. As it had already bought out Pullman in Italy the two concerns henceforward developed in harness, and in the winter of 1925 the roll of European mainland Pullman trains opened with the 'Milan–Nice Pullman'. The following year one of the best-known, the Calais–Paris '*Flèche d'Or*' – 'Golden Arrow' – was added to the list. The only other private entrepreneur to invade the European luxury market was the Canadian

1888 and 1895. At a stroke – and at the last moment, to preclude an immediate counter-stroke – the West Coast cut by an hour the overall time of its day Anglo-Scottish train between London and both Glasgow and Edinburgh from 2 June 1888. The East Coast brethren responded as quickly as they could and for the rest of that summer there was a cut and thrust of piecemeal acceleration until the East Coast train ultimately made Edinburgh in only 7 hours 27 minutes from London, 11 minutes better than the smartest West Coast performance. At that both parties settled for an uneasy truce, recognizing that neither could sustain such performance all year round. But they stabilized on a common 8½-hour timing, which on the West Coast meant that the racing had secured a permanent saving of an hour and a half in journey time between London and the two major Scottish cities.

The contest erupted again in the summer of 1895 after completion of the Forth and Tay Bridges had shortened the East Coast Route to Aberdeen, the new winning post. This time it was the West Coast partnership which took the final laurels, ultimately covering the 540 miles (870 km) from London to Aberdeen in a nineteenth-century world record time for such a distance of 512 minutes – three hours quicker than the public timetable had allowed any West Coast train between the two cities just seven weeks earlier. From then on the British companies knew that everyday passenger train operation in excess of 75 mph (120 km/h) was both practical and safe, and were increasingly to

prove that a mix of speed, comfort and competitive fares could generate travel growth in every sector of the market.

The British were leading the world in their generous provision of upholstered third-class accommodation, at no extra charge, in even their fastest trains apart from a handful of Pullman services, but they were ceding their speed supremacy to the French and Americans at the turn of the century. With the aid of its splendid du Bousquet-de Glehn compound engines the Nord Railway of France had crossed the mile-a-minute start-to-stop average mark with its Paris–Brussels and Cologne expresses over sectors of their route as long as the 112½ miles (181 km) from Paris to Busigny, and the Paris–Orléans as well as the Nord had a rising number of timings in the 55–60 mph (90–100 km/h) average speed bracket to show. The German railways, on the other hand, were only just into the 50 mph (80 km/h) range.

In fairness one ought to add that the fastest French and German start-to-stop speeds were generally over considerably shorter distances than those in the British timetables. British railways were tabling progressively longer non-stop runs to secure quicker transits by the crack trains from London to the principal provincial cities, whereas French and German systems were reluctant to bypass any major town with a *rapide* or a *Schnellzug*. Also influential in this trend was most British railways' adoption of the water troughs devised by the London & North Western's John Ramsbottom; laid at strategic points along main lines between each pair of

Right: The Midland Railway 'corridor luncheon car express' heads towards Scotland in 1900. The threat of this third route to Scotland in the 1870s instigated the Races to the North.
Below: A poster of about 1895 emphasizes the rivalry between the competing East Coast and West Coast routes to Scotland.
Bottom: A West Coast express of the 1890s, headed by a Webb LNWR compound 2-2-2-0, speeds over water troughs.

running rails, they enabled a steam locomotive to replenish its water supply at non-stop speed by means of a tender scoop which the fireman powered by a wheel control to cut into the surface of the shallow trough's water and force the latter up into the tender's tank. In France only the Ouest Railway laid troughs; no German main line ever had them. Thus until mainland European steam power acquired its more capacious tenders of the twentieth century, continental railways were forced to schedule more frequent stops than the British for water, if nothing else. Across the Atlantic installation of troughs, or 'track pans' as they were known there, was limited to a few eastern US railroads.

In 1888, year of the first British Race to the North, British timetables were scheduling nearly 63,000 miles (101,400 km) daily for 40 mph (65 km/h) average running or better, whereas the American books yielded just under 14,000 (22,500 km). But the excited American press reaction to the British exploits of 1888 – 'Flying Over the Rails!' was the *New York Times'* banner headline for its 7 August 1888 account of the culminating run from London to Edinburgh – was taken by railroads on the East Coast of the US as a challenge to close the gap. The New York Central's General Superintendent, for instance, promptly proclaimed that his road would better the British every day between New York and Buffalo.

Needless to say, almost all the US 40 mph-or-better (65 km/h) running of the late 1880s was operated in the East. Almost half of it was concentrated on the fiercely competing routes between Philadelphia and the New Jersey coast mentioned in the previous chapter, where the Philadelphia & Reading already boasted a 54.4 mph (87 km/h) average timing between Bound Brook and West Trenton. Elsewhere the Baltimore & Ohio had four trains daily booked over the 40 miles (65 km) from Baltimore to Washington in 45 minutes at an average of 53.3 mph (85 km/h) start to stop.

Over longer distances, though, travel was no quicker than in mainland Europe. Chicago to Kansas City, 483 miles (777 km), was a sixteen-hour haul by the Chicago & Alton; Cincinnati to New Orleans, 922 miles (1,484 km), a 28 hours 10 minutes traipse by the Louisville & Nashville. Neither New York Central nor Pennsylvania could get one from New York to Chicago in less than twenty-five hours. As for the Far West, with the ballast as yet barely firm about the track of the transcontinental routes, most of the latter were running just one all-purpose train a day. More often than not it was so generously scheduled that the crew were easily prevailed upon to stop out of course in the wilds while some homesteader staked out his claim, long enough even to allow a party of buffalo hunters some sport.

The British stimulus apart, the surge of US train speed was set off in the 1890s by the perfection of the inter-car vestibule. Besides adding a new dimension of safety to faster travel, the vestibule enhanced comfort by keeping the cars more rigidly in line at speed (by closing the inter-car gaps it reduced wind resistance too). Although history records that one Samuel L. Calthrop filed the first US patent application for a 'Streamlined' train as early as 1867 – nothing significant appears to have materialized from it – 'Vestibuled' was *the* promotional word as the century turned. A number of US trains, latterly celebrated under other names such as the 'Capitol Limited' and the 'Northwestern Limited', were premiered simply as the 'Vestibuled Limited', though the Rock Island varied the theme by titling its prime Chicago–Minneapolis and St Paul train the 'Solid Express'.

THE ARCHITECTURE OF LARGE STATIONS

The great termini were conceived as showpieces by the railway companies that built them. Unlike the vast sheds constructed to house the lines and platforms, concourses and offices were available for the architect to design as he and his clients wished. The railway companies often employed the most prestigious architects of their day to build them: Eliel Saarinen for the terminus in Helsinki, Sir George Gilbert Scott for St Pancras in London, and the firm of McKinn, Mead and White for the now demolished Pennsylvania station in New York. Grandeur, monumentality and decoration are the hallmarks of the great Victorian stations; in the twentieth century functionalism takes over, but these stations are nonetheless designed to impress. Never only departure points, railway termini have provided some of the most important architecture of the last 150 years.

The Gare du Nord (left) in Paris, by Jacob Hittorf, 1864. The façade impresses on the traveller that he will journey in style.

Grand Central Station, New York (below), built between 1903 and 1912 by architects Reed and Stern. A classical porticoed appearance was thought suitable for this enormous, two-tier terminus.

Central Station, Antwerp, 1899, designed by Louis de la Censerie. The mixing of styles and love of elaboration reached a height at the end of the nineteenth century.

Volvograd (formerly Stalingrad) Station, 1953, built by A. Khourovskin and S. Briskin in Soviet monumental style, echoing Stalin's Moscow skyscrapers.

King's Cross in London, built in 1852 as the terminus to the Great Northern line. The architect Lewis Cubitt gave the façade a remarkably clean and classical look which leaves the station now as the most modern-looking of the Victorian termini.

Victoria Station, Bombay (above), built 1894–6 by architect F.W. Stevens. The grandiloquence of the station speaks of an empire at its most powerful and most confident.

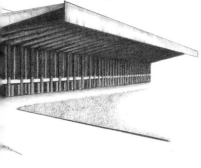

Lens in Northern France, 1926. The architect, Urbain Cassan, has shunned the heavy decoration of twenty years earlier to produce a building more appropriate to the machine age.

Stazione Termini, Rome, built 1947–51 by Montuori Associates. Largely constructed in steel and concrete, this decidedly modern building is free of decorative effect but is still a dominating structure.

Some of the 1890s acceleration was really spectacular. By the end of the decade Boston was closer to New York in time by a full hour, for example, and New Orleans almost ten hours nearer to Chicago than in the late 1880s, when the best Illinois Central train was spinning out thirty-five hours over the journey. Here and there the speed-up was over-ambitious. The Central of Georgia mounted a Southern challenge to British rail speed in 1893 by slashing three hours from the previous best Atlanta–Savannah timecard at the première of its 'Nancy Hawks' and essaying the 191 miles (307 km) from Macon to Savannah in four hours flat, stops included, but within months had to decelerate because of deteriorating track and equipment.

On competing routes railroads vied in speed with each other for passengers or lucrative mail contracts. The Burlington and the Chicago & North Western were racing through the night with the Omaha and Denver mails, and the one-time Plant system and the incongruously named Seaboard Air Line were hustling to be first at the quayside of the Cuba mailboat. The historic struggle for the Chicago–Minneapolis and St Paul passenger business between the Chicago & North Western and the Milwaukee was touched off on New Year's Day 1899 by the C&NW's inauguration of a ten-hour schedule between Chicago and St Paul. Canada was not immune to this new itch for speed, either. A contest for the Montreal–Ottowa traffic was so spirited that the transit time between these two cities came down at a run from $3\frac{1}{2}$ hours to 2 hours 20 minutes.

Most far-famed of all these strenuous rivalries, however, was that of the Pennsylvania and New York Central (NYC) for the New York–Chicago market. Here again it was the British 'Race to the North' which spurred the NYC to fire the opening salvo. At that time the NYC was for all practical purposes run by a partnership of its Locomotive & Rolling Stock Superintendent, an expatriate Scot named William Buchanan, and its acutely publicity-conscious General Passenger Agent, George H. Daniels, whose numerous promotional coups included the inception on the NYC of that American railroad institution, the 'redcap' – porters affording passengers free help with their baggage. Intent on revolutionizing the New York–Chicago passenger service,

Daniels pounced on the traffic-building potential of a major 1893 exhibition in Chicago to instal a new 'Limited', the 'Empire State Express', which connected the two cities in an unprecedented overall time of twenty hours for the 960 miles (1,545 km) via the NYC's indulgently graded 'Water Level Route'. The Pennsylvania's New York–Chicago route was shorter at 908 miles (1,461 km), but quite stiffly graded beyond Philadelphia, and its best New York–Chicago time was all of twenty-eight hours. Buchanan was the last great advocate of the 'American' 4-4-0 for high-speed work, and for the 'Empire State Express' he turned out a special model with 7ft 2in (2,184 mm) driving wheels, No. 999. This was the engine claimed on rather flimsy evidence to have been whipped up to 102.8 mph (165.4 km/h) on 9 May 1893 in pursuit of lost time on the 'Empire State Express' and two days later to 112.5 mph (181.1 km/h). But after basking for some years in No. 999's glory, which won it pictorial honour on a US postage stamp, even the NYC surreptitiously confessed that the top speed almost certainly did not exceed 90 mph (145 km/h).

In June 1902 Daniels astounded the world by hazarding an all-year-round twenty-hour schedule between New York and Chicago with a new luxury train which – with typical acumen – he christened the 'Twentieth Century Limited'. Astonishment was redoubled when the Pennsylvania promptly countered by slashing eight hours, no less, from its best New York–Chicago timecard to compete on level schedule terms through a new 'Pennsylvania Special'. 'Great Speed War' shouted the Eastern and Mid-West press; and for the rest of the decade the public goggled as if at a World Series as the two giants battled for the cream of the New York–Chicago business.

In 1905 both systems lopped another two hours of their timings and all along each route local communities flocked to the tracksides to watch the first accelerated trains steam past. That inaugural day of the eighteen-hour timing, 11 June 1905, the Pennsylvania alleged that its 'Special's' Class E2 Atlantic No. 7002 touched 127.1 mph (204.5 km/h). But again there was no acceptable proof – and in any event steam traction experts are mostly adamant that such a pace was technically impossible given the state of the locomotive design art at the time. The Pennsylvania gave up the

THE ARCHITECTURE OF SMALL STATIONS

Stations in towns and villages manifest a complete variety of forms, ranging from wooden huts to miniature Renaissance palaces. No single functional style has ever evolved as the most appropriate for the design of small stations, and often whim or local characteristics have been the motivating force. Most companies developed a particular look for their lines, but often appearance was left to the architect. The results testify to the great diversity of vernacular architecture.

Nuoro in Sardinia. With its perfectly balanced façade and the steps leading up to it, this building could easily be mistaken for an eighteenth-century villa. The station is now closed.

The colonial engineers who built the railways in the Third World did not always impose the architecture of their home country. The architect of Bobo Dioulasso (below) in Upper Volta conceived of his station as a kind of Moorish fortress.

Stone in Staffordshire, England (above). From the first spurt in railway building, this station looks back to the English Renaissance with its imposing Jacobean appearance.

The imposing appearance of the station at Huancayo in Peru derives from its looking like a grandee's villa. Its impressiveness is underlined by the poverty of many of the buildings around it and the roughness of the ground on which the tracks have been laid.

The illustration above shows a common design for French nineteenth-century country stations. The building on the right was a shed for parcels and lugage.

A railway station may bear no resemblance to a temple in function, but this has not deterred the architect of Hua Hin (below right) in Thailand.

This station at Zuni in West Virginia is a simple wooden construction owing a debt to the Colonial style. As a 'combination' station it serves both passenger and freight traffic.

race in November 1912, reverting to a twenty-hour schedule with the rebirth of the lightweight 'Special' as the heavier 'Broadway Limited', but it never abandoned contention with the 'Twentieth Century Limited' for the title of the most prestigious and luxurious overnight service between New York and Chicago.

THE TOWERING TERMINUS

Most of the world's great passenger stations were erected in the second half of the nineteenth century or very early in the twentieth. From mid-century onwards the handling of passenger and goods traffic on the same premises quickly went out of fashion, but the growth of traffic plus the inclination to build offices, dining rooms and a hotel into the façade quickly inspired bigger and bigger edifices. Eclecticism was the hallmark of mid-nineteenth-century architecture and its railway station exponents were no exceptions. Gothic, Venetian and Byzantine styles were to be seen, though in mid-century the Italianate, with its flourishes of turrets and campaniles, was probably the most popular in Europe and the USA. There early major station builders developed a passion for tall, slender towers; outstanding examples of the early 1850s were those of Baltimore's Camden station and of one of the first Union Stations – those put up jointly by railroads serving the same town or city – at Harrisburg, Pennsylvania.

From now on elephantiasis set in. To match the growing size of the train-sheds spanning the platforms – and also, naturally, to raise a structure more stupefyingly monumental than that of any competing company serving the same city – railways built massive façades. Some, like London's King's Cross, the Gare de l'Est in Paris, Berlin's Anhalter station and one or two of Italy's first big termini, embodied the arch of the train-shed in the outline of the façade. Of those that did not, the outstanding example was Sir George Gilbert Scott's palatial frontage for the Midland Railway's London terminal of St Pancras, completed in the early 1870s, a masterpiece of the Gothic style which by then had just come into vogue.

For size, however, St Pancras and other London termini were eclipsed by the great *Hauptbahnhof* completed at Frankfurt-am-Main in 1888, after nine years' work, which set the style for later central European colossi at Bucharest, Hamburg and Leipzig. At Frankfurt the great triple-section train-shed roof, spanning eighteen terminal tracks, was no less than 549 ft (167m) wide and 610 ft (186m) long. But before long all Europe's stations would be left far behind by the second great two-level Grand Central station of New York, built between 1903 and 1912, with its aggregate of sixty-seven tracks.

The famous 'American' 4-4-0, No. 999, was claimed to have reached 112.5 mph on the 'Empire State Express' in 1893.

THE EVOLUTION OF RAILWAY SIGNALLING

The need of some form of traffic control was patent from the day the first set of points was laid in a public passenger-carrying railway. The first solution was to add control of trains to the peace-keeping chores of the policemen employed by the early British railways. Assigned to station platforms, junctions and road level crossings, they hand-signalled trains away or to a halt, using lanterns after dark, in much the same way as they would road traffic. Unless they happened to be positioned in sight of each other, adjacent policemen had no means of communicating amongst themselves. All they could do was maintain a prescribed time-interval between trains passing their sentry-post – and often their timepiece was nothing more sophisticated than a sand-timer; clocks and watches were not yet commonplace personal equipment.

Given the modest speeds of the early days on most railways this primitive system was surprisingly foolproof so long as train running was incident-free, but it could get pretty hazardous if a train broke down or started losing time heavily in open country between police posts. When that happened the next step was usually to send out a spare locomotive to search for the delinquent. No one had any scruple about resorting to wrong-line working in that circumstance.

Other pioneer European railways followed British practice. But some seem to have been less concerned about the calibre of their policemen. The French, for instance, asked little but signalling 'point duty' of their *gardes*, as they were called, and consequently rated unthinking discipline considerably higher than intellectual faculty. For that reason and also because they were used to roughing it in all weathers, ex-soldiers were most French

Above: In 1844, policemen on the London & Birmingham Railway were using a system of flags to signal trains, as shown in this drawing from the Illustrated London News. Top left is 'all clear', top right 'caution', indicating a train has passed within five minutes, and above two types of 'caution' indicating a defect in the rails. The 'stop' signal is not illustrated but is described as a red flag 'waved backwards and forwards' by the policeman facing the oncoming engine. Right: The exit from Charing Cross station on the SER was guarded by this gantry signalbox and slotted-post signals.

railways' first choice for the job. (Ex-sailors were the favourite French recruits for the brakesmen's job, perched in a box-seat at roof level where they could keep the enginemen in view, because *matelots* should not only be hardened to exposure but impervious to a rough ride.) According to one French historian the ex-soldier *garde* was not even a paragon of discipline. Bored by long periods of inactivity between trains, battered by wintry weather or just satiated with *vin ordinaire*, he often retreated to his rudimentary sentry-box and dozed off until the next train pulled up and its angry, bewildered engineman thumped him out of his stupor to try and discover whether the track ahead was clear.

MECHANICAL SIGNALS

By the early 1840s British railways were starting to make a separate job of traffic policing. At busy traffic centres, too, the traffic policeman was given the assistance of a pointsman to manhandle the switches to his orders. The next step was to supersede hand signals with manually operated mechanical signals. The first devices adopted to convey the basic 'stop' or 'proceed' indications to enginemen were varied, but one of the longest-lived was the Great Western's disc-and-crossbar, employed from 1830 onwards. This mounted the two emblems at right-angles to each other on a rotatable standard; display of the crossbar to the driver was a signal to halt and rotation of the post to show the disc was advice to proceed. Some of these GWR disc-and-crossbar signals, often mounted on posts towering as much as 60 ft (18 m) high, survived almost to the end of the century. Another early type of signal used in mainland Europe as well as England was a ball attached to a rope which, hoisted to the

top of the pole to which it was attached, signified 'all clear'. That was soon discarded in England but it was widely adopted in the USA, where it originated the traditional cry of 'Highball!' as authority to start.

First to use the semaphore signal arm was Charles Hutton Gregory of the London & Croydon Railway in 1841. Tradition has it that the concept was inspired by the Royal Navy's signalling methods, but it seems more likely that it was based on the Chappé overland relay signalling chain which originated in France. At first one signal arm, pivoting within a slot in the signal post, served to convey all three basic signalling aspects: at the horizontal, 'stop'; at an angle of 45°, 'caution'; and dropped vertically so that it was obscured by the post which contained it, 'all clear'. Some anonymous 'bobby' working on the London & North Western at Watford is said to have been the first to hit on the obvious labour-saving ploy of remotely working one of his signals by wire from his hut. The next refinement was to devise a system of rodding that would make a multi-lensed lamp mounted on the post co-act with the movement of the semaphore arm to display a matching aspect for after-dark operation. This was devised in 1847 by one of Britain's first specialist signal engineers, James Stevens, and first employed by the South Eastern Railway, which had been a trend-setter in adoption of the semaphore signal.

As early as 1843 one of Stevens' employees had contrived a semaphore signal in which the lamp was fixed and the

after-dark aspects were obtained by the movement in front of the lamp's single lens of appropriately coloured spectacle glasses co-acting with the semaphore arm. The trouble with this idea was that in the early days the colour code was red for danger, green for caution and white for all clear – this last a natural corollary of the daylight practice of displaying a signal aspect to a driver only when he was required to slow down or stop, and of slotting the arm out of sight to indicate a clear road. As a mnemonic couplet of the day had it:

> White is right, red is wrong
> Green is gently go along.

Above left: A disc-and-crossbar signal as used on the GWR and a few other lines. Most had disappeared by 1890 but a few lasted until the turn of the century, as here on the Somerset & Dorset Railway.
Above: A 'Highball' signal still in use in southern Peru in 1977.
Right: A gantry at Southampton in 1966 with upper-quadrant semaphore signals. Ringed signals indicate entry to sidings.
Below: A 'somersault' signal as used by the GNR, which pioneered the use of the centrally pivoted semaphore arm. With this signal the arm was automatically thrown to danger if a control wire broke.

Many British railways consequently mistrusted movable spectacles, apprehensive that if a glass fell out there was nothing to deter a driver from taking the naked light of the fixed lamp as an 'all clear' aspect. In the north of the country they worried that heavy snow settling on the spectacles could have the same effect. A number of railways therefore persisted with a variety of signal designs relying on movable multi-lensed lamps long after Stevens' 1854 development in essentials of the standard British lower-quadrant semaphore signal, with fixed lamp, spectacle glasses embodied in the arm and a balance weight at the base of the operating rodding.

The British persisted with the dangerous practice of obscuring signals as assurance of a clear road ahead for forty years or more, until a catastrophic accident in heavy snow on the Great Northern in January 1876 glaringly focused the inherent risk of the danger signal not functioning. The Great Northern immediately accepted the recommendation of the Board of Trade's Inspector deputed to investigate the accident that previous signalling procedure be reversed. Until then the 'normal' signal aspect had been 'all clear' – i.e., with the arm obscured; it was only put to danger when a train movement needed protection. From 1876 onwards a signal was normally held at danger and cleared only as necessary to authorize a train movement (one should add that this change was not generally adopted by other European railways; in France particularly 'clear' was perpetuated as the 'normal' signal aspect). Since the advanced warning or distant signal was coming into fashion, the three-position semaphore was becoming redundant; hence the green aspect could supersede white to denote 'all clear'. The Great Northern also recognized that the recession of semaphore arms in a slotted signal post was a prime factor in the malfunctions of apparatus which brought about the 1876 disaster. It pioneered the general use of a centrally pivoted semaphore arm, located clear of the post and coupled to a balance weight which would automatically throw it to danger in the event of a control wire breakage.

Almost to the end of the nineteenth century Britain's railway companies had to be prodded out of either lethargy or sheer tight-fistedness to follow up improvements of safety. Their reluctance to lay out money on continuous braking has already

BLOCK SIGNALLING
AND TRACK CIRCUITING

Bit by bit from just after mid-century the division of a railway running line into successive blocks or sections, each of which had its point of entry protected by one stop signal and exit from which was governed by another, became the fundamental arrangement of railway signalling. 'Absolute' block working, now as then the cardinal principle of the system other than in special operating circumstances, dictated that only one train at a time be admitted to each block section. Thus the maintenance of safe geographical space between trains on the same line superseded control by time interval. 'Permissive' block working infringed the golden rule by allowing two or even more trains into one section in succession, but nowadays

been observed in a previous chapter. In several respects the signalling story is no different. Despite the moral of the 1876 disaster, forests of the old slotted signals and their white-light clear aspects survived until at length, in 1892, the Board of Trade enforced a code of practice which among other things made centrally balanced signal arms and the use of green as the 'all clear' nocturnal aspect mandatory.

It took just as long to standardize the shape and significance of signals within mainland European countries, where each railway had substantially followed its own bent. So far as France and Germany were concerned the powerful stimulus to take the confused situation firmly in hand was the Franco-Prussian war of 1870–71. Bismarck's new Imperial Railway administration was the quicker to react to the occasional delays inflicted on its long-distance military traffic, because enginemen directed to work beyond the boundaries of their own system got bemused by unfamiliar signalling. A universal signalling convention had been imposed on German railways by 1875, whereas the French – who, as described earlier, execrated railway inefficiency as a prime factor in their defeat – did not establish a standard code until 1885.

British and German semaphore signalling practice developed differently in one essential. Whereas British railways were by the second half of the century content with the basic 'stop', 'caution' and 'go' indications and were beginning to give drivers advance knowledge of the route they were to take at a junction, the

Germans preferred to multiply signal aspects to obtain a wider range of speed direction and to prescribe the necessary deceleration for a route divergence that way.

Another conspicuous difference between German and British signalling systems in the nineteenth century was the Germans' early preference for an upper-quadrant rather than a lower-quadrant display of the 'clear' semaphore aspect. One practical advantage was that a raised signal arm could be guaranteed to fall back to the danger position in the event of a control wire breakage.

Above left: French signalling in the 1880s. An 0-4-2 locomotive on the Nord railway prepares to pass a signal turned edge-on to the track – the normal all-clear indication.
Below: The signalbox at London Bridge station in 1866, fitted with manual controls in an interlocking system patented by John Saxby. Block bell telegraph instruments are visible in the background.
Below right: Block signalling instruments in the No. 1 Camden signalbox on the LMS during the days of semaphore signalling. The signals and points were electrically controlled.

its use is generally limited by European railways to special situations where track capacity needs to be maximized and traffic is anyway slow-moving – on the reception tracks leading to a freight marshalling yard, for instance, or in a station where a platform is long enough to accommodate a pair of trains head to tail.

European railways were much slower to adopt block signalling than they need have been. The first essential, concentration of the controls for all points and signals in an area, was realized with the evolution of the earliest British signalboxes during the 1850s. The next step, the interlocking of point- and signal-operating mechanisms to prevent the setting up of routes with which signal aspects conflicted, was initiated by the Englishman Austin Chambers as early as 1843. Another English pioneer, John Saxby, patented a version which was installed in the London area at Bricklayers Arms in 1856. Three years later, on the north side of London at Kentish Town, Austin Chambers installed the first fully perfected example of mechanical interlocking which prevented the clearing of any signals until a previous train movement had been completed and the points had been correctly re-set.

That left unsolved the vital need of instant communication between signalboxes in charge of adjoining block sections. And it was here that railways were yet again slow to adopt what evolving technology had to offer. As far back as 1837 the electric needle telegraph had been devised by William Fothergill Cooke and Charles Wheatstone. The telegraph was a visual, not a speaking, device: each letter of the alphabet was represented by a degree of deflection of the needle and it was claimed that a competent operator would work up a transmission and deciphering rate of at least fifty characters a minute.

Several tentative practitioners of the Cooke and Wheatstone invention in the late 1830s and early 1840s included the Great Western, who installed it between Paddington and Slough. Straight away the Paddington telegraph office attracted as much interest in the capital as, in a later telecommunications age, the city's Broadcasting House or Post Office Tower. The Duke of Wellington headed the nobility who hastened to see this new wonder in action and was reported 'much pleased' by what he saw. The immediate snag inhibiting rapid and widespread adoption of the Cooke and Wheatstone needle

telegraph was the prevalence of illiteracy. Far too many stationmasters and signalmen could neither read nor write, let alone decipher a needle code, and that was still a problem until well into the 1850s.

The 1850s and 1860s were seminal in the evolution of the block signalling system in Europe. The single-stroke block bell telegraph system was devised by Charles Vincent Walker of the South Eastern Railway in 1851. With that the routine messages, which had to be exchanged by signalmen to ensure that a train could be safely despatched from one signalbox block section to another, could be standardized into an easily assimilable, Morse-like code of bell signals. Refined over the years, this bell code was the basic medium for regulation of traffic between signalbox block sections for the rest of the mechanical signalling era, though the single-needle telegraph survived as a supplementary means of communication long after Bell's invention of the telephone. To answer a telephone a signalman would probably have to take his eyes off his instruments, whereas an experienced man would instinctively pick up telegraph messages by mentally decoding the graduated ticks of its flickering needle without moving from his lever frame.

The next of the significant British pioneers was Edward Tyer. As a precursor of the track circuiting of nearly half a century later, to which we will come later in the chapter, Tyer devised in 1852 a means

of automatically registering to a signalman the presence of a train in his block section. This was a treadle mounted just inside the running rail, depression of which by the wheel flanges of a passing train completed electrical contacts and actuated a visual apparatus in the signalbox. While a treadle at the entrance to a section announced the arrival of a train, another at the exit served usefully to advise that it was leaving the block. Tyer's next contribution, in 1854, was a so-called lock-and-key commutator which compelled neighbouring signalmen to attend their instruments simultaneously for an exchange of messages and to check that there was mutual acceptance and understanding. Then for London's Metropolitan Railway Charles Ernest Spagnoletti conceived in 1863 the signalman's first visual aid – generally known as a block instrument – which kept men in adjoining cabins continually advised of the state of each running line as a result of their mutual traffic regulating decisions.

But, as already indicated, European railways by and large reacted very torpidly to most of these clearly valuable reinforcements of railway operating efficiency as well as safety. The first objection was the obvious one: their adoption would cost money on which there was no easily quantifiable return for the shareholders or State. Just as powerful a deterrent, though, was that practically every responsible railway engineer had been grounded in mechanical engineering and regarded the

EARLY TRAFFIC CONTROL

In the earliest days of the railways signalling and control was done by hand, and a signalman was a kind of traffic policeman on points duty. As the railway networks themselves became more complex, precise signalling became more involved and mechanized. Practice varied considerably from country to country, but what remained constant until the modern era was the high level of manpower which was required to keep trains running smoothly and safely.

The use of telegraphy enabled the signalman in his control box to know what was happening further up the line, and made block signalling possible. Before then signalmen were dependent upon what their own eyes showed them. This station at Landres near Nancy in eastern France shows the arrangement on a French station at the time that block signalling was introduced in the 1880s, and semaphore-style block signals have been installed side by side with the old signals. This has not affected the large number of

signalboxes – three – required to control one small segment of track. Two boxes each controlled a half of the station and the area immediately beyond it (shown in the drawing by the yellow and blue tracks); the third is placed where a group of sidings and a private line to a factory all rejoin the main line (its control area is shown in green). Each box is responsible for a few points, the signals with them and the signals controlling the traffic into and out of the station. The points were operated by station crews who would walk out to them equipped with whistles, flags and a keen eye for the trains. The signals pivoted on their axes, so that the message was to be read only if it faced the driver; otherwise the signal was set parallel to the track and indicated 'all clear'.

French practice was centred on the stations, as it is to a large extent still

so today. For safety reasons junctions and signals were not originally built out in the country. All the points were located within or just outside the station, and the lines would run out parallel, often diverging several miles away. The boxes, then, were based on the station platforms and the operators were station staff. Level crossings were managed by special keepers who lived by them.

Although the precise organization of signalboxes differed, it was common practice in all countries that a box could only control the area in its immediate vicinity.

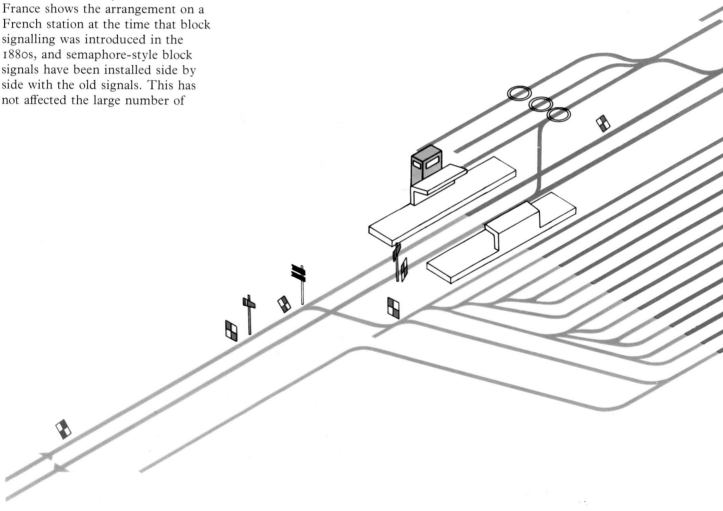

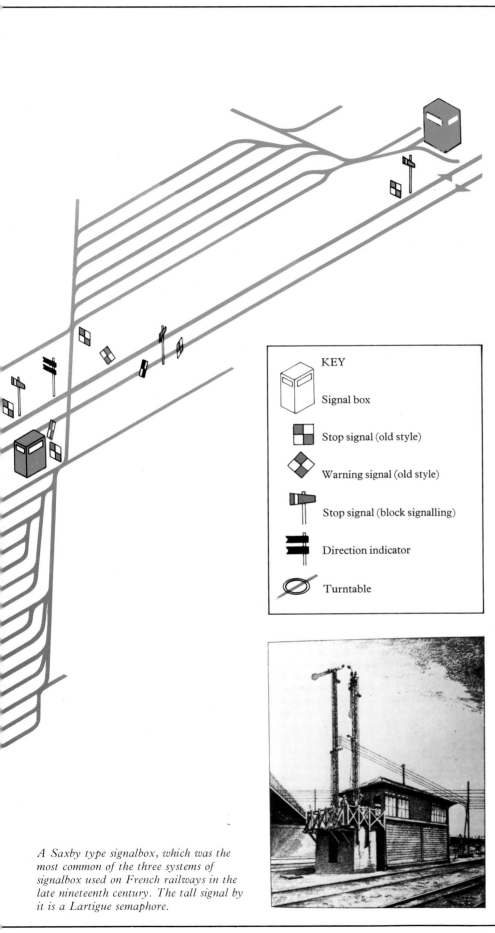

KEY

Signal box

Stop signal (old style)

Warning signal (old style)

Stop signal (block signalling)

Direction indicator

Turntable

A Saxby type signalbox, which was the most common of the three systems of signalbox used on French railways in the late nineteenth century. The tall signal by it is a Lartigue semaphore.

new technologists of electricity as unreliable upstarts. Rare was a railway like the Nord of France, whose Henri Lartigue had had experience in telegraphy and whose block telegraph system was developed in France alongside that of Edward Tyer's.

Both Britain and France needed Government intervention to enforce the block signalling system on all well-trafficked lines. By 1873, when the British Government first stepped in, though at that stage merely to demand progress reports, only three of the country's companies – the South Eastern, London Chatham & Dover and London Brighton & South Coast – had all their double-track route mileage under absolute block system control. The rest, even such major concerns as the London & North Western, could report little more than a 50 per cent installation. It was 1889 before a further Regulation of Railways Act made block working in conjunction with interlocking a statutory requirement. When block working was made mandatory in France in 1881, the only railway with more than 1,000 route-miles (1,600 km) already converted to the system was the PLM; the Nord could show no more than 350 route-miles (560 km), the Ouest, Paris-Orléans and Est even less, the Midi and Etat none at all.

British signalling practice and mid-century signalling inventions were widely adopted in many details by other railways. The most common variance is conspicuously perpetuated to this day by the location of signalling panels within the wayside station buildings of such railway systems as the French, Italian and Swiss, whereas the British developed separate signalbox buildings. To take Italy as an example of how the difference originated, there the telegraph all but ante-dated the supersession of hand signals by mechanical signals. Consequently a station's pointsmen worked as directed by the telegraph operator, who gradually assumed the status of stationmaster, or *capo stazione*. As station layouts enlarged and became more complex, and Italian railways acquired their first British-designed interlocking signal lever frames in the 1870s and 1880s, the signalling work itself became a separate job. But the responsibility for security of the block section remained with the stationmaster and the signalman worked to his direction.

The last major signalling advance of the nineteenth century was the perfection of track circuiting, though yet again the railways were shamefully slow in taking it up. After W. R. Sykes' first experiments on the London Chatham & Dover Railway in the early 1870s, there were comparatively few applications of it until the second decade of the twentieth century. Then a horrifying Midland Railways collision which culminated in a fire at Hawes Junction in the Yorkshire Pennines on Christmas Eve 1910 drove that company to widespread installation of track circuiting, and other railways belatedly followed suit.

As opposed to the intermittent recording of a train's passage on earlier mechanical devices, electrical track circuiting detected its movement continuously. A running line was divided into sections insulated from each other, each section corresponding spatially to the location of signals within the block, and within each section a weak electric current passed through the rails energized an electro-magnet. Passage of a train short-circuited the current throughout the former's presence in the section. The resultant de-energization of the electro-magnet could be exploited electrically to lock the signalbox controls of points and signals conflicting with its passage, and to record its presence continually on illuminated signalbox layout diagrams as it moved from one track-circuited berth to another. In present-day electronic remote-control signalling the track circuit is the basic activator of a wide range of automatic controls and signalmen's visual aids. It is, in fact, the pivotal component of all modern signalling.

At the turn of the century railway signal engineers were at last on terms with electricity and beginning to recognize its revolutionary possibilities. The fading 1890s saw the first practical examples of power-worked points and signals, both straight electrical and electro-pneumatic, and the early twentieth century the first installation of automatic signalling actuated by track circuitry.

NINETEENTH-CENTURY NORTH AMERICAN PRACTICE: SAFETY SECOND

Chapter Four left the North American signalling scene at the mid-1860s point where the New Jersey Canal & Railroad accepted that traffic control by time interval and train despatcher was no longer secure enough for busy lines and had established the continent's first block

signalling system and interlocked signalling plant – though the first perfected, permanent installation of the latter at East Newark, New Jersey, did not materialize until February 1875, by which time the railroad was part of the Pennsylvania system. Five years earlier another American, William Robinson, had also hit on the idea of track circuiting and impressed another constituent of the Pennsylvania, the Philadelphia & Erie, into its almost immediate adoption in 1872.

But as in Europe, and for the same reasons, railroads were in no hurry to

Top: Instrument panel on a pneumatic signalling system at Pittsburgh on the Pennsylvania Railroad, about 1890. All movements were displayed electrically on the track model above the keyboard. Above: A US train despatcher passes up the train orders to the engineer of a moving train 'on the fly'. Above right: Two illustrations of American three-position semaphore signals, with (above) the upper signal in the vertical all-clear position and (below) the Santa Fe 'Super Chief' passing under an angled caution signal.

of the country's railroads still preferred to work purely to timetable and train despatcher's orders – some just by timetable.

Extraordinarily, in view of the rapid growth and size of the national railroad network, the American companies did not really begin to rationalize their signalling systems until the last decade of the nineteenth century. Then the economy was buoyant and the railroads were prepared to spend some money. The first step was to standardize the signals themselves, which the American Railway Association finally achieved in 1897.

Many separate distant signals were eliminated after the turn of the century when the heavily trafficked railroads in the eastern US started totting up the money they could save by combining stop and caution signal functions in a three-position semaphore. The pioneers were the Baltimore & Ohio and Pennsylvania, with lower-quadrant signals in which the caution aspect was 45° from the horizontal, all clear the full 90° parallel to the signal post. Very early in the twentieth century, however, there was a switch to the upper quadrant arrangement, in which the Germans and later the Belgians were the European trend-setters; in the American version the fully vertical display was retained as the all-clear aspect. The Americans took just as long as European railways to substitute a green for an indeterminate white as the after-dark all-clear aspect, but they were quicker than the Europeans to follow the lead of the New York, New Haven & Hartford around 1899 in reserving yellow or amber for caution.

The annals have it that the Cumberland Railway installed a telephone for train despatching as early as 1882, but it was the second decade of the twentieth century before American railroads generally superseded the telegraph with the telephone. Conviction that a train order transcribed from the telegraph was less vulnerable to misconstruction was ingrained, even though the second generation of despatchers was obviously not bothered to work up the same proficiency with the Morse key as their seniors. Too often a characteristically rapid message from a veteran would have a recent recruit either missing words altogether or else fudging up the drift from memory in the hope of masking his ineptitude. Starting-point of a general move into telephone

spend their money on new-fangled gadgetry which would make not a dollar of difference to their revenue, especially as these innovations coincided with the financial panic of 1873 and the crippling rate wars of the 1870s and 1880s. A number of companies did think mechanical interlocking worth the money, especially after 1885 when one state administration after another relaxed its rule that all trains must stop before negotiating a flat diamond crossing if the signals protecting such an intersection were effectively interlocked.

Several eastern US railroads did order track-circuitry installations in the 1870s and 1880s, but few were of the continuous, fully electrical type outlined earlier in this chapter. Most of them were limited to station areas and merely prevented the agent or signalling tower at one station from releasing the despatch signal of the next station in the rear until a train had cleared the control area of the first installation. The track between the two control points was not covered by circuitry and offer and acceptance of trains was still by telegraph. The overwhelming majority

despatching was the Burlington's installation of the system between Aurora and Galesburg early in 1908.

In the dawn of the twentieth century American railroads were already distinguished by one or two impressive power signalling plants. The showpiece was the St Louis Union Terminal, built as the dead-end apex of a triangle which had the seven-track east-west main line as its base and all thirty-two tracks of which were usable for arrivals and departures in either main-line direction. Here the highly complex layout's signal and point operation was entirely electro-pneumatic. On the New York Subway fully automatic signalling, similarly powered, was already in commission. But between the provision for intensively worked areas of railroad, such as these, and that for lightly trafficked stretches of line – even of trunk line – in rural America, there was a world of

BASIC MECHANICAL (SEMAPHORE) AND COLOUR-LIGHT SIGNALS

The first semaphore arm signals were adopted by the London & Croydon Railway in 1841. They were accompanied by red, green and white lights for use at night, but it was not until the 1930s that colour-light signals alone began to come into general use.

Initially semaphore signals operated in the lower quadrant, moving through three positions from the horizontal downwards. But eventually many railways evolved a form of upper-quadrant signalling, since here at least the arm would drop back into the horizontal danger position in the event of a control wire breakage. The two-position semaphore became increasingly popular with the advent of separate 'distant' signals to give cautionary indications (in Britain and Italy, for instance, distant signals have a yellow-painted arm with a vee notch at the end). The Americans, however, continued to use a three-position semaphore.

Semaphore signals appear in different combinations and colours, and, like colour-light signals, can control a variety of situations, such as block sections, junctions or shunting. The block system – a simplified form of which is illustrated here – arose from the need to control trains running on the same line and superseded control by time interval.

The illustration presents in diagrammatic form a few of the basic signals (both mechanical and colour-light) that might be used in a three-block section in the USA, UK, West Germany, Italy and France, together with the colour-light signals for a four-block section in Britain. A train in the bottom left is entering the first (green) section, while the train at top right is passing through the third (red) section. The signals are interlocked, so that the one behind the train at top right immediately goes to 'stop' and the one preceding that to 'caution', while the first one indicates 'proceed', allowing the following train to enter the first section. The four-aspect signal (here illustrated as a British colour-light signal) allows a braking distance over two cautionary signals.

Caution

Preliminary Caution

Proceed

Proceed

British Four-Aspect Colour-Light Signals

Three-Aspect Signals

difference, and a gulf still to be closed. That is sharply pointed by the Interstate Commerce Commission's railroad safety statistics for the period, which show the number of railroad passenger fatalities rising from 303 in 1902 to 537 in 1905, and passenger injuries from 6,089 to just over 10,000 in the same period. Worse still, the odds on a train crewman's survival seem to have been little better than that of an active soldier's; in 1904 one in every 120 lost his life and one in nine suffered some injury.

Left: Interior of a manually operated British signalbox, showing signal and point levers indentifiable by their colours – red for a stop signal, yellow for a distant signal and black for points. On the shelf above are block telegraph instruments.
Right: West German semaphore signals at Bullay with a 'Pacific' behind.

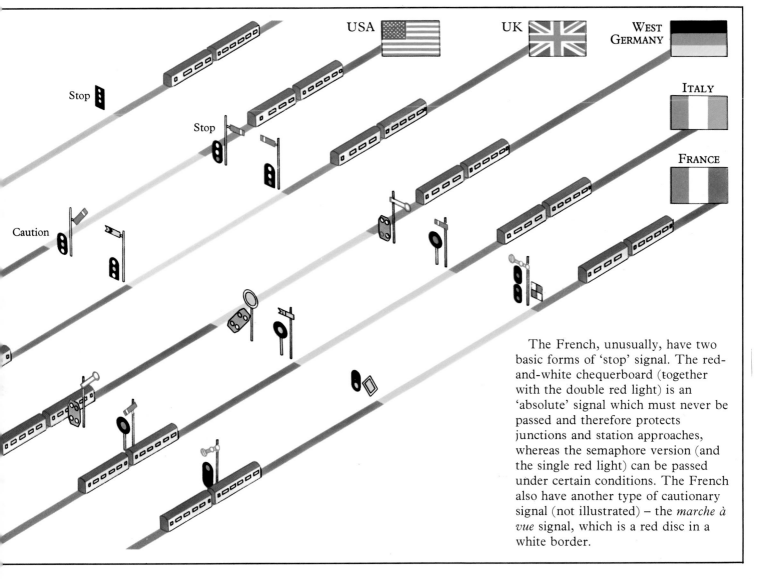

The French, unusually, have two basic forms of 'stop' signal. The red-and-white chequerboard (together with the double red light) is an 'absolute' signal which must never be passed and therefore protects junctions and station approaches, whereas the semaphore version (and the single red light) can be passed under certain conditions. The French also have another type of cautionary signal (not illustrated) – the *marche à vue* signal, which is a red disc in a white border.

ENTER ELECTRIC RAILWAYS

Faraday's discovery in the 1820s that electricity could create continuous motion, and subsequent inventions of the first electric motors and dynamos, prompted several attempts to power railed vehicles electrically in the mid-nineteenth century. Some were essentially models – in fact, the first effectively demonstrated electric locomotive was a miniature. This was a 3 hp narrow-gauge midget which the German engineer Werner von Siemens displayed at the 1879 Berlin Exhibition. Drawing low-voltage current from a centre live rail through a sliding pick-up shoe, it successfully perambulated some thirty visitors at a time on three knifeboard-shaped trucks around a 900 ft (275 m) circle of track at about 4 mph (6 km/h). It was a primitive machine with no graduated control of power, just a simple switchgear, but it initiated far swifter technological development than that of steam in the previous fifty years.

First to be drawn to von Siemens' device in Germany and America were mining railway operators – understandably, because of its mechanical simplicity and minimized safety hazards below ground – but within a few years it had inspired the first electric passenger trams. In Germany a short line was established at Lichterfelde in 1881 and in Britain an energetic and inventive electrical engineer named Magnus Volk won the local authority's assent to lay a 2 ft (610 mm) gauge railway along the foreshore of Brighton, the South Coast resort. Volk's enterprise, which is still operational (though its gauge was later widened to 2 ft 8½ in or 825 mm), is usually acclaimed as the first railway to be built specifically for electric traction, but its vehicles were first cousins to horse-drawn trams, adapted to take 110 V power from a third rail.

Volk's railway generated its own current and the very low voltage sufficed both for the motors of his vehicles and the short distance they had to run. It would not do for longer electrified rail routes because current loses strength the further it travels; persistence with such weak voltage would have incurred heavy cost in the provision of a frequent succession of feeder stations.

By the 1880s higher-voltage power was starting to come on tap from either coal-fired or water-driven generating plant – the USA's first hydro-electric plant was established in Wisconsin in 1882 and Niagara Falls were harnessed soon afterwards – although it was some years more before the science of transmitting the power stations' output over considerable distances was mastered. That immediately broadened the electric railway's horizon.

Use of higher voltage raised obvious objections to use of a naked current-supply rail at ground level. Early in the decade various Americans were experimenting with wire conductors in sub-surface conduits, but the method finally favoured was the overhead wire. An expatriate Belgian sculptor who somehow became absorbed with electric tramway technology, Charles Van Depoele, is usually

Right: City and South London train at Borough Station in 1922. The stock dates from 1890, when the line – the first underground electric railway – was opened. Below: The world's first electric locomotive to be effectively demonstrated was made by Werner von Siemens and ran at the Berlin Exhibition in 1879.

credited with the perfection of overhead current transmission around 1885, though he was certainly not the only American to experiment with it. The original system employed a trolley on top of a flexible, roof-mounted conductor arm to collect the current – hence Americans' adoption of 'trolley car' as a synonym for the European tram.

An American who had still greater influence on the evolution of the electric passenger railway was a young US Navy midshipman named F.J. Sprague, an inventive genius who began to apply himself to electrical engineering in the late 1870s. In 1884 he successfully devised electric motors which could be fitted to the existing bogies of New York Elevated Railway cars. Still more significant was his 1897 application to the Chicago's South Side Elevated of a method of controlling the power and electrical auxiliaries of several coupled vehicles in unison from one cab in the leading car. In other words it was Sprague who pioneered that key component of the modern short-haul passenger railway, the multiple-unit train.

Some years before Sprague hit on that idea, his earlier work and that of Van Depoele had set off an explosive tramway system development in the USA. In 1887 there were only ten electric tramways in the USA (and nine in Europe). By 1890 construction contracts had been signed for over 200 new American systems.

In 1882 Sprague had been in London and pondered the feasibility of electrifying the capital's first sub-surface railway. This was the Metropolitan District, the first stretch of which had been completed by the 'cut-and-cover' method just below street

A Swiss Class Be 4/4 Bo-Bo electric locomotive (a type that dates from 1927) winds down from Nesslau to Wil on the Bodensee–Toggenburg line in 1973.

level between Bishops Road (now Paddington) and Farringdon Street, in the City of London, at the start of 1863. Initially the Metropolitan District was steam-worked. It was not in the event to be London's first electric railway, nor did the first such London project adopt Sprague's practices. The $3\frac{1}{2}$ mile (5.6 km) City & South London, opened from the capital's commercial heart under the Thames to Stockwell in 1890, besides being the first electric underground line in the world, was the first to haul its trains with a fleet of locomotives – diminutive, barrel-organ-shaped machines with a top speed of 25 mph (40 km/h) which worked off 500 volts direct current (dc) via a third-rail supply. Up until then the use of electric locomotives had been confined to a few American experiments.

Ac v Dc

The early tramways employed dc traction motors and low voltages – that is, up to about 500 or 600 V. By the turn of the century, however, industrial supplies of alternating current (ac) at high voltage were being generated in several countries. The normal frequency adopted for these supplies was 50 or 60 Hz (cycles per second), but for technical reasons this posed considerable problems in traction motor design. Consequently, most early electric railways preferred either to transform and rectify the current before it was fed into the conductor, so that it would reach the traction motors as dc, or, from the early 1900s, to use a frequency of $16\frac{2}{3}$ Hz, single-phase, which mitigated the difficulties of ac motor design.

The full frequency and power of the industrial supply could theoretically have been channelled into the conductor and modified on board the traction unit for feeding to dc traction motors, but the practical deterrent was the cumbersome-

ness of transformers and mechanical converters at that stage of electric technology. After the Second World War it was a different matter. The emergence first of mercury arc rectifiers, then of very compact solid state semi-conductor rectifiers coupled with advanced transformer design, allowed the French to build on pre-war German work and evolve lightweight but extremely powerful dc-motored locomotives that could take a direct supply of 25 kV 50 Hz current. That development materially cheapened the first cost of railway electrification because a high-voltage ac traction current supply allows lighter catenary, or overhead wire system, and a smaller number of ground feeder points, and from it much of today's railway electrification has stemmed.

Especially in Central Europe, however, a number of engineers at the turn of the century opted to battle with the problems of operating with the full industrial frequency and three-phase ac motors. In Germany this was coupled with an

Wheel Notation:
Diesel and Electric

For diesel and electric locomotives the number of axles is counted: the driving axles are given letters (A = 1, B = 2, C = 3, D = 4) and the carrying axles numbers. An 'o' after the letter means that the driving axles are

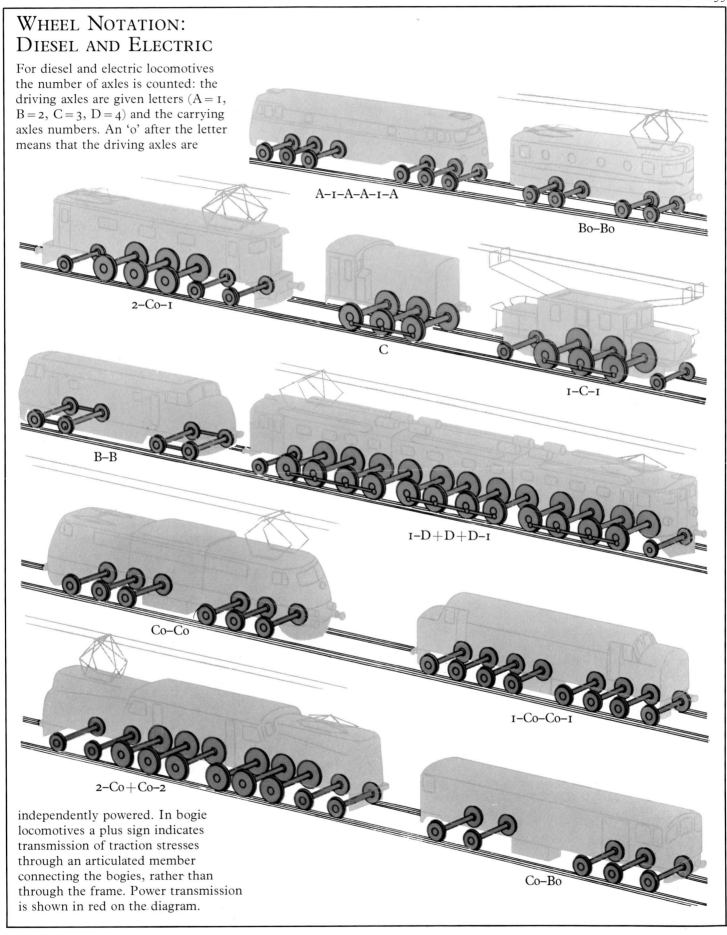

A–1–A–A–1–A

Bo–Bo

2–Co–1

C

1–C–1

B–B

1–D+D+D–1

Co–Co

1–Co–Co–1

2–Co+Co–2

Co–Bo

independently powered. In bogie locomotives a plus sign indicates transmission of traction stresses through an articulated member connecting the bogies, rather than through the frame. Power transmission is shown in red on the diagram.

adventurous pursuit of high speed by an industrial consortium titled the *Studiengesellschaft für Elektrische Schnellbahnen.*

The German research culminated in some extraordinary exploits in 1901 and 1903. The setting was a well-aligned and easily graded 14½ mile (23.3 km) military railway between Marienfelde and Zossen, near Berlin, which was electrified at 15 kV ac; the protagonists were two purpose-built fifty-seat railcars each with 1,000 hp traction equipment, one furnished by Siemens & Halske and the other by AEG. At that early date experience of vehicle behaviour at high speed was negligible. Moreover, the lightly laid track of the military railway had not been fettled up for what was in mind, so the first essays with the heavy and cumbersome railcars was all but catastrophic. Above 75 mph (120 km/h) they pitched and rolled drunkenly, to the accompaniment of violent arcing as their triple-pan collectors lost contact with the three vertically spaced wires of the three-phase conductor, which was unusually erected at the side of the track, not over it. At 100 mph (160 km/h) one of the cars actually bounced a bogie clean off and then back on the track, doing the latter such severe damage that the trials were promptly suspended until the line had been rebuilt to a stronger specification and the cars' bogies had been modified. That done, in October 1903 the cars were unleashed again and progressively pushed up to a peak speed of 130.5 mph (210 km/h). In the afterglow of these records electrification of the Berlin–Hamburg main line for service by high-speed railcars was canvassed, but eventually rejected as too costly.

Normally three-phase ac electrification employed two, not three, separate conductor wires – one of its two major disadvantages, the other being the characteristics of ac traction motors, which debar infinite variation of track speed on the move. Nevertheless, one three-phase system initiated in 1901, that of Piedmont in northern Italy, was not completely converted to the standard 3 kV dc system of the remainder of the Italian State Railways until the 1970s. This Italian electrification was the work of the Hungarian firm which dominated early three-phase technology, Ganz of Budapest. Its chief engineer, Kalman Kando, is almost the only individual – as opposed to companies – to make a durable mark on the earliest electric railway history.

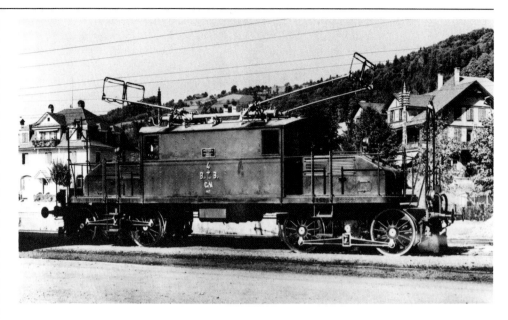

SWITZERLAND AND ITALY
LEAD THE WAY

Electrification touched US main-line railways before 1900, when the city fathers enjoined the Baltimore & Ohio in 1894–5 to eradicate steam from its surface and subsurface lines traversing Baltimore, and 675 V dc overhead conductor was erected. Thereafter 1,440 hp four-axle locomotives ushered trains through the city with their steam locomotives still in place but merely simmering. Electrification of the tunnel approaches to New York's monumentally rebuilt Grand Central station had to be conceded by the New York Central after a catastrophic collision under Park Avenue in January 1902, which was blamed on the clouding of signals by locomotive exhausts.

The New York terminal area was electrified on a low-voltage dc third-rail system, but in 1907 the New York, New Haven & Hartford erected 11 kV single-phase 15 Hz ac catenary from Woodlawn, the point of that railroad's junction with the third-rail, to Stamford; this was later projected to New Haven, 72 miles (116 km) from New York. The New Haven enterprise was the USA's first main-line electrification proper. Its 1,000 hp double-bogie locomotives, built by Baldwin-Westinghouse and equipped for multiple-unit control in pairs, could rouse a 60 mph (100 km/h) pace on express passenger trains, though at a price of boisterous riding which soon had to be remedied by adding single-axle bogies at each end.

The crucial testimony to the potential power and economy of electric traction in

Above: An early Swiss electric locomotive (an F/2 double-bogie machine) built by Brown Boveri and introduced on the Burgdorf–Thun Railway in 1910.
Right, above: The US Great Northern Railway electrified its route through the Cascade Mountains in 1909 after problems with fumes in the steep Cascade Tunnel.
Right, below: Early Italian electric locomotive heads a Rome–Naples Rapido.

both fast passenger and heavy freight haulage had come a year earlier than the New Haven inauguration, when the Simplon Tunnel route in Europe was opened with 3 kV, three-phase 15 Hz ac current in 1906. Brown Boveri, the other major practitioner of the three-phase system at the turn of the century, was the electrical engineering concern involved in the Simplon scheme.

Already, however, a Swiss engineer named Behn-Eschenburg was perfecting 15 kV single-phase 16⅔ Hz ac traction and this technique was triumphantly applied to the Bern–Lötschberg–Simplon Railway. When the BLS was opened throughout in 1913, its new Oerlikon-built 2,000 hp locomotives, weighing only 90 tons, were immediately forging single-handed up the unremitting 1-in-37 gradients to the Lötschberg Tunnel at a steady 30 mph (50 km/h) with over 300 tons on their drawbar. In contrast it needed two steam locomotives weighing almost three times as much as the Lötschberg electric to heave little more than 200 tons up to the Gotthard Tunnel at 20 mph (32 km/h). A year later the Swiss Federal put electrification of the Gotthard route at 15 kV 16⅔ Hz in hand and the rapid conversion of the whole Swiss main-line network on that system – mostly achieved in the first decade after the end of the First World War – was launched (the Simplon route was converted to 15 kV in 1930). This Swiss pioneering was the model for 15 kV ac single-phase electrification in Germany and Austria.

The pace of Swiss electrification was strongly influenced by the country's lack of indigenous fuel but enviable hydro-electric potential. And elsewhere in Europe it was not merely electric traction's capability which stimulated an electrification drive after 1918. In France, for instance, war damage to the country's richest coalfields, aggravated by labour unrest, had sent the cost of coal soaring and made supplies so scarce that by the mid-1930s the French were compelled to import more than a third of their needs. Consequently, the government shared the railways' enthusiasm for electrification and promulgated a law of July 1920 encouraging the Orléans, Midi and PLM to embark on schemes embracing no less than 5,500 route-miles (8,850 km). There was a dual objective, for the railways' hydro-electric generating plant was to supply and cheapen power for industry and agriculture as well as trains. The plan was much too ambitious and it had become a dead letter by 1925, but by 1939 two of the radial trunk routes from Paris were under 1.5 kV dc wires – that to Bordeaux and the Spanish frontier at Hendaye, and the line to Brittany as far as Le Mans.

By 1939 the majority of European railway systems had converted one or more of their main lines to full electric operation of freight as well as passenger traffic – the conspicuous exception was Britain, although some other coal-rich countries such as Belgium and Czechoslovakia had barely opened their account by then. But every continent and sub-continent had at least some electrified mileage operative. In the USA abundance of cheap coal had also discouraged main-line electrification (so, in its turn, would over-cheap oil), except in the mountains of the West. In the Cascade Mountains the Great Northern had little option save to electrify in 1909, after numerous near-tragedies when steam engines gasping at the 1-in-45 gradient through the 2.6 mile (4.2 km) long Cascade Tunnel choked their passengers with sulphurous fumes. The GN example was followed on another transcontinental route by the Chicago, Milwaukee, St Paul

& Pacific, which inaugurated its first stretch of 3 kV dc in 1915 and by the end of that decade had nearly 650 route-miles (1,050 km) electrified in the Rocky and Bitter Root Mountains between Butte, Montana and the west coast. In the 1920s this was the longest, continuously electrified main line in the world.

The most compulsive electrifier of the inter-war years was Italy, after Mussolini had made autarchy and world technological supremacy two of his national goals. From the early 1930s onwards, with the aid of hydro-electric power, the Italian State Railways were electrifying at an annual average of 275 route-miles (443 km). At the same time the Fascist regime pressed to completion two brand-new, well-aligned railways which had

made very halting progress since their conception just before and after the First World War. These were the Rome–Naples and Florence–Bologna *Direttissime*, desperately needed bypasses of the sinuous and fiercely graded lines laid between each pair of cities in the previous century, when economy in earthworks was paramount; the new Rome–Naples line was finished in 1927, the Florence–Bologna in 1934.

The combined effect on the passenger service of electric traction and the shortening and smoothing of the routes between these cities was stunning. For the first quarter of the century Italian train travel had been about the most purgatorial in all Europe. For instance, in 1914 the fastest journey from Naples to Milan, 523

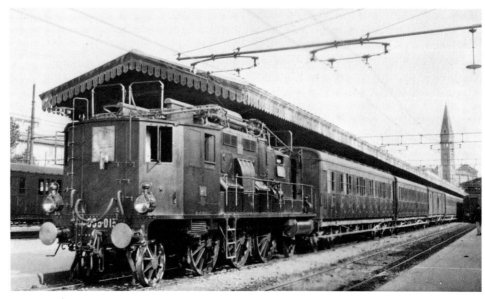

miles (842 km), dragged out seventeen hours or more, but by 1939 it was taking only eight. Opening of the Rome–Naples *Direttissima* had the best time between those cities cut at a stroke from 4 hours 25 minutes to 2 hours 50 minutes (by 1939 it was down to 1 hour 48 minutes, predicating a start-to-stop average speed of $72\frac{1}{2}$ mph [116.7 km/h] – one of the fastest scheduled runs in Europe at the outbreak of war). And in 1939 one could ride from Bologna to Florence in fifty-one minutes, as against almost $2\frac{1}{2}$ hours by the best train before the opening of the *Direttissima*. Not only were Italy's crack trains twice as fast as they had been on the eve of the First World War, but everywhere far more frequent – more than doubly so between Rome and Naples.

For three decades the world's railways had shown bafflingly little inclination to develop the high-speed potential of electric traction, displayed, however crudely and chancily, by the Germans at the start of the century. That lethargy was now being dispelled by the competitive pressures of the automobile and the emergent airliner. Just ahead of diesel traction's dazzling debut and conquest of US railroads by storm, as described in a subsequent chapter, the Pennsylvania had

electrified from New York to Washington in 1933–5 at 11 kV ac and, for its passenger services, invested in the first of the fabled and revered 4,620 hp Class GG-1 locomotives, which had 100 mph (160 km/h) capability. In 1934 French Railways commissioned a quartet of new 4,950 hp locomotives to explore the possibilities of

Above: A Milwaukee electric locomotive at Deer Lodge, Montana, in 1952.
Below: The famed Class GG-1, 4,620 hp electric locomotive heads a New York to Washington and Harrisburg express.
Above right: The all-Pullman 'Brighton Belle' electric multiple-unit on Britain's Southern Region.

machines with a substantially higher output than that of any preceding French design; and in 1938 one of these 2–Do–2s (the wheel arrangement which, in customary non-steam locomotive terminology, signifies that idle front and rear bogies enclose four independently motored driving wheels) was pushed up to 115 mph (185 km/h) on the Paris–Bordeaux main line during tests with a four-car train.

By then the Reichsbahn's streamlined diesel inter-city train-sets were crowding the top places in the European speed table, with Italian and Dutch electric services gaining ground on steam and closing up behind them. Nevertheless the Germans, planning electrification from Munich to Berlin (abortively because of the war and the country's later partition), were also absorbed in high-speed electric traction. It was Germany that unquestionably produced the most consummate electric locomotive design of the pre-Second World War era, the four 5,360 hp Class E19 1–Do–1s built by AEG (two) and Henschel (two) for the Reichsbahn in 1938–9. Sadly they never had the opportunity to show off their specified top speed of 140 mph (225 km/h) in public service, but on trial one achieved it and another demonstrated a maximum short-term output of well over

8,000 hp in hustling a 400 ton load up to 125 mph (200 km/h) within five minutes of a standing start.

The Italians staged the most spectacular finale to inter-war electrification progress. As tools for the greatly accelerated services, tabled with each extension of catenary, the Italian State Railways had preferred self-powered multiple-units to locomotive-hauled trains, and from 1936 onwards had built a range of three-car, 110-ton sets with 1,475 hp motors and 100 mph (160 km/h) capability (Classes ETR201 and ETR221). To signal the opening of the Florence–Bologna *Direttissima* the Minister of Communications and some hundred other guests were invited to sample the length of the new line in an ETR201 set on 20 July 1939.

Clearly some *tour de force* for the greater glory of the republic and Il Duce was pre-planned, since the catenary current had been upped from 3 kV to 4 kV for the day, but one wonders whether a trip quite so startling as that which eventually took place had been premeditated. The *Direttissima* is infinitely better aligned than the old route, but even so has quite frequent curves that check full speed. Those must have been treated pretty cavalierly, for the unit ran the whole 195.8 miles (315.1 km)

from Florence to Milan in 115¼ minutes at an average of 102 mph (164 km/h) start to stop, dismissing the 11 miles (17.7 km) of 1-in-106 grade up to the new line's 11.5 mile (18.5 km) Apennine Tunnel at a steady 85 mph (137 km/h) and touching 126 mph (230 km/h) in the flat Po Valley on the other side of the mountains. Not until the Japanese opened their first Shinkansen, the New Tokaido Line, in October 1964 did any train make a faster journey over such a distance.

URBAN AND SUBURBAN ELECTRIFICATION

Until this Italian inter-city exploitation of the concept, of course, the multiple-unit train had been virtually the preserve of the high-intensity metropolitan operations above and below ground. Their development was powerfully stimulated by perfection of electric traction. London was the only city to proceed from the model of the pioneering City & South London Railway to an extensive system of deep-level 'Tube' railways, all electrified from the outset, primarily because its substratum of blue clay was amenable to the tube tunnelling technique first conceived by Sir Marc Brunel (father of Isambard Kingdom Brunel) in 1818 and some forty

Above: A Swedish three-unit Class Dm3 electric locomotive of 5,500 hp, used to haul iron ore.
Left: An Italian ETR 200 series electric multiple-unit. In 1939 one of these trains covered the 195.8 miles from Florence to Milan at an average of 102 mph.
Above right: An electric Bo-Bo locomotive built for the Metropolitan Railway in 1904/5; these were used to haul trains which had to change to steam. The construction of London's underground railways was left to private enterprise, whereas many European urban (and main-line) railways were State-aided from the outset, giving them the character of an essential social service.

years later elaborated as the Greathead shield by the engineer of that name. Elsewhere in Europe the sub-surface urban railways were built just below the ground on the cut-and-cover system, like London's Metropolitan Railway – from which similar systems worldwide derived their categorization as 'Metros'. The Metropolitan itself began the change from steam to electric multiple-unit operation in 1903, by which time it had European counterparts in Budapest (opened in 1896), Paris (where the first line of what was to be the continent's most tightly knit city-centre network was opened in 1900) and Berlin (initiated in 1902).

Uniquely in Europe British governments had eschewed any entrepreneurial role in the expansion of main-line railways.

London likewise left the construction and financing of its underground railways to private enterprise. Not so the Continentals. The Paris authorities, for instance, footed most of their Metro's engineering bill from the start. So in mainland Europe urban as well as main-line railways always had to a greater or lesser degree the character of an essential social service, the part-financing or subsidization of which from the public purse came to be regarded almost as a law of nature.

Underground electric railways came to American cities slightly later than to those of Europe, for by the turn of the century one or two of the biggest were already served by impressive elevated railways. By 1897 New York's extraordinary 'El',

begun in 1897, was a 36 mile (58km) network operating over 300 steam locomotives and 1,000 passenger cars. Its operation was incredibly quick-fire. Despite the lack of any lineside signalling other than speed-limit indicators on sharp curves, the stumpy little 0-4-4 tank engines ran their trains at little more than a minute's headway from each other. Station stops were rigorously curtailed to fifteen seconds, so that one 9 mile (14.5km) route with twenty-five intermediate stations was covered in a standard time of thirty-five minutes, which represented a better end-to-end speed than the far shorter, pioneer electric underground line, the City & South London, could muster.

Needless to say the 'El's' engines had to be hammered incessantly to operate this sort of service, and by the end of the century New Yorkers had had enough of the aural nuisance as well as the daylong pollution of their city by cinder-laden exhausts. The 'El' was subsequently electrified and its lines sunk below ground from 1904 onwards (though a few elevated sections survive in outlying areas of the city), but before then the first New York Subway route had been put in hand in 1900. One unique feature of the New York system was its resort to quadruple track over the busiest underground sections so that limited-stop expresses could be run past all-stations locals.

Boston began to divert its Elevated Railway underground in 1901 and Philadelphia started a Subway in 1903. In contrast, Chicago was content with its downtown Elevated system until almost mid-century, opening its first Subway route in 1943.

By 1930 the USA headed the world table of electrified surface railways for route-mileage by virtue of its conversion of formerly steam-operated urban lines. At that juncture Britain was in eighth place behind Switzerland, Italy, France, Germany, Sweden and Austria, but ahead of all comers in one respect – the size of its fleet of electric multiple-unit vehicles. That was because its Southern Railway was developing on the southern side of London the most intricate and intensively operated short-haul passenger system in the world.

Competition from spreading urban street tramway systems was a powerful spur to electrify the busiest London commuter lines in the first decade of this century. The Great Eastern (GER) was the railway most heavily burdened with this traffic, steam-hauling some 200,000 north-east London passengers daily into or out of its Liverpool Street terminus and a third of them during each two-hour morning and evening peak, but it resisted the electrifiers' pressure. Its counter-argument was irresistible. The GER's mechanical engineer, James Holden, was encouraged to design and build a behemoth of a tank engine, a three-cylinder, ten-coupled machine nicknamed the 'Decapod', which demonstrated that it could accelerate a 300 ton train from rest to 30 mph (50 km/h) in thirty seconds – precisely the performance claimed for an electric multiple-unit of the period. The fact that after the electrification lobby had been trounced the ungainly 'Decapod' proved much too heavy for regular use was immaterial.

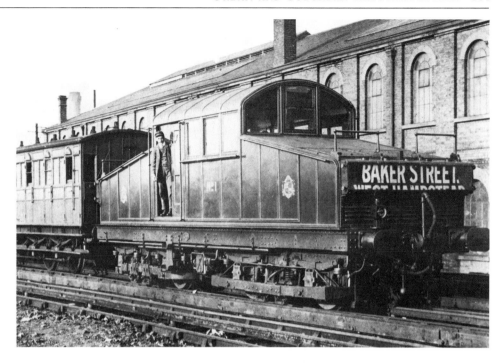

Thus in the 1920s, with north-east London's suburbia yet more densely populated, the GER saddled itself with a local steam service so intensive that in every daily peak it was funnelling twenty-four trains and some 20,000 passengers per hour over each of the two suburban tracks between Bethnal Green and the west-side platforms at Liverpool Street.

The railways on the south side of London, on the other hand, went electric – the London Brighton & South Coast from 1909 and the London & South Western (LSWR) from 1915. Of these the LSWR adopted a low-voltage dc third-rail current system; and it was that which the Southern Railway pursued after its absorption of all railways south and south-west of the capital in the 1923 'Big Four' Grouping of Britain's main-line companies. The Southern's choice was unsurprising, for its first General Manager was the former LSWR incumbent, Sir Herbert Walker.

Walker was arguably the outstanding British railway manager of the inter-war period. By the start of the 1930s he had electrified virtually the whole of the Southern's complex web of London suburban railways, embracing altogether about 900 track-miles (1,450 km), to create the biggest unified system of its kind in the world. Each extension of the third-rail was accompanied by introduction of a standard timetabling concept – the daylong operation of an immaculately repetitive service at frequent intervals (on some lines at less than half-hour headway) with standard multiple-unit train-sets, which were reversed as quickly as feasible at terminals to extract the maximum possible daily mileage from each set. It was the appeal of this Southern train service more than any other factor which induced the much quicker and more far-reaching sprawl of dormitory suburbs south of the Thames than on any other side of London.

The ribbon housing development began reaching all the way to the sea when the Southern moved on to electrification of its main lines from London to the Kent and Sussex coasts, beginning in 1932 with the Brighton line. As implied earlier in this chapter, they were strictly passenger service projects. To each of them the Southern applied exactly the same time-tabling and operating precepts as they had to the suburban lines, marrying reversible multiple-units – of appropriate internal design for the longer journeys and including three unique all-Pullman multiple-units for the 'Brighton Belle' train – to a repetitive regular-interval service.

It was not foreseen at the time, but here was the essence of BR's 'Inter-City' formula, with its economic justification of intensively used standard train-sets for a regular-interval service of strong commercial appeal. And not only the prototype for BR's contemporary passenger operation but for that of all the other European systems – the Belgian, the Dutch, the German, the Austrian and the Swiss – which have successively adopted the same concept since 1945.

THE ZENITH OF STEAM

In the first decade of this century European locomotive designers were put under inexorable pressure for faster, more powerful passenger locomotives. Not only were train weights for any given seating capacity advancing because of the influx of more capacious, more comfortably appointed coaches, but the impulse to travel was intensifying. To stimulate it managements were pressing for more speed. Consequently locomotives with a higher steaming capacity and a bigger firegrate area than the Atlantic layout allowed were an imperative requirement – provided that the tracks were strengthened, and some of the early nineteenth-century bridgework too, if there were to be a substantial growth of locomotive size and weight.

The most influential European designer in the transition from four- to six-coupled express engines was George Jackson Churchward of Britain's Great Western Railway. Uniquely for his day he did not build on accepted local practice to satisfy a short-term operational specification; he embarked upon a step-by-step evaluation of the best in contemporary world technology so as to evolve a limited range of standard locomotive designs that would be a competent match for the foreseeable traffic demands of ten to fifteen years in the future. Thus the GWR did not rely upon received evidence of de Glehn compound Atlantic performance in France, but bought three engines of this type for assessment alongside some simple-expansion Atlantics which Churchward had constructed for comparison. And it was from the American design schools that Churchward imported his characteristic tapered-boiler shell, which he married with a big Belpaire-type firebox.

For the general future of the high-speed steam locomotive the most important product of Churchward's exploratory period was his recognition that efficient steam generation was no more than halfway house to sound performance. 'You can always get steam into a cylinder,' as he himself once put it, 'the problem is to get it out.' The solution was enlargement of steam passages and supersession of traditional slide-valves with long-travel piston valves; with the latter an engine could be worked on an early cut-off of steam supply to the cylinders, so that more of the propulsion could be effected by the expansion properties of steam. Obviously this made for more economical working. Equally it made for a very much freer-running machine at speed.

The de Glehn compound Atlantics had clearly outshone Churchward's own Atlantics in only one particular – smoother riding, which was a function of their well-balanced four-cylinder layout. As a result Churchward adopted a four-cylinder simple-expansion arrangement for his first express passenger masterpiece, the 'Star' class 4–6–0 of 1907. After these engines had been superheated from 1908 onwards they were without British equal for power and economy until the 1920s. Time and again they were logged at a steady 70 mph (115 km/h) or more on the level with 450 tons of train on their drawbar and shown capable of sustaining over 60 mph (100 km/h) up perceptible gradients with similar tonnages. By the time the Great Northern was levering Britain into the 4–6–2 era, in 1922, Churchward's GWR successor, C. B. Collett, had developed the

A Milwaukee Railroad 4-6-2 leads a local passenger train out of Chicago in 1952. The 4-6-2 became known as the 'Pacific' after a series built for the Missouri Pacific in 1902.

came the genesis of the US express passenger Pacific in the Pennsylvania Railroad's Class K with 6 ft 3 in (1,905 mm) driving wheels. By 1914 this Pennsylvania design had evolved via some intermediate stages into the remarkable Class K4s Pacific, of which no fewer than 425 were constructed between then and 1927. Like the 'Castles' on Britain's Great Western, the K4s Pacifics shouldered the brunt of the Pennsylvania's front-rank passenger operation into the early 1940s, long after other US railroads were deploying much bigger machines on their principal trains. In the late 1930s, after some of the K4s Pacifics had been modified with poppet valves and had had their steam passages redesigned to maximize the steam-generating potential of their tubby boilers, they were frequently timed at close on 100 mph (160 km/h) over the level between Fort Wayne and Chicago with trains like the 'Broadway Limited', the 'Manhattan Limited' and the lightweight 'Detroit Arrow'. In some memorable tests of 1938 a K4s accelerated a 1,005 ton train from a standing start to 92 mph (149 km/h).

For severely graded main lines the 4–6–2 was deficient in adhesion, however, and here an eight-coupled arrangement was essential. To fulfil a Japanese specification in 1897 Baldwin had created the 2–8–2 by adding a trailing bogie to the by-then well-established 2–8–0 concept so as to accommodate a wide, deep firebox, and in 1905 the Northern Pacific decided that the Japanese example was the one to follow in its mountain territory. It was the first US exponent of a type which, known as the 'Mikado' in recognition of its Japanese association, was built to the tune of 14,000 or more by 1930. Two years earlier, in 1903, the Santa Fe inaugurated the 2–10–2 layout with some Vauclain

'Star' into a bigger and still more effective 4–6–0 type, the 'Castle'; and the 'Castle' yielded few points to any British Pacific under either power or speed headings until British 4–6–2 design was fully refined in the 1930s by Gresley on the London & North Eastern and Stanier on the London Midland & Scottish.

In the United States the first venture into a bigger format than the Atlantic was the 2–6–2. It appealed to Mid-West railroads as a natural extension of the 2–6–0 which so many of them operated, and its origin in that area was responsible for the 2–6–2 arrangement's 'Prairie'

nickname. But, although the Santa Fe Railroad built as many as 235 such engines, most 2–6–2 operators found that the single-axle leading bogie was not thoroughly trustworthy at speed. The significant event was the American Locomotive Co.'s 1902 construction of a batch of 4–6–2s for the Missouri Pacific – not the first engines of this wheel arrangement to take American tracks, but the first series, hence the fact that it was these engines which inspired the 'Pacific' tag for 4–6–2s the world over.

The Missouri Pacific engines were styled for mixed traffic use, but a year later

tandem compound locomotives from Baldwin, but the first 2–10–2s were prone to mishap on curves and this format had few adherents until its stability had been improved by a new design of leading bogie in 1912.

The 2–8–0, 2–8–2 and 2–10–2 became and remained essentially freight haulers throughout their American careers. It was the Chesapeake & Ohio (C&O) which inspired the near-standard express passenger type of the country's chief mountain main lines in the first quarter of the new century. Rejecting the 2–8–2 as inherently unsuited to speed, the C&O had the American Locomotive Co. (ALCO) build for its Virginian mountain routes the country's first 4–8–2s in 1911. The C&O engines were not, however, the first-born of this genus; two years earlier the locomotive superintendent of the 3ft 6in (1,069mm) gauge South African Railways had requested the North British Locomotive Co. to enlarge the small driving-wheel 4–8–0 design, already proven ruggedly reliable in South Africa, into a deep-firebox 4–8–2 for the taxing mountain lines of his Natal Division.

In this first pair of C&O 4–8–2s, in which each firebox measured 9ft 6in by 7ft (2.9 by 2.1m), North American locomotive development was beginning to demand boilers with a steam generating capacity that was beyond one fireman's resources to sustain. Happily the mechanical stoker had now been perfected and the C&O 4–8–2s were among the first to be equipped with a reliable model. Various nineteenth-century attempts to devise something of

Above left: GWR No. 4066 Malvern Abbey, *one of the last of Churchward's 'Star' class 4-6-0s, speeds through Sonning Cutting in 1930.*
Left: A Pennsylvania Railroad Class K4 Pacific (at the front) and a later Baldwin-designed Class T1 4-4-4-4 locomotive haul a train round the famous Horseshoe Curve at Altoona.
Above: Bound for New York, the Pennsylvania's 'Broadway Limited', hauled by a K4s Pacific, and the New York Central's 'Twentieth Century Limited' race together out of Chicago in 1935.
Below: Two Santa Fe 2-10-2s, built in the 1920s, start the heavy climb out of Victorville, California, in 1946.

the kind, ranging from a blower that blasted pulverized coal at the firehole door to a vaned wheel that paddled coal indiscriminately around the grate, had been abortive, though some of them were more concerned to achieve even combustion and minimize exhaust pollution than to relieve the fireman. Early twentieth-century models, which tried to ram the coal into the grate from below or to chain-feed it into the fire through a tube, were just as profitless. The ultimate answer was a rotating screw feed, laid in a trough from tender to firebox door and powered by an auxiliary steam engine; final distribution of the coal over the grate was by steam jet. Both jet and pace of the rotating screw could be controlled by the fireman to vary the amount and the placing of the coal feed.

That first pair of C&O 4–8–2s, which had 5ft 2in (1,575mm) driving wheels, did not impress. The type – branded the 'Mountain' for obvious reasons – did not make its mark as an express passenger engine until ALCO built a class of ten engines with 6ft 2in (1,880mm) drivers for the Rock Island line in 1920. One should add that thereafter the 4–8–2 was not multiplied exclusively as a mountain-suited express passenger type. Systems

whose main routes were relatively grade-free, notably the Illinois Central and New York Central, built a substantial number for mixed passenger and freight assignments.

Nor should one leave the American scene at this point without remarking that the 4–6–0 – or 'Ten-Wheeler' – retained widespread affection and was still built until the later 1930s, by which time American workshops had turned out more than 17,000 since the debut of the Philadelphia & Reading's *Chesapeake* in 1847. In general, twentieth-century US 4–6–0s were valued as ideal for light general-purpose work; but a few were ordered for fast passenger duty and the Pennsylvania constructed the weightiest 4–6–0s of all American history, its 106–ton Class G5s type with 5ft 8in (1,727mm) driving wheels, for accelerative punch on its toughest city suburban routes.

Mainland European railways stepped smartly into the Pacific era behind the Americans. The pioneer European 4–6–2s were a pair of four-cylinder compounds extrapolated in design from the de Glehn Atlantics and 4–6–0s, which went into Paris–Toulouse service on the

Paris–Orléans Railway in 1907 and soon proved competent to sustain 50mph (80km/h) up the long 1 in 100 gradients at the southern end of the route with as much as 400 tons in tow. In basic outline the de Glehn four-cylinder compound Pacific was subsequently adopted by foreign railways as well as by all the major French systems with the exception of the Paris–Lyon–Méditerranée (PLM), although on the Nord the inception of Pacifics in 1912 was preceded by the delayed emergence of a pair of 4–6–4s which du Bousquet had conceived as the logical successor to the very efficient Nord 4–6–0 when train weights rose. This duo was not completed until after du Bousquet's death and survived in inter-war service only because the Nord was short of motive power; their length and bulk were operational nuisances which would otherwise have condemned them, since as soon as the Pacifics materialized the latter showed equal capability. The PLM elected in 1908 to order for comparative assessment two prototype Pacifics of its own pattern, one a saturated steam four-cylinder compound, the other a superheated four-cylinder simple, and eventually settled for a superheated four-

cylinder compound type of which Henschel built the two dozen standard-bearers in 1911.

The apotheosis of the de Glehn four-cylinder compound Pacific was a Nord design actually drafted before the First World War in anticipation of track reconstruction that would ease the axle-load limit of that railway's main lines from 17 to 18½ tons. But the war temporarily blocked the relaying and, *ipso facto*, the engines' construction. When they did emerge in 1923–4, the prowess which bigger cylinders and grate area, a boiler pressed to 225lb/sq.in (15.8kg/sq.cm) and 10 per cent greater adhesion weight bestowed on them quickly earned them the reverential epithet of '*Les Supers*'. They were no way discomforted by loads of 650 tons on the boat-train workings between Paris and the Channel ports and could keep loads of that size rolling at 75mph (120km/h) – the statutory maximum speed on all French main lines until the 1950s – along the flat between Amiens and Paris, while between Amiens and the coast one was once logged at a steady 53mph (85km/h) up the 1-in-200 Survilliers bank at the head of no less than 760 tons. These Nord 'Super-Pacifics' designed by de Caso

Above left: A Stanier Class 5 4-6-0,
built for the LMS, traverses Lune Gorge
in the north-west of England in 1966.
Above: No. 7029 Clun Castle, a restored
'Castle' class 4-6-0. This GWR design
evolved from the 'Star' type and was first
produced in 1923.
Right: The 4-8-2 configuration was
adopted in Spain in the 1920s to cope
with mountain gradients as well as
lowland plains. For many years
they formed the basis of Spanish
main-line locomotive power.

also powered the Paris–Brussels non-stops, scheduled to cover the 193.1 miles (310.8 km) in three hours flat at an end-to-end average of 64.4 mph (103.6 km/h).

Hard on the heels of the pioneer Paris–Orléans Pacifics the first German 4–6–2, a four-cylinder compound built by Maffei for the Baden State Railway, took the tracks in the autumn of 1907. The thirty-five engines of this type did not long survive their owner's absorption in the Reichsbahn, for they had been built with 5 ft 11 in (1,803 mm) drivers to suit them for the steep gradients of the Black Forest lines and that was too much of a constraint on their suitability for general express passenger duty. By far the most successful of the pre-Reichsbahn Pacific designs, also a Maffei creation, was the four-cylinder compound Class S3/6 of the Bavarian State. After its foundation in 1920 the Reichsbahn picked this type for proliferation until it had settled designs for its own standard Pacifics, and by 1930 the total of Class S3/6 was 159 engines. The majority were built with 6 ft 1½ in (1,867 mm) driving wheels, but an eighteen-strong batch of 1912–13 had bigger 6 ft 7 in (2,007 mm) wheels as they were intended for express traffic between Munich, Nuremberg and Würzburg, the only sectors where the Bavarian State tolerated a speed in excess of 70 mph (115 km/h).

The heaviest and most powerful European Pacifics of the pre-First World War years were the grotesque-looking engines which J.B. Flamme conceived in 1910 for the Belgian State system. A big boiler was a prerequisite for these engines, since they confronted lengthy stretches of 1 in 62½ on

their trips into Luxembourg. But the axle-load limit was a generous 20 tons, so there was no deterrent to imposition of the whole weight of the boiler on the driving wheels to maximize adhesion weight. As a result the smokebox front stopped short of the cylinders, which with the leading bogie projected well clear of the boiler like some outrageous bustle. With this peculiarity and their hulking boilers sunk comparatively low amid the driving wheels, the Flamme engines were fearsome-looking – and sounding – machines on the move. They saw out the steam age in Belgium, though from 1935 they were complemented by a new semi-streamlined Pacific class.

Austria's insubstantial track and indifferent coal resources discouraged Karl Gölsdorf from recourse to a Pacific, because a single rear trailing axle could not support the size of firebox needed to make adequate steam from the miserable fuel on which his engines had to subsist. He resolved the problem by inverting the format in his ten four-cylinder compound 2–6–4s of 1908, on which he bestowed driving wheels no less than 6 ft 10¾ in (2,102 mm) in diameter. The dismantling of the Austro-Hungarian Empire after the First World War left the savagely contracted Austrian railway system with greater need of mountain railway power than of high-stepping Pacifics, however. For that sort of assignment the Mediterraneo Railway of Italy had successfully pioneered the European 4–8–0 in 1903 and the type's potential had been fully realized in eight four-cylinder compounds constructed by Hanomag in 1914 for the

Madrid, Zaragoza and Alicante Railroad of Spain.

In the same year, 1914, the Austrian Südbahn commissioned two 4–8–0 prototypes, the layout of which took full advantage of the generous Austrian loading gauge by pitching the boiler high so that 5 ft 9 in (1,753 mm) driving wheels could be employed and yet room be left above their axles for a capacious firebox. The pair had been intended for the Trieste-Ljubljana route, with its protracted slopes of 1 in 70, but when that was severed by the post-war partition they were diverted to the Semmering line. They attacked the Semmering inclines so manfully that, almost unchanged except for the refinement of poppet valve gear, the design was endorsed for standardization as Class 113 in 1923.

These 4–8–0s upheld the heavy international passenger traffic of the Westbahn and Südbahn until the fulfilment of Austrian main-line electrification after the Second World War. From the mid-1950s onwards they were miraculously rejuvenated by the last significant contribution to steam traction technology, the Giesl oblong ejector. This was the contrivance of an Austrian engineer that took the science of optimizing the exhaust's efficiency in pump-draughting hot gases from the grate through the boiler tubes a stage further than the earlier work in double or multiple-jet blastpipes and chimneys of Kylala, Chapelon and Lemaître. A Giesl-fitted Class 113 was not disconcerted by a load of even seventeen coaches or 700 tons and more on the 1 in 125 grades of its domain.

The 4–8–0's shortcoming was its limitation to 56 mph (90 km/h) at any time, even on the flat. In the later 1920s international travellers were demanding more pace, so in 1928 the Austrian railways' chief engineer of the day, Lehner, resorted to Gölsdorf's ploy by inverting the 4–8–2 layout so as to squeeze a massive boiler and firebox between 6 ft 4½ in (1,943 mm) driving wheels without transgressing a maximum axle-load limit of 17¾ tons. Two of these majestic 115½ ton 2–8–4s were built initially, both simple-expansion, but one with two and the other with three cylinders. The former, designated Class 214, pleased the more, attaining 97 mph (156 km/h) on its preliminary trials, and it was proliferated with twelve more engines between 1931 and 1936. The design also captivated the Rumanian

Above left: The 4-6-2 four-cylinder compound Class S 3/6 was built by Maffei for the Bavarian State Railways and was later adopted by the Reichsbahn on its foundation in 1920.

Above: An Austrian Südbahn 4-8-0 and a Giesl-fitted 2-10-2 tank (at the front) pass over the Hollgraben Viaduct on the Semmering line in 1958.

Below: The French Class 241P 4-8-2 with a Paris–Brest night express in 1964.

State Railway; they built no fewer than seventy-nine similar machines.

Even earlier in the 1920s two of the French railways had come to the conclusion that the quickening schedules and heavier loads of express trains were asking too much of six-wheeled engines when they were faced with recovery from operating delays on up-grades. The Est and the PLM began a draft of 4–8–2 designs almost simultaneously and both

premiered prototypes in 1925. Both were four-cylinder compounds, but whereas the Est engine's driving wheels were of 6 ft 4¾ in (1,949 mm) diameter the PLM's were only 5 ft 10½ in (1,791 mm). Despite the fact that its designer distinguished its smokebox door with an aggressive bullet-nose of German pattern to reduce wind resistance, the PLM engine's small wheels fitted it more for heavy mixed traffic haulage than high speed. As an all-purpose machine it proved eminently successful and 145, designated Class 241A, were built from 1927 to 1931. A subsequent variant constructed with 6 ft 6½ in (1,994 mm) driving wheels was the foundation of the superb Class 241P 4–8–2 standardized by French Railways after the Second World War. Although the Est prototype beat the PLM model to the tracks by a short head it took much longer to perfect and was not passed for series manufacture until 1931.

The Est 4–8–2 was chronologically Europe's first 'Mountain', but the Spaniards are more justly adjudged the continent's earliest practitioners of the wheel arrangement. The Norte Railroad was anxious for a versatile machine that would be as much at home in the plains as on the slopes of the Guadarrama Mountains, so that engine changes from a Pacific

to a 4–8–0 at the threshold of the hills could be avoided. The 4–8–2 looked the part and six four-cylinder compounds built in Germany by Hanomag in 1925 so promptly and effectively met the specification that sixty more were commissioned in fairly short order, initiating a family of 4–8–2s – and later some 4–8–4s – which were the hallmark of high-power Spanish main-line steam.

FOUR GREAT DESIGNERS

Four men dominated European steam locomotive engineering in the 1930s – Gresley and Stanier in Britain, Chapelon in France and Wagner in Germany. The cramped British loading gauge debarred the country's designers from attempting such powerful machines as their Continental colleagues had been evolving since the First World War, even if main station platform lengths and other track layout

and signalling parameters had permitted the lengths of train to justify comparable locomotives in Britain, which they did not. Besides that there was a school of thought, powerfully influential on the London Midland & Scottish (LMS), which preached that in British traffic conditions it was more economical to build small and double-head the heavier loads. Arch-opponent of that theory was Gresley, who built for the London & North Eastern (LNER) Britain's first series of Pacifics, as soon as that railway had been established by the 1923 Grouping. In their youth these three-cylinder engines were not flawless, but Gresley, like Churchward, was receptive to evidence of others' expertise. A 1925 exchange of an LNER Pacific and a GWR 'Castle' for exercises on each other's main lines yielded emphatic proof of the value of Churchward-style long-lap valve gear. When the 1925 lessons were embodied,

along with a higher degree of superheating, in the Gresley Class A3 Pacific of the early 1930s the world's fastest steam locomotive had begun to take shape.

The A3 emerged as British railways were beginning to counter-attack the growing menace of road competition by taking advantage of the country's much more lax attitude to maximum rail speed than Continental European governments conceded. Since 1929 the Great Western had thrust an otherwise rather nondescript Cheltenham–London express to the front of the world stage by steadily accelerating its timing over the almost flat and superbly aligned sector of Brunel's main line from Swindon to Paddington until it held the title of the world's fastest daily train between 1929 and 1933. The 'Cheltenham Flyer', as this almost invariably 'Castle' 4–6–0 hauled train became known, briefly surrendered the claim in 1931 when

Canadian Pacific, battling it out with Canadian National for Montreal–Toronto business, instituted a 68.9 mph (110.9 km/h) average over 124 miles (200 km) between Montreal and Smith's Falls; but in September that year the GWR edgily recaptured the crown by tightening its Swindon–Paddington allowance to attain a 69.2 mph (111.4 km/h) average. Highpoint of the 'Cheltenham Flyer's' career was a pre-planned record attempt of 5 June 1932, when No. 5006 *Tregenna Castle* whirled its six coaches of 195 tons over the 77.3 miles (124.4 km) from Swindon to Paddington in just over 56¾ minutes at a start-to-stop average of 81.7 mph (131.5 km/h) to complete the fastest journey ever recorded with British steam. It entailed averaging 90 mph (145 km/h) for 39 miles (63 km) on end, with two peaks of 92 mph (148 km/h) – a level of speed inconceivable with a public

Above: One of Chapelon's first series of 4-8-0s built for the Paris–Orléans Railway. This design featured a Kylchap double blastpipe and chimney.
Left: A 'Duchess' class engine named after its designer. Stanier had produced the first Pacific for the LMS in 1933.

service train almost anywhere else in Europe at that juncture.

The exception was Germany where, as described in the succeeding chapter, the Reichsbahn was at that moment concluding that Dr Rudolf Diesel's perfection of his art had handed them the wherewithal to achieve a long-cherished ambition to trounce the world in rail speed. A prototype two-car diesel-electric streamliner was unveiled in 1932 and the following spring it initiated Europe's first 100 mph (160 km/h) public service operation as the *Fliegende Hamburger*, or 'Flying Hamburger'.

At Gresley's instigation a high-level LNER mission studied this German operation at first hand and concluded that some similar business service, strictly limited in load, would be a commercial draw between London and both Leeds and Newcastle. The German diesel train builders – WUMAG of Görlitz for the vehicles and Maybach for the engines – were invited to quote, but did not persuade the LNER either that they had proven diesel power plant on the shelf capable of improving on a Gresley steam Pacific's potential with a light train, or that they

could create a train interior which would stand comparison with the two-a-side first-class seating comfort and full diner service of a contemporary LNER locomotive-hauled train. The traction point was made by two trials, one in 1934 when Gresley's No. 4472 *Flying Scotsman* registered Britain's first fully authenticated 100 mph (160 km/h) on rails, and another in 1935 when one of his more sophisticated A3s with a boiler pressure of 220 lb/sq.in (15.5 kg/sq.cm), No. 2750 *Papyrus*, improved on the projected London–Newcastle schedule of four hours for the 268.3 miles (431.8 km) in each direction and touched 108 mph (174 km/h) in the process. At that there was unanimity in the LNER Boardroom that their new high-speed train should be steam.

By the time that Gresley was required to design a specifically high-speed Pacific he was already profoundly impressed by the science of André Chapelon. In the mid-1920s Chapelon was employed in the Research and Development Department of the Paris–Orléans Railway (P–O), which was baffled by the inability of its Pacifics to surpass the performance of their Atlantic predecessors. Chapelon's response was to re-examine the problem from first thermodynamic principles, the outcome of which was a highly scientific elaboration of Churchward's much more empirical convictions about the free flow of steam. When, in 1929, Chapelon's theories were put to practical proof in a specimen P–O Pacific, which had its whole steam circuit totally revised with bigger, stream-lined steam passages, modified valves and draughting and a higher degree of superheat, the engine's output was immediately enhanced by 50 per cent and its thermal efficiency markedly improved as well. The same went for subsequent rebuilding of P–O 4–8–0s. An important component of the Chapelon layout was the Kylchap double blastpipe and chimney, so-called because in it Chapelon refined the earlier work of a Finnish engineer named Kylala.

Chapelon himself retired in 1953, but his technology informed French steam locomotive engineering for the rest of its days. In 1934 the Nord, unashamedly recognizing that its 'super-Pacifics' were outclassed by Chapelon's P–O rebuilds, acquired a new class in the Chapelon mould – the remarkably proficient Class 231E. Chapelon practice also imbued the design of the Nord's subsequent pre-war 4–6–4 prototypes, but what promised to be the most striking Chapelon product of all materialized in the shadow of catenary, too close to the start of French Railways' intensive post-war electrification to make its proper mark in steam locomotive history. In 1946 the SNCF – into which the individual French main-line railways had been grouped in 1938 – authorized reconstruction of an Etat Railway 4–8–2 from an unmemorable class of the 1930s as a 4–8–4 embodying all Chapelon's precepts. The three-cylinder compound result, No. 242-Al, never had the opportunity to exert its full strength in everyday service, but it left some stunning

test performance in the record books – ascents of the long 1 in 125 to Blaisy–Bas summit, north of Dijon on the ex-PLM Paris–Lyon main line, with over 800 tons at a steady 60–70 mph (100–115 km/h), for instance; and acceleration of 780 tons from rest at Creil to 72 mph (116 km/h) on the 1 in 200 of Survilliers bank on the Nord.

To revert to 1935, Gresley applied much of Chapelon's theory – though not at first the Kylchap exhaust – to the streamlined, three-cylinder Class A4 Pacific he created for the first LNER high-speed train, the 'Silver Jubilee'. The benefit was patent when the first A4, No. 2509 *Silver Link*, went almost straight from the Doncaster works production line to a demonstration trip with the 'Silver Jubilee' train-set on

27 September 1935 and surged up to 112½ mph (181 km/h) in the course of running 25 miles (40 km) on end at 100 mph (160 km/h) or more.

Two years earlier, in 1933, the rival LMS had produced its first Pacific. The designer was Stanier, who had been imported from the GWR's Swindon hierarchy to infuse some standardized order into the illogical mixture of motive power – a great deal of it not virile enough for the jobs to which it was assigned – with which the LMS had landed itself as a result of inability to weld its pre-1923 constituents into an organization with amicable unanimity of purpose. Understandably, considering his origins, Stanier's first Pacific essay, the 'Princess

Above left. The Silver Link, *Gresley's Class A4 Pacific, on its record-breaking run in September 1935, with the 'Silver Jubilee'.*
Above: The 'Coronation Scot' made its debut in 1937, the year of George VI's coronation. This four-cylinder Pacific was the LMS answer to the LNER Class A4.
Below left: A French 231E in 1963. It was used on expresses between Paris and the Channel ports.

Royal' type, was basically an enlargement of the GWR 'King' – that railway's final design of express passenger 4–6–0, which exploited the ultimate practicabilities of the ten-wheeler arrangement within the British loading gauge. But when the LMS decided to follow the LNER into the streamlined high-speed train orbit Stanier designed for its 1937 London–Glasgow 'Coronation Scot' a more original machine, a four-cylinder Pacific which outstripped Gresley's A4 for size.

The streamlined version captured the media's interest when it hoisted the British speed record to 114 mph (183.5 km/h) on a demonstration of the LMS 'Coronation Scot' on 29 June 1937 – though at all but catastrophic cost, as Pacific No. 6220 *Coronation* almost ran out of tangent track in a desperate effort to surpass the LNER's mark on the downhill before Crewe. She had been braked only to 57 mph (92 km/h) when she hit the crossovers outside Crewe station, the coaches behind her streaming flames from tortured brake blocks. The train lurched perilously over the point-work, cascading many of its passengers

from one side of their compartments to the other, but mercifully it all ended at the Crewe platform with no worse debit than a few bruises and a voluminous indent for new kitchen crockery.

Far more significant than this rash stunt was the feat of one of the later, non-streamlined versions of the Stanier Pacific, No. 6234 *Duchess of Abercorn*, after she had been fitted with a double blastpipe and chimney. On a test run of February 1939 between Crewe and Glasgow the modified engine humped a twenty-coach train of 610 tons up the 10 miles (16 km) of Beattock bank, which are sloped at a mean 1 in 75, without falling below 31 mph (50 km/h), while on the return from Scotland with the same load she charged Beattock summit at a fiery 60 mph (100 km/h) in the teeth of a blizzard.

Before that epic performance Gresley had fitted a few of his later A4s with Kylchap double blastpipes and chimneys. And with one of these, No. 4468 *Mallard*, he staged on Sunday 3 July 1938 a glittering demonstration of the free-steaming which the device induced. The LNER was methodically testing a new quick-acting vacuum brake valve that had proved an urgent requirement to ensure its streamlined trains could be brought from 90 mph-plus (145 km/h) to a stand within the existing signal spacing and Gresley used one of the regular Sunday trials for a calculated effort to put the rail speed record beyond the reach of any other British railway. On the LNER's ideal race-track, the long descent of Stoke bank south of Grantham, *Mallard* was urged up to

126 mph (203 km/h), a world steam speed record which was never excelled.

Both Gresley and Stanier had projects for bigger engines to uplift the average speed of their heavier, conventional expresses closer to that of the streamliners – Gresley's was for a 4–8–2, Stanier's for a 4–6–4 – but both were aborted by the war and never revived. In 1934, however, Gresley had produced Britain's only eight-coupled express passenger type, his Class P2 2–8–2. On the European mainland this wheel arrangement had been pioneered for express work by the Saxon State Railroad with twenty-three four-cylinder compounds of 1918–22 and the Italians adopted the same layout in their Class 746 of 1921, but for the Continentals these were only useful steps on the road to perfection of the 4–8–2. Gresley's model was Chapelon's Paris–Orléans 4–8–0, which he revised to a 2–8–2 partly to accommodate his preferred wide firebox and partly because he fancied that a 'Mikado' would be better riding over the curves of the sharply undulating Edinburgh–Aberdeen main line of the LNER – the course for which he specifically created his 2–8–2. It was in *Cock o' the North* that Gresley embodied the Chapelon doctrine to its fullest extent, save only that his P2 was a three-cylinder simple, not a four-cylinder compound. The six P2s had no British equal as load haulers in express passenger work, but although they were triumphantly vindicated in concept they were flawed in mechanical detail; and that was not seriously tackled before the war enforced a host of new priorities. Sadly Gresley's successor was so determined not to live in his shadow that rather than attempt to refine the 2–8–2s he ruthlessly ordered their reconstruction as ungainly – and unsuccessful – Pacifics.

In Germany the Reichsbahn had inherited from the state railways over 350 different types of locomotive at its creation in 1920. But at the same time motive power resources had been disastrously depleted by the First World War. Only a few of the individual state classes were sanctioned for continued construction – the outstanding case was the versatile Prussian P8 4–6–0 – while a government-appointed committee of railway and locomotive industry experts hammered out new standard designs. Fourteen of these had been endorsed by 1922 and the first of them, the four-cylinder compound Class 02 and two-

A West German Class 44 2–10–0 at speed with a consignment of iron ore.

cylinder simple Class 01 Pacifics, together with two breeds of freight 2–10–0, the Class 43 and 44, were ready in 1925–6. Experience eventually favoured the simple-expansion 01, which from 1930 was complemented as Pacific power by the 03; this had the same-sized 6 ft 6¾ in (2,000 mm) driving wheels as the 01, but was designed within more stringent axle-load parameters as the 01's route availability was uneconomically restricted by the state of many German main lines in the 1920s.

Although Reichsbahn locomotive design in the 1920s and 1930s was ostensibly a committee product, its thought was dominated by the railway's motive power chief, Dr R.P. Wagner, a man whose independence of mind was as unmistakable as his towering physical stature. The Reichsbahn administration had not shown much zest for speed with steam in the 1920s. Once the new diesel streamliners were on song it was downright apathetic to any suggestion of high-speed steam locomotive development. But Wagner and the steam locomotive industry

would not be rebuffed and in 1935 created two of Europe's outstanding steam locomotives, the fully streamlined, three-cylinder simple Class 05 4–6–4s, with 6 ft 7½ in (2,019 mm) driving wheels and a high 285 lb (20 kg/sq. cm) boiler pressure. In May the following year one was reportedly coaxed up to 124.5 mph (200.4 km/h) on an almost imperceptible downhill of 1 in 333 of the Hamburg–Berlin course. Over that route the pair were deputed in the following summer to haul new lightweight morning and evening business expresses at end-to-end averages of just on 74 mph (119 km/h) for the 178.1 miles (286.6 km). More streamlined designs followed, culminating in the heavy-haulage Class 06 4–8–4s of 1938, but by then Wagner was in serious disfavour. Criticism of his dedication to high-power streamlined steam rather than perfection of simpler workhorses might have bent fewer influential ears had not Wagner been so openly contemptuous of the Third Reich's bombast (he once dismissed the Hitler-Mussolini Axis as 'a cheap tin tube for blowing hot air across the Alps'). With the onset of war opposing policies easily prevailed and Wagner left the Reichsbahn on the pretext of ill-health in 1942.

THE FINAL FLOWERING OF STEAM DESIGN

In the first two decades of the twentieth century North American railroads' priority in steam locomotive development had been increased tractive effort – that is, the quest for means simply to start heavier trains, of freight above all, and to keep them moving. The tool which best met that specification was the Mallet compound articulated and the development of this genre in size and power was rapid and dramatic. As early as 1918 ALCO had built for the Virginian ten 2–10–10–2s of 342 tons, weight apiece, with boilers of a girth that seemed to probe the limits of the American loading gauge; on a continuous tractive basis they were arguably the most powerful steam locomotives in all rail history.

At that time speed on the road was immaterial – in fact, the contemporary average of all but specially cherished merchandise trains was below 10 mph (16 km/h). Standard practice was to tie on to a locomotive's tender as many wagons as it could move, no matter how long freight cars had to hang about a yard until enough had accumulated to make a train that would exert one of the Mallets. It was what

Americans now call the 'drag' era of freight railroading. Except for its exaction of monumental tractive effort from the locomotives, it was abysmally inefficient. Marshalling yards were chronically blocked to approaching traffic as these huge trains were assembled or sorted, adding more transit time to the hours squandered by trains moving so slowly.

The disadvantage of the Mallet compound for railways with more restricted clearances or operating on less than standard gauge was the size of its low-pressure cylinders, quite apart from the fact that a compound had some objectionable traits that were inherent in its principle. Just ahead of American realization that there was virtue in a simple-expansion articulated, the partnership of Herbert Garratt and the builders Beyer Peacock in England proved it in the distinctive Beyer-Garratt layout. This set each unit of cylinders and driving wheels well apart from each other, pivoting them independently to a long frame which cradled a boiler of very large diameter between them; fuel supplies were carried in receptacles front and rear of the boiler and cab, above each of the power units.

Early Garratts – the first was a little 33-ton 0–4–4–0 built for Tasmania in 1908 – were compounds, but a simple-expansion 2–6–0 + 0–6–2 constructed for the 3 ft 6 in (1,069 mm) gauge South African Railways in 1921 so outclassed a contemporary Mallet compound both in performance and in fuel thrift that it established the Beyer-Garratt as the basic power of numerous railways in the continent until the demise of steam. The apotheosis of the South African Beyer-Garratt was the Class GMAM 4–8–2 + 2–8–4 of 1956, which despite its narrower gauge had a tractive effort roughly equivalent to that of any of the final generation of continental European ten-coupled freight engines. Beyer-Garratts did not attract many railroads remote from British influence, but among the exceptions was the PLM of France, which ordered some magnificent passenger 4–6–4 + 4–6–4s with 5 ft 11 in (1,803 mm) driving wheels for its Algerian subsidiary. One of these machines was tested very satisfactorily at up to 85 mph (140 km/h) before it was shipped to North Africa.

In the United States it was the Chesapeake & Ohio, with forty-five 2–8–8–2s of 1923–6, which persuaded American railroads that the simple-expansion articulated, while it lacked the tremendous starting effort of a Mallet, had punch enough: and moreover had a speed potential which the compound's characteristics inhibited. This last was now crucial, for the automobile's erosion of both passenger and freight business was awakening US railroads to a need of greater pace in every traffic sector.

This commercial demand fertilized the final, supreme flowering of US steam locomotive design. The first bloom was 'Lima Super-Power', a concept of the youngest locomotive manufacturer in the USA, the Lima works of Ohio, and its chief designer, W.E. Woodward. He broke new ground by employing a trailing bogie not to enhance stability, as most previous practitioners had, but to carry a stoker-fed firebox with a greater evaporative surface than that of any contemporary Mallet. Moreover, the rear bogie was fitted with a small auxiliary steam engine, or booster,

One of the streamlined 4–4–2s built in Belgium in 1939 to work express services between Brussels and Ostend.

which augmented tractive effort at starting and was cut out soon after the train was rolling. Lima's initial 2–8–4 demonstrator, which featured several other sophistications for improved efficiency, astonished both as a merchandise freight and an express passenger haulier and quickly attracted series purchasers. Because the first customer, the Boston & Albany, bought the 2–8–4 layout for its tortuous and graded route in the Berkshire hills of western Massachusetts, this arrangement was tagged the 'Berkshire'; and when the Texas & Pacific indented for a longer-boilered, bigger-cylinder 2–10–4, that layout was inevitably dubbed the 'Texas'.

A subsequent batch of 2–10–4s built for the Chesapeake & Ohio in 1930, the world's most powerful two-cylinder machines, was potent enough to supplant the 2–8–8–2 Mallets – and moreover to accomplish the Mallets' work on substantially less fuel. The 'Chessie' 2–10–4s needed a helper's shove to get a 160-car, 12,000 ton coal train on the move, but after that they were not strained to keep it moving across Ohio to the Toledo docks. Lima's ultimate accolade was that this

Above: New York Central's first steamlined 'Twentieth Century Limited' pulls out of Chicago on its eastbound trip to New York in 1938. The locomotive is a Class J-3a 'Hudson' 4-6-4, streamlined by designer Henry Dreyfuss.
Below: The Santa Fe Railroad's 'Grand Canyon Limited', hauled by a 4-8-4, overtakes a side-tracked freight.
Above right: A simple-expansion articulated built by the Pennsylvania Railroad in 1919.

2–10–4 was picked as the design to satisfy a Pennsylvania Railroad need as late as 1942, when wartime stringency dictated that new construction be confined to existing, proven models.

From the Lima mixed traffic concept it was a short step to the 4–6–4 and 4–8–4 layout for front-rank passenger assignments. The New York Central pioneered the 4–6–4 arrangement in 1927 with its celebrated 'Hudsons', many of which had 7 ft (2,134 mm) driving wheels and some of which were ultimately streamlined. The Northern Pacific was first with 4–8–4s, in 1927 – hence the 'Northern' tag for the layout, although the New York Central called its 1946 4–8–4s 'Niagaras' – and from then on over a thousand were built.

The ultimate North American steam power had the harshest treatment of any in the world. Not only was it thrashed mercilessly on the move, but the big express passenger engines especially were rostered to unbroken journeys of a length without world parallel, generally with extremely little time off between each trip

for servicing. For instance, in their prime, Santa Fe's 228-ton, 6 ft 10 in (2,083 mm) two-cylinder 4–8–4s of 1938 had six regular assignments to run the 1,772 miles (2,852 km) between Kansas City and Los Angeles unchanged and two, equally without relief, over the 1,235 miles (1,988 km) between La Junta, Colorado, and Los Angeles, an itinerary which was beset with some grades as steep as 1 in 29. Crews were changed every 200 miles (320 km) or so and at some station stops *en route* there was a time allowance for minimum locomotive servicing, while the engines, which were oil-burners, had to have their fuel tanks replenished at least once on the way. Duties of this sort were responsible for the massive tenders with which the last great US steam classes were paired; the Santa Fe 4–8–4s' tenders were mounted on two eight-wheel bogies and weighed 165 tons apiece when two-thirds full with supplies, while the fourteen-wheeler of a Union Pacific 4–8–4 scaled as much as 183.7 tons.

In general the 4–8–4, though easily capable of 80–90 mph (130–145 km/h) on the level with 1,000 tons of train, was a heavy passenger and merchandise freight hauler. The racing thoroughbreds were predominantly the 4–6–4s, above all the New York Central 'Hudsons' and the streamlined 4–6–4s of the Milwaukee. As described in Chapter Twelve, when the trio of railroads contending for passenger business between Chicago and the Twin Cities, Minneapolis and St Paul, got embroiled in a speed race in the mid-1930s, the Milwaukee – like Britain's LNER –

preferred a steam streamliner to one of the new diesel train-sets, and for much the same reasons as the LNER. For the debut of its new 'Hiawatha' in 1935 the Milwaukee surprisingly reverted to a 4–4–2 layout, moulded into some striking streamlined engines with 300 lb/sq. in (21.1 kg/sq.cm) boiler pressure and 7 ft (2,134 mm) driving wheels. The Milwaukee was not alone in harking back to the 4–4–2 as a high-speed machine; in 1939 the Belgians built a small stud of bulbously streamlined 6 ft 10$\frac{1}{2}$ in (2,095 mm) driving-wheel Atlantics to work a service of three-coach flyers between Brussels and Ostend timed between the Belgian capital and Bruges at an average of 75.4 mph (121.3 km/h) start to stop, a schedule which briefly grabbed the world's fastest daily steam train crown from the 'Hiawatha'. But the 'Hiawatha's' appeal soon generated loads that demanded bigger engines, and that in 1938 bred the magnificent F7 4–6–4, with 300 lb boiler pressure and 7 ft drivers. Day in, day out the F7s had to maintain point-to-point timings of up to 90.9 mph (146.3 km/h) average with the nine-car 'Morning Hiawatha', which predicated some consistent running at 100 mph (160 km/h) and more.

The 1930s were also the heyday of the simple-expansion articulated. Its development was spurred by the 'Lima Super-Power's' testimony that, given appropriately proportioned boiler, firebox and cylinders, simple expansion could generate the horsepower for competitive speed as well as a tractive effort not far short of a comparable Mallet compound's.

The trend was set by Northern Pacific's ALCO-built 'Yellowstones' of 1929, 2–8–8–4 behemoths with a huge boiler and firegrate which in one test session was found capable of devouring 25 tons of coal in an hour (the mechanical stoker had to be guaranteed to deliver almost 18 tons per hour to the firegrate). A 179 ton twelve-wheel tender was paired with the 323 ton engine, assembling the USA's first power unit of over 500 tons' aggregate. The 'Yellowstones' were at the time a venturesome solution to the operational problem of a 200 mile (320 km) sector of main line between Mandan, North Dakota, and Glendive, Montana, which was humped by four summits flanked in some cases by 1-in-190 gradient. The spacing of the slopes was inconvenient for attachment and detachment of assistant engines, so the Northern Pacific specified articulateds which would hopefully hoist 3,000–4,000 ton freights over the crests unaided. And they did.

Three other railroads bought 2–8–8–4s, but from the mid-1930s onwards most simple articulated purchasers opted for the greater versatility of larger driving wheels in a 2–6–6–4 or 4–6–6–4 layout. Most extensive user of the former was the Norfolk & Western (also, one should interpolate, the last US railroad to build Mallet compounds in its Class Y6b 2–8–8–2s of 1948–51). With its 5 ft 10 in (1,778 mm) driving wheels an N&W Class A 2–6–6–4 was designed to exert 6,300 hp at 45 mph (70 km/h); it could roll a 7,000-ton freight at up to 60 mph (100 km/h) on the flat and sustain over 75 mph (120 km/h) in the railroad's mountain territory with twenty-coach loads on the N&W's crack 'Pocahontas' and 'Cavalier' passenger trains.

First in the field with 4–6–6–4s, in 1936, was the Union Pacific with its 5 ft 9 in (1,753 mm) driving-wheel 'Challengers'. And the Union Pacific was one of the two railroads which crowned the development of the simple articulated. The other was the Chesapeake & Ohio, for which Lima in 1941 created the 336 ton 'Allegheny' 2–6–6–6 with a gargantuan boiler to sustain an output of no less than 8,000 hp; more were built for the C&O in 1949, but the only other road to invest in these Lima 2–6–6–6s was another major coal hauler, the Virginia. The 'Alleghenies' were just beaten for weight by the biggest orthodox steam locomotives the world has ever seen, the Union Pacific 'Big Boys' of 1941 and 1944 – 345-ton 4–8–8–4s. Built primarily to hump massive freight tonnages over the Wasatch Mountains between Omaha, Nebraska and Cheyenne, Wyoming, they were also designed – in fact, deliberately over-designed – with scope for 70–80 mph (115–130 km/h) pace on passenger hauls, a faculty that Second World War troop train duty called upon them to demonstrate. An awe-inspiring spectacle it was, too.

The Custer's Last Stand of the US steam power industry against the diesel was Baldwin's attempt to create a high-speed, high-power locomotive without the transmission complexities to which orthodox eight-coupled engines were prone or the inherent instability at speed of an articulated, without also the latter's probably excessive maintenance bill if it were put to the stresses of consistently fast running. Baldwin's solution was to revive a

concept of the pre-articulated era: duplex drive – that is, a rigid mounting within the locomotive's frame of two sets of cylinders and driving wheels. The only railroad to embrace the Baldwin theory wholeheartedly was the Pennsylvania, which like most of the other great coal-hauling roads of the north-eastern USA was politically and economically motivated to resist the diesel's encroachment as long as technology kept such a policy credible (the last of these systems to yield to the diesel was the Norfolk & Western). Pennsylvania's effort culminated in its shark-nosed Class T1 4–4–4–4s of 1942 (two prototypes) and 1945–6 (the main production series of fifty). 'They'll outperform a 5,400 hp diesel at all speeds above 26 mph (42 km/h),' Baldwin boasted at the T1's debut. And there seemed to be fair justification for this bravado when T1s were logged at well over 100 mph

(160 km/h) for miles on end with 1,000 tons in tow. But within a year of their appearance Pennsylvania had joined the dieselizers. Not only were the T1s intolerably expensive to maintain, but they murdered the track, especially when they slipped, which was one of their besetting sins at starting and slow speed.

Coal-rich roads like the Pennsylvania and others in the eastern USA were less preoccupied with the steam locomotive's congenitally poor thermal efficiency than systems which had to live on poor or imported fuel. The twentieth century was marked by numerous attempts to improve fuel economy by revision of Stephenson's classic steam locomotive format, but none combined advance in efficiency with technical reliability to a degree that inspired the confidence to mass-produce.

One line of thought was preoccupied with the virtues of very high-pressure

boilers of the kind employed in marine engineering. The outcome was such experimental but short-lived locomotives as Gresley's water-tube boiler 4–6–4 No. 10000 of 1929 for Britain's LNER and, in the USA, the Delaware & Hudson's 500 lb/sq in (35.2 kg/sq. cm) boiler 4–8–0 *L.F. Loree* of 1933. A considerable number and remarkable variety of steam turbine locomotives were attempted from 1910 onwards, the last and most spectacular essays in this genre being Baldwin's three 140 ft (42.7 m) long, 595 ton contraptions of 1946–7 for the Chesapeake & Ohio and the joint Baldwin–Lima–Hamilton/Westinghouse/Babcock & Wilcox creation of 1951 for Norfolk & Western, the whole assembly of which scaled 586 tons. A last-ditch effort to uphold the economic validity of a coal-burning locomotive, *Jawn Henry*, as it was titled, was in essence a mobile, coal-fired power station, since the

Above: A South African Railways' Beyer-Garratt shifts a heavy freight. Left: A French Railways' 141R with a Paris–Brest express. These post-war 2–8–2s, built in North America, were ideal for mixed traffic.

final drive from the turbine was to a generator feeding electric traction motors in the four three-axle bogies of the main power unit.

During and after the Second World War some European designers were still seeking more elegant answers to classically controversial questions of steam locomotive design. The final flourishes of French big-engine development were mentioned earlier. In Britain, in the fading pre-nationalization years of its 'Big Four' railways, the Southern's O.V.S. Bulleid packed a wealth of innovation – over-much, in fact – into his 'air-smoothed' Pacifics, the most egregious element of which was a chain-driven valve gear encased in a notoriously fire-prone oil bath. Too late, in 1956, the post-war German Federal Railway of West Germany produced in its semi-streamlined and very sophisticated Class 10 what might have been one of the continent's classic Pacific designs, had the onset of dieselization and electrification not denied it the scope to realize its promise. Not until the post-Second World War period did one steam locomotive builder come into its finest hours. That was Skoda, in Czechoslovakia, after it had begun a two-way flow

of ideas with French Railways' engineers. Skoda's output of some 1,100 new steam locomotives between 1945 and 1958 was crowned by some superb 4–8–2s with Kylchap double blastpipes and mechanical stokers, and by far the biggest, most powerful and most sophisticated tank engines the world ever beheld – the Class 477 4–8–4 tanks, 124 ton monsters which were also Kylchap fitted and, for a tank engine, perhaps uniquely equipped with mechanical stokers.

But well before war's end in Europe the diesel's sweep of American railroads through its superior performance, versatility and economy over steam had clearly set a term on the life of the continent's front-rank steam power. Within a very short time that lease of life had been curtailed still more by a swift advance of electric traction technology and the consequent enhancement of its economy, despite its high first cost. And for such time as steam was still to be vouchsafed, the unreliable quality of coal, the rapid rise of labour costs and the sharp competition of post-war industry for staff, backed by its vastly improved working environment, put a premium on rugged simplicity of design for easy and speedy maintenance. That was exemplified in the ubiquitous post-war, mixed-traffic 2–8–2s of French Railways and above all in British Railways' range of standard classes. There was thus no longer any future for designers with ambitions of immortality as steam super-power architects.

THE DIESEL ERA OPENS

The application of Europe's railways to the 1914–18 war effort underscored the potentially superior efficiency of nationally administered railway systems far more vividly than the Franco-Prussian War. In several countries, Britain included, unification of the railways as soon as peace had been restored was being politically canvassed well before the end of the war. After the Armistice these pressures were redoubled because of the physically and financially battered state of so many railways and because of unrest in their labour forces, and as the world subsided into the economic slump of the early 1930s the trend towards bigger railway groupings was given a fresh impetus.

For the defeated countries, the Austro-Hungarian Empire in particular, change was inescapable. Whatever the material damage suffered by other European railways, none suffered such economic as well as physical mutilation as the Austrian. At a stroke the Versailles Treaty lopped off almost three-quarters of their route-mileage in its re-drafting of the Balkan map. Simultaneously the greater part of their locomotives and rolling stock was sequestrated and handed over to the new Balkan countries or to the Allies as reparations.

Savagery of its route system by the Versailles provisions crumpled the tenacious resistance to State control · of Austria's great Südbahn, and establishment of the nationwide Österreichische Bundesbahn (ÖBB), or Austrian Federal Railway, followed in the 1923–4 winter. Germany's 1919 constitution vested the country's railways in a new Reichsbahn, State-administered but with financial autonomy (from 1924 to 1930 there was an interregnum of Allied intervention in the overall management of the Reichsbahn under the victorious powers' Dawes Plan for resolution of the vexed reparations question). Today the Reichsbahn title survives in East Germany, but the half of the original Reichsbahn network segregated in the west by the partition of Germany after the Second World War was reconstituted in 1945 as the Deutsche

The diesel streamliner M10005, City of Denver, *at Denver, Colorado, in 1942. It was jointly operated by the Union Pacific and the Chicago & North Western Railroads.*

Bundesbahn (DB), or German Federal Railway.

The progressive State acquisition of private railways in Belgium reached its ultimate stage with the reorganization of the State system as the Société Nationale des Chemins de Fer Belges (SNCB) or Belgian National Railways, but France did not take the ultimate step until 1938. Their wages depressed by the financial straits of the railways after the war, French railwaymen attempted a nationwide strike for nationalization in 1920 but got much less than full-hearted support from their colleagues in the regions, hardest pressed to recuperate from the war. The Nord Railway undermined an effort to follow the neighbouring Reichsbahn's lead and evolve standard locomotive designs, which would have been a modest step towards achievement of the economies of scale. Eventually the 1930s depression defeated the relacitrant companies. The even worse deficits it created drove the Paris–Orléans and Midi into merger in 1934, and after the Popular Front government had brought the companies to the brink of nationalization agreement in 1937, its middle-of-the road successors finished the job in 1938. The main-line systems became the unified Société Nationale des Chemins de Fer Français (SNCF), or French National Railways. In the same year the two

A 'Battle of Britain' class Pacific heads the luxury 'Golden Arrow' in the late 1950s. The service was fully launched by Southern Railway in 1929 to complement the French 'Flèche d'Or', which had opened three years earlier.

companies created by a Dutch grouping of 1890 were united as the State-owned Nederlands Spoorwegen (NS), or Netherlands Railways.

The post-war British government shrank from the total nationalization that had been propounded not only by politicians to the left of centre. It opted instead for a grouping of the existing companies into four big combines (at one time seven were proposed) – the London Midland & Scottish (LMS), London & North Eastern (LNER), Great Western (GWR) and Southern (SR). The government for a period considered making mandatory the inclusion of railway workers on the boards of the 'Big Four', but ultimately preferred to make statutory provision for collective bargaining of wage rates between management and trades unions – and that was a radical enough measure for the times. The grouping was enshrined in the Railways Act of 1921 and the 'Big Four' came into being on New Year's Day 1923.

Britain's railways were the last major European system to be nationalized. The Spanish government had had to take over that country's railways in 1943 to create some order from post-Civil War disruption, and in 1945 the Republic of Ireland moulded the Irish Transport Company (CIE) from the Great Southern Railways and a Dublin bus company. Renewed British experience of the overall control of railways and the resultant economy in working – especially the more productive employment of freight wagons – during the Second World War rekindled enthusiasm for nationalization. This time the companies had much less strength to resist. Only one, the GWR, had been financially fit enough to pay its shareholders a reasonable dividend in 1939 and all had been thrashed into physical decrepitude by the war effort. Moreover, this time a demobilized Britain elected a full-blooded Socialist government in 1945. Inevitably a new Transport Act of 1947 enthroned a British Transport Commission with the objective of a State-controlled, co-ordinated public transport system. That was never realized and some of the components established were dismantled by later right-wing regimes. But not British Railways, in which the 'Big Four' were submerged on New Year's Day 1948.

SIGNALLING IMPROVEMENTS

The first decade of the inter-war period was marked on both sides of the Atlantic by significant advances in signalling technique and method which laid ideal foundations for the comprehensive automation that electronics would facilitate half-a-century later. Roused by the appalling safety record of its railways the US Government, through its Interstate Commerce Commission (ICC), had begun to insist on improvement in 1907.

The ICC's priority was a device that would override a negligent driver and automatically halt a train that overran a stop signal. Fifteen years elapsed while countless inventions were analysed, but finally in the summer of 1922 the ICC had endorsed enough as practicable and reliable to require forty-nine major railroads to start equipping main lines with them. In the later high-speed era of the 1940s the ICC was to ordain an 80 mph (130 km/h) speed limit on any route not equipped both with Automatic Train Control (ATC), as automatic train stop systems became generally – but misleadingly – known, and with automatic repetition of lineside signal aspects in the driving cab.

The first to instal the more sophisticated, continuous form of cab signalling was the Pennsylvania Railroad, from 1927 onwards. In its fundamentals the Pennsylvania technology is still valid for the cab signalling system of the world's fastest railway in the 1980s – the French 160 mph (260 km/h) TGV from Paris to Lyon. A change of signal aspect sent an appropriately coded current impulse through the track circuiting of the section it governed, and the impulse was picked up by a receiver on the locomotive and translated into a repetition of the new aspect on light panels in the cab, one on the driver's and another on the fireman's side. The cab panels continued to display that aspect until the engine passed a signal showing a different one, when the cab lights changed accordingly, a whistle automatically sounded in the cab to warn the driver and it was not silenced until the driver pressed an acknowledgement plunger. Later refinements added an appropriate, automatic application of brakes to bring speed within the range dictated by each signal aspect.

The Pennsylvania, ever independent, maintained that such an elaborate system did not need the supplement of an automatic stop and eventually bulldozed the ICC into granting it a unique dispensation on that score. But other railroads did in time couple continuous cab signalling with the automatic stop, which was obtained by the intermittent form of ATC. In this type of ATC, as its name implies, the enginemen only received advice of a signal aspect at the moment of passing a lineside signal: he had no continuous information of the state of the road ahead.

The great majority of the intermittent systems introduced by North American and European railways in the 1920s were inductive; an arrangement of electro- and permanent magnets laid between the running rails at a signal which exerted a differing effect on a receiver beneath the locomotive according to the aspect of that signal. Of the major railways which made a calculated bid for high passenger train speed between the World Wars the backsliders in ATC were three of Britain's 'Big Four'. In Britain only the GWR applied ATC to its main lines, employing a system of direct contact between locomotive apparatus and energized track-mounted ramps, and even the GWR did not embark on widespread installation until the 1930s. The other companies' systems were not equipped until after nationalization.

Britain's railways were, however, among the front-runners in adopting colour-light signals in place of semaphores, in devising more elaborate methods of communication between signalboxes in heavily trafficked areas by means of train describers, and in bringing wider areas of railway under the more efficient control of a single centre by developing power-assisted operation of points and signals. For single-line railways in the undeveloped world a specially pregnant development under the last of these heads was the 1927 installation on a 40 mile (65 km) stretch of New York Central single

A British Railways poster, entitled 'Signal Success', illustrates the extension of colour-light signalling proposed in the 1955 Modernisation Plan.

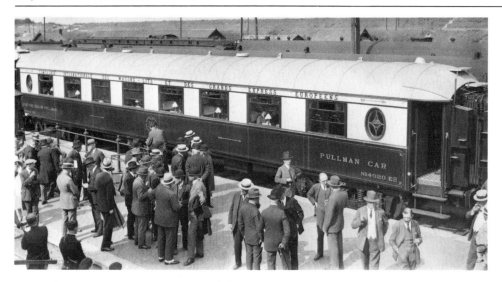

track of the first Centralized Traffic Control, or CTC.

With only one 3-mile (5 km) loop this New York Central line was becoming hard pressed to cope with its throughput of forty trains a day under the classic train-order and despatching system. CTC brought the points and signals of the whole line under the electrical control of one operator, before whom the state of the route and the position of every train within it was continuously displayed on an illuminated track layout diagram linked to the track circuitry. The much more efficient use of track capacity possible with centralized traffic regulation was to make its adoption a vastly cheaper but totally practical alternative to double-tracking for railways traversing unpopulated areas in other continents as well as those of America. Before the Second World War the extent and complexity of track which could be controlled from one centre was governed by the impossibility of transmitting electrical commands to more than one piece of remote apparatus at a time. The possibilities were transformed beyond the wildest conceptions of 1927 when postwar electronics technology not only contrived the channelling of many differently coded commands over a single wire, but could effect each transmission in an infinitesimal fraction of a second.

THE AGE OF LUXURY

For most of the 1920s the emphasis of passenger service development in the developed world was heavily on prestige trains. In Europe the first new service of this kind was created in 1919 at the express wish of the victorious Grand Alliance, which invited the Wagons-Lits company

to devise an illustrious new international train that would link Western Europe and the Balkans without taking the traditional route through ex-enemy territory and thereby help to stabilize the redrawn map of Europe. The Wagons-Lits response was the 'Simplon–Orient Express', which conveyed sleeping cars from Calais and Paris via Switzerland and Trieste to Bucharest, Athens, Sofia and Istanbul, together with a diner which from 1933 to 1939 travelled the entire 1,899 miles (3,056 km) from Paris to Istanbul – the longest unbroken journey ever made by a European restaurant car.

In 1926 the Wagons-Lits company won Near East concessions and thereafter the 'Simplon–Orient' was the first leg of a *de luxe* rail journey all the way from the French Channel port to Cairo, save for interruptions by ferry crossings of the Bosphorus and the Suez Canal and a special bus journey from Tripoli to Haifa. The 'Taurus Express' from the shores of the Bosphorus to Tripoli was as regal as the 'Simplon–Orient', while in the late 1920s the Egyptians began operating palatial Pullman trains between Kantara, on the Suez Canal, and Cairo.

The overland journey from London to Cairo by Wagons-Lits and Pullman occupied seven days – an exercise only masochists would entertain, you might think. But not so. Even in the 1920s the comfort of Wagons-Lits' trans-European expresses, the cuisine of their diners and the assiduous attention to passengers of the company's train staff still endeared them to the pleasure-bent travellers of high society as much as any ship, however palatial its first-class accommodation. Over shorter itineraries within the continent the *train de luxe* was the diplomatic corps' recognized travel medium – and there were several royal figures who customarily hired a separate sleeper and had it attached to a regular scheduled *train de luxe* for their private journeys.

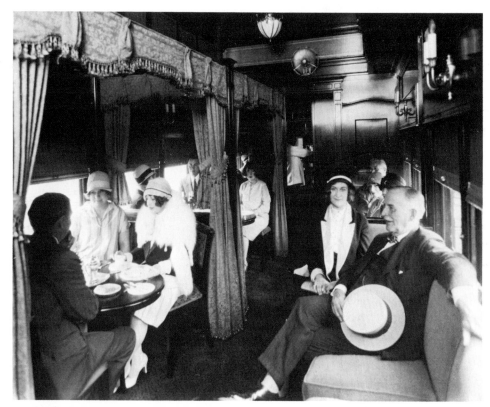

*Above left: The inauguration of the
'Flèche d'Or' in 1926 marked the golden
jubilee of the Wagons-Lits company.
Left: Passenger comfort in 1924 in the
Chicago–St Louis 'Alton Limited'.
Above: The incipient competition from
the air. A Fokker aircraft flies over the
'Twentieth Century Limited' in a 1929
publicity photo.*

With Europe's Pullman operations now
under the same direction as the Wagons-
Lits services the complementary development of day Pullman trains was a natural
consequence in the 1920s. In Britain the
LNER was the front-runner, not entirely
of its own volition. One of its pre-grouping
constituents, the Great Eastern, had in
1914 imported an American general
manager, Henry Thornton. In an un-
characteristic misjudgement Thornton
vainly thought to attract the bluff
farming gentry of England's East Anglia to
the higher tone of Pullman travel.
Inheriting a commercial fiasco but also a
stock of Pullmans and an unexpired

Pullman contract, the LNER reassigned
the cars to the ex-Great Northern main line
from London King's Cross to Yorkshire
and Scotland. After one or two ill-advised
ventures in 1924 and 1925, the LNER's
Pullman trains settled down to a very
successful career that did not end until
1978, when the last survivor had to go with
the reshaping of the East Coast main-line
timetables on a strictly standard, even-
interval pattern with 125 mph (200 km/h)
diesel units, BR's 'Inter-City 125' HST
train-sets.

The starting of sections of both the
'Simplon–Orient Express' and of the
post-war Paris–Nice 'Train Bleu' from
Calais testified to the importance of the
upper-bracket British tourist in the
optional international travel market of the
1920s. That was re-emphasized, as one
new day Pullman after another took the
European tracks in the 1920s, by the
considerable number that were oriented to
the British market. Altogether two dozen
new all-Pullman trains were inserted in
European timetables between the World

Wars. However, some were short-lived,
their business not virile enough to survive
the economic depression, and others
vanished at war's outbreak in 1939 never to
be resurrected.

In North America, as in Europe, the
extra-fare luxury train received all the
attention until the mid-1920s. The coach-
class passenger – the equivalent of
Europe's third class – was complacently
regarded as captive by most railroads. But
in the second half of the twenties, some
time before Europe felt the same impact,
managements were jolted into a change of
policy by the internal combustion engine.
Buses were evolving from comfortless
rural carriers into inter-state expresses,
rolling the highways at a pace that was
beginning to compete keenly with non-
luxury train schedules which in many cases
had not altered since the start of the
century. As early as 1929 private cars were
recording five times as many passenger-
miles as US trains. And the aeroplane was
no longer a once-round-the-airfield sens-
ation but was emerging as purposeful

passenger carrier. While the US population rose by 13.5 per cent in the 1920s, sales of rail passenger tickets slumped by 43 per cent. At the end of the decade passenger train revenue was exceeding direct running costs by only 10 per cent, whereas freight operation showed a margin of about a third.

The reaction had begun before the 1920s were out, but it gathered rapid momentum in the 1930s. Starting in the East, railroads not only began to admit coach-class passengers to their crack trains, such as the 'Pennsylvania Limited', and to order them better-quality rolling stock, but also to introduce all-coach trains on the fastest practicable schedules. The Erie Railroad's coach-class passengers between New York, Buffalo and Chicago, for instance, were stunned to find that they now rated their own club lounge car complete with radio. And journey times were progressively reduced. The depression toughened the struggle to retain passengers, but many railroads combatted boldly by lowering their fares.

At the same time the railroads were busy devising more opulent lounges, observation cars and diners to enhance the appeal of their premium-fare trains. The most important thoroughly practical advance,

without question, was the progressive Baltimore & Ohio's installation of air-conditioning throughout its all-parlour car New York–Washington 'Columbian' in May 1931. That was the first fully air-conditioned train in the world. The B&O's example was soon followed by other companies, although for a number of years air-conditioning was the prerogative of

first-class travellers only, and by 1940 US railroads as a whole were already running over 12,000 air-conditioned passenger cars. As for more fanciful frills, a typical flourish of the period was the Japanese tea room administered by Oriental ladies in full Japanese rig that embellished the Chicago–St Louis 'Alton Limited'.

In 1932 US timetables showed a total of just over 2,000 train-miles (3,200 km) daily scheduled at 60 mph (100 km/h) or more, almost exactly the same as the con-

Above left: The gleaming stainless steel body of the Budd-built Burlington diesel train-set, the 'Pioneer Zephyr', as it appeared in a 1934 film The Silver Streak
Above: Advertisement for Wagons-Lits trains, which in the 1920s opened luxury services beyond Western Europe.
Above right: The German lightweight diesel unit, the 'Fliegende Hamburger', at Berlin before its test run in 1932.
Below: In 1934 the second Union Pacific diesel streamliner, M10001, beat the coast-to-coast rail record by 14½ hours.

temporary British timebooks, but slightly less than those of the French railways. But by 1939 the US aggregate was a stunning 75,000 train-miles (120,700 km), whereas Europe as a whole could muster only some 54,500 (87,700 km) led by Germany and Britain with some 13,600 (21,900 km) and 12,000 (19,300 km) respectively. What had transformed the transatlantic balance was, of course, diesel traction.

ENTER THE INTERNAL-COMBUSTION ENGINE

Railways had been dabbling in internal-combustion engine vehicles from the early years of the century, but the earliest examples were petrol-driven, although a diesel-electric railcar was committed to public service in Sweden in 1913. In the 1920s several US railroads acquired diesel-electric locomotives as shunters, impressed with their availability for continuous work compared with a steam engine's recurrent need of time off for

servicing. But as yet diesel engines were too heavy and cumbersome to compete with steam or electric traction for main-line haulage. For rural passenger work US railroads preferred petrol-electric railcars, nicknamed 'doodlebugs', of which some 700 were turned out in the 1920s.

The turning-point was the near-simultaneous perfection in the USA and Germany of far more compact, high rpm diesel engines. In the USA General Motors' new 201A two-cycle engine of the early 1930s suddenly cut a diesel power plant's weight/power ratio from about 80 lb (36.3 kg) to 20 lb (9.1 kg) per horsepower of output. This advance coincided both with a vogue for streamlining and with the adaptation to rail coach bodywork of the latest lightweight metal techniques of the aircraft and automobile industry devised by the two great US carbuilders, Budd and Pullman-Standard. In 1933 the Union Pacific and the Chicago, Burlington & Quincy independently

decided to integrate these three new developments in train-sets that were to ignite a revolution in US railroading.

First to emerge was the Union Pacific's (UP) quaintly fish-headed and fin-tailed three-car articulated unit, the M-10000, in February 1934. It promptly exhibited 100mph (160km/h) capability and drew over a million engrossed visitors – headed by President Franklin D. Roosevelt – on a barnstorming tour of sixty-eight cities which eventually led it to the 1934 'Century of Progress' exhibition in Chicago. But on the display's opening day, 26 May 1934, the UP train's thunder was stolen by the Burlington's articulated three-car 'Pioneer Zephyr', which was dispatched straight from Denver to the pageant in a calculated transcontinental record attempt and wrapped up the 1,015.4 mile (1,634.1km) journey in a fraction under 13 hours 5 minutes for an end-to-end average speed of 77.6mph (124.9km/h). Moreover, this was done at a fuel cost of sixteen dollars, such was the price of 418 gallons of diesel oil in 1934! The following October the second UP diesel streamliner, the six-car M-10001, slashed the previous coast-to-coast rail record by 14½ hours and the best public service schedule of that year by over 27 hours when it was run experimentally from Los Angeles to New York, 3,259 miles (5,245km), in five minutes under 59 hours.

When the Burlington's first 'Twin Cities Zephyrs' entered public service the following spring they chalked up practically a 100 per cent load factor in the first ten weeks and the Burlington hurried to order roomier units. The resultant Denver–Chicago 'Denver Zephyrs' of 1936, twelve-car sets of which two vehicles were power units with an aggregate output of 3,000hp from three engines, prefigured the luxuries of the ultimate transcontinental diesel streamliner, with a cocktail and observation lounge complementing a diner and a wide range of sleeping accommodation (the first, incidentally, to be equipped with electric razor sockets). On 23 October 1936 a 'Denver Zephyr' set with four of its ten trailers temporarily removed was fettled up for a fresh transcontinental record attempt, this time from east to west so that it faced the long climb from the prairies to the 5,000ft (1,524m) level of Denver. Topping 116mph (187km/h) *en route* it sprinted the whole distance at an average of 83.3mph (134.1km/h), still a world record

for a journey of more than 1,000 miles (1,600km).

By then similar German lightweight diesel units (similar, that is, apart from the fact that the German streamliners were exclusively day trains) had begun to extend European speed horizons dramatically. Introduction in May 1933 of the two-car 'Fliegende Hamburger' on a 77.4mph (124.6km/h) average between Berlin and Hamburg was followed in 1935 by the 'Fliegende Kölner' and the 'Fliegende Frankfurter', each a high-speed business service between the cities of their titles and Berlin. That year a new range of three-car units appeared to be followed in 1938 by four-car sets. In the summer of 1935 the Reichsbahn had already tabled the world's first 80mph (130km/h) average start-to-stop schedules with these diesel flyers; by

1939 German timetables showed forty-nine daily runs timed at over 70mph (115km/h), more than twice as many as all the other European railways put together. Practically all major German cities were interlinked with each other and with Berlin by the diesel streamliners.

The French were even more active than the Germans in developing internal combustion-engined rail vehicles, first petrol and then diesel. By the end of the 1930s, in fact, they were operating more railcars than any European system, including many of the idiosyncratic Michelin type, of which the wheels were steel-flanged but rubber-tyred. This French fleet included some inter-city units with proven 100mph (160km/h) capability, but only in the twilight of the pre-war era was the statutory French rail speed

limit of 120 km/h (75 mph) relaxed to 140 km/h (90 mph) for them. In consequence the quickest French schedule of 1939 – 73 mph (117.5 km/h) for the 219.1 miles (352.6 km) from Nancy to Paris – was well below the best of the German diesel streamliners (and only slightly better than the best German steam timing, the 72.7 mph [117 km/h] average of one of the Hamburg–Berlin business flyers,

Below left: Two examples of French diesels in the 1930s – a rubber-tyred Michelin railcar (above) and a PLM twin-unit built by Bugatti (below).
Below: In 1936 Santa Fe Railroad's first 'Super Chief', built by Electromotive, ran the 2,227 miles from Chicago to Los Angeles unchanged on a regular schedule taking 39¾ hours.

which was Europe's fastest with that form of traction at the outbreak of war).

In Britain the GWR invested in a squad of diesel railcars, chiefly for rural stopping service; the LMS and LNER dabbled in one-off diesel railcar experiments; while as described in an earlier chapter, the SR dedicated itself to third-rail dc electrification. On the longer-haul routes from London to provincial cities, however, the thrust of British inter-city passenger service development up to 1939 was totally reliant on steam power.

Until 1932 advance on the rival routes from London to Scotland was hobbled by the pact, which the East and West Coast Companies struck after the 1888 and 1895 Races to the North, not to outdo each other in speed. The LMS and LNER had to content themselves with competitive

emulation in amenities, such as two-a-side seating in the first-class compartments of their crack Anglo-Scottish trains and the LNER's early essays in train radio, cinema cars and hairdressing salons, or in gimmickry, exemplified by a 1928 contest in length of non-stop running. The LMS muffled the LNER's publicity trumpets on this occasion by running its 'Royal Scot' the slightly further distance from London Euston to Glasgow and Edinburgh without an intermediate call three days before the non-stop London King's Cross–Edinburgh première of the LNER 'Flying Scotsman', but then the LMS rested on its laurels. With the aid of new tenders for Gresley's Pacifics that had an in-built corridor so that the engine crew could change places with another in the train at the mid-point of the route, only the

'Flying Scotsman' made a regular summer practice of running the 392.8 miles (632.2 km) from London to Edinburgh non-stop, a feat never surpassed for distance anywhere else under steam.

In the second half of the 1930s the railways' publicity made much of the high-speed streamliners – the LNER's London–Newcastle 'Silver Jubilee' of 1935, London–Edinburgh 'Coronation' (Britain's fastest pre-war train, timed to average 71.9 mph (115.7 km/h) from King's Cross to York) and London–Leeds/Bradford 'West Riding Limited' of 1937, and the LMS London–Glasgow 'Coronation Scot' of 1937 – but from a strictly commercial viewpoint they were not the most consequential products of the period. The LNER trains, in fact, were almost shop-window loss-leaders because of the inflated costs of carving clear paths for trains so much swifter than the rank-and-file expresses, let alone the ambling, non-brake-fitted freights with which they shared tracks for parts of their itineraries. Of far greater moment for the future were the moves to democratize the accommodation and level up the performance standards of medium- and long-haul passenger trains – the SR's regular-interval service with standard electric train-sets between London and the South Coast; the LNER's pioneering of buffet cars undercutting restaurant car prices; better second-class coaches with compartment armrests; and the GWR and LMS drive to lift overall speed standards, rather than single out a few flag trains for spectacular acceleration. The LNER, in its 'Coronation' streamliner, boasted much the fastest Anglo-Scottish train in 1939, but compared with 1913 its Anglo-Scottish expresses overall averaged only an eighteen-minute saving in transit time, whereas those of the LMS were almost fifty minutes quicker.

The depression's pinching of balance-sheets compelled a number of railways around the world to shelve electrification extensions and kindled interest in diesel traction's possibilities as a heavy haulier. Early applications had clearly established the diesel's fundamental advantages over steam in operating economy and acceleration; and its adoption would avoid the cripplingly high first cost of setting up the current supply for electrification. The crucial question was whether diesel engine technology could come up with a power plant that combined a satisfactory output with the compactness required for accommodation in a locomotive of tolerable weight and bulk.

Since the early 1920s, when the Russian engineer G.V. Lomonossov was percipiently authorized – and capitalized – by Lenin's Russia to embark on the first diesel locomotive essays with the German Reichsbahn (three pioneering 1,200 hp machines were the outcome), several European firms had been feeling their way into diesel locomotive construction. By the start of the 1930s, motivated by the dearth of water supplied in the bleakest areas of the USSR, the Russians were the most extensive employers of main-line diesel locomotives, but several other countries with severely graded routes – India, Japan and several South American states were instances – were sampling the new medium. However, the 800 hp output from an 81 ton, five-axle locomotive devised by British builders Armstrong Whitworth for the Indian continent in 1935 typified the uninviting power/weight ratios European builders were attaining in the mid-1930s state of their art.

The only significant high-power prototype to emerge from Europe's industry before the war was a massive, permanently coupled 4,400 hp twin-unit acquired by the French PLM in 1937 with the aim of running 450 ton trains from Paris to the French Riviera at an end-to-end average for the 700-odd miles (1,125 km) of 69.5 mph (118. km/h). Each half of the locomotive, which grossed 225 tons, was carried on two four-wheel bogies and six powered axles and was powered by a Sulzer diesel engine with a 2,200 hp rating. The newborn SNCF was seriously contemplating a fleet of main-line locomotives with individual outputs of up to 3,000 hp when the war aborted the project.

DIESEL TRIUMPHANT

Reliable, stress-proof and efficient means to transmit the engine's output to the road wheels was a prerequisite to employment of high power. Lomonossov conducted parallel experiments with compressed air, hydraulic, mechanical and electric transmissions and rejected the first two systems. From the late 1930s onwards, however, the emergent German diesel industry made the alliance of high rpm engines and hydraulic transmissions its hallmark, claiming incontestable advantages of high continuous tractive effort in all speed ranges at much less cost in locomotive weight and bulk than with electric transmission. The simplest of all forms of transmission, naturally, was straight mechanical through gears, but its limitation was the power it could handle without components disintegrating; outside of one or two experiments, such as the privately sponsored Fell 4–8–4 locomotive tested on British Rail tracks after the war, mechanical transmissions were confined to railcars and low-power locomotives.

taneous success of General Motors' first main-line locomotive prototypes and the brushfire of cost-saving US dieselization they soon ignited which confirmed the majority European belief in the diesel-electric format.

Arguably the first epochal railway locomotive to be manufactured since Stephenson's *Rocket* was a 240 ton, 3,600 hp twin-unit, embodying two twelve-cylinder versions of the engine that powered the 'Pioneer Zephyr', which the Electromotive Division of General Motors turned out in 1935. On a countrywide demonstration tour this prototype at once proved that it could handle the same tonnage as the average US steam passenger locomotive of the day, but at half the fuel-cost per mile, with less servicing and, from extrapolation of early evidence, at considerably lower repair cost. Before the year was out the Baltimore & Ohio and the Santa Fe were customers and in 1936 the Santa Fe previewed the future by assigning its purchases to run its new 'Super Chief' unchanged over the 2,227 miles (3,584 km) from Chicago to Los Angeles on an

Above: Dome cars on the Union Pacific 'City of Portland' glide through Columbia River Gorge, Oregon.
Below: From 1945 the 'Twentieth Century Limited' (here beside the Hudson river) was powered by diesel locomotives.

Most widely adopted in the late 1930s and ever since was the electric transmission, wherein the diesel engine was direct-coupled to a generator of current for electric dc traction motors. In recent years the availability of compact semi-conductor rectifiers has seen the historic diesel-electric system evolve into the more effective diesel-alternator layout, in which the diesel drives an alternator and the resultant ac is rectified on the locomotive before it is fed to the dc traction motors.

In the 1960s, tempted by the outstandingly high power/weight ratios the Germans were achieving with diesel-hydraulics on their own soil, the Southern Pacific and Denver & Rio Grande Western Railroads each imported a stud of 4,400 hp units for their mountain territory in the west (but discarded them within ten years). Apart from this, US diesel traction was launched with electric transmission and never changed course. It was the instan-

unprecedented regular schedule of 39¾ hours overall.

With other railroads queueing at its shop door, Electromotive now made a sage policy decision. In subsequent decades it was to be worth millions of dollars to General Motors abroad as well as at home. Potential buyers who spread sheets of their own fancy specifications over Electromotive's office tables were politely asked to fold them up and take them home. Electromotive refused to squander the diesel locomotive's economic potential in unnecessary one-off design variations. It would happily paint a locomotive as flamboyantly as the customer wanted and concede minor component changes, but the name of the game was rigid standardization of a very limited range of standard locomotive models, each guaranteeed in reliability and performance because it had not been mass-produced without the protracted and most meticulous 'debugging' of a prototype.

This policy was promulgated in the E range of streamlined passenger units with full carbody that rolled off the production line in 1938. In the E6 of this series Electromotive unveiled the most successful engine of diesel traction history to date, the V12 Type 567, which was to be the prime mover of the company's diesel locomotives for years to come. Nearly 1,300 twin-engined E series units of around 2,000 hp apiece were constructed for US railroads between 1938 and the supersession of the model in 1963. A few of the ultimate E8s and E9s were still serving Amtrak, the US rail passenger operating corporation, at the end of the 1970s.

But could diesels shift as much freight tonnage as a 'Lima Super-Power' or one of the mammoth steam articulateds? The

question was answered empirically. The passenger service-oriented Es had been manufactured both as cab units and as cabless 'booster' units, each of the same power and each mounted on a pair of three-axle, twin-motor bogies. Railroads soon grasped how simple it was to multiple not just one but two or more boosters to one cab unit and create a 6,000 hp or even more potent locomotive without any addition to the locomotive crew. On this 'building block' principle there should be little problem in matching diesel power to the weightiest mile-long freight train. The last lingering doubts of most steam operators were dispelled when, in 1939, Electromotive evolved its 1,350 hp V16 engine in the 567 series and fitted eight of them to a two-cab and two-booster, four-unit demonstrator on two-axle bogies which was put through a year of faultless freight-hauling display in every conceivable variation of terrain and climate which US main-line railroading could oppose to it. More than half the host railroads immediately mailed orders for production versions and in the next two decades Electromotive mass-produced almost 7,000 units of this FT type and its later F refinement.

The Fs had streamlined full-width bodies like the Es. Gradually railroads realized that they were paying too high an operational price for visual symmetry, because the configuration blocked any rearward view from the driving console and consequently any multiple-unit 'block' incorporating only one cab unit needed turning at terminals. Moreover, mechanics had to grope inside the body to get at the machinery. Recognition of these limitations and new awareness of the diesel's inherent versatility spawned the mainstay of today's US railroading, the

Above left: An observation car built in 1938 for the Milwaukee's 'Hiawatha'. Above: The interior of a dining car used on the 'Hiawatha'. Below right: The departure of the first and second 'City of San Francisco' streamliners from Southern Pacific's Oakland Pier station in 1940.

'road-switcher' or 'hood unit' in American terminology: a machine in which aesthetic outline is a secondary consideration and the machinery is housed in a narrower bonnet, or 'hood', to obtain a good view fore and aft from the driving desk of a full-width cab. 'Road-switcher' signifies that the locomotive is adaptable operationally to both main-line and yard work, though the term grew generically nonsensical in the 1960s when Union Pacific bought some gargantuan 6,600 hp locomotives in the nominally road-switcher category. The trend-setting road-switcher was Electromotive's 1,500 hp GP7 of late 1949.

The hectic years of US dieselization were 1946–58. In that period the steam fleets of the country's Class I railroads were massacred from 37,500 engines – still powering 88 per cent of their owners' freight and 78 per cent of their passenger trains in 1946 – to 1,700, for the most part concentrated on ten railroads. Concurrently the diesel locomotive stock climbed to over 27,600 units, which in 1958 had a grip on roughly 90 per cent of all main-line rail traffic. Electromotive dominated the diesel market and still does. ALCO, the merged Baldwin-Lima-Hamilton and Fairbanks-Morse fought for a foothold, but all had given up by 1969; only General Electric, a latecomer with its own road-switcher range in 1960, competes on any scale in today's US locomotive market.

Electromotive's E series of diesel locomotives set off a flood-tide of US express train acceleration from 1936 onwards, of such dimensions that by 1950 the 152,000 mile (244,600km) total of start-to-stop runs tabled daily at average speeds of 60mph (100km/h) or more was six times the 1936 figure. Several short sprints over level track timed in excess of an 80mph (130km/h) average had no world superior. And these were no longer only the comparatively effortless spurts of lightweight, self-powered streamliners, but in many cases the surges of heavy locomotive-hauled trains. The pace was hottest where companies paralleled each other in a busy corridor, above all that between Chicago and the Twin Cities of Minneapolis and St Paul, where three railroads were in fierce contention and there was a choice of seven weighty trains each way daily. Here both Milwaukee 'Hiawathas' and Burlington 'Zephyrs', now locomotive-hauled rakes, had routinely to run at 100mph (160km/h) in order to maintain high average speeds that eventually reached 84.4mph (135.8km/h) over one 57.7 mile (92.9km) stretch in the case of a Burlington 'Zephyr'. To the connoisseur, however, these short-distance exploits were not as impressive as the end-to-end times made by the great transcontinentals like Union Pacific's 'Cities', Santa Fe's 'Super Chief' and the jointly operated 'California Zephyr', since their itineraries required 6,000hp diesel 'blocks' and their fifteen-, sixteen- or seventeen-car trains to surmount summits ranging from 7,622ft (2,323m) to 9,191ft (2,801m) above sea level (in the case of the 'Zephyr') in the mountain ranges of the west before the Pacific coast was reached.

COMFORT MATCHES SPEED

To complement speed the railroads laid out huge sums on opulent new train-sets and staffed them with commensurate extravagance. The Great Northern's transcontinental 'Empire Builder' of the 1950s, for instance, was fifteen cars long, but had living accommodation for only 323 passengers at most because of the space pre-empted for lounges, coffee shop, bars and diner. To minister to those 323 passengers the train deployed a staff of 25, exclusive of all railway operating staff such as locomotive crews. The prodigal pace of equipment renewal was extraordinary, too. How were the Great Northern's stockholders persuaded to accept that the 'Empire Builder', re-equipped with new luxury cars from end to end in 1947 at a cost of some $7 millions, needed another total renewal only four years later for a further $12 millions, then in 1955 was worth an outlay of $6 millions more for the addition of full-length dome observation cars?

The dome car was the last striking addition to the amenities of the great American passenger trains. Its genesis was a General Motors executive's inspiration when he was riding through spectacular western canyons in the cab of a freight-hauling diesel through the Rockies in 1944 (his brainwave is commemorated at the precise spot where it flashed through his mind, on the Denver & Rio Grande near Gresley, Colorado, with a cairn surmounted by a model dome car). His employers were intrigued by the concept of a bi-level car with a glass-roofed upper-storey observation lounge and eventually built a demonstration train-set embodying the idea in conjunction with Pullman-Standard. But before that emerged the Burlington's president had got wind of the idea, had one of his own cars remodelled and premiered the country's first dome car in July 1945. Public response was immediate and before the 1950s were out every prestigious US train was studded with one or more domes.

Only in present-day South Africa's 'Blue Train' has the world still any impression of the long-haul US streamliner in its 1950s heyday, when railroads summoned up every resource and ingenuity of industrial design to stamp their service with a distinctive, unforgettable character. One of the most far-famed through its popularity with Hollywood's elite was the Santa Fe 'Super Chief', which linked Los Angeles with Chicago and, by onward through sleeper, with New York and Washington. In this all-Pullman, extra-fare train every apartment, from 'roomettes' to the suites which could be fashioned by withdrawing partitions between adjoining bedrooms, had its own radio and enclosed toilet. Champagne came with the compliments of the Santa Fe at dinner, served to a menu of a length and sophistication that would handsomely promote any first-class hotel on terra firma. By prior appointment one could take the meal, not in the main restaurant, but in a delicately furnished, ten-seater Turquoise Room on the lower floor of one of the most superb of all dome cars. Upstairs in this vehicle was the palatial observation lounge, with a bar and individual, rotating armchairs; elsewhere, at normal car floor level, another sumptuously furnished lounge with a secluded writing-desk area. In other parts of the train were a barber's shop and ample shower-bath facilities. Valet service was always on call. News bulletins and the latest Stock Exchange prices would be handed in to the train at each stop. They were the less frenetic days when one travelled not just to arrive, but no less to enjoy travel for its own sake.

ADJUSTMENT TO THE MOTOR TRANSPORT AGE

The problems which the Western world's railway systems had to face in the two decades after the Second World War stemmed essentially from an ever increasing and unrestricted competition with the car, the truck and the aeroplane. As an example of the effect these rival modes of transport were to have, Swiss Railways enjoyed 52.2 per cent of the country's total passenger movement in 1950, but by 1960 their share had dropped to 28.7 per cent, and by 1965 to 19.6 per cent. Over the same fifteen years the mileage travelled in private motor cars increased more than fivefold, while the airlines' proportion went up from 0.3 per cent to 4.2 per cent of the total. The figures for freight are less dramatic, but the decline was just as steady: railway's share of total tonnage dropped from 20.3 per cent in 1950 to 18.9 per cent in 1960 and to 15.3 per cent in 1965, while over the same period road freight trebled. And Switzerland had not been devastated by war; the problems in

other countries were further aggravated by the necessity of rebuilding railways either wrecked by bombing or just worn out by the strain the war had imposed on them.

It was the prospect of this changing pattern of transportation which forced the railways to produce their own competitive response, in order at least to match the speed, efficiency and economy that the road and airways might provide in the immediate future. Time was to show, however, that this could not be achieved within the self-financing constraints that the railways' historical status as a commercial carrier imposed. Equating both efficiency and social necessity with a black balance sheet was to prove an impossibility, and for some countries this was a hard lesson to learn.

The railways of the industrialized world sorely needed enhanced performance and economy just to retain their share of both passenger and freight markets in a postwar transport world of upsurging private-car ownership, expanding motorway systems, road freight juggernauts and mass air travel. Furthermore, railway managements needed to rethink their

operating and commercial method, because the easy accessibility and fast-sharpening economy of road transport was making many traditional elements of rail service hopelessly uncompetitive.

And where railways were expected, however sanguinely, to be self-supporting, the common carrier obligations, which had been laid upon them as a safeguard against misuse of their nineteenth-century monopoly positions, had become an anachronism. Maintenance of staff, track and vehicle capacity to convey any goods offered to them – which by now meant mostly freight that other carriers shunned as unprofitable – could be justified only as a State-supported social service.

THE LEGACY OF
THE SECOND WORLD WAR

The scale of the war and its logistics demanded far more of the combatants' railways than the First World War. Nowhere was this more so than in the United States, whose forces were this time committed in the Far East as well as in Europe. With road transport tightly circumscribed by petrol rationing and

rubber shortages, the US railroads had to shoulder more than 90 per cent of organized troop movement and military freight, as well as a considerably higher proportion of civilian traffic (over 70 per cent) than in the preceding peacetime years. From 1942 onwards the total freight-ton-mileage of US railroads was annually at least 50 per cent greater than that registered in the peak 1918 year of the earlier war. Indeed, in 1944 it was 82 per cent higher. And in that same peak year, 1944, the railroads' recorded passenger-mileage exceeded the aggregate of all five depression years, 1931 to 1935 inclusive. Over the whole war period the railroads

transported an average of a million servicemen a month in a total of 114,000 troop trains.

It was all done with far greater efficiency than in the First World War. Of course, the railroads had much more powerful locomotives and higher-capacity freight vehicles, but they were also better operated. A key factor in this was the rapid spread of Centralized Traffic Control over the vital single-track sectors of trans-continental and other routes; in 1929 only 341 route-miles (549 km) had CTC, but by 1945 this had increased to 6,495 route-miles (10,453 km). But most importantly, determined to fend off Federal control

which had been imposed in the First World War, railroad managements fell over themselves to co-operate with each other.

In Britain, where the railways were brought under Government control for a second time, wartime stress was intensified by subjection first to Luftwaffe bombing and later to flying-bombs and rockets. Nevertheless, freight-ton-mileage had soared by 43 per cent above the peacetime norm by 1943. The railways' supreme effort was mounted just before and after the invasion of Normandy; in the two months preceding D-Day almost 24,500 special trains had to be run, and in the ensuing four weeks as many as 18,000.

Hauled by four diesel units, the Union Pacific 'City of Portland' snakes its way through barren terrain near Portland in northern Oregon.

A 'Mistral' express crosses the Rhône at Lyon. France foresaw the advantages of electrification early on, and quickly pushed ahead with its conversion plans after the Second World War. The Paris–Lyon line was one of the first to be electrified by the SNCF who were readily supported by the Government.

Britain's railways emerged from the war physically and financially drained, and shabbily remunerated by the Governmnet for their wartime work. The arrears of maintenance were fearful, but the bomb damage had been made good as it happened and the trains could be kept running by make-do-and-mend. A quick resumption of pre-war service standards was out of the question, for, in their strict control of scarce raw materials, steel and construction, successive governments relegated the railways practically to the end of the industrial queue. They drastically curbed investment in the newly nationalized system and it was not until 1955 that British Railways were at last permitted to spend heavily on modernization and to overtake enforced wartime neglect.

Mainland European railways, on the other hand, were so devastated that if they were to play any significant role in postwar transport they had to be rebuilt. French Railways had lost half their locomotives and freight wagons; Allied bombing, resistance sabotage and finally earth scorching by the retreating Germans had incapacitated six of their ten locomotive works, well over half their marshalling yards and freight depots, a third of their passenger stations, almost 2,000 route-miles (3,200 km) of track, 1,965 bridges, 27 tunnels and 570 signalboxes. The Dutch had more than 60 per cent of their track and 70 per cent of their railway bridges in ruins, as well as 84 per cent of their locomotives and 90 per cent of their rail vehicles purloined or destroyed. The aftermath was much the same in Belgium and Italy.

As for Germany, the problems of reconstruction were compounded by the country's post-war partition. In West Germany the newly created Deutsche Bundesbahn inherited half a railway system that before the war had been focused on Berlin. To re-orientate this to the north-south social and commercial axis of the new Federal Republic involved subjecting a number of routes to volumes of traffic for which they were never conceived. As time went on, moreover, their curvature and gradients would severely cramp the DB's quest for higher inter-city passenger speed. This handicap was to become – and still is – particularly frustrating on the key route from Hamburg and Bremen via Hanover to Frankfurt, Stuttgart and Munich.

The West German railways, like Britain's, were kept on short commons for some years after the war. But in the 1950s, as Dr Ludwig Erhard engineered the country's post-war 'economic miracle', resources were generated to swell the Marshall Aid dollars from the USA which all the war-ravaged countries – except Britain – were now gratefully applying to railway reconstruction as a priority. By the middle of the 1950s even the DB was showing more signs of modernization than British Railways.

ELECTRIFICATION

So, with rebuilding forced upon Europe's railways after the war, it was common sense to modernize at the same time. The result was that, with the exception yet again of British Railways, two of whose pre-nationalization companies' plans for main-line diesel locomotives where shelved in favour of simple, rugged, standard steam design, the major West European railways set course for dieselization or electrification. The few that did continue steam construction did so only as a transitionary move during the spread of the new traction.

The electrification pace was set by the French. SNCF planners had kept their war-interrupted electrification schemes alive during the German occupation and as early as 1946 their centrepiece, the 1.5 kV dc conversion of the ex-PLM main line from Paris to Lyon, was under way with the enthusiastic backing of a Government anxious to economize in consumption of scarce coal. In only six years some 380 route-miles (610 km) of main and avoiding line between the French capital and Lyon were electrified. A re-draft of express passenger services was a priority objective of the scheme from the start, and in the winter of 1952–3 this intention materialized in a dramatically rewritten timetable that restored to Europe its first post-war timings at an average speed of 70–75 mph (115–120 km/h).

The French Government urged the SNCF to pursue electrification as rapidly as human and physical resources allowed – and, moreover, to apply it to secondary as well as main lines. But the SNCF's economists protested that the traffic of many French main lines, never mind their feeders, was not enough to support the heavy first cost of dc electrification, with its necessarily frequent sub-stations and substantial catenary and supporting structures. On the sidelines, however, the SNCF's electrical engineers were on the point of perfecting a new, considerably less capital-intensive electric traction technology.

The post-war Allied arrangements in West Germany had drawn the French occupation zone around the 34 mile (55 km) Höllental line in the Black Forest. In the 1930s the Germans had converted this line into a laboratory for experiments in the use of industrial high-voltage ac for traction. The French were quick to grasp the implications if this system became thoroughly practicable. Not only would its more widely spaced sub-stations and less ponderous catenary greatly reduce installation costs, and its ability to take current straight from the national grid obviate the railways' construction of their own power stations, but, in addition, traction of considerably enhanced performance should be technically realizable.

In 1950–51, after three years of research, the SNCF electrified a line of its own, the 48½ mile (78 km) branch in the Alps from Aix-les-Bains to Annecy and La Roche-sur-Foron, as a 25 kV ac 50 Hz test-bed for their first three prototype locomotives. Within months they had data encouraging enough to proclaim not only extension of this test-bed, but their intention to electrify similarly one of their vital industrial main lines, the north-to-east artery between Dunkirk and Thionville.

Initially traction design was handicapped by the unwieldy apparatus needed to convert the high-voltage ac supply to low-voltage dc for the traction motors on board the traction unit. But, before long, technology came up with non-mechanical current rectifiers – first mercury-arc, then of semi-conductor materials such as germanium and silicon. Soon transformer and rectifier gear was being turned out in packages slim enough to fit under the frames of a commuter multiple-unit power car. A new railway electrification age had opened.

However, the economies of the new system were not so monumental that it paid every railway already part-electrified to convert to it. The case for change was even less a few years later when multi-voltage locomotives had been developed which could work with equal facility and very disparate power outputs under two, three or even four different ac and dc catenaries. A traction unit would soon be able to operate on any electrified main line throughout Europe.

The French, however, continued to electrify on both systems, at first applying the new 25 kV ac 50 Hz to projected schemes which would extend catenary across the northern half of the country, but continuing with 1.5 kV dc south of Paris where the system was already widespread. But later, when the ex-PLM main line was electrified beyond Marseilles along the Côte d'Azur, 25 kV ac was tacked on to the existing 1.5 kV dc between Marseilles and Paris.

The lead taken by the French was followed by nearly every railway which embarked on its first main-line electrification after 1950. They were all persuaded by the example of French performance to standardize exclusively on high-voltage ac at the industrial frequency. Even BR, within months of reaffirming pre-war dedication to 1.5 kV dc, experimentally converted as a 25 kV ac proving ground the short Lancaster–Morecambe–Heysham

line, which had been uniquely electrified at 6.6 kV ac 25 Hz by the Midland Railway in 1908. And in 1956 BR was to pronounce high-voltage ac the standard for all future electrification outside the low-voltage dc third-rail territory of its Southern Region.

And today the list of countries taking the same ac electrification path is lengthening. Only in 1979, for instance, Denmark, embarking on its first electrification beyond the limits of the Copenhagen suburban area, was added to a number that includes Czechoslovakia, Hungary, India, Japan (for its high-speed Shinkansen passenger railways), Yugoslavia, Luxembourg, Pakistan, Portugal, South Africa, Turkey, the USA (for the Boston–New York–Washington main line), the USSR and Brazil. For some of these countries, especially those in the underdeveloped world, the lower first cost of the ac system has economically justified electrification projects that would have been barely conceivable with dc.

For all these railway systems, there were two main sources of appeal. Firstly, the technical characteristics of electric traction achieved smarter acceleration, more sure-footed adhesion and greater power from a given tonnage of locomotive weight

Electric locomotives in India. The advantages of high-voltage ac electrification are being recognized by many countries.

Now part of railway history, this small branch-line station was one of hundreds that closed in Britain in the 1960s as part of the Beeching plan to cut all unprofitable lines and services.

than diesel traction – and that ratio was to widen significantly with the advance of ac traction technology, especially when it could incorporate developments in electronics. Secondly, but no less attractive in the post-war world of inflating labour and materials costs, was the electric traction unit's minimal need of time off haulage work for maintenance, which allowed an electrified route or area to be operated with considerably fewer traction units than diesel traction permitted, let alone steam. This clearly diminished the need for maintenance establishments and staff, but it could also effect economies in train crews. Electric traction's almost continuous availability for revenue-earning work enabled locomotives to be turned round much more quickly between jobs, with the corollary that their crews might be capable of rostering to an additional trip within a single duty shift. The only deterrents to worldwide electrification of heavily-trafficked lines, in fact, were the availability in the immediate post-war years of cheap and plentiful oil – above all in North America – and the formidable capital cost of installing a supply system and the catenary.

BEECHING AND THE NEED FOR RATIONALIZATION

Even in those cramped days of the 1950s, to rely on cheap oil supplies in an attempt to minimize costs in a modernization programme was an obviously short-sighted economy. For electric traction very quickly demonstrated better performance and economy, which gave the operator at least one edge in the rapidly changing post-war transport world. However, it quickly became apparent that what the car and the truck could provide was door-to-door transport; better roads now made that a swifter operation; cheap oil made it economical. Thus, in a short space of time, the railway was to become the second alternative for the transport customer, the carrier of last resort.

Britain was the first country to square up to the implications for railways of road transport's new versatility. This, however, was not surprising, not so much because the country's close-packed urbanization originated so many short-distance journeys which favoured use of the road – that was equally true of Belgium and Holland – but because Britain's railways were the only ones in Europe with no tradition of support from public funds. In fact, it was not until the Transport Act of 1968 that the principle of subsidy for socially defensible but inherently unprofitable passenger services became politically recognized. The many laborious legislative essays in

railway finance and management from the 1947 nationalization onwards had always set self-sufficiency as their target.

Consequently, political anxiety was acute when the first fruits of BR's Modernization Plan failed to stem the deficits into which BR had slid from the start of nationalization, and the balance sheet reddened more garishly as the country's heavy road freight vehicle capacity soared 60 per cent between 1958 and 1963. This was mainly a result of the Conservative Government's 1953 deregulation of own-account transport, which basically removed all restrictions on the size and operational range of own-account lorries (road vehicles owned and operated by the trader himself for the movement of his own goods, as opposed to those of a haulier plying for general hire). The Conservatives reacted to BR's financial decline at the start of the 1960s by recruiting as Chairman of a reconstituted British Railways Board an industrialist with a brilliant track record of rationalization in the chemicals industry, Dr (later Lord) Beeching. His brief was to probe the whole of BR's activity and to set the system on a course guaranteeing ultimate viability. Beeching's findings were embodied in a document – officially the 1963 Reshaping Plan, but popularly dubbed the 'Beeching Plan' – which was to make his name familiar far beyond his own country because of the relevance of its dogma to efficient railway operation practically anywhere in today's developed world. The railway had become a political problem, as well as an item in a Government ledger.

The essence of the Beeching Plan's doctrine was that, particularly in what was becoming an era of steady if not yet runaway inflation, the railway was a highly capital-intensive medium that could never be viable unless it made the most of its disciplined ability to move traffic in bulk. It must renounce its nineteenth-century role of common carrier, available to ferry half a coachful of passengers down country branch lines and to deliver single wagonloads of coal and parcels to each and every wayside station. Those were now jobs done far more economically by road and there was no way a railway could compete without losing money heavily. Nor could the railway any longer afford to maintain its traditionally generous provision for traffic fluctuation. Thousands of coaches lay idle for two-thirds of the year and were only mobilized for holiday extra workings that did not even repay their upkeep. Traditional methods of dealing in freight by the wagonload, which wasted so much time and money in intermediate marshalling that the average wagon was starting a fresh loaded journey only once in twelve days, were abysmally unproductive. Track layouts were over-indulgent; they must be slimmed down to what was necessary to handle efficiently a stable throughput of worthwhile traffic.

The worthwhile business was what could be moved in an intact train from source to destination. Railwaymen must no longer regard the individual vehicle as the unit of rail movement: it was the train, for it was when a train was on the move with 500 passengers or 1,000 tons of freight, employing only two or three operational crew, that the modernized railway was optimizing its characteristics. And the more intact or unit trains that could be concentrated on a single route, the greater the financial contribution to that route's

fixed track, signalling, ground staff and other indirect costs. The easier it would be, too, to finance a rolling modernization programme on the key trunk routes.

Since 1963 the name of Beeching has been a synonym for ruthless axeing in Britain. Over the next five years BR underwent the most drastic surgery yet applied to any national rail system as passenger stations, freight depots and lines generating inadequate traffic volume were closed; coal and small-lot freight were concentrated on a few strategic mechanized depots which could be served by complete trains and from which local delivery was by road; duplicate routes and facilities inherited from the unregulated railway competition of the nineteenth century were rationalized; and track layouts thinned out. A stop was ordered to construction of any more of the big automated marshalling yards that were a key component of BR's 1955 moderniz-ation plan. There would be greatly reduced

use for these anyway in the drive for a high degree of unit train operation. Between 1963 and 1968 BR trimmed its passenger coach stock from 33,821 to 19,544, freight wagons from 862,000 to 437,412, passenger stations from 4,306 to 2,616, route-mileage used by passenger trains from 12,915 (20,785 km) to 8,471 (13,633 km), freight depots from 5,165 to 912 and total track-mileage from 47,543 (76,513 km) to 33,976 (54,679 km). Perhaps most import-ant of all, in the same period staff was cut from 476,545 to 296,274.

Even such grim amputations as these, however, failed to staunch the deficits. That was partly because it took a few more years to evolve a scientific appreciation of rail service costing – in the 1960s there was no certainty where the money was being

A typical British Railways freight train of the early 1960s with individual wagonloads. This was the kind of uneconomic service that Beeching abruptly ended.

Clearing snow on the Gotthard line in Switzerland. This high-altitude line is extremely expensive to maintain but, equally, is an essential route.

lost – and partly because even the Beeching regime underestimated the cost of change on a railway. Closure of a branch line, for instance, did not save as much as expected for a number of reasons; some of its fixed costs were shared with a main line, even if only at a junction station; some of its traffic was fed into main-line services; and redundant staff had to be compensated or re-located. Nevertheless, the Beeching cuts did start a commercial re-orientation which in the 1980s would make BR by far the least expensive system in Western Europe in terms of service rendered per million pounds of grant aid from public funds.

By the 1960s no railway was immune from the effect of sharply escalating wage costs as well as a drain of traffic to the competition. Even mainland European governments also sought to be rid of those country lines which could barely fill a couple of passenger trains and a short goods train each way daily with the traffic left them by rising private car ownership and cheaper, more convenient trucks – situations where, as one British Transport Minister discovered, it had become a better bargain to buy a car for each of the residual regular train-users than to go on running and maintaining the railway. In Western Europe only the Swiss Federal

managed to report a surplus of revenue – including subventions – over expenditure until the mid-1970s. Finally it too succumbed in the aftermath of the mid-decade oil crisis as both its tourist traffic and especially its transit freight slumped through the combined effect of the worldwide recession and the then impregnable strength of the Swiss franc.

But by and large, the railways of the European mainland escaped the political probing to which BR was subjected during the 1950s. They were shielded in part by their historic status as a state-supported social service, in part by the fact that restoration of their wartime depredation was still incomplete. And unlike BR, most of them were also protected to some degree from the unfettered competition of new, high-capacity road freight vehicles which, with the benefit of the new highways, were developing a greatly superior productivity to traditional rail freight working in wagonloads. France and Holland, for instance, set quantitative limits on long-haul road freight operation, and Switzerland curbs on the international road freight it would allow to use its roads as a transit land-bridge. Consequently mainland European systems were not losing freight business as precipitately as BR. The need, however, to rationalize in the face of competition and costs was never in dispute; it was more a question of method. Few governments needed, or would allow, a knife as sharp as Beeching's. The example of the West German railways over

the past dozen years puts the problem in perspective.

In 1968 the Social-Democrat Transport Minister in West Germany's coalition government of the day, Georg Leber, attempted to close some 3,200 route-miles (5,150 km) of the DB as a component of what became known as the Leber Plan, the other controversial element of which was a proposal to ban entirely heavy road vehicle movement of bulk freight such as coal, aggregates and steel with the dual aim of environmental protection and more productive use of the railway. But the post-war Federal Republic, with its careful balance of power and financial control between Bonn and the provincial *Land* governments, and its ambivalent reverence for the environment but dedication to the road vehicle and citizens' rights, was no place for such revolution. All Leber won was agreement to some seasonal and local prohibitions on heavy road freight and a special tax on the bigger lorries engaged in long-haul freight that was weighted against the particular scourge of post-war railways – deregulated own-account transport. Few closures were secured in the face of virulent self-interested opposition from the provincial administrators.

The same happened to far more drastic proposals advanced late in 1975 by the DB itself, which advocated virtually halving the West German national system to the 10,000 route-miles (16,100 km) carrying 90 per cent of all its traffic. The DB was desperately anxious to escape from the demoralizing extent of its dependence on public money and the distraction of its management from major tasks by the need to keep up so many hopelessly unremunerative services as a social obligation. What was regarded as the official annual deficit was not extraordinary, given the size of the DB and the volume of its traffic; but if to that one added its total intake of subsidies, grants, compensation for heavily discounted fares to some passenger categories, schoolchildren especially, and aid to cover interest on vast sums already borrowed for post-war rehabilitation and modernization, then the DB's reliance on public money was on the way to a total of DM14 billions by the end of 1981. Another particular DB difficulty was the established civil servant status accorded a high proportion of its operating railwaymen, which made natural wastage through age or voluntary retirement the only hope of reducing labour costs in such cases as these.

Nevertheless the West German Government accepted only a fraction of the DB proposals. And even this heavily watered-down cure was pigeonholed in the closing 1970s, apart from agreement to transfer the traffic of a few rural and for the most part freight-only lines to road, as West Germany agonized over the long-term energy prospects and marked its railways inviolate. However, in 1981, with the government searching for palatable ways to trim social expenditure and check the worsening imbalance of the Federal budget, Bonn was moving towards loading provincial administrations with more of the cost of the loss-making rail services which they insisted on retaining.

And the story has been the same in other countries of Europe, too. Switzerland and Austria have perforce accepted the rural railway as a social necessity, because it is the only dependable winter transport in their high mountain valleys. In these two countries post-war rail closures have been negligible, though one should add that in neither do the railways consider they are adequately compensated for their essentially social operations. Every other Western European country has attempted to prune its railways, some quite severely and some more than once. Only France, under President Mitterand's socialist regime, has now firmly barred further rail closures and even moved to reopen some previously abandoned rural services.

As recently as the late 1970s the Belgian Government considered a Beeching-style truncation of the SNCB to check the railways' rising calls on public money; the inevitable closure of almost 350 passenger stations together producing only 4 per cent of all SNCB travel, of nearly 200 freight depots and of 25 marshalling yards, with the inevitable corollary of a 10 per cent staff reduction, was advocated in a plan to reshape the railway as a bulk carrier of people and goods, and thus extract the maximum benefit from the cash invested in it. Since, however, it was all too easy to read into this scheme another political ploy to nourish the more densely populated Flemish area of the country at the expense of its French-speaking territory, the plan's chance of execution in full looked remote.

In 1980, too, the Norwegian Government threatened a heavy cut in its support for the railways, which sounded like a second attempt to butcher its rural lines.

But, up to 1980, political sensitivity to constituency opinion had limited cuts to the most extreme cases of unviability and minimal use in every Western European country except Britain during and immediately after Beeching's presidency. Since then even British governments have been reluctant to bare the knife.

So few of the rationalizing options tried in post-war years have gained much public approval: the rural community is hopelessly vulnerable without its local service; the road hauliers throw up their arms at 'discriminatory' legislation; the taxpayer digs deep into his pockets for the subsidy. But the drive to cut costs has not always needed external stimulus. Few railwaymen have found job satisfaction in the compulsion to run financially hopeless and poorly patronized trains, however readily some public body balances the books at the end of the day.

In the case of the loss-making but socially necessary and politically sensitive rural services, the alternative to complete closure was to inject some commercial viability into the operation, principally through cutting its costs. And one of the first post-war ideas to inspire hope of bringing the cost of these rural services under control was the lightweight, four-wheeled railcar with an underfloor bus-type engine, the so-called railbus, which the West Germans developed for their own network and also exported in quantity. Railbus operation certainly trimmed costs, especially when the use of railbuses was

British Railways flirted briefly with railbus operations in the 1960s. This survivor has found employment on a privately owned line in Yorkshire.

accompanied by every conceivable economy in staff and fixed equipment on the lines concerned – one-man staffing of trains, removal of station staff and level-crossing keepers, reduction of signalling to very basic essentials, and so on. But many of these economies were feasible only if the train service was sparse; and that, coupled with the increasingly spartan feel of a railbus ride as road vehicle comfort improved, discouraged the resurgence of rural rail travel so many had optimistically expected from the concept. By the 1970s the railbus operators had concluded that it was more sensible to run such services with standard, off-the-shelf railcars.

However, BR, which in the 1960s had tried but soon discarded a small railbus stud of mixed German and British manufacturing parentage, was pondering a return to the passenger four-wheeler at the start of the 1980s. One of BR's many perplexities at this time, in face of the Government's tight rein on its investment, was how to replace the big fleet of diesel railcars it had amassed under the 1955 Modernization Plan. It had evolved a sophisticated new diesel-electric railcar design, but in Britain's arctic economic climate the production cost of that looked acceptable only for key inter-urban and conurbation commuter services that were not electrified. For the rest of the railcar-worked services, BR's research centre at Derby came up with a much cheaper alternative. To a four-wheeled, long-wheelbase frame and running gear which had been scientifically developed as part of a high-speed train research programme they adapted the bodywork and power plant of a standard British Leyland single-decker bus. The result, known as the Light Experimental Vehicle or LEV, proved smoother riding at 80mph (130km/h) (it has been tested at 100mph) than the ageing BR bogie railcars at half that speed. Besides its domestic potential, the LEV soon had export prospects.

DEVOLVED RESPONSIBILITY AND ACCOUNTING

Even in the 1960s not every operation of a country's railway system was running at a hopeless deficit – the healthy were always trying to sustain the weak. But inevitably among the weak, and two of the great drags on cost effectiveness, were the rural lines and short-haul conurbation services. The need to maintain these kinds of operation had gone hand in hand with the increasing recognition of their political sensitivity. So the services were maintained for the main part. But how could the subsidized rail travel of a minority be justified on a minor service which sapped the strength of the healthy ones?

To relieve the national taxpayer of an open-ended obligation to subsidize the few and to preserve the strength of the viable operations (or in some cases to satisfy regional pressure for more autonomy), more countries devolved responsibility for shaping and financing the inherently unprofitable short-haul passenger services to city and provincial administrations in the 1960s and 70s.

Britain's 1968 Transport Act, for example, attempted a devolved account-ability programme for BR's passenger – but not freight – services. However, the more complex, tight-knit character of the British rail network made the precise allocation of costs highly controversial where the socially necessary services shared tracks with, or fed traffic into, the trains which were required to be self-supporting. The 1974 Transport Act therefore dropped the individually calculated subsidy of social services in favour of a global grant for all BR's passenger operation, though in 1980 the Government decided to set BR a specific target figure for the Inter-City services' contribution to BR's fixed costs and a year later demanded that they become fully self-supporting of indirect as well as direct costs. Otherwise BR would be denied further main-line electrification.

The 1968 Act, however, also established Passenger Transport Executives in the areas of the country's chief conurbations to integrate and rationalize all local bus and rail services, and to shoulder the losses of all the rail operations that the Transport

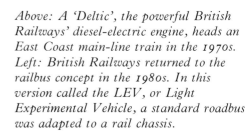

Above: A 'Deltic', the powerful British Railways' diesel-electric engine, heads an East Coast main-line train in the 1970s. Left: British Railways returned to the railbus concept in the 1980s. In this version called the LEV, or Light Experimental Vehicle, a standard roadbus was adapted to a rail chassis.

Executives concluded were essential to their overall transport plan.

Similarly in France in the 1970s, the regional authorities were given power to replan their public transport services as they thought fit within a fixed envelope of financial support from the central Government (which had previously been the arbiter of rural rail services' quality and extent); and municipal authorities were encouraged to contract bilaterally with the SNCF for expanded local service. As a result several areas agreed to finance an improved and more frequent train service

and some invested quite heavily in new rail passenger equipment, liveried in their own colour scheme, in order to make the use of their trains more attractive and to relieve the pressure on their roads.

Although the annual budget set by the Austrian Government makes separate financial provision for socially necessary rail services, the Austrian Federal Railway (ÖBB) was encouraged in the 1970s to strike deals with provincial administrations for the financing of extra local trains, track and signalling improvements to accommodate them, and ancillary facilities such as enlarged station car parks. And in Sweden those services deemed socially necessary but commercially unviable have been divorced financially from the main operations of SJ. The Swedish Government found itself unable to close the lines in the rural north of the country, even where one of over 400 miles (640 km) carried just one passenger train a day. The

services have now been maintained, but as a separate entity from the rest of SJ operations, and their only brief is to operate at minimum cost. Running costs have been cut to the bone but are otherwise dependent on Government subsidy. The remainder of the main SJ operations have to function as a commercial enterprise. And Spain concluded a similar agreement with RENFE in 1979.

The prime example of the subsidized service is Japan, whose railways have been overburdened with more social obligations than any other since the last war. Consequently no railway has had a harder job of adjustment to the economics of latter-day operation than the Japanese National Railway (JNR), which by the end of the 1970s was annually failing to cover its total costs from fares and freight charges by £1¾ billions and had run up an astronomic accumulated loss of over £7 billions. To most of the outside world JNR

conjured up the glistening image of its pioneering 130mph (210 km/h) Shinkansen, the network of new purpose-built passenger-only, standard-gauge railways in Japan's principal population corridors which was inaugurated in 1964 with the Tokyo–Osaka New Tokaido Line. But Shinkansen profitability, derived from the labour-saving, largely automated operation of a patterned, intensive service with high load factors the whole day long, was submerged without a trace in the huge deficits of the 3 ft 6 in gauge (1,067 m) system which constitutes the bulk of JNR.

The narrow gauge itself was a factor in the dismal slump of JNR's share of the national freight market from over 50 to little more than 10 per cent between mid-century and 1980, because it prevented JNR from developing the high-capacity vehicles and speed essential to compete with the road. JNR's need of both was particularly desperate because the country's phenomenal post-war industrial activity quickly denuded its natural resources. The imported coal and minerals which replaced them could be seaborne almost to the door of the plants crowding the coastal belts, so that the inland transport market was increasingly dominated by high-tariff merchandise.

But passenger traffic was JNR's millstone. In Japan as a whole the volume of JNR rail passenger business outstrips freight by five to one, and the proportion is still higher if one takes account of the country's numerous private railways. JNR's daily commuter traffic in the Tokyo area is an astonishing six to seven times heavier than that of London's main-line termini, such has been the population growth of Japan's capital conurbation since the last war.

Until 1976 not one passenger on JNR's 3 ft 6 in gauge system was paying anywhere near an economic price. It was bad enough that the basic fare scales trailed far behind the rate of inflation, but these were statutorily discounted by amounts of up to 90 per cent to key groups such as commuters and students. The JNR was powerless to raise fares. For both passengers and freight prices were proposed annually by the Government, then subject to approval by the Japanese Diet, a procedure that virtually guaranteed equivocation, given the assembly's delicate political balance. Year after year politicians lambasted the railway management for a catalogue of sins ranging from mismanaged investment to failure to trim its labour force, then themselves voted to aggravate JNR losses by curbing fares and freight rates for a further twelve months.

And that was not all, for, besides obdurately resisting closures within the rural 40 per cent of the JNR system that generated a beggarly 4 per cent of rail revenue and was responsible for about a quarter of the annual deficit, Diet members were far too nervous for their seats to resist local clamour for new country railways. At the end of the 1970s JNR was still stuck with almost all the 1,600 route-miles (2,575 km) it had sought to close as financially hopeless in 1968, while at the same time almost as much new rural railway was under construction, only a proportion of it warranted as a bait to coax population away from the teeming coastal areas. These new lines were being built entirely at political behest, yet successive governments rejected the Swedish format

of a railway system financially segregated into social and profit-centred sectors, so that the losses of the social network would be clearly identified as a political responsibility.

This explains JNR's paradoxical coolness to the full draft network of no less than 4,350 route-miles (7,000 km) of new high-speed passenger railways which the politicians euphorically proposed following the first Shinkansen triumph, at a time when most national railways in Europe would have given their eye-teeth for the same Government support of technological advance. Some of the projected routes had an essentially social purpose, to encourage dispersal of people and industry; the railwaymen, however, saw no chance of finding enough traffic to cover running costs for years to come.

Confronted with JNR deficits that were soaring into the stratosphere, and aggravated because the accumulated loss was attracting phenomenal interest charges (like West Germany's DB, JNR was caught in the spiral of borrowing more heavily by the year to repay previous loans), the Government at last acted resolutely in 1976. The Diet was pressured not only into acceptance of an overnight increase of all JNR fares and freight rates by 50 per cent, but also into renouncing its right of veto on JNR prices. Henceforward JNR would need only Transport Ministry approval for price rise proposals; moreover, it was subsequently allowed to

reduce the rates of fare discount – for example to students – quite substantially. But since JNR was forbidden to outpace the rate of inflation, it had no scope to repair the financial damage already done. Thus the Transport Ministry's 1980 budget still provided £1¼ billions purely for subsidy of rail operation, apart from investment cash for continuing high-speed and other railway construction.

The obvious remedies had little hope of realization. In 1980 the Transport Ministry sanguinely advocated a 2,200 route-mile (3,540 km) reduction of JNR's 13,000 route-mile (21,000 km) system but the political response was mute. It also urged JNR to reduce its 420,000 staff by 70,000 within five years. Given Japanese mastery of automation technology, that and more was feasible, and highly desirable too, for the powerful railway unions had extracted wage rises at double the rate of JNR's permitted price increases since the 1950s, so that pay was absorbing 80 per cent of

Two aspects of the Japanese National Railway – a rural passenger train (above right) and a commuter train in the Osaka area (below). Despite the glittering image of the Shinkansen 'Bullet Trains', the JNR as a whole has been suffering from huge operating losses. The victim of often conflicting political pressures, it was for a long time unable to set economic fares or make necessary reductions in staff and services.

JNR's revenue – the highest proportion recorded for any national railway in the industrialized world. In the spring of 1981 it looked as though some sensible steps to contain JNR's deficit were at last approaching achievement, among them a 4 per cent per annum reduction of staff by natural wastage and redeployment, and closure of seventy-seven rural lines. But, although the Transport Minister's new plan, the third attempt to rationalize the JNR network since 1960, passed the Diet, it had made no headway by the summer. Yet again the powerful political forces in the provinces were successfully blocking even the start of hearings on individual line closures.

FINANCIAL DECLINE OF THE AMERICAN RAILROADS

The ill-health of US railroading displayed many of the symptoms seen in Europe during the two decades after the Second World War. The companies were even robbed of their lucrative merchandise freight by a road transport system whose operating logistics were frighteningly extensive. The result was that by the 1960s the average financial return on US private enterprise railroading had fallen to below 3 per cent. The problem, however, was compounded by other peculiar characteristics: fuel oil was cheap, and was expected to remain so; domestic aviation in a country with such vast transport

corridors was a great attraction – one which Europeans had yet to experience; and any national rail network as such was in practice a fragmented conglomeration of individual private companies and tracks, a tradition reinforced by the American's reflexive fear of monopoly. So there was no Beeching to wield the axe and the companies had to produce their own schemes to survive. In many cases survival depended on mergers, take-overs and conglomerates. But at the end of the day, with the airways full of aircraft and the highways trembling with convoys of forty-ton Macks, it was clear that there was not much profit if any that could be squeezed from the railroads, and in some cases only Washington could ensure their continued survival.

Among the companies to diversify into more profitable businesses such as oil and real estate were Union Pacific, Sante Fe and Illinois Central; each one of them today is the railroad member of a wide-ranging industrial conglomerate. Others sought greater financial strength in mergers that either rationalized parallel and competing systems or created longer-haul opportunities by stitching two railroads end-to-end. The Norfolk & Western's takeover of the Virginian, for instance, combined two of the major coal hauliers from the eastern US pitheads to the coast. The other kind of alliance assembled in the spring of 1970 what is

currently the biggest US railroad, Burlington Northern, by knitting together the Chicago, Burlington & Quincy, the Great Northern, the Northern Pacific and the Spokane, Portland & Seattle in a system of 23,000 route-miles (37,100 km) covering the territory from the Great Lakes to the West Coast.

The unlikeliest marriage of all, only consumated after ten years of litigation by apprehensive competitors and customers, was that of the arch-rivals, the giant New York Central and Pennsylvania. But this merger, which in 1968 produced the Penn-Central (PC), never achieved the anticipated economy. In part this was because the jealousies of three-quarters of a century and more were irreconcilable and almost every attempt to agree on standard practice disintegrated in acrimony, even at board level. But it was also because the Pennsylvania element of the Penn-Central's top brass dissipated such savings as there were in real estate diversification, just at a time when the US economy was reversing into recession.

Soon there was no cash to meet the wages as well as the costs of the merger, fearsome losses on passenger business (of which PC was the last long-haul operator, with three-quarters of the surviving business) and the interest on the massive loans that had been run up at escalating rates to try and hold the financial pass. In the spring of 1970 US banks took fright and slammed the doors on PC. So did Washington. PC had no option but to file for bankruptcy.

That quickly had a domino effect. In short order six more railroads in the North-East declared insolvency and the risk of a total rail shutdown in the region was real – but politically intolerable, of course. Washington reacted by passing the Rail Reorganization Act of 1973. As a first step this created the United States Railway Association (USRA) to work out a rationalized rail network in the area and ways of making it financially viable. Its plans were crystallized in the Rail Revitalization & Reform Act of 1975, which established the Consolidated Rail Corporation – generally known as Conrail – to run an amalgam of the bankrupt systems. Aggregating 19,200 route-miles (30,900 km), the Conrail dominions became the country's second biggest rail system, second only in geographical size to Burlington Northern. Besides giving birth to Conrail, this legislation also took tentative steps to solve the spreading inability of US railroads to generate enough cash to keep their plant in good working order, by setting up funds which would part-finance track renovation in deserving cases.

Few doubted that the main reason for Penn-Central's going bust in 1970 was its perseverance with long-haul passenger business, a business which had been in retreat before the airliner since 1950. During that brief but false dawn in the few years after the war, investment was high to maintain the momentum and the streamliners slid from coast to coast with a speed and luxury which was the envy of the world. In 1949 the railroads had over 80 per cent of an aggregate of their own and the airliners' passenger-mileage – by the end of the fifties it had contracted to less than 40 per cent. And in the period between 1946 and 1953 the railroads' net loss on passenger operation quintupled to over $700 million a year.

Given the USA's geographical size and its scarcity of corridors of 500 miles (800 km) or less in length, the airliner's triumph was predictable, though railway managements complained bitterly that it was made quicker and easier by the extent of Federal subsidy of the airlines' ground and control facilities. But although the railroads had begun petitioning for service withdrawals in the 1940s – and to such effect that passenger train route-mileage had already been trimmed by almost a third between 1945 and 1947 – they were slow to tackle their cost overruns.

Even in the late 1950s, when regular dining-car workings were down to about 1,400 a day, staffing and catering were still so prodigal that on average restaurant car costs were outstripping revenue by a third. On the labour side there was not the slightest inclination to relax archaic rules which hallowed 100 miles (160 km) as the basic day's work for a locomotive crew and 150 miles (240 km) as the daily stint for other train crew, so that a transcontinental streamliner was halted about eight times on a 16-hour journey just to change crews.

One or two railroads in the East tried to stem the tide with energy- and cost-saving lightweight rolling stock. The Rock Island, for example, had bought the Spanish-developed Talgo train in the mid-1950s. It was based on a low centre-of-gravity, guided axle system, in which each short, very lightweight body was carried on a single axle at one end only and at the

Above: The Chicago Los Angeles 'Super Chief' was one of the few passenger services that Santa Fe did not withdraw on losing US Post Office custom in 1967.
Left: A Pennsylvania freight, headed by two Baldwin 2–D–D–2 'centipedes', at Horseshoe Curve in pre-merger days.
Right: Two Conrail road-switchers. The formation of Conrail in 1975 was designed to create a rationalized freight network after a spate of railroad bankruptcies.

other was articulated to its neighbour. Rock Island unveiled the train in 1956 as the Chicago-Peoria 'Jet Rocket', and at the same time two other companies, General Motors and Pullman-Standard, produced their own lightweight trains. But even the enthusiasm of the irrepressible Robert R. Young, chairman first of the Chesapeake & Ohio and later of the New York Central, for Pullman-Standard's short, low-slung 'Train X' could do little to persuade Americans that the wayward riding and cramped interiors of the lightweights was the price to pay for the trains of the future. Americans still preferred a Cadillac to a Beetle. All the lightweights were abruptly retired after a very brief service life.

The last straw for the US long-haul passenger train was the desertion to road

Diesel locomotives built for Amtrak.
Amtrak was set up in 1971 to save some
of the US inter-city passenger services
threatened with closure.

and air of the US Post Office, whose mails had generated so much revenue. Until 1967 the Santa Fe refused to join the gadarene rush to end passenger service, content with modest retrenchment and prepared to shoulder a passenger loss of $30 millions. But in 1967 the Post Office withdrew from almost all Santa Fe trains, with the result that the Santa Fe immediately petitioned for discontinuance of every passenger service except on its flagships – the Chicago–Los Angeles 'Super Chief' and 'El Capitan', Chicago–San Francisco 'San Francisco Chief' and Chicago–Houston 'Texas Chief'.

At that the 15,000 daily US long-haul passenger trains of the late 1930s shrank to barely 500. Total extinction was a very real threat, but by now environmental concern had roused public interest, especially among those living in the fume-choked cities and beneath the overcrowded airlanes of the North-East. Throughout 1969 an assortment of schemes to rescue and financially support inter-city passenger services was mulled over by Congress. President Nixon's Office of Management & Budget did its best to stall discussion, but in October 1970 the legislation was voted which from 30 April 1971 created a Federally subsidized corporation, later titled Amtrak, to run a slender, rationalized network of inter-city passenger trains

to Government specification. At the start that specification nominated a timetable of just 184 trains on twenty-one routes. Only three railroads – Southern, Denver & Rio Grande Western and Rock Island – elected not to hand their few remaining trains over to Amtrak.

Whereas the passenger-operating corporation, Amtrak, was created with political acceptance that it would be forever reliant on public money to cover both operating costs and investment, the idea of a fully nationalized freight railroad such as Conrail was political anathema. Conrail was given only a third of the start-up money it needed from Federal funds and bidden to borrow the rest on the open market. As it was, the 1975 legislation had a tough passage both with Congress and the administration, where President Ford was at one point meditating a veto. The fond expectation was that, within a few years of its operational takeover on 1 April 1976, Conrail would have taken an axe both to the many duplicated routes and profitless branches and also to the surfeit of staff which it had inherited. Once it had broken even, USRA, which was kept in being as an overseer of Conrail's first steps, would be disbanded and Conrail would float financially without more buoyancy aids from the Treasury. But four years and $3.3 billions of Federal investment money later, Conrail was still seriously in the operating red, and in need of $900 millions more aid up to 1985; and USRA still had a job to do as monitor, besides its other function of sorting out the value of the

bankrupt railroads' plant with their creditors and stockholders.

One reason for the still critical state of railroading in the North-East was that Conrail was handed track, traction and rolling stock that was for the most part appallingly run-down. To a degree, rationalization hopes were frustrated by characteristic political stalling on closures, but Conrail management itself was slow both to prune the overlapping facilities of the previously competing systems it had absorbed and to develop new operating strategies that would maximize the productivity of a slimmed-down network. And that failure was in part attributable to the difficulty of staff reduction in face of the job-protection agreements Conrail had had to conclude with the labour unions as the price of their co-operation in its take-over of the former companies. Finally, Conrail suffered badly in North America's horrendous winters of 1976–7 and 1978–9 and was also affected by a drift of industry from the North-East, though as the decade closed that was offset by the rising demand for coal as industrial and generating plant fuel. As 1981 dawned, Washington could no longer escape grappling with the alternatives of allowing Conrail to cut its system down to a much smaller and viable size or else of enacting the previously unthinkable – unashamed nationalization, with Conrail's reconstitution under the wing of the Department of Transport's Federal Railroad Administration (FRA). But that, under President Reagan, was out of the question. Conrail was given two years to balance its books if it wanted to be sold as a complete unit – assuming a buyer could be found to take it on whole – otherwise it would be auctioned off in pieces. The Reagan administration was determined to get Conrail off the Federal books by mid-decade.

The Conrail experience was a deterrent to any similar rescue when the long-threatening bankruptcy of two major Mid-West railroads, the Milwaukee and the Rock Island, became conclusive in 1979. The Rock Island was left to sell off the useful parts of its system to its neighbours and then disappear, the Milwaukee hopefully to contract to a viable core as Conrail should have done but did not.

By then the majority of major US railroads were in uncertain financial health. Although the average rate of the industry's return on investment had climbed from a 1977 nadir of 1.24 to 4.20

per cent, thanks chiefly to the new industrial enthusiasm for solid fuels, analysts calculated that only thirteen of the thirty-six Class I railroads were generating enough cash to sustain their operations long-term, let alone content their stockholders and attract fresh capital. Only in the west and south of the country were railroads recording a reasonably healthy operating ratio and obtaining margins sufficient to keep their track in sound order and free of the rash of severe speed restrictions which had occurred simply because renewals were badly in arrears.

One important Washington reaction to the gathering crisis was the adoption of a more co-operative attitude to inter-railroad mergers. In the first three post-war decades US transportation was still muddled by the contradictions of a belief in private enterprise, amounting to religious fervour, and of an inherited complex of statutory procedures and regulations dating from the late nineteenth-century reaction to blatant cases of monopolistic exploitation. Thus, although the merger of neighbouring railroads might lead to a single system of greatly enhanced productivity, each and every claim against the combine had to be heard and dissected by the Interstate Commerce Commission (ICC). If the ICC findings displeased, then the objectors had subsequent recourse to the courts – the last hurdle the Penn-Central merger had to surmount, in fact, was the US Supreme Court. As recently as the 1960s and early 1970s the ICC took twelve years to pronounce on Rock Island's request to merge with Union Pacific. By the time the ICC felt it could approve, Union Pacific had understandably lost interest in the proposition and the 'Rock' was left to slither on into bankruptcy.

In the mid-1970s, however, Congress streamlined the ICC procedures. Washington had been taught a chastening lesson: on the one hand by the catastrophic outcome of its failure to anticipate and unravel the mess in the North-East; on the other by the impressive increase in transcontinental rail transport efficiency that was resulting from the voluntary merger into the Burlington Northern (BN) of four healthy railroads to provide a unitary end-to-end system stretching from the West Coast to the Great Lakes. So BN's request to add the St Louis–San Francisco RR, better known simply as the Frisco, to its family took only two and a quarter years to clear all its regulatory hurdles by the spring of 1980. 'When carrier operations can be made more efficient and less costly,' commented the ICC judgement, noting that this merger was forecast to save $20 millions in running costs and raise $33 millions more in annual net income, 'it is in the public interest to approve the result.' It would extend the BN network to 29,200 route-miles (47,000 km).

Encouraged by Washington's more amenable attitude, the railroads laid more giant merger schemes on the table during the years 1978–80. Union Pacific sought to gather in Missouri Pacific and Western Pacific, extending its trackage to almost 22,200 route-miles (35,400 km). Santa Fe (SF) and Southern Pacific (SP) announced a merger plan, but within a few months struck a disagreement and dropped the idea. Had it been pursued the western USA would have been almost monopolized by three huge combines, BN, UP and SF-SP, with the Denver & Rio Grande

A Western Pacific freight train travels through Utah on its way to California. At one time Western Pacific was part of Union Pacific's merger plans.

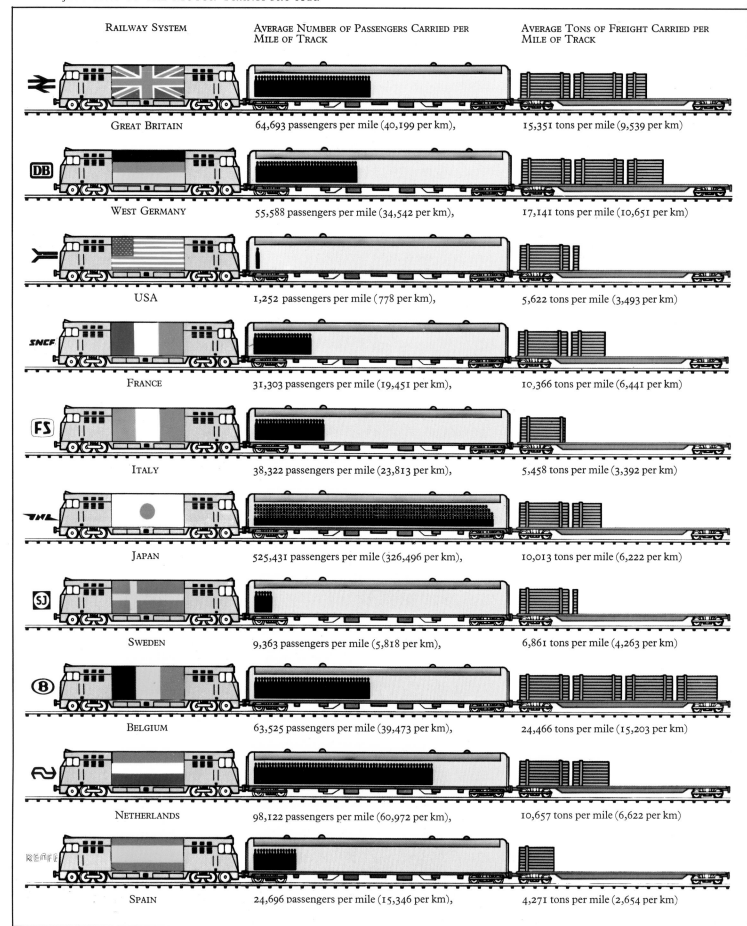

RAILWAY SYSTEM	AVERAGE NUMBER OF PASSENGERS CARRIED PER MILE OF TRACK	AVERAGE TONS OF FREIGHT CARRIED PER MILE OF TRACK
GREAT BRITAIN	64,693 passengers per mile (40,199 per km),	15,351 tons per mile (9,539 per km)
WEST GERMANY	55,588 passengers per mile (34,542 per km),	17,141 tons per mile (10,651 per km)
USA	1,252 passengers per mile (778 per km),	5,622 tons per mile (3,493 per km)
FRANCE	31,303 passengers per mile (19,451 per km),	10,366 tons per mile (6,441 per km)
ITALY	38,322 passengers per mile (23,813 per km),	5,458 tons per mile (3,392 per km)
JAPAN	525,431 passengers per mile (326,496 per km),	10,013 tons per mile (6,222 per km)
SWEDEN	9,363 passengers per mile (5,818 per km),	6,861 tons per mile (4,263 per km)
BELGIUM	63,525 passengers per mile (39,473 per km),	24,466 tons per mile (15,203 per km)
NETHERLANDS	98,122 passengers per mile (60,972 per km),	10,657 tons per mile (6,622 per km)
SPAIN	24,696 passengers per mile (15,346 per km),	4,271 tons per mile (2,654 per km)

TRACK LENGTH AND AMOUNT ELECTRIFIED

11,188 route-miles (18,005 km), 21%

17,821 route-miles (28,679 km), 37%

224,337 route-miles (361,025 km), 0.6%

21,452 route-miles (34,523 km), 28%

10,181 route-miles (16,384 km), 52%

13,316 route-miles (21,429 km), 38%

6,996 route-miles (11,259 km), 63%

2,688 route-miles (4,326 km), 30%

1,797 route-miles (2,892 km), 61%

8,386 route miles (13,496 km), 36%

INTERNATIONAL MILEAGE COMPARISONS AND SUBSIDIES

Electrification is seen by many to be the way forward for the railways, producing an economical, energy-conserving system that will attract more passengers and more freight. Yet degrees of electrification vary widely in the industrialized world between Sweden, where 63% of the track is electrified, and the United States, where the proportion is less than 1 per cent.

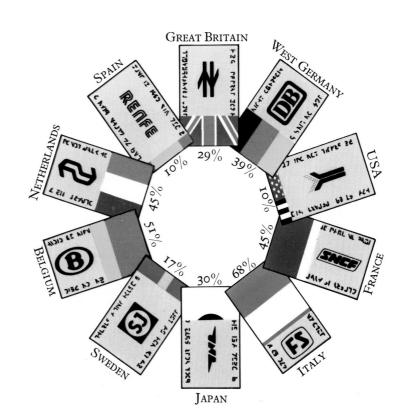

SUBSIDIES

State subsidies are now seen to be essential to the efficient running of railways, even in countries committed to free enterprise. Through various Federal and state aid programmes and government-backed loans American railways receive support to about 10 per cent of their capital and running costs; the highest amount in the Western industrialized world is Italy's 68 per cent.

Off-peak hours at Peking station, 1976. For China an efficient and comprehensive railway is accorded high priority. Route-miles have doubled since 1949 and electrification is proceeding apace.

Western the only independent major carrier. But in any event, approval of the SF-SP alliance was improbable. The ICC was prepared to smile on the mergers of systems abutting each other, where the principal gain was the creation of longer through routes under unified management and the simplification of freight handovers at former railroad frontiers; but public opinion was not yet ready for amalgamations of intertwined, competing systems where the main objective was rationalization of rival routes. That was clearly the goal of SF and SP, stern opponents in earlier days, whose merger would have deprived very large tracts of California, New Mexico and Arizona of competitive rail services.

On the other side of the country, two systems that were already the product of earlier mergers, the Family Lines and the Chessie, banded together under the enigmatic initials of CSX to unite their systems as one 28,200 route-mile (45,380 km) network – the sum of no fewer

than sixteen one-time railroad companies – from the Great Lakes south to New Orleans and Miami. Between them they moved almost a third of the coal carried by US railroads. That spurred the neighbouring Norfolk & Western and Southern to reactivate their plan, pigeonholed the previous autumn, to coalesce as one 19,440 mile (31,285 km) system between the Mid-West and the Gulf of Mexico.

The CSX merger was approved by the ICC within twenty months, in mid-1980, and few US observers doubted that the other two big mergers would eventually be sanctioned. Few believed either that they would ring down the curtain on mergers. The betting was that by the century's end US long-haul freight would be shared by fewer than ten giant consortia.

THE THIRD WORLD

In many parts of the Third World the main preoccupation in the 1970s was not the competitiveness or otherwise of railways, but the fact that they simply did not exist where they were needed to keep pace with post-war development trends. In the central tract of the African continent, for instance, the original railway builders had only one objective – to establish the cheapest system consistent with efficiency

for haulage of their territory's raw materials from the interior to the coast. Very few of them gave a thought to the possibility that one day their economy might demand interdependence of their railway with the one next door. So the rapidly evolving industries of Africa and its aspirations to economic solidarity in modern times have had to contend not only with a multi-gauge network, but with one where operation method varies, influenced from one country to another by the national railway practice of the colonial powers under whom they were constructed. Of Africa's 58,000 miles (93,300 km) of track in 1979, 60 per cent was 3 ft 6 in (1,067 mm) gauge, 16 per cent 3 ft 3½ in (1 m), 19 per cent standard gauge, and the rest a medley of other narrow gauges.

The first moves for new international links followed closely on the Second World War. Construction of a railway from landlocked Northern Rhodesia (today's Zambia) to the East African coast was discussed as early as 1947, but, though one survey after another was undertaken by the British Government during the next two decades, progress was held up because traffic prospects failed to encourage any prospective source of finance, private or governmental. At last, in 1967, China offered to finance and build the railway for Zambia and Tanzania, and three years later the details of the project were agreed. The 1,156 mile (1,860 km) 3 ft 6 in gauge railway, popularly known as the Tan-Zam, was finished in the summer of 1975, but its performance for the rest of the decade was chaotic. Within two years less than half the railway's rolling stock was serviceable and the Chinese had to return to run the system until 1980. The Tan-Zam experience taught every African country the vital importance of staff-training in step with capital investment; that has become a priority item on the agenda of the African Union of Railways which was founded in 1972.

China itself has doubled the route-mileage of its railways since 1949. Here the railways absorb about 64 per cent of all passenger travel and just under 60 per cent of the country's freight transport. By 1978 every province had at least been brought within the railways' orbit with the sole exception of Tibet, but that gap was being closed under a fresh eight-year plan which budgeted for contruction of six fresh trunk railways, including the completion of a route to Lhasa, and a crash programme of electrification. China did not begin electrifying (at 25 kV ac) until 1958 and twenty years later well over 80 per cent of the country's rail traffic was still steam-hauled, but reduction of the steam element to no more than 40 per cent by 1985 is the goal. This immense Chinese railway activity, needless to say, has opened up another enticing market for the railway industries and specialists of the West and of Japan – possibly the most lucrative market of all.

THE ROLE OF GOVERNMENT

The history of railways in the democratic industrialized world over the past twenty years has underlined the inability of governments to embark on a fundamental reconstruction of transport law, financing and taxation to reflect the internal combustion engine's transformation of the transport world. The railways of the West have had to live with the dichotomy of regulation and increasingly unbridled competition and with the problems of reconciling social duty with political pressures to reduce calls on public money through greater competitive efficiency.

The lessons of the Eastern bloc, of course, can well illustrate what railways can achieve when all its competitors are subject to state regulation within a national economic plan. Even sluggish road transport investment cannot account for all the near-capacity loading of the Eastern bloc's freight trains.

In 1980 East Germany's DR, for instance, still little more than 10 per cent electrified and on many routes single-track (the Western powers and the USSR between them lifted almost 4,000 route-miles, or 6,440 route-km, of the country's second track after the war), was straining under 65 per cent of the nation's freight. In Poland some PKP routes were groaning with freight amounting to 14 million tonnes a year, as against maxima on West Germany's DB of 8.3 millions and on France's SNCF of 7.6 millions.

And no railway system in the industrialized world dominates its country's overland transport to the extent of the USSR's, which moves 75 per cent of Soviet freight and half the nation's passengers. In fact, the USSR railways claim to shift over half the whole world's total rail freight tonnage over only 10 per cent of its rail route-mileage. The railways are such a part of Soviet life that when construction of the second Trans-Siberian railway, the 1,995 mile (3,210 km) Baikal–Amur Magistral, began in the late 1970s, Moscow could proudly report that 150,000 members of the Young Communist League were clamouring for construction jobs, despite the fact that the route largely traverses the perma-frost belt, where temperatures of minus 60°C (– 108°F) are not rare.

But in the West such directing of transport policy was obviously an impossibility. The operators of the West's railways are left with a virtually insoluble problem and their role can only be to find the balance between social desirability, fair subsidy and equitable legislation.

Two areas of traditional concern to railway operators – the costing of infrastructure and the regulation of rates and charges – have in recent years prompted some governmental response. It has always been the duty of the railways of the West to maintain and signal its tracks, whereas its competitors are not directly charged with all the infrastructure and policing costs they incur (and that includes air transport in the matter of air traffic control and sometimes the full range of airport services it employs as well). In the nineteenth century these restraints were justifiably imposed on the industrial world's railways to prevent monopolistic exploitation of customers on the one hand, and unfair competition with rival media on the other. Since the middle of this century, however, it is the railways who have been crying foul – especially in the USA, where the private enterprise railroads are taxed on their property in the same way as other entrepreneurs.

One country which has long been comparatively fair-minded on the infrastructure cost issue is France. Here the State's nineteenth-century involvement in

A Soviet electric multiple-unit in Moscow. Fifty per cent of the nation's passengers travel by rail.

*An electric locomotive-hauled passenger
train on the Swedish National Railways.
To combat dwindling traffic the Swedish
Government cut off-peak fares by half.*

provision of railways has evolved into a
substantial annual grant for track upkeep,
which in 1982 was worth £500 millions.
But elsewhere aid is mostly confined to
State responsibility for level crossings or
the partial use of general investment grants
for track renewal. In contrast waterway
operators both in Europe and the USA pay
at best a negligible contribution to their
infrastructure costs, while study after
study on both sides of the Atlantic has
proved that road freight juggernauts cause
vastly more infrastructure damage than is
recovered from their operators through
tolls or taxes.

A method of equalization canvassed but
rejected both in Britain and in West
Germany in the 1970s was to take the
railway infrastructure entirely into State
care, leaving the railways only to run trains
as fee-paying tenants. France, as already
mentioned, makes a handsome State
contribution to the SNCF's infrastructure
upkeep. In addition, it also makes an
annual grant to the SNCF which is
considered a further necessity to equalize
the terms of competition. The complicated
formula which determines the annual
amount was revised in the new contract

which the SNCF agreed with the French
Government in 1979 and since then it has
been steadily reduced. Even so, the figure
agreed for 1982 was £280 millions.

Assumption of total responsibility for
the national rail infrastructure by the
State was also a recommendation of a Swiss
national transport plan, the Conception
Globale Suisse des Transports (CGST),
which a Federally appointed commission
submitted to the Berne government in
1978 after six years' deliberation. This
draft also propounded the original idea of a
national transport tax, possibly extracted
by way of an addition to value added tax, on
the grounds that even an inveterate
pedestrian benefited from public transport
expenditure to some degree every time he
took delivery of a consumer good.
Concerned to relieve the Federal authorities of more of the cost of socially
necessary services, the CGST also proposed to delegate to the Cantonal
administrations a larger measure both of
decision-making and of its financial
consequences in the provision of local
public transport. In the summer of 1981
the Federal Government took the first
steps towards realization of the CGST by
assuming responsibility for further development of the Swiss Federal Railway's
infrastructure; it forecast a new tax on
heavy road transport to equalize the terms
of competition still more effectively, and

reshaped the national railway's mandate so
that it would act as a purely commercial
enterprise in its main sectors.

The most bizarre approach to the
question of fair shares of infrastructure
costs so far has been Sweden. Unable to
devise any politically acceptable or
pragmatic way of saddling road users with
their just costs, and anxious to break their
national railways, the SJ, out of the Catch
22 of an increased-charge reaction to
dwindling traffic, the Government decided to balance largesse with largesse.

If the Swedish Government was to
subsidize the SJ's financially hopeless
rural lines, then it would equally subsidize
its passengers. So, in the name of
equalizing the terms of competition, it
financed a rail-fare reduction scheme that
slashed the price of off-peak travel by
almost 50 per cent to those passengers who
were prepared to commit themselves to
regular use.

The other contentious area where
governments could intervene was in that of
pricing. The regulation of rates and
charges was seen as an out-dated constraint
which usually determined the floor as well
as the ceiling level of charge – it was thus a
simple matter for competitors to consult
published railway tariffs and undercut
them. In Europe, only BR obtained
through the 1962 Transport Act near-
complete licence to fix its fares and rates,
and thereby to price off the railway the
unsuitable traffic it had previously had to
accept under common carrier legislation;
but then Britain also had Europe's least-
regulated road transport. Otherwise the
only significant development was in
France. There, in 1979, the Barre
Government, dedicated to allowing free
play to market forces, concluded a new
contract with the SNCF which, although it
retained the Government control of
maximum rates which in Europe only BR
was relieved of, at last allowed the railways
to bargain for business some way below the
ceiling, provided any deal made was not a
loss-leader. The reverse of the coin was a
new duty laid on the SNCF to break even –
within its envelope of agreed grants and
compensations – by 1982. Even then there
were ambivalences in the French approach. For instance, the Government
could require priority for electrification to
benefit a politically sensitive area of the
country such as Brittany, and arrange the
loan money for the investment so as to
relieve the SNCF's budget for the years

concerned. But in subsequent years interest on the loans would be the SNCF's responsibility, even though the original investment decision was not of its making.

Perpetuation of price control and regulation of competition in the rail freight sector may still claim some justification where railways are a substantially state-aided utility – but not much, considering the general failure to equalize track costs for all competitors. This has long been an anachronism in the USA, where railways (Conrail partially excepted) are reliant on private enterprise and capital and, as already implied, Class I railroads have become desperate for increased traffic to finance reparation of deteriorating assets. After 1955 not one of these systems was earning enough to cover the costs of its capital – in other words, interest charges on loans exceeded the return on the investment. Yet the railroads were not only debarred from mergers and the abandonment of uneconomic services without ICC approval, but were also economically

regulated by statute and the ICC throughout almost all their freight activity.

It was not until Carter's presidency in the late 1970s that moves were made to deregulate all forms of transport, railroads included. Despite counter-lobbying, a Bill was passed in October 1980 which promised the railroads more pricing freedom, though still less than its rivals had been ceded. The Bill's most important provisions allowed the railroads new scope to conclude long-term contracts at freely negotiated rates with major customers (previous constraints were concerned to protect small customers from the absorption of railroad capacity by high-tonnage shippers); and, on a scale rising in steps up to late 1984, to price up to 180 per cent of direct operating costs for any traffic without fear of ICC intervention.

On the other side of the 49th Parallel the two big Canadian systems, Canadian Pacific and Canadian National, gained full commercial freedom in their freight activity – with one significant exception –

much earlier, under a National Transportation Act of 1967. That spurred both companies to develop a marketing expertise which has made them two of the most profitable railroads in North America. The State-owned Canadian National, in particular, has benefited to such an extent from the 1978 transfer of loss-making passenger operations to a new government agency, Via Rail, that it is now – after two decades of continuous loss – hoisting itself to a profit level challenging that of the private enterprise Canadian Pacific. The exception to the two railroads' marketing freedom is the grain sector. There rates are still Federally pegged at an abysmally uneconomic level under an 1897 agreement that was framed to stimulate grain exports from the prairies and safeguard their world market prices.

Two road-switcher diesels head a Canadian Pacific freight train. The private enterprise Canadian Pacific is renowned for its profitability.

THE HARD SELL OF INTER-CITY

The American experience of the 1950s had shown that inter-city passenger services could no longer rest on past laurels to safeguard their share of the market. The inroads made by road and air transport meant that these operations, still deemed inherently or potentially competitive, would have to be subjected to the most urgent requirements not only of speed and efficiency but also of financial viability.

Radical innovations were thus necessary to attract or even keep the inter-city traveller from the comfort and economy of his car, or from the speed of the now safe and civilized wide-bodied jet aircraft. For just as the competition from the road and airway had changed, so had the demands of the traveller. The post-war years were followed by a gradual revival in national economies. As business began to boom and people enjoyed increasing affluence, travel became a commonplace part of everyday life. More than ever before, ordinary families rather than the privileged rich demanded a high quality of service and comfort from their transport systems.

As we have seen, one important legislative outcome of the struggle for survival in the post-war years was the partial freeing of competitive operations from regulated price constraints and even, in a few cases, from any undue financial responsibility for network infrastructure. This allowed the passenger service operators to create a significant marketing strategy, for now a wide-ranging scheme of attractive fares could be applied to the inter-city operation. Indeed, as these services across Europe developed, their operation was to become as much a marketing exercise as an application of progressive rail technology. The inter-city services were to incorporate all the key features of price, flexibility, comfort, speed and efficiency in a package, designed and promoted to attract premium-fare business and second-class domestic passengers alike. Thus the image of today's inter-city rail service is a function of contemporary marketing strategy, based on 'hard sell' and 'consumer' research.

The concept, however, goes back to the immediate post-war years and saw its first realization in the Trans-Europ Express. Although air travel development has now outpaced TEE's ability to compete on international itineraries, its aspirations, and indeed many of its features, were those on which the services of today depend.

THE TRANS-EUROP EXPRESS

This first major effort to create a modern inter-city rail system concentrated on the premium-fare first-class market. TEE was a concept developed in the early 1950s by Dutch Railways President F.Q. den Hollander. He based his ideas on the belief that the out-and-home-in-a-day business market could be extended to international travel if trains were able to cross frontiers as freely as airliners, and if the railways could offer a network of suitably timed international trains fulfilling this condition, that were also of unvarying standards of speed and comfort. Den Hollander won his first point with the agreement of border authorities to conduct their customs and passport checks on TEEs as they moved at normal speed through frontier areas, but not what he wanted for the trains themselves – a standard design operated by a financially autonomous, international company representing the participant railways, those of France, Western Germany, Luxemburg, the Netherlands, Switzerland and Italy. Standardization was stymied by the SNCF, which insisted on contributing to the TEE pool the RGP diesel multiple-unit created a year or two earlier for its own domestic services. And the countries' transport ministers vetoed the idea of supra-national management.

When the TEE network was launched in 1957, therefore, about the only standard features of the equipment were air-conditioning and an external livery of red and cream. Four different types of diesel multiple-unit were in use, ranging from the very handsome diesel-hydraulic sets with separate restaurant and bar specially created by the DB to unimpressive two-car diesel sets representing the SNCF and Italy's FS, in which meals were served at seats.

The initial TEE equipment was diesel multiple-unit because catenary was not yet continuous from end to end on most TEE routes and multi-voltage traction was still in its infancy. But the latter technique had progressed sufficiently by 1958 for the Swiss to order four-voltage electric TEE multiple-units and fill a gap in the TEE system enforced by the unsuitability of diesel traction to the hard grind over the transalpine main lines. In the summer of 1961 these Swiss sets premiered the 'Cisalpin' TEE from Milan to Paris via the Simplon route and the 'Gottardo' and 'Ticino' TEEs between Milan, Zurich and Basle via the Gotthard.

The Swiss multi-voltage train-sets lifted the TEE concept into a more distinctive grade of speed and comfort, soon to be consolidated by new West German and French equipment. The DB had revived the 'Rheingold' in 1951, but

A Paris–Brussels–Amsterdam TEE. In 1963 this lucrative service was re-equipped with stainless steel coaches hauled by the French CC40101 electric locomotive.

not in much more than name, for in its early post-war career it was three-class and steam-hauled all the way to the Swiss border. But in the 1950s the Dutch and Germans electrified with such rapidity that by the early 1960s catenary was all but continuous on the 'Rheingold' route. That encouraged the DB in 1962 to regenerate 'Rheingold' as a first-class-only train and re-equip it with the most opulent air-conditioned stock Europe had yet seen in public service. Its most eye-catching components were vista-dome observation-bar cars (since sold out of DB service) and double-deck kitchen cars, but the most significant vehicles were compartment and reclining seat coaches; their superb appointment and riding quality, the latter the product of an extended 86 ft 7 in (26.4m) length and a new type of bogie, made them the model for a great deal of subsequent European coach design. Among the 'Rheingold's' amenities were a train secretarial service and a passenger's telephone kiosk, both of which the DB has since made a standard facility, unique on European railways.

The most lucrative of the first batch of TEE services was that between Paris and

Brussels, especially after the latter's ennoblement as the administrative head-quarters of the European Economic Community. The 195 mile (314km) distance between the two capitals was a near-ideal distance for competitive rail service and traffic soon saturated the first-generation multiple-unit TEEs. Completion of electrification throughout the route in 1963 justified re-equipment and the Belgian railway, SNCB, joined the TEE scheme to share with the SNCF the

Above: A Swiss four-voltage TEE electric multiple-unit just prior to its inauguration in July 1961.
Right: A West German diesel-hydraulic unit TEE speeds through Wörgl on the journey from Salzburg to Innsbruck.
Below: A southbound 'Rheingold' express. When this route was electrified in the early 1960s, the DB introduced new standards of passenger comfort in a first-class-only service, including air conditioning, dome cars and telephones.

cost of a fleet of new air-conditioned, locomotive-hauled coaches with stainless steel bodies. To go with this fleet, both systems ordered multi-voltage locomotives, since the French sector of the route was 25 kV ac, the Belgian 3 kV dc and portions of two trains continued over Dutch 1.5 kV dc to Amsterdam. The four-voltage French machines, of a six-axle 4,540 hp CC40101 type, were particularly striking. Apart from previewing the dashingly raked, horizontal 'Z'-form cab front, subsequently standardized by the SNCF's designers on the grounds that inward-sloping cab windows protect a driver from glare and distracting reflections, these locomotives were Europe's first to be arranged for a maximum speed of 150 mph (240 km/h). For reasons elaborated later they have never been regularly operated at that speed, but the provision reaffirmed the SNCF's long-range objective.

The adoption of locomotive-hauled equipment for the Paris–Brussels–Amsterdam TEE operation signalled the temporary eclipse of the multiple-unit as a European inter-city tool, except for short-haul services with distinctive characteristics, such as those of the

Netherlands Railways, of which more shortly. Its operational virtue was the double-ended format's facility for quick turnround at the not inconsiderable number of stations on domestic and international routes – Frankfurt, Stuttgart, Munich, Marseille and Zurich are conspicuous examples – where piecemeal railway development in the previous century had bequeathed twentieth-century operators the inconvenience of through train reversals. But the reverse of the coin was the inflexibility of the fixed formation when traffic fluctuated. At the start of the 1980s this disadvantage was still manifest every week on the Austrian Federal Railway, the ÖBB, where much of the domestic inter-city service is furnished by Class 4010 six-car electric multiple-units. To cope with abnormal traffic the ÖBB has either to couple on a second six-car unit, extravagantly manning the restaurant cars in both because there is no passenger access through the end cars of a unit, or else couple on up to two locomotive-hauled coaches and deny the latter's occupants access to the 4010's diner.

This apart, in the 1950s and 60s no railway designer managed to achieve the

same smoothness of ride in a multiple-unit propelled as well as pulled by its power plant – or in some cases with traction motors dispersed over several vehicles in the set – that was by then being attained with hauled coaches. And ride quality had become commercially critical as the automobile industry transformed the comfort of the average family car and jetliners mitigated some of the displeasures of air travel.

From the mid-1960s onwards den Hollander's original TEE concept grew more and more blurred. The title ceased to connote international trains exclusively when the SNCF's crack Paris–Riviera 'Mistral' was admitted to membership in 1965; four years before, the 'Mistral' was re-equipped with stock of the same pattern as the Paris–Brussels TEEs, but with the additional frills of a buffet-bar, fancy goods shop, unisex hairdressing saloon and train secretary, though the last two were soon discarded for lack of custom. The DB's 'Rheingold' and its companion Dortmund–Munich 'Rheinpfeil' (which with an 85 mph/135 km/h average timing from Freiburg to Karlsruhe briefly stole the 'Mistral's' crown as Europe's fastest train in 1963) were sensibly crowned TEEs

in 1965. But from the start of the 1970s the
DB began to build identical stock for its
domestic, supplementary-fare inter-city
operation. In 1969, after they had
perfected a variable-gauge axle for the
Talgo system to overcome the difference
between the RENFE 5 ft 6 in (1,676 mm)
width and the West European standard,
the Spaniards bartered a Talgo operation
into the network – the Barcelona–Geneva
'Catalan Talgo'.

More and more of the premier internal
trains of the member railways won TEE
status, some of them such as the Italian
'Settebello', introducing a fresh pattern of
equipment which allowed the image of a
standard European express service to
disintegrate still further.

At the same time the very long-distance
international TEEs were being denuded of
custom by wide-bodied jetliners and
aggressive airline marketing. In the later
1970s, as individual railways became
increasingly preoccupied with revitalization of their domestic services, these
prototypical TEEs were steadily fading
from the timetables. By the 1980s TEE had
degenerated into a not particularly ap-
posite brand-name for a first-class-only,
supplementary-fare train generally superimposed on a basic express service as an
exclusive peak-hour facility for the
business market.

INTER-CITY TIMETABLING:
THE BREAKTHROUGH

Before the end of the 1960s one European
railway after another had grasped the
necessity of reshaping its inter-city
passenger service if it was not to surrender
the bulk of its second-class business to the
increasing convenience, comfort and
economy of motoring, as each country
invested heavily in new highways and as
modestly priced family saloons acquired a
quality not far off the Jaguar or Mercedes
standard of a few years earlier. As an earlier
chapter described, the model for re-
gularized service had been assembled on
the pre-war Southern Railway in Britain,

where the percipient Herbert Walker saw how travel over the short inter-urban distances between London and the South Coast could be stimulated by a frequent, fixed-interval service of standard-format electric multiple-units.

The first railway to follow his example after the war was the NS of the Netherlands. The NS allied rapid electrification with development of patterned, standard multiple-unit operation for all but international and a few long-distance services. Today the working at every sizeable Dutch station is cyclic from hour to hour, save for the irregular incidence of international trains. The country's forty key towns and cities are interlinked by limited-stop express services at never less than strict hourly frequency, and often half or even quarter-hourly in the Ranstad, the 3,000 square-mile (7,770 sq. km) agglomeration of towns and cities in the west of the country where main NS traffic flows merge. The rest of the NS passenger

Above, far left: An Austrian Federal Railways inter-city express, formed of a Class 4010 electric multiple-unit.
Above left: The 'Settebello' electric multiple-unit – an Italian TEE.
Above: A shop on the French 'Mistral'.
Left: The 'Mistral' ran between Paris, Lyon, Marseille and Nice. In 1961 it was re-equipped with the same stock as the Paris Brussels TEEs and, although not an international train, it was accorded TEE status four years later.

service is equally regular-interval and is arranged to connect into and out of the fast trains, so as to open up convenient rail journeys between almost any pair of towns in the country.

The NS method justifies near-total reliance on multiple-units, both because of the service's sharply timed turnrounds at terminals and also because the railway maximizes track capacity by joining units from different points of origin to run them as one train over its busiest stretches of main line. Each multiple-unit is fitted with the patent Scharfenburg coupler, which on contact instantly combines coupling with connection of traction, braking and other electrical control lines (to uncouple, all the driver has to do is depress a foot-pedal in his cab). Consequently, a unit can run into one half of a Dutch main station platform (divided for just such operation), nudge up or back on to a unit already arrived in the other half, and be coupled and ready to depart as one train within moments.

In Britain the pre-war timetabling principle was naturally applied to post-war main-line extension of the Southern third-rail electric system from London to the Kent coast in 1959. But more significant was the same year's profitable application of the method to its steam locomotive-hauled London Liverpool Street to

Norwich service by BR's Eastern Region. From then on BR's main-line passenger timetables were progressively redrafted on the basis of frequent regular-interval operation. The extra train-mileage which that postulated was economically supportable only if more daily work could be extracted from coaching stock. And to be adaptable to traffic demand throughout the day, coaching sets had to be standard; that inevitably spelt the demise of through

Above: One of Spain's lightweight Talgo inter-city trains.
Left: An inter-city electric multiple-unit in Holland. Major Dutch cities are linked by express services at regular intervals as part of a well integrated and comprehensive passenger network developed by Netherlands Railways.

coach workings and of Pullman trains which could only pull in satisfying business in the morning and evening peaks. It meant, too, that a train-set which on one journey served a noble name like 'Flying Scotsman' would be turned round to form an anonymous London–Newcastle express on its next trip. The process was aided and encouraged by BR's belated and hectic transition of the 1960s from steam to diesel traction because of the latter's proclivity for longer spells of continuous work between programmed servicing and because of its theoretically predictable performance, which simplified standard timetabling with fixed-formation train-sets.

The key year in this BR development was 1966. In the previous four years, by intensive use of what were then the world's outstanding diesel-electric locomotives in terms of power/weight ratio, the 103-ton, 3,300 hp, 105 mph (170 km/h) English Electric Deltics, the BR Regions operating the East Coast route from London to the North and Scotland had accumulated encouraging new traffic with an amplified and considerably accelerated regular-interval service. With these machines and with the track now fully reconstructed, stretches could for the first time be passed for regular 100 mph (160 km/h) running. The Deltics' achievement, however, was overshadowed by the results from BR's first 25 kV ac main-line electrification, which became fully operative from London Euston to Liverpool and Manchester in 1966, and from London to the West Midlands a year later.

For rapidity and scale of market response to the inception of an accelerated, intensified and regular-interval inter-city service, nothing in Europe has yet exceeded the impact of BR's first all-electric service between London Euston and the North-West. In four years the railway doubled its passenger business on the route. Granted, the quality of travel on this line had deteriorated deplorably in the immediately preceding years as the electrification engineering work inflicted delays on schedules that were already well lengthened to allow for it. Granted, too, that besides vastly increased speed and frequency, the route's second-class as well as first-class users were offered air-conditioned comfort – BR was the first in

Europe to standardize air-conditioning in new inter-city coach construction – and at first an over-generous array of bargain fares. Nevertheless, this increase, which meant that it captured three-quarters of the total travel market between London and the North-West, was a considerable achievement.

West Germany's DB took another ten years to realize that it was neglecting the most lucrative sector of the inter-city market. The DB, in fact, was one of the earliest European systems to appropriate the 'Inter-City' brand-name from British Rail, although it was for an elegant, air-conditioned service that was exclusively first-class and scheduled primarily for the convenience of the business market. By the start of the 1970s, however, this operation was not attracting enough passengers to cover its average direct running costs. Too much of its longer-haul business was being lost to the air, a still more attractive medium with the influx of wide-bodied jets, especially because the DB's ability to shorten end-to-end times was severely limited by the unsuitability of so much of the West German half of the old Reichsbahn for its post-war role. Simultaneously, the DB was barely holding its own in the mass travel market which was at the time relegated to a timetable of D-trains. Service was generally sluggish and random in overall structure, and had been untouched by any comprehensive, market-based reorganization since the DB's foundation.

The DB remedied that in one of the most far-reaching overnight timetable reconstructions ever seen. From the start of the DB's 1979 summer timetable the thirty-three principal cities of West Germany were each interlinked by a dual-class IC train every hour from dawn to late at night. Broadly speaking, the 152 daily trains fulfilling this specification followed four routes, achieving the aim of multiple, fixed-interval links between so many centres by tightly timed connections with each other at key stations in the heart of the DB network.

Given the end-to-end distances of the IC routes, the volume of freight and other traffic contending with the IC trains for track space, and not least the physical handicaps of some of the DB's key trunk routes, the precision of the new IC timetable was extraordinary. Before 1979 – and since – no other railway has managed to sustain rigidly patterned

timetabling throughout an itinerary of more than 150 miles (240km). The longer the distance involved, the harder it becomes to mould more and more complexes of local traffic to suit a grand scheme. For instance, in Britain it is comparatively easy to send London-bound trains away from Edinburgh and Newcastle at precise intervals in the early afternoon, but much harder to keep the same perfect spacing right through to London, where they arrive in the middle of the evening commuter peak. But even over a route as long as the 508 miles (817.5km) from Hamburg to Munich, heavy with freight all the way and disturbing scores of local traffic hives, variations in the intermediate station and destination times

of the day's IC trains in each hour were kept to three minutes at most.

Needless to say, efficiency of passenger exchange between IC trains at the connectional stations was crucial. To the maximum extent practicable, connecting trains were programmed to meet on each flank of an island platform and marshalled so that passengers changing trains would generally find the same category of coach to the one they left immediately opposite them on the other side of the platform. Many of these exchanges were successfully allowed less than ten minutes. Even so, on-time workings of such a complex, tightly-timed service demanded special measures in traffic control, which was greatly helped by the installation (the first in Europe) of

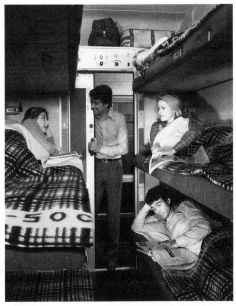

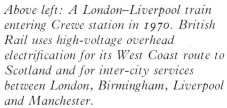

Above left: A London–Liverpool train entering Crewe station in 1970. British Rail uses high-voltage overhead electrification for its West Coast route to Scotland and for inter-city services between London, Birmingham, Liverpool and Manchester.
Left: The DB provides secretarial services on its inter-city trains. Although it may seem a modern innovation, similar services were provided on London to Birmingham trains in the early years of this century.
Above: The spacious interior of a West German first-class inter-city coach.
Above right: Six passengers are comfortably accommodated in a French Railways second-class couchette.
Right: A public telephone on a West German inter-city train.

two-way track-to-train radio. The end of the 1970s saw this facility available over almost 10,000 route-miles (16,000 km) of the DB's system with the cabs of every electric traction unit and most of the diesel fleet fitted to work with it.

At a stroke, simply by widening the benefit of existing IC speed standards, the DB cut an *average* of 25 per cent from second-class rail journey times between any of the country's chief cities. Not surprisingly, the DB's second-class long-distance traffic soared almost 25 per cent in the remainder of the year. The DB had expected that at least 15 per cent of the first-class IC clientele would bridle at deprivation of their exclusivity and decamp to other modes, but the loss was

not more than 2.5 per cent – further proof of the appeal of a reliable, intensive regular-interval service in its own right.

INTER-CITY PASSENGER FACILITIES
An essential ingredient in the modern inter-city package is the comfort and convenience it offers its passengers. This includes the design of suspension systems to ensure a smooth ride even at high speed, large windows to give passengers good views, air-conditioning, good food and other fringe benefits, even if loss-leaders.

Such an example is the telephone facility now standardized on the DB's inter-city services. In the 1950s the French and Italians also added this equipment to some of their business trains, but discarded it

when the apparatus needed renewal on the grounds that demand was nowhere near sufficient to warrant the cost. The DB, however, argued that in the business travel market both this and a train secretarial service were justifiable loss-leaders in the IC shop-window display. Now a coin-in-the-slot, self-dialling telephone kiosk with radio-link access to all the normal facilities of the national network is appearing in every dual-class IC train, and each train's telephone number is listed in the DB's IC service brochures so that passengers on the move can be called. Incoming calls are first taken by the trainboard staff, who page the recipient to the phone over the train's public address. The Austrian and Belgian Railways were beginning to follow the DB lead in the 1980s.

The DB's readiness to meet the loss on such a fringe benefit contrasted oddly with its long-held conviction that air-conditioning was not a crucial sales factor outside the first-class market – though admittedly air-conditioning is a far more costly extra, besides which the plant adds substantially to car weight. Thus for second-class trade the dual-class IC system has operated almost entirely with conventionally ventilated cars of a design updated in nothing more than detail since its introduction in the 1950s. Only on the eve of the new IC era did the DB unveil forty prototype air-conditioned saloons of comparable quality to the handsome first-class cars that had been standard IC equipment for years past; the series order, placed subsequently for 750 more, would not completely re-equip the IC network until 1982 or 1983.

The French, on the other hand, took the British view that air-conditioning was becoming such a commonplace in stores, restaurants and cinemas that trains could no longer sustain an up-to-date image in the mass market without it. Throughout the 1970s the SNCF consequently re-equipped both classes on all its prime domestic inter-city routes with an elegant new breed of air-conditioned car, fleet-named 'Corail' – a contraction of 'Confort' and 'Rail' – and later adapted the 'Corail' body-shell to develop the Continent's first fleet of air-conditioned couchette cars. This was another significant move in the drive to 'democratize' the long-haul train's appeal and entice the young professionals and their families out of Renaults and Citroëns, and one that gained more strength when the SNCF later narrowed

THE PROGRESS OF SPEED

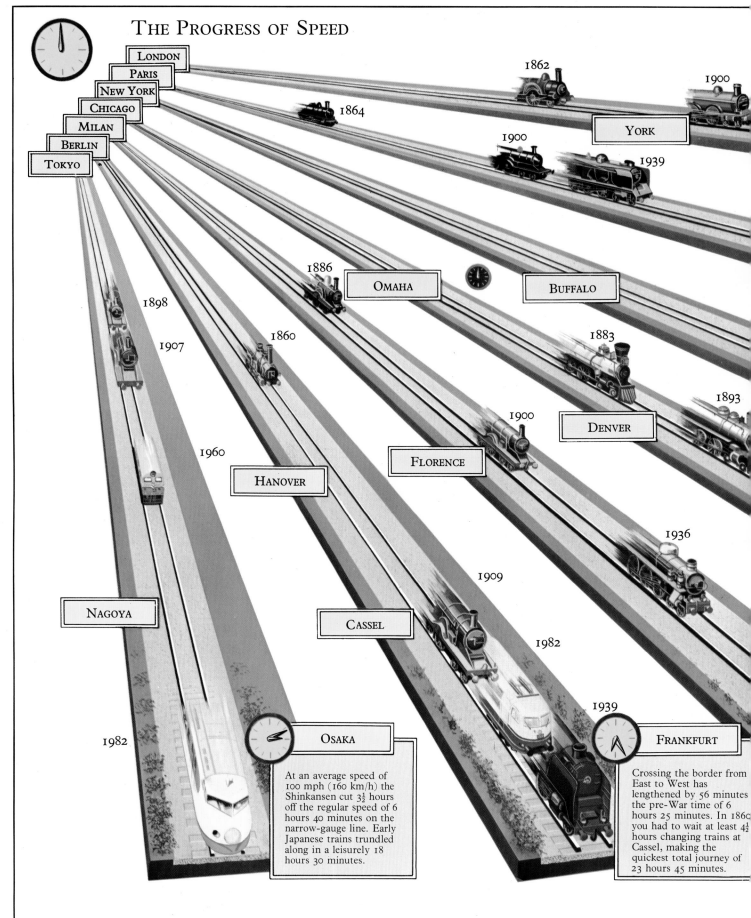

LONDON
PARIS
NEW YORK
CHICAGO
MILAN
BERLIN
TOKYO

1862

1900

1864

YORK

1900

1939

1886

OMAHA

BUFFALO

1898

1883

1907

1860

1893

1960

1900

DENVER

FLORENCE

HANOVER

1936

NAGOYA

1909

CASSEL

1982

OSAKA

At an average speed of
100 mph (160 km/h) the
Shinkansen cut 3½ hours
off the regular speed of 6
hours 40 minutes on the
narrow-gauge line. Early
Japanese trains trundled
along in a leisurely 18
hours 30 minutes.

1982

1939

FRANKFURT

Crossing the border from
East to West has
lengthened by 56 minutes
the pre-War time of 6
hours 25 minutes. In 1860
you had to wait at least 4½
hours changing trains at
Cassel, making the
quickest total journey of
23 hours 45 minutes.

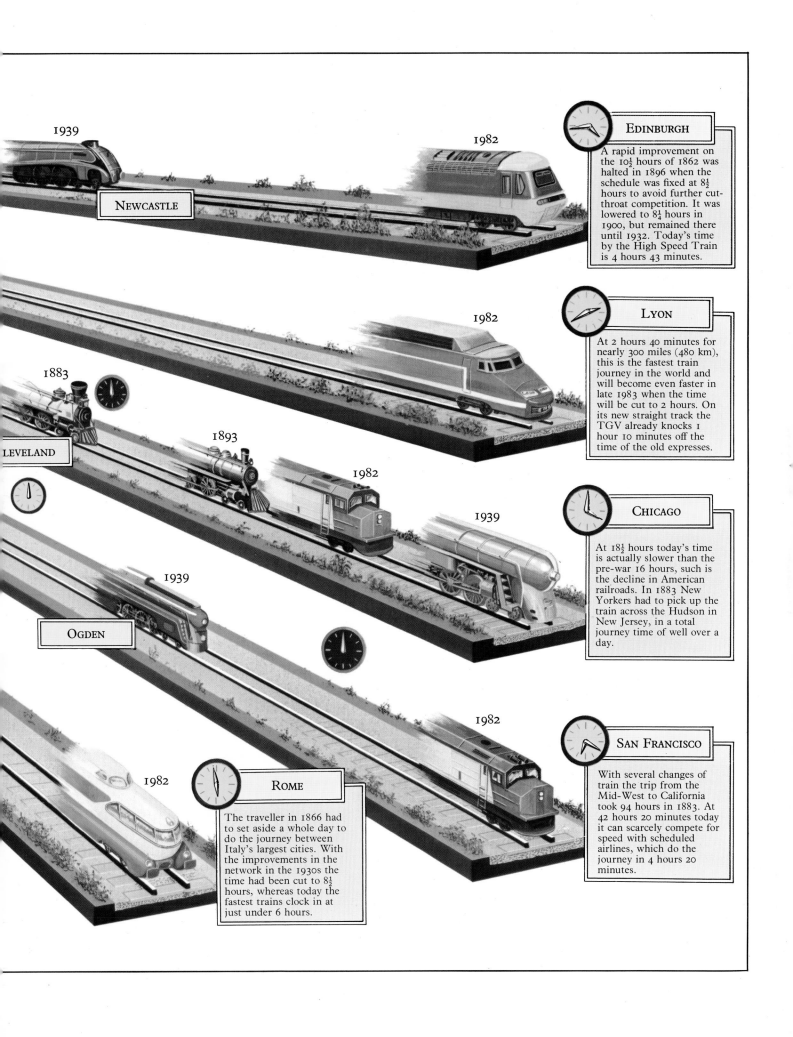

1939

1982

NEWCASTLE

EDINBURGH

A rapid improvement on the 10½ hours of 1862 was halted in 1896 when the schedule was fixed at 8½ hours to avoid further cut-throat competition. It was lowered to 8¼ hours in 1900, but remained there until 1932. Today's time by the High Speed Train is 4 hours 43 minutes.

1982

LYON

At 2 hours 40 minutes for nearly 300 miles (480 km), this is the fastest train journey in the world and will become even faster in late 1983 when the time will be cut to 2 hours. On its new straight track the TGV already knocks 1 hour 10 minutes off the time of the old expresses.

1883

LEVELAND

1893

1982

1939

CHICAGO

At 18¼ hours today's time is actually slower than the pre-war 16 hours, such is the decline in American railroads. In 1883 New Yorkers had to pick up the train across the Hudson in New Jersey, in a total journey time of well over a day.

1939

OGDEN

1982

1982

ROME

The traveller in 1866 had to set aside a whole day to do the journey between Italy's largest cities. With the improvements in the network in the 1930s the time had been cut to 8½ hours, whereas today the fastest trains clock in at just under 6 hours.

SAN FRANCISCO

With several changes of train the trip from the Mid-West to California took 94 hours in 1883. At 42 hours 20 minutes today it can scarcely compete for speed with scheduled airlines, which do the journey in 4 hours 20 minutes.

The SNCF pioneered self-service catering on Europe's railways. The 'Gril-Express' was very successful and prompted other countries to follow suit.

the quality gap between couchette and sleeper travel by making sheets as well as blankets standard couchette equipment.

RESHAPING

The SNCF's 'Corail' reshaping included perhaps the boldest attempt of the 1970s to grapple with a major anxiety of post-war inter-city rail operators, the soaring cost of train catering and the marked change in the taste and habits of its customers. On the supply side inflation was dramatizing the high first cost of a specialized vehicle loaded with expensive cooking equipment, but which earned no mileage revenue from its first users; that made the replacement of obsolescent dining cars harder to justify by the month. Post-war industrial conditions of work, moreover, were escalating the costs of lodging crews away from home between long out-and-back trips. As for the customers, dietary concerns at one end of the market and economy or surrender to the emergent fast-food salesmanship at the other were diminishing the demand for substantial mid-day meals, producing a fresh imbalance in the economics of traditional dining car operation. As early as 1962 these trends forced the International Wagons-Lits company to cease actually owning catering cars and confine its role to staffing and supplying them. In that year its client European railways took over full responsibility both for maintenance of the existing fleet and for their renewal. And in 1971 similar agreements were concluded for all but the Austrian operations of the Wagons-Lits company's international sleeper network.

Before 'Corail' the French had attacked train catering costs that were doubling annually by introducing Europe's first self-service cafeteria cars, known on the SNCF as 'Gril-Express', which supplemented an array of cold wares with hot dishes economically produced by re-heating pre-prepared and pre-frozen packs. Other railways followed suit and by the end of the 1970s the concept had been best realized, both in quality of cuisine and in layout and furnishing, by the DB in its 'Quick-Pick' cars. But although the self-service car's continuous turnover for a greatly reduced staff cost erased a good deal of red ink from the catering account and the second-class trade was happy, the first-class market was not, however hard the interior designers tried to efface the image of a fast-food bar.

In its 'Corail' trains the SNCF tried to satisfy both ends of the market at acceptable cost by standardizing an airline-style service of prefabricated tray meals from galleys built into some of the cars. But that was shunned by the second-class passengers, so snack bar cars were added to the 'Corail' fleet and the tray meal service was limited for first-class and abandoned altogether in trains with a self-service cafeteria. At the start of the 1980s the only French trains still running traditional waiter-served, multi-course meal service were the first-class-only TEEs. Many modern air-conditioned vehicles were among the large number of dining cars made prematurely redundant. Several, however, in another instance of the modern railways' readiness to adapt to market trends, were earmarked for conversion into 'bar-dancing' and 'bar-disco' cars, with all the trappings of strobe lighting and demonically-powered amplifiers, vehicles by then in increasing demand for the charter trains of European package tour operators. No other European railway has yet gone as far as the SNCF in economical reconstruction of its train catering, but all have gone some way in substituting buffet or self-service cars for full restaurant car operation.

The importance of reshaping the post-war passenger railway to interconnect smoothly with road transport dictated adequate parking space at stations and convenient interchange with public road transport. But this was not the only way in which railways were to accommodate motor vehicles. As waves of new private cars and commercial vehicles started to clog the trunk roads of Europe in the 1950s, the passenger management of BR's Eastern Region hit on a fresh inter-modal idea – the accompanied car-carrying train, offering stress-free rail transport for motoring parties and their cars all the way from the big conurbations to railheads in prime holiday areas.

A prototype service was improvised from London to Perth for the Anglo-Scottish tourist traffic in the 1955 summer, coupling to sleepers converted parcels vans for the cars and a diner for their passengers. Public response was immediate. It was the same with a Boulogne–Lyon operation which the SNCF promptly set up the following year, and within a few years Western Europe was criss-crossed by a network of such trains. For the most part they catered for car tourists from the big cities of the north-west to the resort areas of central and southern Europe, though some were chiefly for the convenience of the business market, like the DB's 'Cristoforus', a day train between Düsseldorf and Munich.

INTER-CITY SPEED:
THE FRENCH PIONEERS

Although fixed-interval convenience, improved rolling stock and adept marketing were prime factors in the protection and gradual rebuilding of European railways' inter-city passenger business in the 1960s and 1970s, increasing speed was just as influential. In fact, BR's experience in the second half of the 1960s evolved a rule of thumb that a one per cent rise in the average speed of all trains on an inter-city route generated a one per cent increase in the volume of traffic. But the higher the schedules were raised in the 70–80mph range of average start-to-stop speeds, the further trains needed to run at 100mph or even faster to keep time; and that was becoming steadily more difficult and more expensive to contrive.

The achievement of faster inter-city passenger services was an integral component of French Railways's post-war electrification planning. Though all services would benefit to a degree from electric traction, however, the primary aim was to establish a fleet of peak-hour trains, first class only and surcharged as well, which would substantially outpace the rest of the trains on each route and be styled essentially for the business market. The best-known of them was the Paris–Lyon–Marseille–Nice 'Mistral', which by 1959 was Europe's first post-war train timed at an average of 80mph (130km/h) and was scheduled to cover the 195.3 miles (312km) from Paris to Dijon in 146 minutes.

With the need to solve the technical problems in producing faster trains in mind, the French set themselves to probe the ultimate speed horizons of flanged wheel on steel rail in a study that would eventually have a profound significance for the mass travel market. In the mid-1950s a co-ordinated research programme was started with the objective of assessing the practical performance limits of orthodox electric locomotives, studying the high-speed behaviour of rolling stock, and determining the resilience of the track, the efficiency of the current supply apparatus and the capability of the electrical equipment – fixed as well as mobile – to withstand the maximum loads imposed upon it by the abnormal current demands of locomotives making well over 100mph (160km/h).

Track tests got under way in February 1954 with a new world record of 151.9mph (244.5km/h) on a practically dead straight and level 23 miles (37km) of the Paris–Lyon main line between Dijon and Beaune, achieved by one of the SNCF's first post-war locomotive designs with all axles motored, the 106-ton, 4,740hp No. CC7121. These locomotives had already revolutionized the Paris–Lyon service with their ability to romp up inclines as steep as 1 in 125 in the Burgundy hills above Dijon at 80mph (130km/h) with a 700-ton *rapide* in tow.

The climax followed in March 1955. As astonishing as the speeds attained was the fact that the test track on this occasion, a stretch of the former Midi Railway between Bordeaux and the Spanish border at Hendaye, had been electrified in 1927 and that its catenary, suspended from the Midi's idiosyncratic arch supports, was comparatively slender and never previously subjected to regular traffic travelling faster than 75mph (120km/h). But one 52¾ mile (85km) stretch of this route south of Lamothe, 25 miles (40km) from Bordeaux, was the ideal course for high-speed trials – dead level and bent by just one curve, which was anyway of a generous 2¼ mile (3.6km) radius.

After months of proving the fitness of track, traction and current supply capacity with tests of increasing severity, the SNCF's engineers were ready in March 1955 to go for the target set at the start of the programme – 186.5mph (300km/h). Two locomotives had been specially prepared for the exercise with modified gearing and running gear, and with re-designed pantographs. One was another of the post-war Co-Cos, No. CC 7107; the second, No. BB9004, was one of the first lightweight four-axle locomotives evolved in 1952–4 to set the parameters for latter-day SNCF electric traction design, packing a continuously rated output of just over 4,000hp into a unit of only 80 tons weight. Each in turn was set at the racetrack with a set of three coaches which had had their running gear specially fettled up, every protruding fitment removed from their exteriors and rubber fairings stitched between them to streamline the train down its raked tail nearly 8ft (2.4m) long, which was fixed to the rear of the end coach.

After a preliminary canter by BB9004 at 171.5mph (276km/h) on 26 March 1955, its companion was given first crack at the ultimate objective two days later. For 7 miles (11km) on end CC7107 had the featherweight test train hurtling at 185mph (300km/h) and more, in the

Wires glow red hot as French locomotive No. BB9004 hits the top speed of 205.6mph recorded during speed trials in 1955.

course of which a peak of 205.6mph (330.9km/h) was recorded.

But not without trauma. One of the imponderables was the resilience of the locomotives' current-collecting strips atop their pantographs in face of phenomenal power loading, and whether they could maintain firm, constant contact with the overhead wire at very high speed. The record speed was the point at which the red-hot strips finally melted, bringing the frame of the pantograph itself into contact with the overhead wire and compelling the engineers to order a shut-off of power and deceleration. Just the same happened the next day when BB9004 was run up to an identical maximum speed – or so the French have always insisted, though they have never entirely dispelled doubt that things could be so immaculately judged at such phenomenal speed, especially when the attention of many of the engineers must have been transfixed by the sight of liquescent metal streaming like glowing lava from the pantograph.

These first 200mph exploits were one-off performances in minutely controlled conditions, the climax of a long and meticulously prepared research and development programme. They had boldly identified the possible horizon, but not what was immediately practicable in everyday working. Nor had they done anything to show how the frequent curves of most European trunk routes could be magically straightened to create stretches long enough for trains of 400 tons or more to accelerate to 150, let alone 200mph.

Moreover, the technical problems of developing thoroughly dependable and economical high-speed traction and rolling stock were by no means the only barriers to 100 mph-plus inter-city speed. Optimal economic use of a trunk rail route's operational capacity depends on the breadth of its traffic's speed band. Ideally, all trains should be of standard vehicles with a standard length, weight and power – as on a Metro – so that they can be timed at common speed to maintain a constant headway from each other over the whole length of the line (parameters which also simplify signalling for close headway working, of course). If the average speed of the top flight of traffic is sharply increased, but that of the slower trains sharing its running lines is unchanged, then obviously the headways both in front and in rear of each express or group of express trains must be widened and track capacity is wasted. A further discouragement to the widening of the speed band is that the superelevation of curves has to be a compromise between the ideals at each end of that speed band: the degree of cant must not be so sharp that a slow-moving train wears the inner rail severely, nor so slight that the passengers of an express are subjected to discomforting centrifugal force.

The French needed another decade to translate the findings of that elaborately prepared 1955 exploit into standard hardware that could withstand daily operation at even 125mph (200km/h) without fallibility or incurring intolerable upkeep costs. Almost two decades of methodical research and development were required to prove every component of a railway designed for standard operation at 160mph (260km/h) – the Paris–Lyon TGV, discussed in the last chapter.

From the 1950s onward every railway ambitious for 100mph (160km/h) and more in regular passenger service was to learn that a one-off experiment in controlled conditions took them only a foot or two down a very long technological trek

Above: The cool and slightly clinical interior of a Japanese Shinkansen coach. Below: Across a landscape dominated by the sacred Mount Fuji, a 'Bullet Train' shoots along the New Tokaido Line. This, the first of Japan's entirely new high-speed lines, was inaugurated in 1964.

in search of traction, running gear and track structure – and not least the correct match of running gear and track – that could absorb stresses which multiplied as they sought to advance further into the three-figure speed range. Not only that, but the resilience had to be obtained economically.

INTER-CITY SPEED: THE JAPANESE EXPERIENCE

The first to prove that intensive and reliable day-to-day rail operation at over 100mph was mechanically practical were the Japanese. But they only did it at the high cost of custom-building a new railway for the exclusive use of standard train-sets, creating, in fact, what was virtually a long-haul Metro line in so far as its operating characteristics were concerned. That was the New Tokaido Line, the first of Japan's Shinkansen ('New Railways'), widely known in the Anglo-Saxon world as the 'Bullet Trains' because of the projectile-like styling of the train-sets' noses.

The genesis of the New Tokaido Line, which was not inaugurated until October 1964, was the Government's acceptance in 1957 that the existing 3 ft 6 in (1,067mm)

*The high-speed Shinkansen cut through
city and countryside alike.*

gauge main line between Tokyo and
Osaka, severely handicapped by curvature, gradients and countless level crossings, could never be adequately adapted
to the demands of the Tokaido coastal belt
between the two cities. This strip of land
teems with almost three-quarters of
Japan's industry and 40 per cent of its
population. The only solution, despite the
deterrent costs of construction through
such densely populated territory, was to
build a new, ideally aligned standard-
gauge railway – electrified, of course, but
at 25 kV ac instead of the previous Japanese
National Railways 1.5 kV dc standard.

Originally, the new railway was to be
traversed by night-time container trains as
well as daytime passenger services, but the
freight proposal was dropped. It was
unlikely to attract enough business to
justify interference with track and catenary
maintenance, which would have to be done
at night because of the intensity of daytime
passenger service envisaged. In time even
the nightly six-hour shutdown of the new
railway was to prove inadequate for all the
upkeep work and today the New Tokaido
Line still has to be closed for whole
mornings eight times a year to give maintenance crews more time undisturbed.

In a remarkable feat of construction,
considering the scale of the enterprise, the
320 mile (515 km) track was completed in
five years. With the historic 3 ft 6 in gauge
main line left to cater for short-distance
passenger journeys between Tokyo and
Osaka, only ten intermediate stations
serving the major cities and townships
were needed on the new line. They could
be of the simplest layout, with no more
than loops of the through tracks for trains
booked to call at them. There were no
junctions whatsoever and the train-sets
were standard. Consequently, the whole
route could be controlled from a single
centre in Tokyo. In view of the high
running speeds contemplated, drivers
could not be left reliant on intermittent
observation of lineside signals. Thus the
New Tokaido Line was the first railway to
be governed entirely by a continuous
display on driving cab consoles of signal
aspects; the displays were actuated by
coded frequencies transmitted through the
track circuitry, which were also employed
to supervise the drivers' responses.

From its inauguration on 1 October
1964 this first Shinkansen immediately set
standards of passenger service – and of
economic performance – which astounded
the world. Even though the original target
top speed of 160 mph (260 km/h) was
lowered on second thoughts to 130 mph

(210 km/h), the line's 'Hikari' expresses,
calling only at Nagoya and Kyoto en route,
were soon linking Tokyo and Osaka in 3
hours 10 minutes at an end-to-end average
of 101 mph (162.5 km/h), thanks to the
most generous powering of a train-set yet
seen. With every axle motored, the total
output of the ultimate sixteen-car Shinkansen unit was a prodigious 15,875 hp for
a total train weight of 834 tons! As for
return on investment, the strictly patterned high-speed service, that was
quickly built up to a level of eighty trains
each way daily, so magnetized the Japanese
that on one single spring day in 1969 the
trains shifted over half a million passengers. In the following year the Shinkansen
moved into healthy financial surplus on its
central financial charges as well as on its
running costs.

Euphoric projections of a 4,350 mile
(7,000 km) Shinkansen network were
issued in 1973, but the catastrophic losses
on JNR's 3 ft 6 in system meant that the
proposal met with political disfavour. Also
the oil crisis affected Japan more than most
countries, and the subsequent inflation
sent the cost of new railway building
skyward, especially in urban environ-
ments. And, in addition, ecological
concerns were growing. Suddenly the
Shinkansen were a noisy environmental
menace and JNR was coerced into very
costly erection of sound-deadening barriers around the high-speed lines.

However, in 1975 the original line was
extended by the New Sanyo Shinkansen
into Kyushu island to complete a 664 mile
(1,069 km) route from Tokyo to Hakata
(Fukuoka). The New Sanyo traverses very
different terrain from the New Tokaido; its
final 247 miles (397.5 km) pierce 111
tunnels aggregating 138 route-miles
(222 km), and among them is the 11.6 mile
(18.7 km) tunnel under Kammon Strait
between Honshu and Kyushu islands.
This, however, is almost unremarkable
when set against the 33.4 (53.8 km) Seikan
Tunnel which the Japanese were completing underneath the Tsugaru Strait between Honshu and Hokkaido islands, in
the north, at the start of the 1980s. Whether
the Seikan Tunnel will eventually carry a
Shinkansen, as originally intended, rather
than a 3 ft 6 in (1,067 mm) JNR line has yet
to be confirmed.

The Tohoku Shinkansen from Tokyo to
Morioka, the first step in the northerly
direction, was heading for completion in
the summer of 1982 but at least five years

behind schedule because of the problems outlined earlier. Also due for completion in 1982 but equally belated was the Joetsu Shinkansen, cutting through the spinal Mukumi mountains of Honshu from Tokyo to Niigata on the north coast and thereby incurring some more formidable engineering which included a summit tunnel 13.8 miles (22.2 km) long, the Dai-Shimize. These two latest Shinkansen, the Tohoku and the Joetsu, have been constructed to 160 mph (260 km) design parameters like the original New Tokaido Line, but, in view of the re-laying and re-wiring of the whole New Tokaido route enforced on the JNR after only ten years' pounding by an intensive 130 mph (210 km/h) service, and also because of nervousness about the environmentalists' reactions, the Japanese balked at a commitment to operate daily at this higher speed. During 1979 it was apparent to the Japanese that the French were securely on course from the autumn of 1981 for standard operation at 160 mph (260 km/h) on the first half of their new Paris–Lyon high-speed line. Dislodged from their pinnacle as the world's fastest railways, 130 mph (210 km/h) Shinkansen might cost the Japanese rail supply and consultancy industry prestige in the glittering markets of the developing world and forfeit some of the worldwide business originally generated by the 'Bullet Trains'.

Abruptly, in the autumn of 1979, a fresh series of high-speed trials with a prototype unit was ordered over a finished stretch of the Tohoku line, but, even though the French record was challenged with a peak speed of 198.3 mph (319.1 km/h) on one January 1980 trip, the Japanese finally decided that the two new Shinkansen would have to operate at 130 mph (210 km/h). The higher speed remained an objective for some unspecified date in the future, but, nevertheless, the announcement would clearly not help to boost Shinkansen's domestic image, which had already lost some of its commercial sheen owing to a combination of wide-bodied jet competition and the relaxation in 1976 of the government's severe curbs on railway fares. An overnight fare hike of 50 per cent, succeeded by further rises to pace inflation, hoisted Tokyo–Osaka fares close to the price of an air ticket and drained traffic to the extent that in late 1979 some thinning of the train service was deemed essential.

As the New Tokaido Line's track-bed wilted under the hammering of a high-speed service, JNR decided to lay the greater part of the subsequent Shinkansen in a cast-concrete slab bed, instead of on traditional sleepers set in ballast. Several railways have lately adopted this method where traffic is heavy but track upkeep is difficult – for instance, in commuter line tunnels – but none so extensively as JNR.

Since the middle of this century track design and maintenance to stringent standards have become increasingly crucial to the performance of major railways in face of commercial clamour for higher passenger speeds and more capacious freight vehicles. At the same time pressures to reduce the high labour content of traditional track inspection and maintenance have been unremitting. The development of a whole armoury of very sophisticated mobile apparatus to mechanize every phase of tracklaying and repair, and to detect, precisely locate and identify flaws from inspection vehicles travelling at up to 100 mph (160 km/h) has been an outstanding money-saving achievement of rail technology since the last war. The semi-permanent solidity of slab track cuts maintenance expense still more, but its capital cost is at least twice that of conventional track and to renew the latter with slab track shuts the line concerned for twice as long as like-for-like replacement.

INTER-CITY SPEED: THE AMERICAN EXPERIENCE

Japan's New Tokaido Line made a profound impression in the USA. Its success reinforced a powerful lobby urging Federal support for a rail revival in the populous north-east corridor between Boston, New York and Washington to prevent its skies and highways being overrun by planes and automobiles. In September 1965 President Johnson signed a High Speed Ground Transportation Act

An Amtrak 'Metroliner' on the New York to Washington run.

MODERN TRAFFIC CONTROL

One of the major breakthroughs in running a complex modern railway has been provided by the computer, and a large mileage of track can now be controlled from one centre by only a handful of staff. An example of modern electronics at work in the railways is given by British Rail's Southern Region where two electronically linked signalboxes will control the whole network between London and Brighton – some 551 track miles (882 km). Gone are the old levers and bells, and gone too are the seventy-one signalboxes that used to house them.

The complexity of the job to be performed can be seen by examining just one section of the track, at East Croydon station, a busy part of the commuter route into London. Such are the precision and efficiency of the new equipment that it has been possible to remodel the station layout to cope better with the flow of traffic. Trains running at $1\frac{1}{2}$-2 minute intervals will be directed to almost any of the platforms, which are on reversible track, thereby enabling best use of them according to which direction the traffic is the heavier.

The diagram shows a typical situation in the morning rush-hour, when most of the traffic is on the up lines. Fast lines are indicated in red, slow lines in blue, and reversible track in green. Movement of the trains is controlled by four-aspect signals with, in addition to red and green, a single yellow and a double yellow aspect. The single yellow indicates that the next signal is either on red or yellow, and the double yellow that the next signal is on yellow or green. Several of the signals have direction lights on top; when these are lit they indicate that the train is being directed to a track to the left or right, or even to one two or three tracks away.

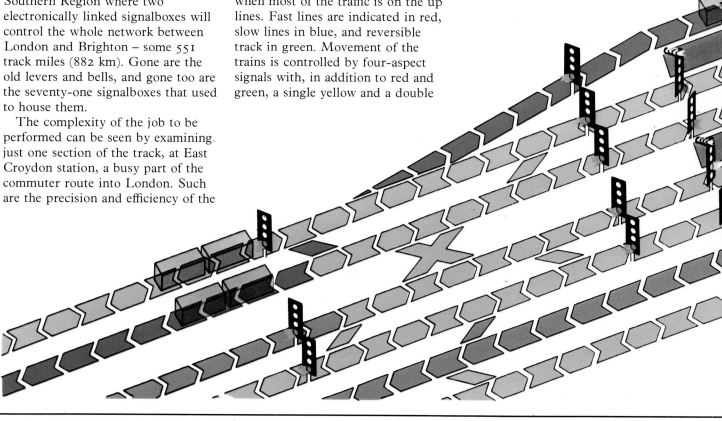

which authorized a demonstration project between Boston and New York with United Aircraft Turbotrains, and between New York and Washington, over the electrified Pennsylvania main line, with new high-speed multiple-units, known as the 'Metroliners'.

Over-ambition and lack of experience doomed the 'Metroliners' to a very troublesome youth. The builders were handed a specification demanding acceleration to 150mph (240 km/h) in three minutes on the level and a top speed of 160mph (260 km/h), capabilities that were quite beyond the state of the track in the north-east corridor. And, despite total innocence in high-speed electric traction, the designers packed the 'Metroliners' with virtually untried technology. Teething troubles were so acute that the full demonstration service could not begin until 1971, four years late. But once it was fully operative, with schedules exacting average speeds in excess of 90mph (145 km/h) between intermediate stops, public response was enthusiastic. The 'Metroliners' became Amtrak's responsibility in 1971.

Uniquely among US trunk rail routes, the north-east corridor is predominantly a passenger line, heavily weighted by short-distance services in the urban areas it traverses. Consequently, it did not fit logically into the network of Conrail, the corporation created in 1975 to take over primarily the freight system of the bankrupt north-eastern railroads. Congress therefore decided to reverse roles and in this instance to make Amtrak the landlord and Conrail the tenant where the latter needed to run freight trains over the route. It was a matter of no little consternation to former Penn-Central creditors, those most affected by the north-east bankruptcies, when the major part of the Boston–New York–Washington main line (some of the commuter sections had already been purchased by state or city authorities) and its installations were sold to Amtrak for a knock-down price.

Amtrak dreamed of reconstructing the whole route to Shinkansen standards, but President Ford's administration would tolerate only partial upgrading, renewal and extension of the electrification. The North-East Corridor Improvement Project (NECIP) got under way in the later 1970s on a budget of $1.75 billions and conclusion was set for 1981. But at the end of the decade the estimated cost had

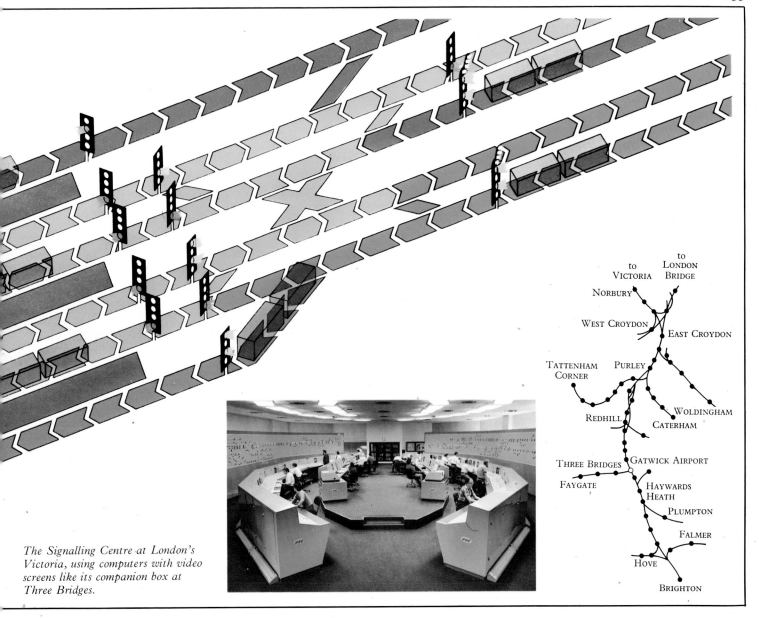

The Signalling Centre at London's Victoria, using computers with video screens like its companion box at Three Bridges.

swollen to $2.5 billions and completion was improbable before the end of 1983 – and that despite sacrificing the plan to convert the former Pennsylvania 125 kV 25 Hz ac catenary to the 25 kV 60 Hz ac system being installed from New Haven, north of New York, to Boston. The delay and cost overrun were partly attributable to inflation, but in considerable measure to mismanagement through involvement of too many bureaucratic agencies in the project. At the end of the day the end-to-end speed of the Boston–New York service in particular would have fallen some way short of Europe's best even on the original prospectus, but President Reagan's determination to trim Federal expenditure on Amtrak may lower sights still further.

Just possibly, though, the USA will have a passenger route or two to compare with Europe and Japan's fastest by the end of the century. One more expression of Americans' new warmth towards all forms of rail transport at the close of the 1970s was the determined moves in some individual states to establish high-speed passenger railways of their own. Coupled with irritation that so much Federal tax money should be lavished exclusively on the north-eastern states was impatience at the time it took to get agreement to the additional Amtrak services which one state after another was anxious to part-finance. These were the '403(b)' trains, so-called after a clause in the founding Amtrak Acts which offered tapering Federal grants to any states prepared to fund additional Amtrak routes that failed to qualify for full Federal subsidy. In 1980 some Ohio politicians were eager to create a high-

speed railway to interlink eight of the state's principal conurbations; Ohio had already spent $1 million in preliminary research and as the year progressed it moved on to discussion of a test-track's design parameters with consultancies in Europe and Japan. Other mid-western states such as Michigan were peering intently over Ohio's shoulder, and Texas and California were seriously examining the case for new high-speed tracks in their key inter-city corridors.

INTER-CITY SPEED:
THE WEST GERMAN EXPERIENCE

West Germany's DB led Europe into the 125 mph (200 km/h) era, but edgily. In the mid-1960s sections of the main lines between Hanover and Celle and between Munich and Augsburg were fitted with a form of continuous cab signalling and automatic speed control, and in May 1966 the Munich–Hamburg 'Blauer Enzian' was authorized to cover them at 125 mph (200 km/h). But very soon the DB was troubled by excessive wear and tear. The limit was pulled back to 100 mph (160 km/h) until the spring of 1978 when, following refinements of track structure and vehicle suspension, a number of sectors in the plains of North Germany and in the Upper Rhine Valley were passed for regular negotiation at 125 mph by 'Inter-City' trains with Class 103 electric locomotives and coaches with supplementary electro-magnetic track brakes.

At the start of the 1970s the DB was promoting its 'Neubaustrecken' – seven new by-passes aggregating 590 route-miles (950 km) – which it was anxious to build around speed-restricted bottlenecks in its trunk system before the century's end, primarily as 150 mph (240 km/h) passenger railways. But since then the Neubaustrecken have also become vital components of the plan to accelerate freight transits. To maximize their operating capacity the speed range of trains sharing their tracks must be kept as narrow as possible; consequently the DB has had to drop its 'Inter-City' speed sights to 125 mph for the immediate future.

But progress with the Neubaustrecken has been agonizingly slow. At first the stumbling-block was Government misgiving about the wisdom of such massive investment in the railways' future. It was 1977 and 1978 before construction of the first two lines was authorized, from Mannheim to Stuttgart and from Hanover as far as the Kassel area, as anxiety deepened about the future of energy. Two years later extension of the second line to its full planned extent, to Würzburg, was approved. But whereas both these Neubaustrecken, and a third from Cologne to the outskirts of Frankfurt which by-passes the sinuous Rhine Gorge route via Bonn and Koblenz, were once programmed for completion by the end of the 1980s, only the Mannheim–Stuttgart route is now likely to mature by then.

The problem is neither shortage of money nor Government disinterest – its Neubaustrecken are now a keystone of Bonn's forward transport policy. It is more the strength of West Germany's environmentalist factions and the checks and balances painstakingly built into the country's post-war constitution. Incon-

gruously in a land which in mid-century allowed so much of its surface to be ripped apart by road-builders, the intrusion of new electric railways has been stigmatized by numerous local authorities as a threat to the quality of life. In two cases in the late 1970s, one in north and the other in south Germany, this resulted in the DB's inability for several months to run electric trains over a newly electrified railway, simply because local authorities blocked the extension of current grid cables to energize the catenary. And the Neubaustrecke between the Cologne and Frankfurt areas was hamstrung almost entirely by interminable argument over the line of route. Worse still, even when consensus had been reached at administrative level, the German constitution provided for formal hearing of any individual objections to what had been agreed, however frivolous. A general effect of this environmental sensitivity is that a substantial mileage of the new Mannheim–Stuttgart line is now being sunk just below ground level and concealed by cut-and-cover tunnelling for no pressing civil engineering reason, but purely to mollify the environmentalists. The impeded progress of the Neubaustrecken – which incongruously at this juncture of railway history had the DB sitting on vast Federal investment grants it was unable to spend – frustrated the Government as much as its railway management, so much so that in 1981 the Government was preparing new legislation to relax the constraints on DB planning.

THE HARD SELL AND ITS IMPACT

It was not only frequent, regular service and timings up into the 80 mph (130 km/h) average range, thanks to the more sustained 100 mph (160 km/h) running made possible by electric traction's rapid acceleration to top speed, which doubled rail passenger carryings between London and the North-West and routed the competing airlines before the end of the 1960s. For the first time a regenerated rail service was promoted with the full panoply of modern marketing techniques, from TV advertising, direct mail campaigns and brand-naming – for this was the genesis of the 'Inter-City' tag – to research-backed market pricing. This last was to court new business for the greatly increased off-peak capacity of the service, which was justified to maximize the economic advantage of electric traction's unrivalled availability for continuous work. Because of improved productivity, the additional trains were run at only marginal extra operating costs; and that created the scope for adept price variation to stimulate optional travel in trains outside the daily business peaks.

In the next few years the commercial impact of BR's regular interval 'Inter-City' operation and the devices by which it was marketed made a profound impression on continental European managements. One after another the NS, DB, SBB, ÖBB, DSB and SJ began to recast their main-line timetables on the same principles, in

The DB's 'Blauer Enzian', hauled by the 125 mph Class 103 electric locomotive.

several cases borrowing the 'Inter-City' brand-name untranslated. Some of the State-owned railways already had the licence to vary their prices provided that at year's end their gross income met the budgetary target set by their governments, but France's SNCF, to cite a major exception, did not gain it until 1979.

The 'hard sell' effect on inter-city passenger services has been nowhere better demonstrated than in Holland over the past ten years. And this was all the more striking as Holland was forging one of the most highly developed inter-urban highway networks in Europe; furthermore, the bulk of NS coaching stock was until the end of the 1970s past its prime and an unappealing alternative to the majority of modern motor cars. After major reorganization in 1970, its success, which added about 30 per cent to the volume of rail journeys of 100 miles (160 km) or more, has depended on day-long and intensive regular-interval timetabling, achieving high productivity of rolling-stock, in a period of escalating oil prices yet worsening urban road traffic congestion. But as influential as these reasons, if not more so, was the Dutch Railways' 1975 reorganization of its commercial department as a marketing organization, which combined a drive to improve the quality of train travel and some service reorganization to minimize changes of train on the most popular itineraries with bold fare offers to encourage regular use of the railway. Under this last head the emphasis since 1978 has been on offers designed to wed whole households to train travel. One scheme requires one member of a family to buy a qualifying card for about £500, allowing that person a year's unlimited rail travel without further outlay, and after that anyone in the same family is entitled to purchase for only £25 or so a card allowing him or her a year's freedom of the railway. Alternatively, for a much smaller investment of about £85 by one member, everyone else in a Dutch household automatically gets a card with which they can buy all their rail tickets for the rest of the year at 35 to 50 per cent off according to type – single, return or season.

These Dutch offers are the most liberal of the 'membership' ideas recently devised by European railways' new marketing departments. Most widely adopted are those for students and pensioners, which uniquely offer the individual purchaser a reduction on all his ticket purchases.

British Rail's 'Inter-City' service is *heavily advertised.*

British Rail markets a family railcard, but it is effective only where an adult travels with at least one child. The BR card does, however, have a much lower first cost than the Dutch, and one must also remember that the British system offers to any traveller a more ramified general range of cheap off-peak tickets than anyone else except Swedish Railways. At least a third of its passenger revenue derives from them.

Marketing is much more than mere market-pricing, of course. In the latter-day railway context its 'packaging' side has innumerable facets. From the starting-point of enticing the public into trains, through aggressive and emphatic advertising, it ranges from easily read timetable layouts and provision for smooth change into a train from car and bus (or in the Dutch case, cycle – one or two Dutch city dormitory stations have room to park as many as 1,000 cycles) to crystal-clear signposting of every facility within the station itself. On train the concerns run from methodically researching the most relaxing internal colour schemes as well as the most ergonomically satisfying seat contours to styling a refreshment service that best compromises the inclinations of a mixed clientele at a tolerable running cost.

Though the Dutch fell behind their neighbours in quality of rolling stock, they were front-runners in other aspects of 're-packaging' rail travel, especially in station layout and passenger briefing. This wrapping on the regular-interval convenience and smart inter-urban speed of the train service, made more appealing still by market-pricing, had the volume of NS rail travel rising at a steady 5 per cent per annum by the end of the 1970s. Within this overall increase, moreover, the NS was recording some remarkable upsurges in first-class travel, despite the basically mass-market orientation of the train service plan. Between Alkmaar and Amsterdam the first-class rate of growth was as much as 40 per cent, hard statistical support for other signs of a pronounced tide of Dutch public opinion in favour of higher investment in railways and a reduction in the level of expenditure on the country's roads.

It was therefore as a result of a service which was genuinely promoted by its marketed image that the Dutch Government at last endorsed the overdue modernization of NS traction and coaching stock on a substantial scale. It also authorized a start on the first of several much-needed projects to enlarge the NS system's tightly stretched operating capacity: a new direct railway from Amsterdam to Leiden and The Hague, serving Amsterdam's Schiphol airport *en route* to relieve pressure on the more circuitous route via Haarlem; and the driving of a new multi-track tunnel under the North Sea Canal to avoid the constant interruption of rail traffic by the opening of a new swing bridge on the existing and very busy route from Amsterdam to North Holland. Construction of an entirely new railway, the Zoetermeer line, to cater for The Hague's outer suburban development was approved and completed; and another, to Lelystad and possibly Groningen to serve the new Zuyder Zee polders (land reclaimed from the North Sea) should be operational by the late 1980s. At the beginning of the 1980s there was evidence, too, that Dutch legislators had accepted NS forecasts that the rate of passenger traffic growth would choke the nodal points of the rail system within a predictable timespan and were prepared to invest in additional trackage and flying junctions at the heart of the network – an expensive business in Holland's flat, highly urbanized terrain, with the extra complication of a dense canal system as well as a highly developed road complex.

THE FIGHT FOR FREIGHT

The post-war world strengthened challenges to the railways' market share of their staple freight traffics – coal, iron, steel, mineral ores, oil and (in some countries) grain. New inland waterways sharpened the competitiveness of waterborne transport or even, in the outstanding case of North America's St Lawrence Seaway, allowed ocean-going ships to penetrate deep inland with their cargoes intact. And new pipeline technology threatened some heavy-tonnage hauls of oil.

Much more at risk was the traffic not always bulked to a single consignee or that which was reliant on prompt, reliable delivery for ultimate saleability – perishable foodstuffs, for example. They were desperately vulnerable to the new door-to-door efficiency and economy of high-capacity road vehicles which were exploiting their speed potential on the expanding motorway networks. This, moreover, was the fastest-growing market by far because of the post-war boom in consumer goods, and the biggest freight prize because revenue per ton was several times higher than that for bulk goods where quality service was not the paramount concern.

It was in the 1950s and 1960s, however, that rail transport looked at its most vulnerable. Road transport, traditionally freer of government restrictions, was easily able to maximize efficiency in its fragmented commercial structure to take advantage of the motorways that were beginning to spread across the landscape of the industrialized world. It was a development that the ever-alert truck manufacturers were geared up to and it needed no great investment for the hauliers to seize the initiative and re-equip their fleets. The investment looked all the more attractive as industrial operations diversified and relocated, and the first post-war affluence set economies into overdrive. Unlike the railway operators, bogged down with outdated plant, financial constraints and governmental pressures, the hauliers could invest with no great difficulty and simply grasp what was put in front of them – highways, vehicles, cheap fuel and traffic – and of course they were quick to demonstrate their advantages. As yet, this was the age of the truck.

It was not until well into the 1960s that the rail operators could properly fight back and challenge the truck for freight. And the railways had to fight on the hauliers' own ground – on rates and efficiency. Some operations inevitably had to be conceded, particularly small-lot/short-haul traffic. Ten tons across 200 miles (320 km) was a winner for road every time – a rail operation would involve transshipment, hauling, marshalling and transshipment yet again; the truck could load and deliver door to door.

But the changes in the transport world of the 1960s and 1970s and especially the escalation of fuel prices began to swing the advantage pendulum back towards the railways, and especially as recession slowed world industry in the early 1980s. The most important of the transport changes was the introduction of the container, a facility primarily instigated by the shipping companies and port authorities, and its effect was to revolutionize cargo handling. Ship turnaround times were halved overnight, even in ports

Above left: Loading a container onto a US COFC (Container-on-Flat-Car) train.
Below: A TOFC (Trailer-on-Flat-Car), or 'piggyback', train in Echo Canyon, Utah. Introduced in 1955, TOFC traffic soon held a major share of US rail freight.

Trailers are loaded onto a Santa Fe Railroad 'Ten-Pack' (ten skeletal frames articulated over single axles).

without the specialized container handling equipment of today's Tilbury, Rotterdam or Norfolk, Va. For in the latter ports a vessel drawing a payload of, say, 10,000 tons in 500 to 800 containers can be discharged and ready for reloading in as little as forty-eight hours. A far cry from the old days of just twenty years ago when dockers with their hooks in hand would be crawling around ships' holds and man-handling cargoes on to pallets for the quay cranes. Of course, containers provided yet more work for the haulier – they still had to be moved from quayside to customer and vice versa – but the standardized unit of the container was to provide a challenge as well as a tempting opportunity for the railway operators.

But it was not until the era of perpetual inflation and oil crises that the road hauliers began to feel the pinch and lose their competitive edge. The problem for them was really one of costing, despite the fact that they now had the big rigs and the super-highways. For when it came for their customers to allocate their freight to either road or rail, once door-to-door efficiency had been allowed for, the final decisive factor was one of cost. And the hauliers could no longer operate cheaply. Fuel prices were not the only reason (for

vehicle standing costs had escalated dramatically) but they played a major part. Today the big 350 hp Volvos and Mercedes of Europe, or the massive 420 Macks and Kenworths of the US, are running at as little as 6 or 7 mpg (2 km/litre) when fully freighted – this a mere 20 ton payload in the UK, or up to 35 tons in the US and on the Continent. So with diesel oil today approaching something near £2 per gallon, the fuel costs for a haulier running a 20 ton, 40 ft (13 m) container from Tilbury to Glasgow would not be far short of £100. It's a safe bet that a haulier would not take on the job for much less than £300 (especially with the additional risk in today's recession of being unable to load his lorry home from Scotland). By contrast, Freightliner, the container-handling subsidiary of BR, would ship the same container from Tilbury to Glasgow for £200.

In the USA it is not feasible to make such cost comparisons, because of the complexity of US railroads' 'piggyback' freight tariffs. However, a comparison of energy consumption can be made, as is shown in a 1980 analysis, by the US Federal Railroad Administration, of two years' working of the Milwaukee Railroad's 'Sprint' freight train over the 410 miles (660 km) between Chicago and St Paul. This demonstrated that on average the 'Sprint' service was generating 172.9 revenue-earning ton-miles per gallon of fuel as against 86.9 by

road vehicles shifting equivalent tonnage over the route. This rail superiority could increase substantially with widespread use of the latest US inter-modal technology. Protracted trials with trains of the 'amphibian' RoadRailer (trailer with interchangeable road and rail running gear) have indicated that fuel consumption can be halved. The fuel consumption per vehicle in a RoadRailer train over 1,000 miles (1,600 km) would be 39 gallons, whereas the US Department of Energy estimates that a typical road trailer rig needs 196 gallons to cover the same distance.

This very fuel efficiency is not just an issue that the transport customers alone have taken advantage of. The ever-vociferous anti-road haulage lobby can now make genuine environmental claims against the diesel-guzzling and road-wrecking juggernauts. Today therefore, as the railways liberate themselves from a tradition of over-restrictive regulation, the road hauliers are increasingly bound by governmental legislation.

INTER-MODAL OPERATIONS

North American railroads were the first to be edged out of their profitable business by the new age of trucking. But it was on this very basis of costing that the railroad operators made their first significant challenge. It depended on the simple yet ironical fact that a train could carry a loaded road trailer over a long distance more efficiently and thus more competitively than the individually crewed tractor unit designed to pull it. With this in mind, the US railroads were the first to devise a system designed to pair their respective trump cards, the rail's long-haul efficiency with the road's doorstep collection and delivery facility.

With the benefit of the generous North American loading gauge, the Pennsylvania in 1955 spearheaded the creation of Trailer-on-Flat-Car (TOFC), or 'piggyback': the use of 85 ft (25.9 m) long rail flatcars to trunk-haul road trailers between suitably equipped transshipment railheads in main industrial or population centres. Over the subsequent years TOFC traffic growth was such that, by the end of the 1970s, inter-modal freight had become the US railroads' second biggest freight business, surpassed in volume only by coal traffic.

For two decades American TOFC was primarily a long-haul operation, thriving above all over such distances as New York–Chicago or the 2,000 miles-plus (3,200km) between Chicago and California. In the autumn of 1979 Conrail and Santa Fe combined to install the USA's first coast-to-coast through TOFC service, a five times-weekly train between Los Angeles and New York that bypassed Chicago and halted only at Kansas City and Albany to detach or attach cars in the course of its five days' long journey.

This transcontinental was one of the trains dedicated exclusively to intermodal freight, which the acknowledged front-runners in the efficiency league of 1970s US railroading, such systems as Union Pacific, Santa Fe and Southern Pacific, were now operating with the same devotion to immaculate performance as they had once accorded their passenger streamliners. Where TOFC traffic was consigned in lots via the general freight services and exposed to the schedule hazards of marshalling yard processing from train to train during transits, its reliability was much less predictable. That was one reason for the railroads' inability, even over the longest hauls, to capture much more than a 30 per cent share of the potential market. Until the later 1970s another reason was the inhibiting provisions of regulatory laws, which included a ban on the railroads' operation of their own road vehicles (a restraint not shared by the two big Canadian railroads, incidentally). Finally, TOFC running costs were comparatively high because of the extra dead weight of road trailer body and chassis with each payload and the expense of the specially equipped transshipment terminals needed.

If rail's TOFC market share was unsatisfying in the long-haul sector it was downright dismal where the potential market was greatest, over distances of 1,000 miles (1,600km) or less in the more densely populated areas of the East and West. Here running costs were disproportionately inflated by the frequent changes of train crew, each on a full day's pay, enforced by archaic work rules. A single stint might cover no more than 100 miles (160km). However, at the close of the 1970s, with energy anxieties deepening and the price of oil distorting road truckers' balance sheets, the unions did cooperate with the Federal Railroad Administration and two mid-western railroads in TOFC field-tests over inter-city distances of less than 500 miles (800km). Blessed with unprecedented union concessions both on size of train-crew and on length of their duty, one of these experimental services was launched over the 410 miles (660km) of the Milwaukee line between Chicago and the Twin Cities of Minneapolis and St Paul, the other over the 298 miles (480km) of the Illinois Central Gulf between Chicago and St Louis. Both demonstrated conclusively the competitive validity of the concept over the shorter distance – so much so that the 'Sprint' exercise, as it was titled, on the Milwaukee was at one stage expanded into a six-times-daily shuttle with fixed-formation flatcar sets, each completing a round trip of 820 miles (1,320km) every twenty-four hours. Even with the eventual withdrawal of the Federal start-up money for the experiment, the 'Sprint' trains were breaking even.

However, despite high load factors, the 'Sprint' trains were unable to generate much return on their running expenses – their short terminal-to-terminal runs were to highlight the other high-cost elements of TOFC. This realization intensified an interest in the development of more economical equipment, which was already stimulated by an appreciation of the wider TOFC horizons that deregulation and costlier and scarcer oil would open up. But, even though the classic rail flatcars and road trailers were aerodynamically inefficient and handicapped by the weight of a second vehicle undercarriage, an impartial Department of Transportation study of TOFC trains on several railroads proved them to be roughly twice as economical of energy as a comparable number of tractor-and-trailer rigs making the same run on the highway. The trains' fuel consumption averaged 2.86 road-trailer miles per litre, as against 1.18 to 1.68 by the road rigs sampled.

At the onset of the 1980s almost a dozen US companies, some of them railroads, others railroad car builders, were sufficiently enthused by TOFC prospects to sink large amounts of their own capital into the development of new inter-modal freight vehicles with improved payload/unladen-weight ratios. The outstanding practical result at the start of the decade was Santa Fe's 'Ten-Pack', an articulation over single axles of ten skeletal frames with projecting lateral platforms to carry the rear wheels of ten road trailers. Besides trimming 35 per cent of the weight of an orthodox TOFC rake of ten flatcars, the 'Ten-Pack' close-loaded the road

A large Burlington Northern freight consignment rolls out of Seattle headed by four locomotives. The train consists mostly of piggyback cars.

	AVERAGE NUMBER OF PASSENGERS PER TRAIN	**AVERAGE LOAD PER FREIGHT TRAIN**
INDIA	diesel 709, electric 525	diesel 1,620 tons, electric 1,592 tons
SOUTH AFRICA	diesel 536, electric 598	diesel 1,402 tons, electric 1,286 tons
FRANCE	diesel 400, electric 494	diesel 618 tons, electric 858 tons
NETHERLANDS	diesel 201, electric 290	diesel 491 tons, electric 829 tons
JAPAN	diesel 252, electric 373	diesel 1,620 tons, electric 1,592 tons
SPAIN	diesel 284, electric 451	diesel 560 tons, electric 609 tons
SWEDEN	diesel 196, electric 277	diesel 396 tons, electric 779 tons
POLAND	diesel 278, electric 408	diesel 1,209 tons, electric 1,483 tons
WEST GERMANY	diesel 177, electric 291	diesel 560 tons, electric 858 tons
EAST GERMANY	diesel 252, electric 286	diesel 953 tons, electric 1,050 tons
ITALY	diesel 267, electric 444	diesel 471 tons, electric 730 tons
GREAT BRITAIN	diesel 437, electric 477	diesel 553 tons, electric 504 tons
BELGIUM	diesel 208, electric 372	diesel 817 tons, electric 820 tons

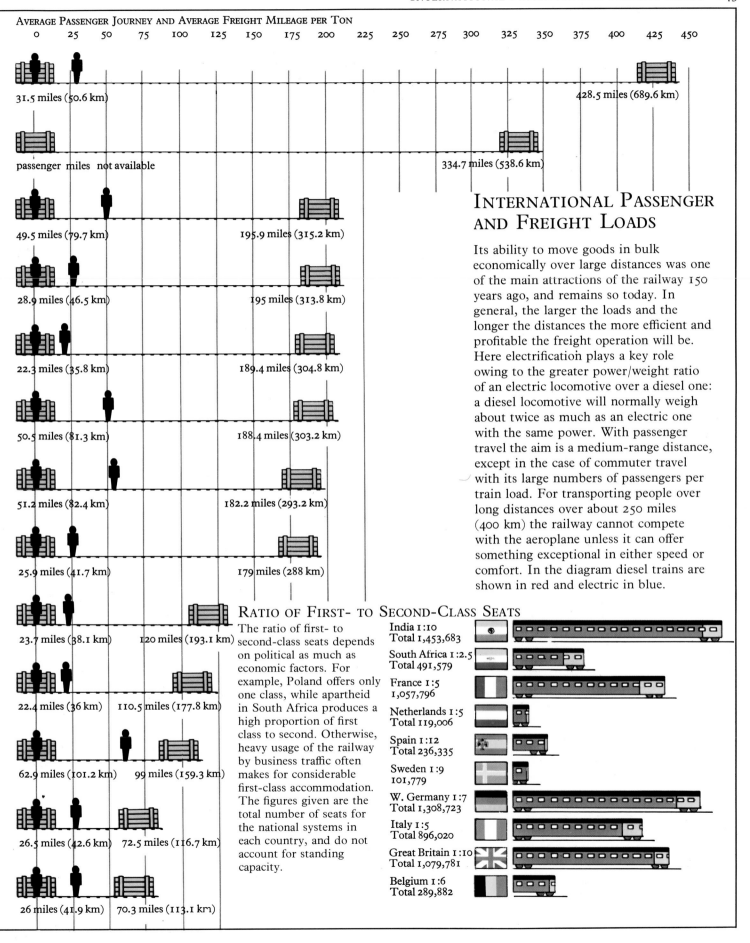

AVERAGE PASSENGER JOURNEY AND AVERAGE FREIGHT MILEAGE PER TON

0   25   50   75   100   125   150   175   200   225   250   275   300   325   350   375   400   425   450

31.5 miles (50.6 km)   428.5 miles (689.6 km)

passenger miles not available   334.7 miles (538.6 km)

49.5 miles (79.7 km)   195.9 miles (315.2 km)

28.9 miles (46.5 km)   195 miles (313.8 km)

22.3 miles (35.8 km)   189.4 miles (304.8 km)

50.5 miles (81.3 km)   188.4 miles (303.2 km)

51.2 miles (82.4 km)   182.2 miles (293.2 km)

25.9 miles (41.7 km)   179 miles (288 km)

23.7 miles (38.1 km)   120 miles (193.1 km)

22.4 miles (36 km)   110.5 miles (177.8 km)

62.9 miles (101.2 km)   99 miles (159.3 km)

26.5 miles (42.6 km)   72.5 miles (116.7 km)

26 miles (41.9 km)   70.3 miles (113.1 km)

INTERNATIONAL PASSENGER AND FREIGHT LOADS

Its ability to move goods in bulk economically over large distances was one of the main attractions of the railway 150 years ago, and remains so today. In general, the larger the loads and the longer the distances the more efficient and profitable the freight operation will be. Here electrification plays a key role owing to the greater power/weight ratio of an electric locomotive over a diesel one: a diesel locomotive will normally weigh about twice as much as an electric one with the same power. With passenger travel the aim is a medium-range distance, except in the case of commuter travel with its large numbers of passengers per train load. For transporting people over long distances over about 250 miles (400 km) the railway cannot compete with the aeroplane unless it can offer something exceptional in either speed or comfort. In the diagram diesel trains are shown in red and electric in blue.

RATIO OF FIRST- TO SECOND-CLASS SEATS

The ratio of first- to second-class seats depends on political as much as economic factors. For example, Poland offers only one class, while apartheid in South Africa produces a high proportion of first class to second. Otherwise, heavy usage of the railway by business traffic often makes for considerable first-class accommodation. The figures given are the total number of seats for the national systems in each country, and do not account for standing capacity.

India 1:10
Total 1,453,683

South Africa 1:2.5
Total 491,579

France 1:5
1,057,796

Netherlands 1:5
Total 119,006

Spain 1:12
Total 236,335

Sweden 1:9
101,779

W. Germany 1:7
Total 1,308,723

Italy 1:5
Total 896,020

Great Britain 1:10
Total 1,079,781

Belgium 1:6
Total 289,882

trailers into a much cleaner aerodynamic outline. Operating ten 'Ten-Packs' in a dedicated Los Angeles–Chicago TOFC train called 'The Chief' – its inheritance of the name of the hallowed Santa Fe passenger train of mid-century underlined TOFC trains' latter-day assumption of the streamliners' status – Santa Fe found that it was saving some 6,000 gallons (27,000 litres) of fuel on every 4,400 mile (7,080 km) round trip by comparison with the consumption of a hundred-car train of traditional TOFC rolling stock.

The first European practitioners of TOFC, or 'piggyback' as it is best known on the eastern side of the Atlantic, were France's SNCF as early as 1945. Their experiment, however, was with standard flatcars, so that to keep within the stricter confines of the European loading gauge SNCF was confined to carrying a purpose-built, low-slung road trailer of un-competitively restricted load capacity. It was the French again who evolved the first design of rail vehicle capable of low-loading a standard road box trailer within loading-gauge limits. This again il-lustrated the rail operators' readiness to fight the hauliers on their own ground. For European road haulage, unlike the domes-tic operations of the UK or US, was becoming an international operation for which the industry had developed its own specification of trailers for cross-frontier traffic. These skeletally reinforced canvas-covered trailers, known in Europe as 'tilts' and adhering to the 37 ft (12 m) length, 8 ft (2.5 m) width and 7 ft (2 m) height of the standard box trailer, could be stripped for overhead and side loading but could also be sealed for customs clearance, thus enabling drivers to avoid the prolonged delays of minute inspection at every border they crossed. To seize this traffic, therefore, and to take advantage of their better cost efficiency, the rail operators had to devise a method of accommodating these rapidly standardizing tilts. With this equipment SNCF set the subsequent European fashion in piggyback operation, and could combine with road haulage interests in the establishment of a separate company to market and manage inaugural Paris–Lyon and Paris–Bordeaux services.

But the high-cost elements of piggyback encountered in North America also loomed large in the economics of European operation because of the shorter inter-city distances. In all countries but West Germany, moreover, it is only on key

Above: A West German 'Huckepack' (or piggyback) train at Mannheim container depot. This method of transporting rail freight has grown dramatically in West Germany, largely because of high levels of Government investment.
Above right: The French 'Kangarou' wagon has a floor lowered below wagon-frame level, on which the trailer's rear wheels rest. This was designed to solve a loading-gauge problem where clearances were not sufficient to accommodate a trailer's extra height.
Right: The ultimate drive-on/drive-off piggyback trains are being used in West Germany. In this system the whole road unit – truck and trailer – is loaded on low, small-wheeled flatcars, which are fit for a speed of 75 mph.

routes that clearances are generous enough to admit loaded piggyback wagons (BR's uniquely constricted main-line loading-gauge prohibits any piggyback). These factors have therefore focused most European piggyback development on international traffic over long and import-ant trade routes, such as the Low Countries and the Ruhr to south Germany, Austria, Italy and Yugoslavia, though the SNCF has regular piggyback services plying between Paris and French provin-cial centres such as Bordeaux, Toulouse, Lyon and Marseille.

West Germany is the only country with a comprehensive, still developing tracery of internal as well as international piggyback routes. This is partly because West Germany is the exception with a significant proportion of its national rail system capable of clearing loaded piggyback trains, and partly because of a decision by the Bonn Government in 1978 to step up rail investment on environmental and energy-saving grounds, backed by a special grant of some DM1,000 millions with which the DB was bidden to triple its inter-modal traffic by 1985. The money could be applied both to investment in equipment and to keen rate inducements to attract new business. The Government also exempted all road vehicles committed to piggyback transport from the country's massive per-axle tax on heavy road transport; this was a particularly powerful stimulus to switch to the inter-modal medium. With its annual volume of container and piggyback traffic aggregat-

ing over 12 million tons by 1980, the DB had its 1985 target of 18.5 million tons crystal-clear in its sights. Throughout Europe, in fact, piggyback was the fastest-growing of all rail freight activities in the late 1970s, accumulating business at the rate of 20 per cent per annum in country after country, although its tonnage was climbing from a small base by comparison with the volume of container traffic and was greatly inferior to the TOFC carryings of US railroads.

The French solved the piggyback loading-gauge problem by creating what they called a 'Kangarou' wagon – so named because it had a hinged floor lowered to pouch the road trailer's rear wheels below wagon-frame height when it had been

complete unit-and-trailer rig of standard size. A train of these cars could be roll-on/roll-off loaded or unloaded just like a drive-through car ferry on the short sea passages, or like the shuttle trains conveying private cars through the Alpine rail tunnels, and would have a couchette couch for the drivers. The attraction for the road haulier of being able to send the unit and driver as well as the trailer by rail to the destination was the availability of man and machine for a return load on delivery. Branded 'Rollende Land-strassen' – 'Highways on Wheels' – by the DB, trains of the Talbot twin-sets were launched on routes from North-West Germany on the one hand to Munich and Switzerland on the other, and from both North-West Germany and Rotterdam on one side of Europe to Italy and Yugoslavia on the other, during 1981.

The railways' need to refine convenience, reliability and rates in the complete door-to-door transportation package was vital to their deeper penetration of the market in high-tariff merchandise, and it was the desire for greater economy in this area that inspired the resurrection of the RoadRailer at the end of the 1970s. This had been invented by some engineers of the USA's Chesapeake & Ohio Railroad in the early 1960s, but its reception was tepid at the time. It is an 'amphibian' trailer with interchangeable and retractable road and rail running gear, each with its own braking and suspension system. All that is needed to change modes is a concrete surround of the track at the transfer point, to provide support for the road wheels during the changeover, and a compressed air supply to raise one set of wheels and lower the other. In the rail mode the RoadRailer runs on its rear axle. Its front is coupled to and supported by the rear end of its neighbour. An eighty-unit train of RoadRailers can be operated on rail at up to 75 mph (120 km/h).

The RoadRailer was reincarnated as a risk venture by a US freight wagon company, North American Car, with a body more akin to the capacity of an orthodox road trailer than the 1960s prototypes. After exhaustive tests had convinced the Federal authorities that it could be operated in trains at up to 75 mph, its sponsors boldly committed themselves to an initial 250-car production run without a single railroad's signature on a leasing contract. After demonstration train services in 1980–81 over four

rolled into position by an end-loading tractor. But at the end of the 1960s the continent was sprouting new rail terminals employing massive 40 ton-capacity gantry cranes to handle the rising flow of ISO (International Standards Organization) containers. That prompted the consolidation of both types of inter-modal traffic in the same terminal and the use of the cranes to top-lift piggybacked trailers into place on their railcars. As a result the piggyback wagons' pouches could be fixed slots (rather than tracks along the wagon), a cheaper manufacturing proposition; moreover, it was easier to make the wagons adaptable to carry containers or demountable bodies as traffic peaks and troughs dictated. This is now the most

widely used European type of piggyback wagon, but at the start of the 1980s the DB was deploying the ultimate in drive-on/drive-off piggyback trains.

The Austrian locomotive and car builders SGP were first in the field with a rail flatcar using such small wheels that its floor could be sunk low enough to carry a road box trailer within the loading gauge, but this initial version had some operational limitations. The type which the DB eventually standardized (it was also adopted by the Austrian ÖBB and Swiss SBB) was devised by the German firm Talbot of Aachen. An articulated twin-set carried on four-axle bogies with wheels of only 14 in (35 mm) diameter, yet fit for 75 mph (120 km/h), had the floor space for a

movement between British ports and inland depots.

BR dreamed of a Continent-wide Freightliner system linked to its own via the cross-Channel train ferries and priced, like its own, to entice new business to the railway with a very simple framework of charges without regard for existing tariff practice. It was frustrated. Unlike BR, which would have been happy to persuade all its wagonload traffic into Freightliners, the mainland European railways were not prepared to prejudice their wagonload business and the activity of their marshal-

railroads (including a 57-hour operation over the 1,742 miles [2,803km] of Burlington Northern's line from Chicago to Seattle, which showed a 19 per cent operating-cost economy over orthodox TOFC) the RoadRailer's sponsors signed their first leasing contract with Illinois Central Gulf in mid-1981.

A train of RoadRailers was acquired by British Rail in the early 1960s. But the Beeching regime, well aware that BR must develop a new door-to-door system, decided to concentrate on containerization to stay in the merchandise market, and the RoadRailer was suddenly abandoned on the brink of public service between London, Newcastle and Edinburgh. Instead, the marriage of the container with the Beeching regime's dedication to the unit train and intensive use of assets gave birth to the Freightliner, which was inaugurated with a London–Manchester service in November 1965.

The essence of the Freightliner concept was high productivity of every component. It was to operate only along the trunk routes with a large flow of freight capable of containerization. Transfer depots would be few and strategically sited to draw road-borne traffic from a wide hinterland; that should theoretically ensure them of the volume to justify investment in high-capacity container handling equipment.

Concentration on the prime traffic flows would also generate the volume to warrant

Above: Transferring a container from road to rail at a Freightliner depot in Britain. This door-to-door system, inaugurated by British Rail in 1965, uses strategically sited transfer depots.
Right: A Canadian Pacific freight train, with a second 'slave' locomotive, climbs through the Rocky Mountains.

expenditure on custom-built, 75mph (120km/h) trainsets of permanently coup-led flatcars that would shuttle at express train speed between the transfer terminals like a conveyor belt, without intermediate marshalling. That would add the selling-point of freedom from damage or theft in transit to the guarantee of overnight delivery at a competitive trunk-haul price.

So far as the domestic market was concerned, the Freightliner prospectus was not completely fulfilled. The expected tonnage did not wholly materialize, partly because the spread of motorways and Government incentives encouraged many likely customers to move away from the big conurbations and partly because BR underestimated the consideration cus-tomers would attach to the costs and time of road shunting to and from Freightliner terminals. The shortfall on internal traffic, however, was more than made good as the container quickly became the universal tool for seaborne merchandise and Freightliner trains were able to build up almost a half-share of deep-sea container ling yards, on which they were spending heavily, by a special play for container traffic. Nor would they endorse BR's determination to deal with containers only in unit trains. On the European mainland, therefore, the greater proportion of container traffic is moved by wagonload methods and its handling is not inflexibly confined to expensive, custom-built transfer depots as it was on BR throughout the 1970s.

Perhaps because of this greater flexibility, the use of containers in Europe has been very extensive. By the end of the 1970s Intercontainer, the unitary marketing company set up to administer European international traffic, represented twenty-four railways from Scandinavia to Eastern Europe and the Middle East, and between 1969 and 1979 quadrupled its container movement. To put this growth in a different perspective, the company was in 1969 achieving slightly less than 200,000 TEUs in the year (TEU is the 20 ft container module in which the volume of this inter-modal traffic is normally measured); but in 1979 the year's gross was 761,567 and in 1980 811,560 TEUs. Well over half Intercontainer's traffic was distribution or collection of deep-sea containers, but in the later 1970s it was advancing in such areas as the inter-factory movement of components and assemblies for the motor industry.

One ought perhaps to add that containers are not necessarily boxes. They can be flats – for the overhead loading of steel, for example – or tanks – for chemicals or drinks. Under the last head BR Freightliners distribute Guinness stout, while Intercontainer does regular trade in the shipment by unit container

The BR 'Merry-go-round', or MGR, trains supply coal to Britain's power stations, like this one at Didcot, in a continuous system without stopping.

train of milk from the Bavarian farmlands to Italian cities, including Rome.

Container movement has become a new factor in the freight operation of every major railway in the world. In some cases the BR unit train model has been adopted, as for instance by Japanese National Railways and South African Railways, the latter between its ports and the industrial area of the Transvaal. So-called 'land-bridge' container operations have ironically even become a threat to shipping, outstandingly between the Far East and Europe via the USSR's Trans-Siberian Railway, though in this instance there is a prevalent suspicion that the Russians have stimulated the traffic by below-cost pricing to build up tonnage.

BULK TRANSPORT

The other striking development in freight operation since the Second World War has been the more efficient movement of bulk minerals – coal and ore especially – in unit trains of modern wagons with greatly increased payload capacity, an area where the railway has always had a distinctive advantage over road. Technological progress in other modes such as pipelines and waterborne transport as well as road juggernauts, has thus compelled the railways to make bigger payloads a priority. Consequently, civil and mechanical engineers the world over have been preoccupied with the perfection of stronger track and more sophisticated running gear so as to make allowable axle-loads of well over 20 tons and permit operation of wagons grossing 100 tons or more.

The scope for improvement in specific tasks of bulk haulage was shown by BR's 'merry-go-round', or MGR. Although the gross train weights operated are unimpressive compared with the maxima of other systems and the cramped layouts of many British collieries dictate the use of four-wheeled hopper wagons, the system is a remarkable translation of the unit train into a conveyor belt. MGR was one of the inspirations of the Beeching Reshaping Plan of 1963. It was basically a translation to full-size practice of the never-stop toy railway circle of track on the living-room floor. To feed Britain's big new coal-fired electricity generating plants, the theory ran, fixed sets of bottom-door discharge wagons should be in continuous circuit between pits and power station. At the pits the trains would be overhead-loaded and at the power stations, where the track layout would be circular, they would be unloaded on the move, their wagon doors automatically opened and closed by lineside devices as they were hauled over below-track bunkers by diesel locomotives with a special gearing to hold them at 0.5 mph (0.8 km/h).

Since its inception MGR has been refined by the computerized timetabling of each week's operation. This ensures that the weekly feed of some half-a-million tons of coal from seventy collieries – the selection of which varies from week to week – to ten power stations is achieved with the minimum possible number of locomotives, train crews and train-sets. As a result the ratio of MGR's running costs to revenue has been reduced to a phenomenal 25 per cent. The same principles have since been applied to the input of imported ore from ports to major British steelworks. This operation employs bogie wagons with rotary couplers so that they can be discharged by individually tipping each one in succession, but without any uncoupling of the train at its destination.

The heaviest European unit trains are deployed by West Germany's DB, which has been compelled to go for very high payloads on its principal routes for imported iron-ore because of the strength of barge-train competition. The heaviest trains, grossing 5,300 tons, are run from Hamburg Hansaport and Nordenham, north-west of Bremen, to the Salzgitter steelworks south-east of Hannover. Almost as weighty are the 4,900 tons gross trains operated from the Rhine port of Duisburg to the Hütten steelworks in the Saar, a 211 mile (340 km) haul which confronts the two 6,000 hp Class 150 electric locomotives that pull each train with a grade of 1 in 100 in the Moselle valley beyond Koblenz. To obtain a payload capacity as high as 101 tons per vehicle, the DB has produced for this traffic an unusual six-axle wagon, in order to spread its gross weight of 133 tons. A fully laden train can thus be run as fast as 50 mph (80 km/h) without detriment to the track.

But all European unit train performance pales against what has been achieved elsewhere, sometimes in an infinitely more difficult operating environment. Since the early 1960s US railroads have steadily developed unit train feeds of coal in 100 ton-capacity wagons, mostly to public utilities, and these now account for half of all rail movement of coal in the country. Many of them gross up to 10,000 tons and a number run remarkable distances. The record at the close of the 1970s was an unbroken haul of 2,073 miles (3,336 km) from Utah to the Mississippi, taking in the tracks of four different railroads.

In 1980 the major coal-shifting railroads were expecting a huge increase of this traffic as a result of the energy crisis. By 1979 Burlington Northern's tonnage had already tripled since the start of the decade while Santa Fe's had more than quadrupled, but both were budgeting for a doubling of the 1979 figure in the next decade. Burlington Northern, in fact, was investing heavily in infrastructure improvements to cope with the anticipated tide of new traffic – too heavily, in fact, to make a decent return because of the then controlled price of coal movement by rail.

The most spectacular North American movement in the late 1970s was Canadian Pacific's transport of export coal for Japan from mines on the eastern slopes of the Selkirk Mountains to Roberts Bank on the west coast. The coal was aggregated into trains of no less than 12,000 tons gross weight, despite the fact that they had to be hoisted up the long 1-in-38 grade of CP's transcontinental route to Rogers Pass *en route* to the shipment port. To make the climb each train needed the 36,000 hp output of twelve diesel locomotives.

Some of the locomotives in these huge CP coal trains were unmanned 'slaves', remotely controlled from the fully manned power at the front end. The 'slave' technique has been adopted by a number of heavy-haulage North American railroads since dieselization. To avoid the risk of jack-knifing a long train on a sinuous route and to reduce coupling strain, it is inadvisable to concentrate power at the front and rear of the formation. Slave locomotives are therefore inserted within the train at points carefully judged in relation to its total length, and remote control ensures that they react in exact harmony with the lead locomotives. A radio transmitter is linked to the manned controls of the lead locomotive and, with each movement of the latter, transmits coded signals to a receiver on the slave that translates them into matching commands to the slave's controls.

At the start of the 1980s the heaviest regular trains in the world were being operated in South Africa and Australia. Incredibly, in the former country they were running over 3 ft 6 in (1,069 mm) gauge. Loads have built up to 180 wagons grossing over 9,500 tons on the first South African Line to be electrified at 25 kV ac 50 Hz under SAR's 1974 high-voltage electrification plan (SAR's previous conversions had been at 3 kV dc), that from the Transvaal mines south-eastwards to Rich-ards Bay, on the coast above Durban. But those loads have been made to look almost puny in comparison with operations on a new 534 mile (859 km) line which SAR absorbed in 1977. It had been built and electrified on an almost unique 50 kV 50 Hz ac system by the South African Iron & Steel Corporation from the Sishen ore mines west of Johannesburg to Saldanha Bay, north-west of Cape Town. On this purely industrial railway the ore is despatched in trains of up to 220 bogie wagons grossing just over 22,500 tons each, hauled by a trio of 5,070 hp locomotives.

Loads just as gargantuan are standard on one of four railways privately built in the mid-1950s to ferry export ore from the rich Pilbara deposits some 1,000 miles (1,600 km) from Perth, in Western Australia, to coastal ports. This is the Hammersley Iron Railway, which was

The seemingly endless lines of coal wagons at Bluefield, West Virginia. With the huge increase in oil prices since 1973 there has come a new demand for coal.

audaciously designed to cope with axle-loadings as high as 30 tons. In practice the stresses were too great, and proliferating defects in equipment and track have required a great deal of subsequent strengthening at heavy cost. However, these track problems have been success-fully overcome, and research is now being carried out into the feasibility of $34\frac{1}{2}$ ton axle loads. To power its huge trains the Hammersley railway employs trios of 3,600 hp US-style 'hood' diesels, which are some of the most powerful traction units in Australia.

THE IMPACT OF NEW TECHNOLOGY

A great majority of the world's railways cannot afford to discard their wagonload freight traffic, either because so many goods move in small lots and unit train potential is limited (the situation, for example, in Japan), or simply because its revenue is too valuable a contribution to total costs. For these railways a paramount concern in the 1970s was acceleration of wagon transits throughout from consignor to consignee. That demanded a minimum of marshalling *en route*, which could only be achieved by a reduction in the number

of marshalling yards. The sorting of incoming and outgoing wagons for much wider areas had to be concentrated on fewer yards which were adequately automated and of a size to cope with the whole of a hinterland's output and input in a few hours. A wagon picked up from a local depot in the afternoon must be sure of attachment to a trunk train the same night, and conversely a wagon arriving overnight of delivery next morning. The fewer the yards, moreover, the greater the scope for fast and economical block working of wagonload traffic between them by overnight trunk trains. The target had to be assurance of twenty-four hour transits between most areas of a country the size of France or West Germany, thirty-six hours over longer distances, and at worst, and only in extreme cases, forty-eight hours. Equally vital to these goals, of course, was high performance freight stock; France's SNCF was one country which by the end of the 1970s was building only bogie freight wagons.

The composition of DB's freight traffic in West Germany epitomized the signific-ance of wagon processing in the achieve-ment of a reliable service. At the end of the

1970s between 50 and 60 per cent of the DB's traffic was consignment in single wagonloads or at best in wagon groups of less than trainload size. They were moving between as many as 4,500 different points, which also determine the DB's scale of charges, but the real sum of origins and destinations was much greater, because the DB served well over 10,000 private sidings as well as its own freight depots. With the exception of BR, which was compelled to break even on its freight working without benefit of any state aid or grant for track upkeep and was thus forced to set very stringent traffic volume conditions for service of private sidings, every Western European railway was courting new private siding customers capable of generating a reasonable number of freight wagonloads weekly. The competitive importance of this reliable door-to-door capacity in a motor transport age has already been stressed.

Between 1975 and 1980 the DB reshaped its freight working so that the total of its main marshalling yards could be cut from 135 to fifty-nine. But there was further to go, for the final objective was a total of forty-eight, on which investment in

Above: A coal train crosses the White Umfolozi River in Natal, South Africa. Despite the narrow 3ft 6in gauge, South African trains are among the heaviest in the world, some grossing up to 22,000 tons.

Left: A Southern Pacific freight train makes its way through the Sierra Nevada in California.

Right: A quiet time at Noranda station in the sparsely settled northern region of Quebec, Canada.

automation would be concentrated. At the conclusion of the programme the DB anticipated that 60 per cent of its long-haul wagonload freight would pass through only two yards *en route*, those which assembled and distributed trunk freight trains in the originating and destination areas of each transit. The proportion of traffic requiring two or more re-sorts during its trunk haul would then contract to 5 per cent or less. And no more than 7 per cent of the traffic should need an excess of thirty-six hours to complete its trunk haul.

The most striking fruit of the DB policy in 1980 was the vast automated yard that sprawls over 692 acres (280 hectares) at

Maschen, outside Hamburg. Planned to amalgamate the work of five other yards in this area of teeming rail freight activity, Maschen comprises 64 sorting sidings in its south-north yard and 48 in the parallel north-south yard. The whole complex has 190 miles (305 km) of track interconnected by 1,014 sets of points.

Every phase of train sorting and remaking at Maschen is computer-controlled to guarantee smart handling of peak throughput of 11,000 wagons in a day. The make-up of a train to be processed in the north-south yard, for instance, and comprehensive data on each wagon in it – size, weight, destination – is wired to the Maschen computer complex in the outskirts of Hamburg well in advance of a train's arrival; this can be done from one of numerous input terminals at originating points up to the Scandinavian border. Consequently, the Maschen operations control has detailed marshalling orders available as soon as the train pulls in. At the same time the computer is casting a continuous forward projection of the build-up of onward traffic by destination, to guide human operators in efficient planning of outgoing train services. When the incoming train is propelled over the yard hump, the route selection to the appropriate siding for each 'cut' of wagons, the judgement of its weight and the distance it has to run, and hence of the brake pressure to be applied to it by the

track-mounted retarders below the hump – all this is entirely computer-controlled. So is the calling into play of track-mounted 'mules', one of which is installed in each siding to move on any wagons that have misled the automatic sensors and have not run far enough to buffer up to wagons already in place.

The automation governing the functions of Maschen is only one illustration of the revolution that electronics have wrought in railway operation since the mid-twentieth century. A railway's efficiency is heavily dependent on the disciplined co-ordination of many departmental organizations; its operation has to

Above: Aerial view of the DB's automated marshalling yard at Maschen, outside Hamburg. This computer-operated complex spreads over some 700 acres and can handle as many as 11,000 wagons a day. There are 112 sorting sidings and almost 200 miles of track.
Left: A computer-controlled wagon retarder at Maschen with the yard hump in the background.
Above right: The whole of BR's freight operation is continuously monitored at this control centre for the Total Operations Processing System (TOPS) in London, which can provide reports of where each vehicle is at any given time. Such sophisticated monitoring enables the precise allocation of vehicles to demand.

be conducted to a timetable, with finite resources over a strictly policed right-of-way which equally has limits of capacity. Consequently, optimum operational decision-making derives from a vast amount of data.

Earlier discussion of BR's 'merry-go-round' coal operation showed how access to modern computers has accelerated the planning of that exercise from week to week and optimized its productivity. From early applications to basic data-processing jobs, such as seat and sleeper berth reservation, the use of computers has now progressed to economic optimization of a railway's entire resources.

Typical of such modern apparatus is TOPS (Total Operations Processing System), which the Southern Pacific Railroad in the USA evolved in the 1960s and British Rail installed in more elaborate form in the 1970s. At BR the TOPS central computer is capable of continuously monitoring, recording and reporting on every detail of resource use throughout the system. From the data it is routinely fed on every locomotive and freight vehicle movement, it can instantly pinpoint the location of every loaded and empty wagon and its status. Consequently, interrogated to supply equipment for traffic on offer, it can precisely match the deployment of resources to demand. The by-products of its capability are countless. For instance, since it banks the mileage covered on each locomotive journey, it can call in particular locomotives for mileage-based servicing when they have accumulated the governing distance. In pre-computer days it was customary to set a standard time-based interval between servicing appointments for a class as a whole, derived from the mileage which the average class member was likely to cover within that period.

No technology, therefore, has had more impact on railway method since the Second World War than electronics. And no industry has welcomed it more, because the inherent discipline of railway operation demands more monitoring, policing and quick translation of data into effective decision than a medium like road transport. Before the electronics revolution, all this was labour-intensive in relation to the traffic units of work actually recorded. And as earlier discussion of Japanese National Railways has underlined, each twist of the post-war inflation screw has worsened the ratio of railways' labour costs to total expenditure. Hence the eagerness to adapt electronics technology to every conceivable railway routine, irrespective of its more rapid and precise functioning, from revenue collection and accounting to track inspection and fault-finding.

To the lineside observer the impact of electronics on railways has been most conspicuous in signalling and traffic control. So compact have the components of a push-button signalbox console and its associated interlocking apparatus become, and so incredible the number and rapidity of command impulses which can be transmitted over a single wire, that up to 500 track-miles (800 km) of a busy railway

area can be supervised from a single control room. One of BR's installations nearing completion at the beginning of the 1980s, that at Edinburgh, is ultimately to oversee 220 route-miles (355 km) and almost 440 track-miles (700 km); the push-buttons on its control room console will finally cover a total of 1,200 different route-settings.

Signalmen could not intelligently command such a wide tract of railway unless, on the modern signalbox's panoramic illuminated track diagram of the whole territory in their care, they had a continuous picture not only of the location of every train but also of its identity. Once a signalman at the point of origin has fed a train's individual reporting number in to the train-describer apparatus, that code moves automatically in step with the train's occupation and release of track circuits, and is successively illuminated in apertures alongside the corresponding track circuit berths on the signalbox layout diagram. Apart from the immeasurable improvement in train operating efficiency which this wider traffic view can effect, the other benefit of the wider signalbox has been its labour-saving facility. BR's new installation covering the busy approaches to London's Victoria terminus, for instance, is making thirty-six older signalboxes redundant.

Add computers to signalling installations of this kind and the fully automated

railway is in sight. On a metropolitan rapid transit or underground railway, where the route layout is simple, the trains completely standard and the timetable strictly patterned, it has not been too difficult to programme a computer to regulate the traffic – routes can be set as the timetable prescribes, and, once it has verified each train's identity, human controllers can be advised on the best course to take, if the train running gets out of schedule. Automatic driving of the trains is achieved by transmission through the track circuiting, through separate track-mounted wires or – in the latest West German installation – through radio microwaves, of coded electronic signals which are picked up by on-train receivers and translated by micro-processors into appropriately graded acceleration, deceleration and braking commands. On the simplest of railway layouts these commands can be actuated by the trains themselves. The occupation of track circuits by one train will dictate the speed at which the following train should be running.

As described in the next chapter, the conditions for full automation have already been realized on some metropolitan railways. Thorough-going automation of the main-line railway, however, with its diverse traffic, junctions and conflicting flows, will take a good deal longer to achieve.

URBAN RAILWAYS TODAY

The upsurge of private motoring after the Second World War was a cause of no small concern to the metropolitan authorities as they saw the increasing congestion of motor vehicles putting a life-sapping strain on their city centres. To create a more efficient and attractive public transport system that could pass both into and through them might well avoid eventual strangulation. The effect of such thinking is that whereas only twenty of the world's cities had underground railways or Metros in 1939, by 1979 the total had passed fifty and was still increasing. Those cities already operating railways were for the most part busy with network extension schemes, and a further twenty at least looked set to open their first lines before the end of the century.

City-centre underground lines, however, were not the whole answer. Many cities were rapidly changing character. For sheer growth, for example, there was nothing to touch Tokyo, where industrial development had added 50 per cent to the population in the 1950s alone. In most cases the dominant reason for this was the emigration of metropolitan residents to the newly created peripheral suburbs. This was especially apparent in Paris and the bigger Italian cities. Particularly to the north of the French capital, lines radiating from the main termini were attracting a commuter traffic far in excess of pre-war levels. Not only was enlargement of their carrying capacity urgent but also a smoother means of interchange was needed between the commuter lines and city-centre transport to sustain the convenience of a journey from home to place of work – or, for leisure travellers, to the city's shops and entertainment. Another new cause for concern, with the popularization of air travel, was the

threatened paralysis of roads from downtown to city airports.

Simultaneously, the expense of improving urban railways grew more daunting. As wages and material costs inflated, the economics of augmenting capacity for just two hours of peak commuter movement at each end of the day looked more and more illogical, especially as most of those commuters were traditionally carried at heavily discounted fares. For the rest of the day a high proportion of the train-sets and operational capacity was at best underutilized, and quite often idle. Furthermore, soaring metropolitan property values were sharply escalating the capital cost of any railway construction scheme that encroached on fresh ground.

THE METROPOLITAN SCHEMES: FINANCING AND OPERATING

Essential urban railway development could only be pursued with greater injections of money. Americans of the eastern seaboard cities had to face up to that very soon after the war. In the Mid-West the three railroads providing Chicago's suburban service somehow managed to keep their commuter operations in the black. And in the late 1950s and early 1960s the Chicago & North Western even increased its commuter business by 50 per cent – and at an operational profit too – by investing over $50 millions in new double-deck passenger cars. C&NW succeeded in persuading its passengers to pay more for the satisfaction of brand-new equipment, and derived revenue benefit by conveying substantially more passengers per train because of the two-level vehicles' increased passenger space. But in the East the country's busiest commuter railroad, the Long Island, disintegrated physically and financially

into bankruptcy in 1949. A succession of fare raises failed to finance desperately needed modernization, and after several years of heavy financial support from the sidelines the State of New York had to take over the system early in 1965. Charged with having embraced 'creeping socialism', Governor Nelson Rockefeller retorted that he had no other option.

Chicago was also the US pioneer in establishing the kind of unitary body to integrate a city's entire public transport system, which European cities had begun to evolve before the Second World War. The London Passenger Transport Board, for instance, was established by a Labour Government Act of 1933, and Paris unified its bus and Metro systems in 1941 as the Régie Autonome des Transports Parisiens (RATP). However, the real model for the future was drawn up by Hamburg. In 1937 a public company, with the city and state as controlling shareholders, was founded to reshape Hamburg's tramways, underground railways, bus services and waterborne passenger transport as a system offering a coherent alternative to the most frequently made journeys by private car. At the end of 1965, this Hamburg metropolitan transport administration became a component of a bigger authority, the Hamburger Verkehrsverein (HVV), which took in the city's hinterland to a total area of some 2,000 square miles (5,200 sq. km) and brought main-line suburban services and peripheral road transport within the orbit of a carefully co-ordinated inter-modal timetable and simple, zonal fare scheme.

The new Hong Kong Metro operates in a highly constricted urban environment and is designed to cope with the heaviest passenger throughput in the world.

In 1945, forming a body something like the Hamburg model, Chicago established the Chicago Transit Authority (CTA). The newborn CTA was soon nurturing schemes for new rapid transit lines from the outskirts to the city centre. Within a few years, in fact, one North American city after another had corroborated the findings of a Toronto research study that a new rapid transit railway, even if it were partly underground, could be constructed for less money than a system of reserved busways capable of the same speed and efficiency of service; a road operation of equivalent standard, the researchers concluded, was impossible without massive expenditure on additional roadways and raising or burrowing road junctions.

But the amount of money needed to build new urban railways was already a handicap. Financial difficulty almost crippled the biggest North American scheme of the immediate post-war years. That was the Bay Area Rapid Transit, or BART, an ambitious project for the most highly automated – and luxurious – railway the world has yet seen. It was to link San Francisco, Oakland and Berkeley with a part-elevated, part surface and part sub-surface network adventurously crossing San Francisco Bay in twin tubes sunk as much as 135 ft (41 m) below water level. The objective was to thin out road traffic over bridges. In fact, the scheme was to be financed in part by the imposition of tolls on bridge users, but the main source of construction money was to be local bond issues, the interest on which would come from property taxes.

BART was heading for a financial morass as soon as the start of construction was seriously delayed by controversy and litigation, chiefly over the routeing of the railway. When it finally got going in 1964, inflation had already added 100 per cent to the scheme's cost estimates of the mid-1950s and by 1966 BART was short of $150 millions to meet its bills. For a time completion of the railway as planned was threatened, but eventually the California legislature agreed to float another bond issue. And just in time to underwrite a fifth of the final cost of BART came one of the pivotal developments in post-war rail history: American Congressional agreement in 1964, under the Johnson administration, to an Urban Mass Transportation Act providing for Federal finance to cover up to two-thirds of the first costs on investment in fully worked-out

urban redevelopment and transportation plans. By the beginning of the 1980s the Act had already stimulated construction of an impressive new rapid transit railway in Washington, D.C. and its suburbs, and another in Atlanta, while a third was under construction in Baltimore.

A dilemma confronting designers of new underground railways after the Second World War was whether to discard the orthodox flanged wheel-on-steel rail system for rubber tyres. French Railways had experimented quite seriously on their main lines in the 1930s with Michelin railcars that combined metal flanges and rubber surfaces on their wheels, but after

the war a revolutionary new system was devised for Paris Metro trains. The Paris Metro is famed for the close spacing of its stations which, in conjunction with the intricacy of the network itself, puts a Metro station within comfortable walking distance of practically any point in the heart of the city. That sets a premium on acceleration ability in the design of its train-sets. Hence the attraction of rubber-tyred wheels, from which maximum adhesion efficiency is guaranteed underground where the rails are always dry (conversely, exposure to damp discourages the use of rubber tyres above the ground).

Below left: A train in Oakland West, part of California's Bay Area Rapid Transit scheme (BART). Construction of this ambitiously automated railway, linking San Francisco, Oakland and Berkeley, began in the 1960s but the first section was not opened until 1973.
Bottom left: Some Paris Metro lines use rubber-tyred units to give maximum adhesion. These have horizontal guide wheels next to the running wheels.
Below: The Metro at Baku, on the shores of the Caspian Sea, is typical of Soviet design – spacious and imposing.
Bottom: An overground section of the Hamburg U-Bahn, or Underground.

The RATP had a Paris Metro line, No. 11 from Châtelet to Mairie de Lilas, fully converted to the new rubber-tyred system in 1957, and since then has similarly reconstructed three more. No further conversions were in prospect at the beginning of the 1980s, however. The main reason for hesitation, claimed the RATP, is the time a Metro line is out of commission while it is adapted to rubber-tyred trains. Concrete runways over the whole length of a route have to be laid outside the orthodox steel rails to carry the rubber-tyred running wheels; the latter are mounted outside a car's conventional steel wheels, which only come into play for

negotiation of pointwork or if the tyres become deflated. At pointwork the concrete runways are inclined down below the surface level of the steel rails, then graded back to their original height, so that the train gently subsides on to its steel wheels and then resumes rubber-tyred traction when it is beyond the junction. Since the concrete runways are entirely flat, there has to be a guidance system in place of that normally provided by wheel flanges. The Metro trains are thus steered by more rubber-tyred wheels, for this purpose mounted horizontally on each bogie and bearing on continuous flat strips laid with their surfaces facing the train at a fixed gauge just above the level of the concrete runways.

France's new post-war Metros in Lyon, Marseille and Lille, have all used the rubber-tyre system, but elsewhere only Montreal, Mexico City and Santiago have adopted it. However, there are two major disadvantages of rubber-tyred trains which offset their remarkable rate of acceleration, their quietness and their smoothness of ride. One has been their bigger appetite for energy than conventionally wheeled train-sets. The other disadvantage, which Montreal learned the hard way, is the excessive heat generated by the friction of tyres and runway; Montreal Metro stations were insufferably stifling until extra and decidedly costly ventilation plant was installed to moderate their temperature.

In the 1960s and 1970s most metropolitan authorities of the industrialized world became more preoccupied with enhancing the convenience of public transport for the maximum distance of each urban journey than with the construction of new railways as an end in itself. The layout of suburban stations to offer ample parking space, to encourage the public to transfer from motor-car to train as soon as possible after leaving home, or plenty of room in the forecourt for what the Americans tagged as 'Kiss-'n'-ride' – a brief pause by a motorist to deliver a passenger to the trains – became all-important. In the USA the Chicago Transit Authority combined satisfaction of this new demand with constructional economy, and also set a fashion for other American rapid transit builders by projecting rapid transit railway extensions down the median strip of new automobile expressways. That made it easier to induce motorists to make for the rail stations, and equally to focus

Like some Paris Metro lines, the Montreal Metro has rubber-tyred trains.

re-planned local bus services on these railheads.

The model of co-ordinated development, however, was Stockholm. When in the 1950s the Swedes laid out the routes of their capital's new T-Bana (for 'Tunnel Railway', despite the fact that two-thirds of the resultant system was above ground!), they were careful to project them outwards from the centre through the gaps in the radial suburban lines of SJ, the Swedish national railway system. That ensured that the two networks would be

COMMUTER TRAVEL

The efficiency of a major city depends upon the ease with which people are able to travel around it. All metropolitan centres depend upon a combination of four basic transport modes: railway, bus, private car and metropolitan or underground railway. As city centres have become clogged up with traffic the role of the metropolitan railway has been widely seen in recent years to be crucial, and several cities have built or are building new systems, while new lines are being added to many of the older networks and new technology introduced.

KEY

Metropolitan or underground railway (subway)

Surburban railway

Bus

Tram (streetcar)

Trolleybus

Private car

Taxi

Ferry

Motorcycle

Bicycle

Pedestrian

30.8% 28.6% 10.7% 9.8% 17.5% 2.6%

LONDON Data: average daily peak travel into Central London, 7 a.m. to 10 a.m., 1980. Total peak-time travellers: 1,049,000.

15.1% 16.5% 12.4% 48% 8%

HAMBURG Data: average weekday travel throughout the city, 1978.

18.5% 7.9% 57.4% 15% 1.2%

CHICAGO Data: average weekday travel throughout the city, June 1981. Total daily travellers: 2,800,000.

complementary, not competitive. Since then the SJ lines have become almost exclusively express routes from the outer suburbs to the heart of Stockholm.

The SJ lines were relieved of catering for shorter-distance inner suburban traffic by a complete reorganization of the city's bus services in 1967. In that year Sweden changed from a left- to a right-hand rule of the road, and the Stockholm Transport Authority grasped this unrepeatable opportunity to reorganize the whole bus service in the inner suburbs and the city centre so that in each case it was primarily a feed into and out of the T-Bana. At the end of the exercise most conceivable journeys into or across the city within the inner suburban periphery had been shaped into a convenient bus-rail-bus sequence. Provided that a journey was completed within a specified time, it could be undertaken throughout with a single ticket under a zoned fare scheme that disregarded the number of modes employed.

As the 1970s progressed almost every major European city was rating it a social necessity to improve the convenience of local rail systems for radial journeys so as to protect the quality of life in their centres, and at the same time to simplify movement to and from the new outposts of their spreading suburbia. In almost every case, too, national governments as well as municipal authorities recognized a social obligation both to fund new development adequately and also to curb fares by annual subsidy to levels that made the cost of door-to-door travel by public transport more attractive than even the perceived costs of motoring. The conspicuous exception was Britain. There the public support for local railways at the beginning of the 1980s was still so circumstantial that London Transport's rail network was by far the most expensive underground system to ride in all Europe.

When the social cost of dispensing with urban railways was quantified, any failure

NEW YORK   Data: average weekday travel into the Manhattan Business District, 1979. Total daily travellers: 2,956,000.

PARIS   Data: average weekday travellers in the Paris metropolitan area 1980. Average daily travel in this area: 20,372,000 journeys.

MOSCOW   Data: average daily travel in Greater Moscow, 1975. Total average weekday journeys in 1979: 14,980,000.

TOKYO   Data: average weekday travellers in the Tokyo-Yokahama metropolitan area. Total average weekday journeys: 29,140,000.

Charing Cross, a recently enlarged station on the London Underground. Owing to lack of public funds, this is the most expensive system in Europe to ride on.

to finance their proper upkeep and renewal and to moderate the cost of their use to the public became quite illogical. At the end of the 1970s the Netherlands Railways demonstrated this with a thorough research of the effect on Amsterdam if the city's central and suburban railways did not exist to perform 45 million passenger journeys entailing about $1\frac{1}{2}$ billion passenger-kilometres a year. Were it transferred to motor vehicles, so the NS calculated, the traffic created would demand 75 new route-miles of road in the city centre and almost 250 more in the suburbs, in addition to 12,000 fresh private car parking spaces and 100 extra bus stations, for a combined capital cost of at least £1 billion – to which would be added substantial recurring costs in policing, increased road accidents, environmental pollution, and so on. The final NS calculation was that the extra annual costs faced by a rail-less Amsterdam and its suburbs would be around £175 millions ($315 million), or more than six times the contemporary deficit on the city's suburban rail services that was met by the State.

In 1979 ordinary ticket purchasers of the Paris Metro were paying only 38 per cent of the system's total running costs (in fact the ticket revenue of RATP was meeting no more than 58 per cent of its wages bill). Some of the deficit was covered by an annual subvention paid to justify RATP's operation of a few routes regarded as irredeemably loss-making but socially essential. Just over half of the bill, however, was straight compensation for RATP's obligation to keep its fares down to levels prescribed by the Government for its own socio-political purposes. Part of this subsidy closed the gap between prices actually charged and a theoretically viable fare structure multiplied by the year's projected number of RATP journeys; the rest offset the heavily reduced fares statutorily available in France (and in many other European countries) to categories of passenger such as mothers, school children and students, apprentices and the militarily disabled. Because of its power over fares, the Government bore 70 per cent of the compensation for uneconomic pricing, the local authorities only 30 per cent.

The metropolitan peak-hour travel surge and the costly excess of part-used railway operating capacity it demands is arguably created by the employers who mass their offices or plant in a city centre, not by the commuters who have to travel where the work is. In 1970 the French accepted that argument and levied a payroll tax on all employers of ten or more staff at a rate of 1.9 per cent in the French capital's densely populated suburbs, and of 1 per cent elsewhere in the Paris transport region, so as to finance the issue

of very attractively priced period tickets for rail and combined Metro-SNCF rail-bus work journeys. A similar tax, but at a standard 1 per cent, has been extracted from all employers in the Lyons and Marseilles conurbations to help finance the start of those two cities' Metros.

As for investment, in the second half of the 1970s the annual outlay on the Paris rail facilities of both SNCF and RATP was averaging £250 millions a year. The RATP was spending twice as much as London Transport, for example, but was required to find only a quarter of the money from its own resources. Roughly equal grants from the State and the Île-de-France regional authority accounted for a further 20 per cent; the rest was realized through long-term loans, partly on the open market, partly from the national Fund for Economic & Social Development, partly from the Île-de-France administration.

The enterprises absorbing the RATP and SNCF money, along with those transforming the rail systems of West Germany's cities, outclass all other urban rail schemes of present-day Europe for scale. Although several lines of the Paris Metro have been projected beyond the old city limits to nourish new inner suburban development, the system's admirably close spacing of stations within the city sets a limit to such extension; the more the number of stops on a journey to the centre, the less appealing the use of the train. As far back as 1920 a plan was formulated to offset this limitation by remoulding the city's surface suburban railways as a 'regional Metro'. Little was done, however, until the post-Second World War growth of new dormitory suburbs well beyond the old city periphery forced the issue. The outcome was a master plan in 1960 for the Réseau Express Régional (RER) that would drive new deep-level, main-line-sized, limited-stop railways under Paris, in part to establish new routes between outer suburbs on different sides of the capital, and in part to create through running from one quarter of the SNCF's Paris suburban network to another.

The first step in the RER project was the construction, completed in 1977, of a new full-size, sub-surface east-west line burrowing deep under the old city via La Défense, Châtelet-les-Halles and Gare de Lyon. Its stations in the heart of Paris are arguably the most spectacular yet built underground in Europe, with cavernous circulating areas for interchange with the Metro, and island platforms at Gare de Lyon wide enough to accommodate the spacious seating areas of two buffet-bars in their centre as well as room for passengers to stand perhaps twenty deep on each working side.

This is not mere grandeur. By the end of the 1980s the Châtelet–Gare de Lyon section of the line will have a morning and evening peak-hour load of forty-eight trains each way. With the progressive connection of more surface suburban lines to the RER, particularly from the driving of a tunnel from the SNCF suburban station at Gare de Lyon, eleven different outer suburban branches on all sides of Paris will eventually have through RER trains interconnecting with each other and with the Metro system at the Châtelet subterranean nexus. Hence the provision at the deep-level RER station of four platforms serving seven tracks and a total of no fewer than thirty-four escalators to interlink them with the huge 820 ft (250 m) by 260 ft (80 m) subterranean concourse and the Metro routes which interconnect at Châtelet. One valuable product of this great 'Interconnection' project, as it is known, will be a direct rail service between the French capital's two main airports, Charles de Gaulle in the north and Orly in the south-east.

West Germany, together with several other European countries since the Second World War, has blurred the distinction between classic street tramways and underground railways. Tramways began to take something of the shape of a railway when numerous continental European authorities, forced to rebuild bomb-damaged systems and contemplating the likely growth of motor traffic, re-located their tram tracks whenever possible on a reserved right of way. This happened mostly in suburban areas.

The boundary between tram and railway became practically extinct with the birth of the 'Pre-Metro' concept. Rather than face the formidable cost of constructing new underground railways of conventional parameters from scratch, several administrations opted to drop their city-centre tramways below ground. So the tram tunnels, as well as their accompanying stations and signalling, were engineered on a scale that would enable fairly simple conversion of the system to a full-scale Metro should traffic and social demands eventually justify a step-up.

Such a development has already happened in Brussels, where in 1976 a Metro proper blossomed from the earlier 'Pre-Metro'.

The splendid subterranean stations built for these underground city tramways shame many on surface suburban railways. Nor would the performance characteristics and appointments of their articulated two- and three-unit train-sets have disgraced a main-line electric multiple-unit of the pre-war era. Benefiting nowadays from the latest refinements in traction technology, such as thyristor control of traction motors and dynamic braking, these vehicles commonly deploy a total output of 500–600 hp for a total

Top: A station on the RER (Réseau Express Régional) in Paris. This system provides direct routes from outer suburbs into Metro stations and the centre of Paris, and is linked to the main line. Above: A tram on the Brussels Metro descends into an underground section.

weight of less than 40 tons and may have a top speed as high as 60 mph.

It is scarcely surprising, then, that, in German-speaking countries particularly, classic terminology in this sector of rail transport is none too clearly defined. At the bottom of the scale is the traditional narrow-gauge street tramway system, sharing roadways with other traffic, known as a Strassenbahn. The standard-gauge successor with its reserved right-of-way and modern high-capacity vehicles – at least 50 per cent more productive than the Strassenbahn mainly because of the greater precision of working on tracks segregated from other road transport – is known as a Stadtbahn. But some cities which have dipped the Stadtbahn below the surface in their downtown areas, such as Stuttgart, designate it a U-Bahn, or underground railway, which terminologically equates it with systems originally built as sub-surface metropolitan systems.

As West German cities' new Stadtbahnen and U-Bahnen developed, the next step, as in Paris, was to project full-size connections from the DB's surface network underground to interchanges with the U-Bahnen in the heart of each metropolis. Suburban passengers could thus make easy connection and be dispersed to their metropolitan destinations without clogging traffic above ground. First in Munich, then in Frankfurt and Stuttgart, the DB's suburban railways on all sides of each city were eventually to be linked with each other and with the U-Bahnen by new lines tunnelled through the downtown areas. (The essentials of a similar system in Hamburg had been established before the war.) These integrated DB city systems are today classified as S-Bahnen (Schnellbahnen).

By the close of the 1970s the Munich scheme had already brought 250 route-miles (400 km) of suburban railway into direct contact with the S-Bahn underground transversal in the city centre, and on its completion in the late 1980s the Rhein-Main S-Bahn network centred on Frankfurt will have done the same for peripheral towns and cities as far afield as Hanau, Darmstadt, Mainz and Wiesbaden. In every city the subterranean interchanges with the U-Bahnen are breathtaking, with batteries of escalators between the surface and each rail system, and with very handsome and spacious shopping centres at a mezzanine level between street and the first layer of rail platforms.

Frankfurt Airport, biggest and busiest on the European mainland, has been plugged into the S-Bahn by a loop off the main DB route from the city's main station to Mainz. In the later 1970s additional tracks were threaded out of the main

station approaches and over the Main river to the start of the loop at a cost of some £20 millions to free the airport train service from operational conflict with the other busy flows of rail traffic in the area. As a result, the train frequency to and from the airport is as generous as ten minutes throughout the peak hours, and twenty minutes during the rest of each day, and the 75mph (120km/h) Class 420 electric multiple-units which furnish the service glide air travellers straight from the airport terminal to the underground city centre station of Hauptwache, almost on the doorstep of Frankfurt's principal hotels, in a journey time of fifteen minutes.

At the start of the 1980s Zurich, London's Gatwick, Frankfurt and Düsseldorf were the only European airports with railway service, thus combining the needs

Above: The distinctive design of the double-decker units which were introduced on Toronto's GO Transit commuter services during 1979.
Left: A Rock Island line commuter train with double-decker coaches leaves Chicago.

of speed, frequency and an airport station only an escalator's rise from the air terminals. At the same time, however, the S-Bahnen of Munich and Stuttgart were in course of penetrating their cities' airports in the same fashion as Frankfurt's. Ideally sited stations were in being at Amsterdam's Schiphol and Vienna's Schwechat, but concern for the fabric of the city was preventing the Netherlands Railways from driving a line from the airport to the business centre of Amsterdam, although all parties concerned have now agreed to a more circuitous route involving conversion of a goods line round the city's western periphery, to join up with the Amsterdam Central passenger railway. Schwechat had a railway direct to a junction with Vienna's S-Bahn in the heart of the Austrian capital at Wien Mitte, but its trains ran only at hourly intervals. London's Heathrow, too, had a convenient station, but in 1970 a short-sighted Government preferred the low-cost option of extending London Transport's Piccadilly Line to serve it exclusively by cramped all-stations Tube trains from the city rather than a Frankfurt-like scheme for a segregated BR main-line railway from West London; the ludicrous outcome is that today Gatwick, some ten miles further

from London's West End, is almost ten minutes closer in rail journey time than Heathrow. Both the Paris airports have an admirably fast and intensive service, but the stations at each are a bus-ride from the present terminals – an absurdity in the case of the newer, Charles de Gaulle, where the operating authority perversely insisted that the new railway laid to it in the mid-1970s should terminate in an area between the airport's inaugural complex and the provisional site for a possible second terminal, now taking shape.

Such prodigious projects as the West German S-Bahnen would be inconceivable without substantial support from public funds. The new-found public concern for the urban railway in many countries is typified by the provenance of the huge sums of money invested in the Frankfurt-based Rhein–Main S-Bahn development. When it was launched in 1968, the final bill was estimated to be around £600 millions, but the full cost on conclusion in the late 1980s will surely be nearer £1 billion. At the end of the day the DB's share of the account will have been confined to the costs of supervising the engineering and providing the train-sets, or probably little more than one tenth of the total. Sixty per cent of the rest will have been covered by the Federal Government and 40 per cent by the public authorities which derive the benefit: the cities of Frankfurt and Mainz and the provincial governments of the Hesse and Rheinland-Pfalz Länder.

Public support does not stop there. The Federal Government subsidizes some 85 per cent of the DB's suburban passenger operating costs in the Hamburg, Frankfurt, Munich and Stuttgart conurbations as compensation for the massively discounted fares for many categories of passenger which German citizenry has long taken for granted as a birthright. Even standard fares on the S-Bahnen and U-Bahnen are cheap by comparison with rates where public authorities are still dedicated in principle to the attainment of self-sufficient public transport.

THE APPROACH OF AUTOMATION: ELECTRIFICATION TO ELECTRONICS

In the first decade or so of urban passenger service development after the Second World War most railways concentrated their train-set construction on self-powered multiple-units, either diesel or electric. Evolving electric traction technology gradually made it possible to reduce very high performance power plant to a size and weight that left practically the entire car-body space available for passenger accommodation. One of the most striking examples of this development is the DB's Class ET420 electric multiple-unit, the tool of most of its S-Bahn operation. An ET420 packs as much as 3,200 hp in the traction motors of each three-car set, so that it can glide up to its top speed of 75 mph (120 km/h) within a remarkably short distance from each stop.

Double-decking as a means of improved train seating capacity without an unacceptable increase in length is a concept almost as old as the passenger railway, but lately it has been reproduced in multiple-unit format for the first time. Since 1970 New South Wales has been progressively re-equipping its 1.5 kV dc Sydney commuter network with a stainless-steel-bodied design, fully air-conditioned, that was created by the Australian railway suppliers, Commonwealth Engineering, with Mitsubishi electric traction gear from Japan. In 1979 the SNCF commissioned a multiple-unit version of their elegant locomotive-hauled design; the latter, seating up to 175 passengers per vehicle, had already been deployed to the extent of over 500 examples in the busiest Paris commuter services during the previous few years. The French design has since been copied by the Italians for their North Milan railway, and the Dutch, the Danes and the Swiss are to buy squadrons of bi-levels, though of their own design, for their busiest city commuter services. The

dramatically lozenge-shaped body-ends of new bi-levels fashioned by Hawker Siddeley Canada for the Toronto Area Transit Operation Authority's GO Transit commuter operation in 1979 also betokened that design's adaptability to electric multiple-unit orders.

Metros and rapid transit railways, as was suggested in the previous chapter, have provided tempting scope for full automation because their route systems are uncomplicated and enclosed, their trains standard in performance, their timetables repetitive, and not least because automation trims the number of extra staff

otherwise necessary to handle peak traffic. The first operator to perfect fully automatic train operation (ATO) on a public system was London Transport on its Victoria Line in 1968. Acceleration, shut-off of power to coast and save energy where gradients permitted, respect for signals and permanent speed restrictions, and deceleration to station stops – all this was appropriately actuated by coded impulses transmitted through the track circuitry and picked up by receivers on the trains. But in this and every subsequent ATO installation elsewhere, operators in the 1970s were reluctant to test the public's

Above left: The DB Class ET420 electric multiple-unit provides the trains for most S-Bahnen in West Germany.
Below left: The railway connecting Amsterdam with Schiphol airport. The growth of air travel has created a need for fast and efficient railway links between cities and their airports.
Above: Australian double-decked multiple-units with stainless steel bodies work Sydney's commuter network.
Above right: A BART train operator in San Francisco. BART uses all kinds of automated systems, including automatic train operation and fare collection.

nerve with driverless trains, except in the more restricted case of what are now termed 'People Movers' – small, crewless cars moving in continuous circuit between, for instance, the widely separated terminals of a major airport such as Dallas (where there is as much as 14 miles of guideway). The new Lille Metro, however, due to open in the early 1980s, is the first metro to take the plunge and build its train-sets without any driver's or conductor's compartment.

But all-embracing automation of the sort possible on a simple, segregated system like an individual Metro route in London, Paris or Washington is not yet a practicable proposition for complexes like the Paris RER 'Interconnection' or the S-Bahn network of a German city. These are funnelling trains through a central underground channel from a number of different routes covering an area spanning 50 miles (80 km) or more, and additionally handling trains which in their progress through

suburbia may be sharing tracks with mainline freight and passenger traffic. But the intensity of the peak-hour flow in the central bottleneck – twenty-four convergent trains each way on the Munich and Stuttgart S-Bahnen, for instance, and ultimately as many as forty-eight in the crucial Châtelet–Gare de Lyon sector of the Paris 'Interconnection' – would be inconceivable without the aid of electronic data processors for efficient traffic control.

In the control rooms off the Munich and Stuttgart S-Bahn systems computers automatically pick up from the electronic train-describer apparatus of the signalling system the individual data of each train as it enters the controlled area. From then on, automatically interrogating the signalling circuitry to monitor a train's progress, the computers deduce its speed and forecast its time of arrival at critical junctions. At his desk each control room operator has a battery of full-colour VDUs on which he can call up from the computers a simultaneous display not only of the actual position of each train and the general traffic situation in any area of the system but also of the predictable progress of each train to pressure points ahead. That way the operators can anticipate conflict at nodal junctions and take advance action to avoid it. On a less complex rail system, of course, the traffic regulation can even be taken out of human hands and the computer's projections translated into automatic, electronic commands to a train defaulting on schedule to accelerate or decelerate to regain its timetabled path.

The wise operators have progressed step by carefully prepared step to full autom-

ation. The folly of going for broke was underscored for the whole rapid transit world by BART, which from the start integrated ATO with every other conceivable automated device, from computer-based route-setting and traffic control to automatic fare collection (AFC). Scarcely any of the apparatus had the warranty of previous service, and in 1979, six years after the opening of its first section, BART was still incapable of operating a train service as intensive as its prospectus had envisaged. Happily, an $8 million Reliability Improvement Programme, launched that year to attack thirteen critical areas of fallibility, has paid off, and in 1981 BART was at least in sight of its originally planned capacity, carrying a daily average of 173,000 passengers and moving about 30 per cent of all trans-Bay commuter traffic. Its creation is reckoned to have been the main stimulus to a doubling of office space in downtown San Francisco in the 1970s.

BART was the first railway in the world to install AFC, development of which has been spurred by the ability to pack a wide range of instantaneous checking procedures into ticket-issuing machines and ticket readers at platform turnstiles through use of micro-processors. By interlinking the machines and readers with a central computer, moreover, revenue accounting and control can also be automated. So far, however, a reliable, high-capacity AFC system has proved one of the hardest items of a fully automated railway to perfect. Operators naturally insist on near-100 per cent financial and functional precision, since one defective

A MODERN METRO – WASHINGTON D.C.

With simple, segregated lines, a steady flow of traffic, and no disruption by freight trains or expresses, the modern metropolitan railway system is an obvious subject for automation. So when the Washington Metro was opened in March 1976 it enjoyed all the benefits of automatic computerized control. Eventually planned to run to 98 route-miles (158 km) and with trains running as fast as 75 mph (120 km/h) and at intervals as low as two minutes, the whole network is run from a single building in the city centre. The trains have no need of drivers, and once the conductor has signalled that the train is ready, the journey is handled automatically.

Instructions to the train and communication with the central computer are given through boxes known as Wee-Z® bonds. They are placed between the tracks at regular intervals, dividing the line up into blocks. An audio frequency is fed into the track from a transmitter through the bond, which can then register the presence of a train in its block. The audio frequency also sets up magnetic fields coded with instructions which are picked up by receivers on the train. These instructions take the form of speed commands determined by what the transmitter records of the state of the track ahead and the nature of the track itself. Equipment inside the train registers the command,

compares the speed imposed with the speed of the train, and then if necessary slows the train down.

The Wee-Z bond also plays a major role in the movement of the trains in and out of stations. The bonds at the stations have an extra channel linking them to the Automatic Train Supervision system (ATS). When a train stops in a station it transmits its number and destination through the bond. A computer compares its position with other trains on the track and against its schedule. It then calculates the speed needed for the train to arrive at the next station in the correct time and transmits this to it through the Wee-Z bond. If instructions conflict the train selects the slower speed. Operators at Central Control monitor the whole system and only take corrective action as necessary.

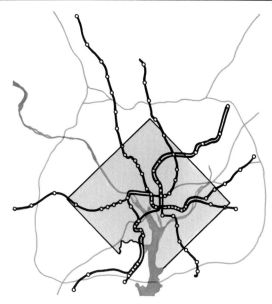

Map of the Washington Metro system showing also the Beltway road that goes round the city.

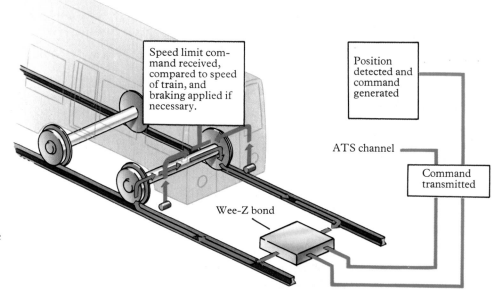

Speed limit command received, compared to speed of train, and braking applied if necessary.

Position detected and command generated

ATS channel

Command transmitted

Wee-Z bond

Far left: Two-carriage train on one of the sections of elevated track.
Left: Video display units at the Central Control showing the progress of each train.
Top: Train in the Rhode Island station, one of the stations equipped with a car park for the 'park and ride' service for motorists.
Above middle: Train console, showing the top speed allowed by the protection system, the 'regulated' speed set by the ATS and the train's actual speed.
Above: Wee-Z bond and electric switch machine.

apparatus in the travelling peak will quickly clog a station concourse with angrily frustrated commuters. That has been none too easy to achieve when the ticket-readers are frequently confronted with tickets that have been pulped in sweaty palms or even chewed out of recognition. So disillusioned was the Chief of the Washington Metro that in mid-1980 he seriously recommended his directorate to write off the $52 millions invested in the system's AFC, complaining that it cost twice as much to keep functioning correctly as the simple, token-operated turnstiles of the New York Subway.

The Washington Metro was the second of the modern generation of North American urban railways, and one of the world's most striking to date. The full project called for a five-route, 98 route-mile (158 km) network, of which roughly a third had been commissioned by the start of the 1980s and the ultimate cost of which is estimated at about $7.5 billions. It was the first US Metro to be planned from the start with a concurrent re-routeing of the operating authority's bus services so that the latter would feed passengers into Metro stations and not parallel Metro trains into the heart of the city. The resultant multi-modal transport network is made the more appealing by a ticketing system that covers through bus-rail journeys. Besides this public transport co-

Rapid Rail Cars of the Chicago Transit Authority on old 'Elevated' tracks. Set up in 1945, the CTA was the USA's first such unitary public transport body.

ordination, the Metro's designers were lavish with provision for 'park-and-ride' travel: by the mid-1980s parking lots at the Metro's out-of-town stations would have space for around 30,000 cars in total. The Washington Metro's 75 mph (120 km/h) train-sets have cabs that are manned by a conductor, but normally, once the conductor has signified that the train is ready to start, they accelerate, decelerate and brake entirely in response to coded commands transmitted electronically through track-mounted devices by a computer-based Automatic Train Operation (ATO) system.

Similarly automated is the second of the USA's new full scale Metros, the MARTA system of Atlanta, which opened the first stretch of a proposed 53 mile (85 km) network in 1979. Next to join this league was Baltimore in 1981. But even though Los Angeles, the city which two or three decades earlier had been cited worldwide as proof that the twentieth-century urban man could live the good life without benefit of railed transport, had in mid-1980 come to the point of surveying the first route of a new Metro, the prospects of more full-scale Metro construction were dimming.

Light Rail Vehicles such as this one in Canada have appealed as a realistic choice for cities that do not require a large-scale metro scheme.

And many Georgians were dubious that the MARTA network would be finished as originally conceived.

The reason for the doubt was Washington's anxiety at the huge cost of new full-scale Metros and their automation trappings, especially when these were set in such grandiose fixed structures as the Washington city authorities had conceived for their Metro stations. President Carter himself had railed at what he called the 'over-design' of this and other Metro schemes. Energy-conscious Americans were generally amenable to a small percentage addition to local petrol or sales taxes to part-finance public transport improvement (although Denver voted down such a proposition in 1980), and urban railways in both Boston and Chicago had particularly benefited from the so-called Interstate Transfer clause added to the 1973 Highway Act, which allowed transit authorities to claim money saved if local administrations were prepared to forfeit expressway road projects. Many

cities and states were also prepared to vote for and support bond issues to raise urban transport improvement capital. Even so, almost every major project was ultimately reliant on a generous Urban Mass Transport Act (UMTA) grant even for its preliminary engineering studies as well as its execution. And with UMTA's annual budget scaling $4.5 billions (£250 million) at the beginning of the 1980s (not all of it for public rail transport, of course, and some of it earmarked for operating grant aid as well as capital investment funding), it was a ripe target for President Reagan's onslaught on public expenditure – especially as Reagan was on record as holding that 'there is no reason for someone in Sioux Falls to pay Federal taxes so that someone in Los Angeles can go to work on time by public transportation'.

The new administration promptly ordered a progressive reduction of UMTA grants towards operating costs that would end all subsidy under this head by 1985. A degree of stringency was salutary, for most of the big US cities had been charging rather ludicrously low fares (most were raised in the wake of Reagan's first budget) and were also allowing themselves to be plundered for high wages and grossly

indulgent fringe benefits by their staffs. But to cut off all support seemed certain to force fares to a level that would drive many users back to their cars. And although Reagan committed himself to some further extension of the Washington Metro – but not to completion of its planned network – he embargoed use of UMTA money for the start of any fresh full-scale US Metro schemes.

Ironically, the one city which through the 1970s managed to finance much of its public transport improvement without heavy calls on UMTA resources was New York, despite its imminent bankruptcy throughout the decade; it was, however, helped by substantial aid from the New York State administration. But New York will surely need to draw heavily on Federal money if it completes all the subway extensions it plans for the 1980s, as well as a mammoth exercise already under way to conduct the trains of the one-time Long Island Railroad right to Manhattan's heart at Grand Central station by the construction of a new bi-level tunnel – one pair of tracks for the LIRR trains, the other for a subway line – under the East River. In total these New York schemes have been costed at about $15 billions (£830 million).

A more circumspect financial attitude had already developed in the Carter era, and that persuaded several cities to embrace a cheaper alternative. Instead of a full-scale Metro, Light Rail Transit (LRT) and Light Rail Vehicles (LRV) were adopted by one administration after another. LRT is broadly the equivalent of a German Stadtbahn and employs similar vehicles. In fact, firms like Düwag of Dusseldorf which were front-runners in the development of the rolling stock of modern European Stadtbahnen and U-Bahnen are now accumulating a rich export business in the equipment of LRT systems emerging not only in North America (where statute requires half or more of the manufacturing content to be of US origin) but in the plans of some African and Middle Eastern countries. In this as in other railway development fields of the Third World, European manufacturers confront fierce competition from Japanese industry.

An LRT system has no more than half the carrying capacity of a full-scale Metro, but in Canada, for instance, its vastly lower first cost has made it a feasible economic proposition for the traffic demands of Calgary and Edmonton, which could not have sustained the expense of a traditional rapid transit railway. To cite just one of the US cities which have elected for a new LRT system, San Diego found that it could create a 14 mile (22 km) LRT line through its chief suburban corridor, adapting a near-redundant Southern Pacific freight track over much of the distance, for $86 millions (£53 million). That contrasted sharply with the $1.2 billion price-tag on a full Metro scheme for the city that had been aired and rejected earlier in the 1970s.

The only major addition to Britain's metropolitan rail systems in the past quarter-century has been an LRT project, the Tyne Metro centred on Newcastle-on-Tyne. This is a planned network of 33.4 miles (54 km) partly appropriating tracks that previously carried a loss-making BR train service, of which the first section was inaugurated in 1980. Whereas the ortho-dox BR trains, expensively operated in accordance with main-line railway prac-tice, were unattractively infrequent and did not touch the centre of Newcastle, the lightweight two-car Metro LRVs, seating only eighty-four passengers but capable of taking 125 more standing, will eventually thread the tunnel section beneath Newcastle's heart at a peak-hour headway of only 2½ minutes.

The Tyne Metro trains set their own routes automatically. Each driver registers his train description and route on his cab controls before starting a trip and the data is absorbed by an underfloor device that is thereafter interrogated electronically by tracks apparatus at key points. The readings of the apparatus are then variously translated into commands to junction points, reports to the illuminated track diagram in the Metro's control centre and impulses that set the platform train indicators at stations ahead of the train.

But though LRT was the majority choice of world cities contemplating their first essay in urban rail transport in the late 1970s and early 1980s – and there was one capital, Brussels, which regretted its decision to advance from 'Pre-Metro' to a full-scale Metro and hinted at a switch to LRT for further development – some specifications still on file could only be met by a full-scale Metro. Such a case was Hong Kong's, with its tight-packed mass of buildings squeezed into a narrow corridor between the mountains of Kowloon and the port, and where nearly four million people jostle for living and working space around the harbour. Here, in the autumn of 1979, the first line was opened of a Metro designed for the heaviest passenger throughput over a single line of railway the world has yet experienced – up to 60,000 an hour each way. Largely British-built and equipped, this comprehensively automated system uses the most generously proportioned cars yet seen on a Metro to cope with its load. Seats are sparse and car doors numerous, with as many as five sets of double doors in each car side, so that each vehicle can quickly cope with up to 350 commuters per stop in the rush-hour. Passengers are thus relieved of inter-minable queuing for buses or trans-harbour ferries and can cut the time of their longer commuting journeys by almost two-thirds. This is the extreme measure of a modern urban electric railway's cap-ability as an economical mass mover of people.

Opened in 1980, the Tyne and Wear Metro is a Light Rail Transit system centred on Newcastle-on-Tyne. Each two-car unit can hold some 210 passengers.

THE NEW AGE OF THE TRAIN

Only fifteen years or so after the Second World War the future of the industrialized world's railways was hanging in the balance. As the American railroads discovered as early as the 1950s, the competitive edge of the railways had been blunted by motor vehicles that were fast, comfortable and efficient, and could deliver door-to-door. Nor would it be long before the airliner would supersede them over the long-haul passenger routes. But to add darkening gloom to the railways' prospect of the future, any investment programme, however lightly sketched, was severely constrained by the legacy of the war itself, whether strain from capacity-use of outdated plant or destruction from bombing, and by the demand for financial self-sufficiency. Revenue could never meet the cost of necessary investment.

It was only in the transport of bulk materials to industry or of mass commuters to their city offices that the railways could offer a service whose cost and speed were beyond the competition of other modes. This apart, however, the railways of the West looked set to be yet another milestone left behind on the forward-march of industrialization and technology. The Beeching principle thus looked the harsh but necessary treatment, and in its wake operations were rationalized throughout the developed world. Few European governments, however, would wield the Beeching axe as did Britain and ignore the political and social sensitivity of ripping up miles of track and of cutting their services to the bone. Nevertheless, none could ignore their problems and nearly all were running in the red.

It was thus a time to pay respectful attention to any scheme which might reduce the liability of a railway and still cope with the ever-rising flood of motor vehicles. Britain's Department of the Environment, for example, even commissioned a serious academic study of the feasibility of turning one of London's busiest commuter railway systems into a network of reserved busways. The academics did not even blink at the prospect of free-steering buses storming at up to 70 mph (110 km/h) in close formation along lanes with almost 75 per cent less side clearance than that specified for British motorways; or at their vision of a Liverpool Street terminus where some 450 passengers a minute would be streaming across tracks of buses arriving or departing at ten-second intervals. Not surprisingly, the idea died with its publication.

In addition to the railways' determination to meet the challenge of the road on its own ground oe speed, efficiency and cost, exemplified in piggyback and container transport or the marketed package of inter-city, two other factors have provided considerable stimulus for the railways in recent years. One is the impact of the oil crisis in the 1970s, the effect of which created a cost advantage which the rail operators were eager to demonstrate; the other was the recognition of the social and environmental claims of a railway when compared with its equivalent road route or air corridor. It was for this latter reason that governments felt justified in their subsidy of loss-making rural services or in their financing of integrated urban transport systems. For at the very time when the flat-earth study of the British academics was proposing the conversion of a commuter railway into

British Rail's APT – ushering in a 'new age of the train' or marking the end of high-speed development on existing track?

busways, Los Angeles, a city entirely dedicated to road transport, was already reversing course. What concerned the Californians was not just safety, although the railway's uniquely low death and injury rate per number of overland passengers carried is a statistic that is too often taken for granted in weighing transportation options (the superior claims for air travel are disingenuously based on total passenger *mileage*, so that one intercontinental journey may be equated with a hundred or more city commuter trips). What exercised the Americans and was very quickly to agonize every industrialized country was the extent to which indulgence of road and air transport had been allowed to degrade the environment. City centres had been sterilized to carve more and more room for new roadways and parking lots; and the skies above inter-city corridors were being fouled by aircraft, let alone becoming hazardously overcrowded with them.

The drift had to be halted. As we have seen, the United States first recognized, as other countries have since, that a modern Metro or S-Bahn can ferry people *en masse* into and out of city centres with negligible claim on surface space; and that if the interchanges with public and private road transport on city peripheries are convenient, the door-to-door journey can be just as efficient as private road transport – more so if city parking lots are scarce.

A measure of the environmental benefit of a modern, rail-based urban transport system came from Munich during the 1970s. There, five years after the establishment of an S-Bahn system converging on an underground tunnel beneath the city centre and its careful co-ordination with other transport modes, the usage of public transport in the conurbation had jumped from 900,000 to 1.5 million people daily. Air pollution in the area of the city was down by 25 per cent, as was the number of recorded street accidents.

The Americans grasped, too, that rail technology was breeding the means to make centre-to-centre inter-city journeys competitive in speed with air travel for up to 300 or 400 miles (500–650km). The inter-city railways to exploit this potential were already in place. To realize it, entice travellers out of the sky and control pollution would demand only investment in the improvement of the corridor railways. It would ask no fresh sacrifice of the environment.

TRACK DEVELOPMENTS AND TILT-BODY SYSTEMS

Despite the environmental and social justification of railways, however, governments and operators could never ignore the reality of financing them or the demand for their commercial viability. The search for speed in the post-war years was nothing but a response to the competition from air and road and relied on the technical promise that higher speeds were possible within acceptable levels of investment in existing railways infrastructure. But the belief that speeds maintained well above 100mph (160km/h) would be attainable only at the cost of custom-building a new railway like the Japanese Shinkansen spurred the pioneers of alternative tracked systems. The traditional monorail was not in the running; its scope for development as a high-speed carrier had been exhausted without achieving the anticipated results. The serious contenders now were derivations of hovercraft technology – what can be generically grouped as tracked hovercraft, moving within channelled guideways and, in their ultimate versions, using linear electric motors for propulsion and reverse magnetic force for levitation (this last system is commonly known as

Above: The 'Transrapid 04', Krauss-Maffei's magnetic levitation research vehicle, on a test track at Munich.
Right: The Grumman tracked levitation research vehicle at the US Department of Transportation's test centre at Pueblo, Colorado. Alternative tracked vehicles, using hovercraft technology, have been able to attain very high speeds.

MagLev). Until 1973, when the British Government ended its support for the research and development work, it was an open question whether tracked hovercraft or a conventional railway would be the choice for a high-speed passenger transport link between the third London Airport, then contemplated on the Essex coastline at Maplin Sands, and the capital.

Development of MagLev systems continues in Germany and Japan, where a test vehicle and track have proved capable of 500mph (800km/h). Nothing is known, however, of their comfort or reliability at even half that speed. And as the very environmentally conscious Germans and Japanese now fret even at the environmental disturbance of a 125mph (200km/h) electric train, they are most unlikely to countenance fuselages hurtling across their countryside at 500mph. Another discouragement is that the energy consumption of such devices, which need power for suspension as well as propulsion, must be considerably greater than that of an orthodox train with comparable seating capacity. But above all, what little logic there was in investment in fresh infrastructure has disappeared with the crystallization of at least 150 mph as a practicality on existing rail tracks. And perhaps even more important is the margin of extra carrying capacity which the disciplines of conventional railway operation are gaining from a combination of electric traction and the ever-widening application of electronics to traffic control and complex, instantaneous decision-making. One should add that MagLev does have a practical future, but as an economical system for airport 'People Movers'.

It was the Japanese experience with their Shinkansen which for many sealed the fate of alternatively tracked systems. For while they had proved conclusively that operation at well over 100mph (160km/h) was possible, they had also highlighted the prohibitive capital cost of the investment needed. Thereafter, the

search for speed was generally conducted along existing track and within prevailing infrastructure, with one outstanding French exception. However, the use of existing track imposed its own problems. Although the years since the war had seen the universal introduction of long, continuously welded rail sections which gave passengers a smooth ride and eliminated the battering of rail ends – always a prime cause of rail failure – the major difficulty still lay in the nature of the track itself. For while the railway operators might have the locomotives for high-speed running, the curvature and gradients of lines, often laid down by piecemeal nineteenth-century commercial development, were not conducive to consistently maintained top speeds. Research was thus initiated into lightweight, aerospace body-building techniques and new forms of running gear which would reduce the high-speed trains' stresses on existing track; and into systems that would automatically tilt vehicle bodies through curves, artificially increasing their cant so that the curves could be taken faster without subjecting passengers to intolerable effects of centrifugal force. It is this comfort factor which dictates a

conventional passenger train's speed limit through a curve; the limit at which derailment is a risk is considerably higher.

Controlled cornering stress was an engineering problem faced initially by the pioneers of turbo-powered traction. The gas turbine in particular attracted the railway engineers because of its much smaller number of moving parts by comparison with a diesel engine, its low mass and its theoretically greater efficiency as a generator of energy. The first application of the research was in the Turbotrain conceived by United Aircraft Corporation (UAC), one of several US aerospace companies which saw revived US interest in rail technology as an outlet for research and manufacturing capacity surplus which the reduction in demand for defence equipment had caused. A revolutionary arrangement of very short and light low-slung bodies, the Turbotrain was taken on by Canadian National for high-speed Montreal-Toronto service in 1968, and by the US Department of Transportation for the Boston-New York leg of its demonstration project the following year. But far too much untried innovatory detail was packed into the UAC design. At the

squadron for US passenger service. And in West Germany the DB adopted the new style of turbine as an auxiliary 'booster' for some of its main-line diesel locomotives.

At the start of the 1970s turbine power was the likely choice for BR's 150mph (240km/h) Advanced Passenger Train (APT) and SNCF's *Train à Grande Vitesse* (TGV), proposed for 160mph (260km/h) working over the Paris–Lyon route. Only a few years later, however, the oil price explosion and the comparative reduction in the cost of electrification shattered the economic advantage of turbine traction, although at the close of the decade the French were still able to find a buyer (Egyptian State Railways) for the export model of their RTG turbine-powered train-set. But from now on this form of traction was confined to an effort to lower the now costly fuel consumption of the SNCF and Amtrak sets by installing a higher-powered engine in place of two smaller ones. In 1981 the DB abandoned turbine boosters in its diesel locomotives.

But British Rail's research into its turbo-powered APT had developed one of several variations on the automatic body-tilting theme to emerge in the late 1960s and 1970s. The idea of artificially exaggerating the inward tilt of a vehicle on a curve so as to add to the cant imparted by the track's superelevation, thus tempering the effect of centrifugal force on passengers when a bend was taken at speed, had originated in the USA, where the Pacific Railway Equipment Co. produced experimental vehicles that were evaluated by a number of railroads in 1938–41. The first European specimen was a test vehicle created by the SNCF in 1947.

end of the 1970s, two of the CN's three nine-car sets were still commercially operational, but only after an ill-starred career notorious for a period of almost three years when the units languished in the UAC workshops for remedy of deep-seated faults. They were not expected to survive 1981.

Another railway to invest in a fleet of gas turbine-powered locomotives was Union Pacific, which between 1952 and 1961 evolved with General Electric a series first of 4,500hp gas turbine-electrics, then a class of huge 8,500hp machines that needed three units to carry all their

engineering and fuel supplies. But the dawn of the turbine looked brief when diesels of superior power/weight ratio staked their claim in the 1960s.

Interest was revived, however, with the evolution of light and compact turbines for helicopters. A nest of them was built into the UAC Turbotrain. At the same time French Railways completed successful trials with similar turbines and invested in a fleet of turbine-powered multiple-units with 110mph (180km/h) potential, first the Type ETG, then the higher-powered RTG; the second of these designs attracted Amtrak and led to the construction of a

Above left: Interior of a first-class coach on a French RTG turbine train.
Above: Amtrak adopted the French RTG train-sets for their Turboliners. They were launched on the Chicago–St Louis route in 1973 and were immediately successful, boosting business by some 50 per cent.
Below: The Canadian UAC Turbotrain. Canada was one of the first countries to use Turbo units on high-speed inter-city services, which are now run by VIA Rail. These trains were also the first in regular commercial use to be fitted with body-tilting equipment.

These early prototypes – and some of the more recent versions of the concept – were based on a 'passive' tilting principle. This works pendular-fashion: the car body does not react until the vehicle has entered the transitional superelevation from straight to curve, which sets up lateral acceleration that eventually swings the base of the body outward and sets up the extra tilt. The limitation of 'passive' tilting, naturally, is that the attitude of the car-body is a response to the character of the track, not an anticipation of it. The evolution of powerful electro-hydraulic servo mechanisms and of sophisticated

electronic controls prompted a move into 'active' body-tilting systems, which detect the onset of curvature and instantaneously set up a controlled action of hydraulic rams to cant the body by the graduation of angles specifically needed to offset lateral acceleration. A number of the latter-day 'active' systems can generate between 8 and 10 degrees of tilt in addition to that imparted by the cant of a curve.

The UAC Turbotrains of Canada were the first automatic body-tilting equipment in the world to be accepted for regular commercial service. They embodied a passive system, as did the forerunners of

what is now a substantial Japanese National Railways fleet of 3 ft 6 in gauge electric multiple-units. The tendency to abrupt response of a passive tilt mechanism is not a drawback on the JNR trainsets, as they are not designed for very high speed, but to gain schedule time on some very sinuous and otherwise low-speed routes in the mountainous interior of the country; on one such route their use has saved 37 minutes on a 157 mile (252 km) journey, although the end-to-end schedule is still as much as $3\frac{1}{2}$ hours.

Active tilt mechanisms are complex and costly, which are two reasons for the halting progress from prototype to mass production, or, in three cases, for abandonment of development. The three railways to discard the idea are the DB, SNCF and Switzerland's SBB. The SNCF and SBB designed a new line of inter-city coaching stock – the former its 'Grand Confort', the latter its Mk III type – for subsequent installation of active body-tilting with a view to operation at up to 125 mph (204 km/h). But they stopped short of fitting the tilt equipment after its experimental application to a handful of

cars. What chiefly deterred each management – the French after the difficult experience of threading a pair of 125 mph TEEs, the 'Aquitaine' and the 'Etendard', through the ruck of conventionally timed traffic on the Paris–Bordeaux route – was a fuller appreciation of the cost of widening the speed-band on an existing line carrying a mixed traffic. The cost of signalling

Above: A Swiss inter-city train between Basle and Zurich. The Swiss decided against installing body-tilting equipment.
Right: The 125 mph Canadian LRC train incorporates an active tilt-body system, but not in its diesel locomotive.
Below: The Italian electric multiple-unit, the 'Pendolino', also has an active tilting system.

modification or elaboration to cater for just a small number of very fast trains, and the disruption of other traffic incurred in carving out a clear timetable path for them, were too high a price to pay for the commercial benefits of shaving a half-hour or so off a few inter-city transits. Within a year or two the French had Government approval for the Shinkansen alternative, the construction of a brand-new railway tailored exclusively for high-speed passenger operation along France's major commercial axis, from Paris to Lyon. And at the end of the 1970s mounting Swiss concern for optimal use of energy and environmental protection was aligning political opinion with the SBB argument that high-speed by-passes of the worst curved stretches of its key Geneva–Bern–Zurich transversal deserved higher priority than more unbridled expenditure on motorways.

In the mid-1970s Fiat created a prototype Italian electric multiple-unit misleadingly dubbed the 'Pendolino', since it embodied an active tilting system. This looked a heaven-sent tool to shorten the tedious inter-city journeys over routes winding through Italy's dorsal mountains. But though the Pendolino cut time handsomely on the Rome–Ancona service

to which it was assigned and seems, after some modification, to have fully satisfied its FS operators, no production order was placed because of the priority call on available investment funds for measures to enlarge freight operating capacity.

A near-identical unit was produced in Spain, but there the Fiat concept had a competitor – Talgo's development of a low-cost, passive tilt-body version of their patent low-slung, single-axle vehicle. Exhaustive tests of a prototype set of the new Talgo design (during which 143.8 mph [228 km/h] was reached on Spanish tracks) convinced RENFE that it fulfilled its specification of comfortable 125 mph (200 km/h) operating capacity. As a result RENFE shelved its ambitious plan to lay a new 455 mile (730 km), 4 ft 8½ in (1,435 mm) gauge high-speed passenger railway from Madrid through Zaragoza and Barcelona to the French border at Port Bou and ordered almost 200 of the new Talgo cars, mostly day coaches but some of them sleepers. With trains of this new lightweight Talgo type and with the aid of some curve realignment to create the opportunities for sustained high speed, RENFE, for so long a decided back-marker in the European rail speed race because of its sinuous inter-city routes and

often indifferent track, would join the 125 mph (200 km/h) league in the 1980s (though initially it was limiting the new Talgo stock to a maximum of 110 mph (180 km/h).

Elsewhere Sweden's SJ, another national system handicapped by trunk route curvature but fighting against powerful internal air service as well as road competition for its inter-city passenger market, was on the brink of bulk-ordering tilt-body equipment at the start of the 1980s. Only lacking was Government authorization for the investment in vehicles derived technologically from a prototype electric multiple-unit, the X15, which SJ had produced in conjunction with the Swedish electric traction manufacturer, ASEA, and submitted to protracted tests. But the most powerful contenders for any emerging world market for proven tilt-body technology were likely to be the Canadian LRC and British APT, which both employ active systems.

The LRC – 'Light, Rapid, Comfortable', which in French is conveniently served by the same set of initials – was the private venture of a Canadian industrial consortium that is now built and marketed by the country's Bombardier group. Conceived as a superior response to the need of higher inter-city speed on the existing tracks of Canada's eastern inter-city corridors, where the Turbotrains had failed to operate reliably, the LRC is not a semi-permanent train-set but a flexible match of a low-slung 100 ton, 3,700 hp diesel locomotive (without body-tilting) and independent passenger cars. Its planned top speed is 125 mph (200 km/h). Its first major customer is Canada's Federally financed long-haul passenger operator, VIA Rail, which is taking twenty-one power cars and fifty trailers.

BR's HIGH-SPEED TRAIN AND ADVANCED PASSENGER TRAIN

The most radical of all tilt-body train designs to date is unquestionably British Rail's Advanced Passenger Train (APT). The extent of the concept's innovatory content is one reason for a long, chequered history of translation from drawing-board to public service – but only one among many reasons running the gamut from a succession of technical reappraisals through industrial action to scarce investment resources. Born in 1967 of the most fundamental research ever conducted into the interaction of flanged wheel and rail, and of the grim acceptance that the expense of driving a new purpose-built Shinkansen-type infrastructure through urbanized Britain could never be justified, the APT did not carry a revenue-earning passenger until late 1981.

As recorded earlier, the prototype APT-E unit – which was purely a test set never used in public service – was abortively gas turbine-powered, but it served to probe successfully the APT's design for a top speed of 155 mph (250 km/h) on the straight and an ability to negotiate curvature up to 40 per cent faster than orthodox rail vehicles without passenger discomfort. Besides automatic body-tilting, its handling of curves was also determined by a scientific design of self-steering running gear that adjusted itself easily to track irregularities and minimized wear when curves were taken at enhanced speed.

Pending the debut of the APT, much of its new engineering was applied to a final essay in orthodox inter-city equipment in the High-Speed (Diesel) Train, or HST. A push-pull unit, with a pair of streamlined 2,250 hp diesel locomotives enclosing seven or eight of BR's 75 ft (22.9 m) Mk III coaches, the HST moved from draft in 1970, via lengthy testing of a prototype, to

THE ADVANCED PASSENGER TRAIN

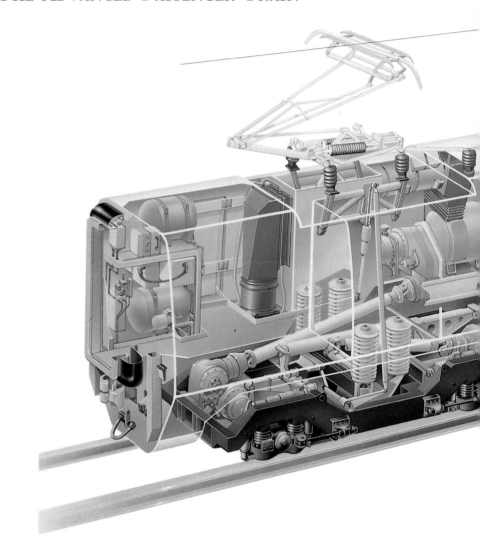

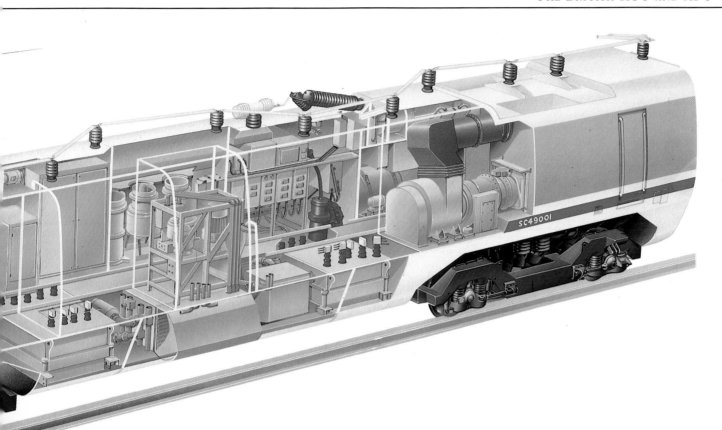

The Advanced Passenger Train that first went into service at the end of 1981 (the APT-P) is powered from the middle, instead of from the customary front. Although one power car is generally sufficient for a maximum speed of 125 mph (200 km/h) for a twelve-carriage set, two are necessary for higher speeds and greater adhesion, but British Rail did not want to link them by a power line running through the train. However, the final form of the train (the APT-S) may well have power cars at either end.

Built of steel with two two-axle bogies each power car has a 4,000 hp rating. The APT-P carries two braking systems – a traditional shoe brake for speeds below 30 mph (50 km/h), and a revolutionary hydrokinetic brake which is located within the power car and which brakes the axles through long shafts. Pantographs have been specially designed not to tilt on curves and lose contact.

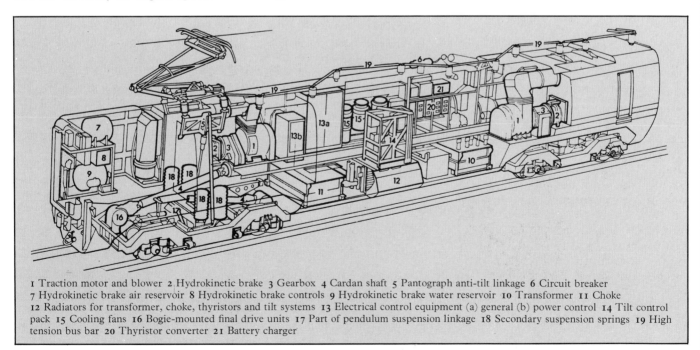

1 Traction motor and blower 2 Hydrokinetic brake 3 Gearbox 4 Cardan shaft 5 Pantograph anti-tilt linkage 6 Circuit breaker 7 Hydrokinetic brake air reservoir 8 Hydrokinetic brake controls 9 Hydrokinetic brake water reservoir 10 Transformer 11 Choke 12 Radiators for transformer, choke, thyristors and tilt systems 13 Electrical control equipment (a) general (b) power control 14 Tilt control pack 15 Cooling fans 16 Bogie-mounted final drive units 17 Part of pendulum suspension linkage 18 Secondary suspension springs 19 High tension bus bar 20 Thyristor converter 21 Battery charger

public service in October 1976. This debut was on the main line from London Paddington to Bristol and South Wales, its first stretch being over Brunel's superbly aligned route. In that environment the rapid acceleration and 125 mph (200 km/h) top speed of the HSTs immediately enabled BR to establish the 'Inter-City 125' operation, as the service was branded, on a level of speed and frequency excelled only by Japan's Shinkansen, with over eighty trains daily, timed start-to-stop at average speeds of 90 to 101 mph (145–163 km/h). In 1979 more HSTs were inaugurated on the trunk route from London to Yorkshire and Scotland, where modernization had fettled up long stretches of track for continuous high speed. Edinburgh, 392.8 miles (632.2 km) away, was brought within 4 hours 37 minutes'

journey time of King's Cross by the 'Flying Scotsman', Newcastle, 268.3 miles (431.8 km), within 2 hours 55 minutes, while a start-to-stop timing which demanded an average of 106.5 mph (171.4 km/h) was for a while tabled for two HSTs daily over the 48.8 miles (78.5 km) between the outer London railhead of Stevenage and Peterborough. Both Inter-City 125 services were to demonstrate the sharp commercial effect of higher speed and regular-interval frequency: between King's Cross and the West Riding, for instance, they quickly recorded a 13 per cent growth in passenger traffic.

On their inaugural London–Bristol and London–Newcastle routes the HSTs enjoyed the best operating conditions for orthodox train-sets with high-speed potential that was obtainable in Britain.

Although BR was debarred by Government curbs on investment from building sufficient train-sets to transmute the entire inter-city service out of King's Cross to HST working, enough were available on both routes to standardize the timetabling of a whole sequence of trains at critical periods. On each route either the four tracks existing for a considerable way out of London or the availability of alternative routes kept slower-moving freight out of the HSTs' way. Finally the incidence of curvature was, by British standards, negligible and gradients insignificant. All this was conducive to sustained 100–125 mph (160–200 km/h) running most of the way.

However, when the third squadron of HSTs was drafted to the London–Plymouth–Penzance route, primarily

to standardize BR Western Region's inter-city equipment in the London–Bristol–Plymouth area, the persistent curvature of the line west of Reading and the incomplete modernization of its signalling (another consequence of straitened investment circumstances) limited them to 90mph (145km/h) at most for all but 36 miles (58km) of their itinerary. The cuts in overall journey times were nowhere near as dramatic as those the HSTs had achieved at first. The Government, therefore, sharply queried the sense of further investment in HSTs which, besides costing about £2¼ millions to build, were more expensive to maintain than the train-sets they superseded. So by 1981, although the HST had earlier been billed as BR's standard inter-city equipment of the 1980s pending perfection of the APT,

the end of the HST production line was in sight. The future of BR's inter-city speed progress was to hinge chiefly on the APT, the only hope of securing schedule improvements on the remainder of the network striking enough to warrant investment in new equipment.

But at that stage BR had only three pre-production APT units, designated APT-P. Following the eclipse of the gas turbine as a traction medium, re-design of the APT for electric traction had been slow and intricate, once more bedevilled by Government lethargy when it came to investment in hardware. Furthermore, full satisfaction with the tilt mechanism's performance took much longer to achieve than anticipated. To be fair to BR's engineers, however, one must emphasize that the APT has been set the toughest

specification of any tilt-body equipment to date. Other versions have been designed for maximum speeds in excess of 100mph (160km/h) but so far none has been ordered for daily services demanding end-to-end averages of 100mph and more. This is the requirement for APT in BR service, as well as a reliable and an immaculately comfortable performance. In the final BR version this has been safeguarded by fitting the sensors which motivate the tilt mechanisms to the leading bogie of the car ahead of the one in which the mechanism responds, so that tilting is

British Rail's HST 'Inter-City 125' – the London Newcastle express near Durham and (inset) the interior of a second-class MkIII coach, the type used on the HST.

appetite for current of a number of 8,000 hp traction units simultaneously on full bore in the same supply section. (The same problem was one influence on the SNCF's long restriction of 125 mph [200 km/h] operation on its Paris–Bordeaux route; when a pair of dual-class *rapides* was eventually timed at the same pace in 1980–81 they had to be formed of fewer cars than the rest of the line's 'Corail' services, not because the 8,000 hp Class CC6500 locomotives'

Left and below: Interior and exterior of the world-beating TGV. Like the Japanese, the French have built a completely new line for their high-speed service from Paris to Lyon.

power might be outstripped but to restrain their demand for current.) Second, BR's desperate shortage of investment resources had dashed any hope of installing the continuous cab signalling system that was a prerequisite for regular working at 150 mph. A final deterrent was the extra cost of the traction current itself – a cost which could not be commercially justified in view of the comparatively small cut in journey times the higher speed would secure. So at the start the APTs would be limited to 125 mph (200 km/h), but later 130 mph (210 km/h) or just possibly 135 mph (215 km/h) might be feasible without extra expense. But even with the 125 mph ceiling, and despite the difficulties of contriving a clear path for only

still more finely graduated. Obviously this benefit is denied the leading car of a train-set, but in the final production version, the APT-S, that will not be a passenger-carrying vehicle.

The head-end car of an APT-P does carry passengers because the three units of this type were designed to the full original performance specification which called for 150 mph (240 km/h) capability. That demanded two 4,000 hp power cars to move twelve passenger-carrying cars. It was deemed desirable to couple the two power cars to each other because current collection is more efficient through a single pantograph and – unlike the French in their TGV train-sets – BR did not fancy carrying a 25 kV ac power line through the train between power cars at each end. But with power cars in the centre of the train-set, the two passenger-carrying sections of six cars were devoid of inter-communication, requiring each to be extravagantly supplied with its own catering cars and subjecting passengers to obligatory seat reservation in advance of travel. Consequently the end cars of each APT-P are unpowered driving trailers and have passenger space.

In the ultimate APT-S, however, a single power car will sandwich nine passenger trailers between itself and a driving trailer housing only luggage space and auxiliary equipment besides the control cab. The reduction in power results from recognition that in the foreseeable future the APT-S will never operate in public service at the full 150 mph (240 km/h). First, BR's existing traction current supply system would need costly enlargement of capacity to satisfy the

two APTs each way daily through a timetable otherwise served by trains limited to 100mph (160km/h) on the straight and lower speeds through curves, the inaugural APTs could immediately cut 45 minutes from the previous best five-hour schedule of a locomotive-hauled, orthodox train over the 401.5 miles (646km) between London and Glasgow.

Sadly it would be 1985 at least before APTs became the standard form of inter-city travel even on one BR trunk route, from London Euston to north-west England and Glasgow. So much innovative detail had been packed into the APT that the Government balked at authorizing a series production line until the three APT-Ps had completed a year's reliable passenger-carrying service. The highly publicized malfunctions which humbled the APT-P's first week of public service in December 1981 were an unpromising augury. Shortly before this ill-starred debut, BR itself had reappraised the wisdom of staking so much of its inter-city future on the APT and launched a design study of a new high-power 125mph electric locomotive.

SNCF's *TRAIN À GRANDE VITESSE*

In enviable contrast, BR's French neighbours moved smoothly towards the unveiling of 160mph (260km/h) European rail travel in the autumn of 1981. The SNCF had followed West Germany's DB into the 125mph (200km/h) club in May 1967, but with a single train, the Paris–Toulouse 'Capitôle' over a 31 mile (50km) stretch near Orléans, specially equipped with an elaborate cab signalling and automatic speed control system. Experience persuaded the French that such expensive safety provision was unnecessary up to 125mph so in 1971 125mph was extended to a second route with much more modest signalling modification. This time the French picked their topographically most favourable route, the Paris–Bordeaux, perhaps the best-aligned main line in all Europe. Two-thirds of it were so free of curves or junctions that they could be passed for 125mph (200km/h) at little cost in track work. That permitted use of French

Railways' then new 8,000 hp CC6500 Co-Co electric locomotives to bring Bordeaux, 359.8 miles (579 km) distant, within 3 hours 50 minutes of Paris at an end-to-end average of 93.8 mph (151 km/h) by two new flyers, the 'Aquitaine' and 'Etendard', which were subsequently graded as TEEs.

For reasons already discussed, the SNCF was content to limit 125 mph (200 km/h) working to these three prestige trains for the rest of the 1970s, until imminent completion of an autoroute over the whole Paris–Bordeaux distance dictated the addition of a couple of 125 mph dual-class 'Corail' services. Long before then, however, the French had grasped their unique advantage in north-western Europe of a vast central area where major population centres were widely dispersed and contours for the most part gently spaced. There new railway-building would be vastly less expensive than in Japan's Tokaido belt, for example. So the SNCF stopped striving for much higher speed on existing infrastructure and won Government support for a concept of new lines, configured for the exclusive use of 160 mph (260 km/h) passenger trains, in the country's busiest corridors.

Foremost of the latter was the artery from Paris to Lyon which, with its offshoots to Marseille and the Riviera, to the cities of south-eastern France, the Alps, Switzerland and Italy, has to satisfy more than 40 per cent of the French passenger and freight movement demand. If the annual increase of its rail traffic in the 1960s and early 1970s continued, the old PLM main line from Paris to Lyon via Dijon would be choked before the century was out. So Paris–Lyon was the obvious course for the first of France's new high-speed railways, the TGV. A multi-faceted programme of research and development, both in laboratory and with experimental vehicles on the track, was conducted to perfect every detail of the project's fixed equipment and rolling stock before construction was started in December 1976.

Because the new railways are used only by standard passenger train-sets, their curvature is ideally canted to allow negotiation at the maximum speed without any discomfort to passengers, so that recourse to costly tilt-body devices is unnecessary; and given the high power/weight ratio and accelerative punch which designers can now build into a lightweight self-powered electric train-

set, the civil engineers can accept gradients as steep as 1 in 28½ without prejudicing the trains' speed. These considerations have thus allowed the TGV builders to follow the ground contours closely and keep their earthworks to a minimum. There is not a single tunnel in the 241 miles (388 km) of new track, the whole of which is safely negotiable at 160 mph (260 km/h).

The French have further avoided the costliest features of Japan's Shinkansen and West Germany's Neubaustrecken. The TGV trains use the existing main-line from Paris Gare de Lyon to the capital's outskirts and within the area of Lyon. But since the historic PLM Paris–Lyon route via Dijon remains to cater for intermediate traffic, the new railway avoids all towns *en route* and serves only two stations on the outskirts of industrial Le Creusot and Mâcon. Consequently no path for additional tracks had to be carved through urbanized areas. The new line was confined to the great rural and agricultural tracts of central France, so that it could be built at vastly less cost per mile than the Shinkansen. The SNCF has reported the total infrastructure cost to be just over £500 millions at 1980 money values.

The TGV is fully compatible with the rest of the SNCF, since it was a principal item of the specification that it must benefit not only the Paris–Lyon traffic but as many other French cities – and traffic with neighbouring countries – as possible. Thus all the TGV train-sets are dual-voltage, though on 1.5 kV dc they are on

only half their full power output – but still sufficient to keep their light weight moving at the maximum permitted speed on the routes beyond the new TGV route-mileage. To sustain an unbroken 160 mph (260 km/h) irrespective of gradients under the 25 kV ac of the new track, the total output of the six powered bogies in each ten-car, 360 ton train-set (two of the vehicles are power cars) is 8,570 hp, which represents a muscular power/weight ratio of 23.8 hp/ton. A few three-voltage sets have also been built for working into Switzerland. The new line has been engineered for a maximum of 300 km/h (185 mph), but for the present the SNCF considers 160 mph gives them the best marketing value in terms of traction current cost.

On the TGV as on Japan's Shinkansen there are no traditional lineside signals. Drivers are guided solely by a continuous driving-desk display of signal aspects, the latter automatically activated by coded, low-frequency currents passed through the running walls and decoded by apparatus on the train-sets. Self-driving is thus almost automatic. The sharply switchbacked character of the new railway's gradient profile demands constant adjustment of the power controls to sustain a steady 160 mph (260 km/h) without waste of energy. So to relieve the

A new programme of electrification has been under way in France since the mid-1970s.

driver of that responsibility and avoid distracting him from other concerns, not least the state of the road ahead, the train-sets are fitted with a device that automatically detects gradient changes and varies the current feed as necessary to hold the driver's selected speed.

The production TGV train-sets started to emerge in 1980 for running-in on the existing SNCF lines, in advance of inauguration of the southern 165 miles (265 km) of the new railway from one of its junctions with the Dijon route to the outskirts of Lyon in September 1981. At that juncture eighteen trains each way daily (two of them running to and from Geneva) were routed over the completed section, where they began their running at the full 160 mph; eight were non-stop between Paris and Lyon in 2 hours 50 minutes, already 56 minutes less than the quickest non-stop train by the Dijon route, the 'Lyonnais'. But with commissioning of the whole of the new route in October 1983 and launch of the full planned service of twenty-five daily trains each way, the Paris–Lyon time would be clipped to a flat two hours for the 265.5 miles (427.3 km), which represents an un-precedented inter-city rail speed average of 132.3 mph (212.9 km/h) from start to stop. TGV journeys from Paris continuing beyond the new line to cities like Grenoble, Marseille and Geneva would be anything from one to two hours faster. French Railways preceded the September 1981 inauguration of the new line's public service by running one of its train-sets up to a new world speed record of 236 mph (380 km/h) on February 26 that year.

This increasingly rapid rise in practic-able rail speed needs to be seen in perspective. It took roughly a hundred years from the dawn of railways to achieve average journey speeds of 60 mph (100 km/h). In 1933, for instance, the fastest European end-to-end schedule over a run of more than 100 miles (160 km) required an overall average of 59.7 mph (96 km/h), between Berlin and Hamburg. But it took only fifty years more to make over twice that speed a daily commonplace on the French TGV. Not only does the French TGV's pace leave Paris–Lyon autoroute motoring far behind, but it will also clip airline wings. Even French domestic airline managers have glumly conceded that as much as 75 per cent of their Paris–Lyon traffic will probably be swept out of the sky in 1983.

THE CONSEQUENCES OF THE ENERGY CRISIS AND ELECTRIFICATION

The far-reaching scope which new methods and technology were opening up for the redeveloping railways as an economical and market-oriented bulk carrier was already patent when the 1973 oil crisis broke. Sudden confrontation with the reality that the industrialized world could be starved of oil whenever OPEC felt politically outraged was just as traumatic as the stratospheric climb in the price of oil or the first global compulsion to recognize that oil resources were finite.

The effects on the world's railways which the oil crisis had were numerous, but combined they were to have a major impact in the reviews of transport structure by governments now determined to channel resources into the mode of transport that used energy most economi-cally. A joint BR/Department of Trans-port study, for example, published in 1980, estimated that at 1980 prices electrification of 13,610 (21,776 km) of BR's 21,892 (35,027 km) single-track miles, bringing 83 per cent of its passenger and 68 per cent of its freight traffic under wires, would save £165 millions in fuel costs alone at the scheme's completion. The crisis provided railways with two benefits. Firstly, the comparative costs of motor transport gave the railways a tariff advantage, which commitment to electrification would even

In Spain, where electrification is also proceeding rapidly, the latest Talgo designs incorporate body-tilting.

further enhance; and secondly, the new-born public concern for energy conserv-ation recognized the cost-efficiency of railways and established them more favourably within the transport policies of their governments and within the sym-pathies of their users. The principal initiative, however, was to trim fuel costs.

The first of many to decide that the crisis demanded an abrupt change of heart on national investment in railways were the Spanish. This was not surprising, con-sidering that Spain's proportion of primary energy consumed in transport was the highest of any country in Europe, running at 27 per cent compared with 14.7 per cent elsewhere. As much as 78 per cent of it was accounted for by road transport because decades of sparing investment in railways had not effectively modernized the national railway system's tortuous, ill-equipped and frequently single-line trunk routes or their traction and rolling stock.

Within a year of the 1973 Arab-Israeli war the Spanish Government had decided to finance a rail electrification plan that by 1980 had doubled the route-mileage of RENFE under wires to 5,000 miles (8,000 km). This figure embraced almost all RENFE's trunk routes and had almost two-thirds of the railway's freight entrusted to electric traction. Then at the end of the 1970s the Spanish Government endorsed a fresh investment programme on an even grander scale. Besides backing the extension of catenary to almost 1,700 more route-miles (2,740 km) of track, some of it new line to double-track trunk routes, the Government approved expenditure on heavy civil engineering to raise speed limits, the expansion of numerous suburban and inter-city passenger services, and the purchase of substantial new fleets of locomotives and vehicles to meet the augmented demand and update existing services. At the same time the financial structure of RENFE was comprehensively revised to make the railway's socially necessary services a clear Government charge and leave the railway management with a financial framework for profit-centred market-pricing of its potentially commercial activities. A White Paper of 1980 affirmed the increasingly important role foreseen for RENFE in the national economy. For its part, RENFE management stepped into the 1980s with a published objective of quadrupling its freight traffic and raising its passenger business from 16.6 billion to 40 billion passenger-kilometres by the end of the century.

Earlier chapters of this book have recounted West Germany's reaction in 1978 to the DB's financial crisis in the light of environmental and energy concerns. Not only were closure proposals dismissed but investment in railways was significantly increased; in 1979, in fact, the Bonn Government issued a transport budget for the 1980s which envisaged enlarging the DB's share of investment funds from 16½ to 29 per cent and a concomitant cut of the roads' allocation from 53 to 42 per cent. Objections that this was pouring good money after bad were firmly rejected; the Government was convinced that the outlook demanded a streamlining of DB with new, well-aligned routes, competitive methods such as inter-modal freight techniques, and the whole gamut of electronics technology to maximize its commercial capacity as quickly as physical rather than financial resources would permit.

To many the most striking volte-face in the industrialized democracies was the USA's. Previously apt to regard State-supported railway systems as the next step to socialist perdition after a national health

service, the USA disbursed over \$11¼ billions of Federal money to its main-line rail services in the 1970s, much of it to fund Amtrak and Conrail, the rest in grants for improvements or the overhaul of maintenance arrears. And a further \$1.6 billions had been shelled out to augment locally raised money for urban rapid rail transit schemes. Equally remarkable was individual Americans' rediscovery of the long-haul as well as the metropolitan passenger train. Even in the most auto-oriented state of all, California, the public

accepted a modest addition to their petrol tax to create money for rail passenger service development. 'People like trains', California's Transportation Director, the enthusiastic Ms Adriana Gianturco, told a US railroad trade magazine in 1979. 'They ride them. They want them. We've tapped a popular emotion.'

That was patent in the 1970s turnround of Amtrak's fortunes. The national passenger train operator's appetite for both operating and investment dollars had outrun Washington's expectation by a

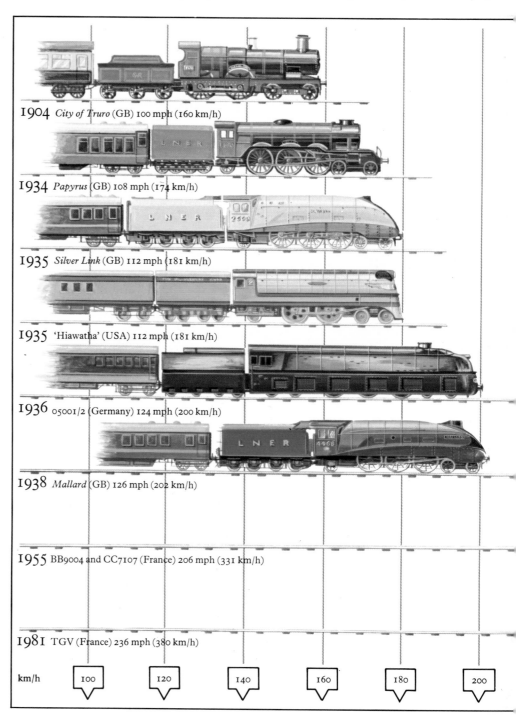

1904 *City of Truro* (GB) 100 mph (160 km/h)

1934 *Papyrus* (GB) 108 mph (174 km/h)

1935 *Silver Link* (GB) 112 mph (181 km/h)

1935 *'Hiawatha'* (USA) 112 mph (181 km/h)

1936 05001/2 (Germany) 124 mph (200 km/h)

1938 *Mallard* (GB) 126 mph (202 km/h)

1955 BB9004 and CC7107 (France) 206 mph (331 km/h)

1981 TGV (France) 236 mph (380 km/h)

km/h   100   120   140   160   180   200

wider margin from year to year, so much so that by the later 1970s each Amtrak traveller was costing taxpayers an average $40 more than the price of his ticket. Obvious causes were inflation and the explosion of oil prices, but another key factor was the increasing fallibility of Amtrak's outdated passenger cars, inherited from the streamliners, and the mounting cost of keeping even a proportion operational.

Sensing Amtrak to be an easy and little-lamented sacrifice to its aim of a balanced Federal budget, the Carter administration, badly in need of convincing victims for credibility, asked Congress in late 1978 for a 43 per cent butchery of the Amtrak route-system, a cut of a third in its annual train-mileage, major fare increases and elimination of numerous sleeping and full dining-car services. But early in 1979 the Iranian revolution abruptly cut the USA short of oil. Congress deliberated the White House proposals to an accompaniment of howls from their constituents snarled in gas station queues or unable even to get a phone call to Amtrak, its switch-boards jammed by enquiries for space and many of its trains already booked solid for as much as a month ahead.

Unsurprisingly, Congress eventually accepted only abandonment of Amtrak's most thinly patronized routes, and they amounted to 17 rather than 43 per cent of the system. Much less expected was Congress's substantial uplift of Amtrak's operating subsidy, its near-doubling of Amtrak's capital investment allowance, and its offer of a considerably higher

THE RECORD BREAKERS

World-beating speeds have been achieved over short distances by locomotives pulling specially pared-down sets in speed trials. When both CC7107 and BB9004 broke the existing record in 1955 they were pulling only three lightweight, streamlined coaches.

Mallard's 126 mph (202 km/h) remains the fastest speed achieved by a steam train. This speed was, however, passed by a German diesel running at 133 mph (214 km/h) in 1939. The world record diesel speed is now 143 mph (230 km/h), set by a British High Speed Train in 1973, but diesel does not achieve the speeds of modern electric traction. Experimental magnetic-levitation hover-trains have gone even faster, registering speeds in excess of 500 mph (800 km/h).

Mallard *in April 1963, her last month in service.*

A German Class 05 locomotive.

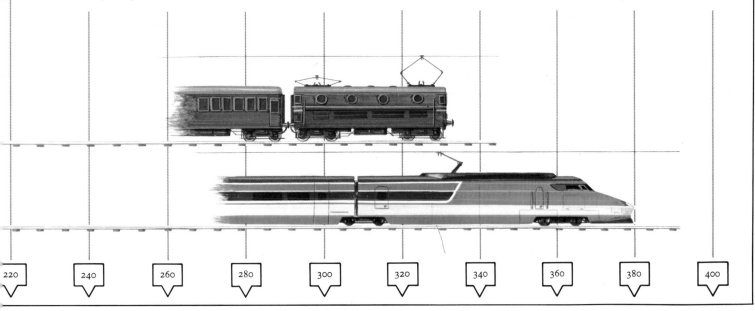

proportion of Federal start-up money to states agreeing to subsidize new routes under the Section 403(b) provision of Amtrak's founding act. Not only that, but Congress was further spurred by two of its more influential members into a request for Amtrak and the Federal Railroad Administration (FRA) to evaluate and rank those inter-city corridors, other than the North-East's between Boston and Washington, which might best repay intensified investment in rail passenger service.

By then eight states were making good the operating losses on thirteen '403(b)' routes producing 6.5 per cent of Amtrak's traffic, which in August 1980 notched up a new monthly passenger record of almost 2.2 million on all its trains (on the transcontinental Chicago–Seattle 'Empire Builder', newly equipped with Amtrak's bi-level 'Superliner' cars, busi-

ness was double that of the previous August). Some of the eight states already in the state-supported passenger train business, plus others new to it, were queuing with applications for a total of twenty-four more '403(b)' services in 1980, but Amtrak lacked the locomotives and cars to satisfy them. However, Connecticut was to show the way by buying thirteen new Budd SPV2000 diesel railcars for Amtrak to operate on '403(b)' services in the Springfield–Hartford–New Haven corridor of New England. But California was the most impressive showcase for the '403(b)' concept; there, state support by mid-1981 had helped to swell the daily trains between Los Angeles and San Diego to eight each way.

A much more serious attack on Amtrak was mounted by President Reagan as soon as he had taken power. His first budget proposed an immediate cut of more than a

third in Amtrak's subsidy and a tapering off of a further third of Amtrak's financial support by 1986. This would almost certainly have cut off all Amtrak services bar the North-East Corridor, either by forcing a massive increase of fares that would have driven away passengers or by depriving Amtrak of enough cash to sustain its operations. But yet again the White House was forced to give ground. Although Congress did agree to trim Amtrak's 1982 funding by about a quarter and to vary the '403(b)' terms of Federal support, it safeguarded 90 per cent of the existing Amtrak network for the immediate future, although the White House quickly made it clear that it took this only as one lost battle, not a lost war.

Another mark of energy concern was the serious prospect in 1981 – at last – of trunk route electrification on the grand scale in the USA. Inevitably, the energy crisis

Above: The Budd SPV2000 diesel railcar, thirteen of which have been bought by Connecticut for Amtrak to operate on '403(b)' services in New England.
Left: An EC60CP electric locomotive on Amtrak's North-East Corridor route between Boston and Washington.

spawned a shoal of claims for the superior energy-efficiency of an electrified railway, some of them more dogmatic than scientific. But the supremacy of electric power in a number of bulk transport roles has been irrefutably proved by both impartial analysis and practical experience. A French Transport Ministry study, for instance, (see below right) came up with comparative figures of fuel consumption, measured in petroleum gramme-weight, for different forms of passenger transport in alternative conditions of full and average loading (the latter was assumed to be 44 per cent for an express passenger train, 65 per cent for an airliner, and one or two persons in a private car in town and on a motorway respectively).

Two comparisons in this tabulation were enlightening. One was the superior efficiency of a TGV to a conventional inter-city train, notwithstanding the former's 160mph (260 km/h) as against the latter's maximum of 100mph (160 km/h) – a testimony to the efficacy of lightweight, aerodynamic construction but much more to the benefits of a railway purpose-built for optimal operation by standard train-

sets. The other was the marginal difference between a bus and a Metro in an urban situation, suggesting that on a purely energy count railways had the advantage only where a substantial off-peak passenger patronage was guaranteed. US analyses tended to confirm this appreciation.

The energy issue aside, electrification was more economically appealing by the year to trunk railway operators because diesel traction technology had few options left to continue the considerable reduction of power/weight ratios that its scientists had managed between the late 1930s and 1960s. The latest designs of the 1970s featured engine modifications which increased thermal efficiency, thereby

cutting fuel consumption, and more sophisticated fault-detection systems that simplified maintenance and cut its cost. But there was no fully proven engine development offering a reliable and not overweight power unit with an output in excess of 4,000hp.

The latest single-engined diesel-electric locomotives at the start of the 1980s, General Motors' four-axle GP50 and six-axle SD50 for US railroads and British Rail's Class 56 and promised Class 58, were not rated higher than 3,500hp, but in both cases for a total weight of well over 100 tons. Simultaneously, however, the Austrian firm of Simmering-Graz-Pauker was building for the Austrian Federal Railway four-axle Class 1044 electric locomotives with a peak output of 7,250hp for significantly less than 100 tons total weight, while the six-axle 8,000hp German Federal Class 103 electric was no heavier than 106 tons. The only draft of an equivalently diesel-powered locomotive in circulation at the time, the speculative prospectus of the French manufacturers Alsthom-Atlantique for a 7,200hp machine incorporating a single eighteen-cylinder engine yet to be tested in rail traction, envisaged a goliath of 201 tons total weight which would necessitate two four-axle bogies to spread the load. This design was drawn up for potential export to the broad gauge of the Soviet Railways. A standard-gauge 6,400hp version of the same design, employing a sixteen-cylinder version of the same power plant, was not expected to come out at less than 178 tons.

In sharp contrast, electric traction technology was still progressing in step

COMPARATIVE FUEL CONSUMPTIONS (in petroleum gramme – weight)	Consumption per vehicle-km with average load factor	Consumption per seat-km with 100% load factor
Paris-Marseille Airbus	52	35
Paris-Marseille Airbus with high density seating	37	31
SNCF electric Paris-Lyon TGV at 160mph (260km/h)	17	11
SNCF supplementary-fare electric *rapide*	20	12
Ordinary express train	15	7
Large private car on motorway	50	20
Small private car on motorway	35	20
Bus	21	7
Paris Metro	23	5.3
Large private car in town	93	23
Small private car in town	67	17

with the apparently limitless possibilities of electronics. One such development was the application of thyristors (a form of transistor) to traction motor control. Initially, the thyristor proved costly and troublesome to apply – stray current interfered with lineside signalling and telecommunications cables – but they were eventually able to achieve an uninterrupted acceleration which was decidedly more efficient and economical of current than the traditional method of building up power by progressively switching out resistances and varying the interconnection of the motors. Thyristor control also made it simpler to utilize dynamic braking – when the current supply to the traction motors is cut off, the latter can be turned into dynamos that oppose momentum and decelerate the train. In this form of braking, the build-up of current is dissipated through resistances; in regenerative braking, however, it can be fed back into the supply line, but only if the current can then be absorbed by another traction unit. Demands on catenary are thus heavy, the main reason why this form of braking tends only to be used on mountain main-lines.

At the start of the 1980s the railway world was particularly intrigued by five prototype electric locomotives undergoing a protracted evaluation on the German Federal Railway. These Class 120 units, each with a continuous power rating of 7,500 hp for a total weight of only 79.6 tons, held promise of extraordinary versatility. Forecast to be as comfortably at home on 75 mph (120 km/h), 1500-ton freights as on 700-ton inter-city expresses making at least 100 mph (160 km/h) and possibly 125 mph (200 km/h), they could enable a main-line railway to cover its entire locomotive-hauled traffic, except possibly the heaviest mineral trains, with a single type.

Once again electronics have been the technological catalyst. In the case of the 120s they have provided the availability of compact apparatus able to transmute the single-phase 15 kV $16\frac{2}{3}$ Hz ac current of the catenary into a feed for three-phase motors. It is this which has been the foundation for the 120s' achievement of such striking power/weight ratio without loss of adhesion.

Alongside these traction refinements, moreover, the real costs of both building and running an electric railway have been reducing. Experience has evolved lighter

forms of catenary, which make use of cheaper metals for the conductor wire, and less elaborate lineside apparatus for the feed of current to the overhead supply. It has also proved the safety of tighter clearances between high-voltage ac wires and overhead structures – the need for rebuilding over-bridges before the installation of catenary has thus been minimized. And operators are still being surprised by the opportunities for further maintenance staff savings; the availability of electric traction for continuous work

allows fulfilment of a traffic specification with even fewer locomotives than thought feasible.

So from the mid-1970s onwards several major railways which seemed to have come to the end of economically practicable electrification abruptly remustered their electrification teams for a fresh programme. In France the SNCF set out to convert 2,500 route-miles (4,000 km) more before the century's end, so that whereas only 9 route-miles (15 km) had been newly electrified in 1976, the yearly pace had

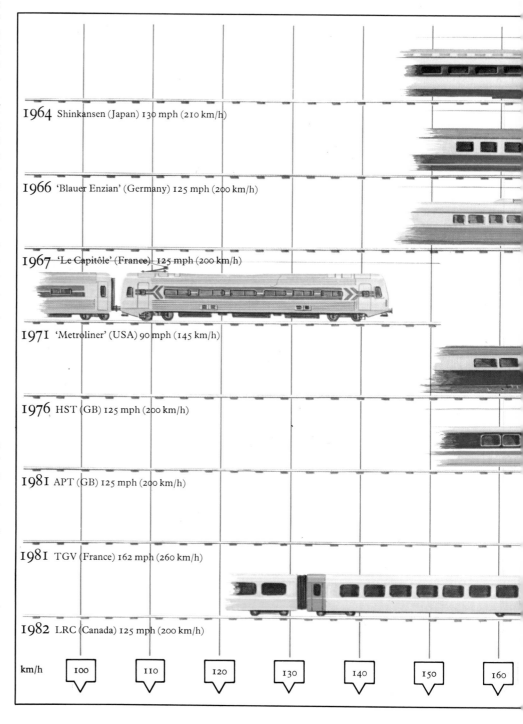

1964 Shinkansen (Japan) 130 mph (210 km/h)

1966 'Blauer Enzian' (Germany) 125 mph (200 km/h)

1967 'Le Capitôle' (France) 125 mph (200 km/h)

1971 'Metroliner' (USA) 90 mph (145 km/h)

1976 HST (GB) 125 mph (200 km/h)

1981 APT (GB) 125 mph (200 km/h)

1981 TGV (France) 162 mph (260 km/h)

1982 LRC (Canada) 125 mph (200 km/h)

km/h   100   110   120   130   140   150   160

stepped up to about 185 (300 km) by the 1980s. Besides putting important cross-country routes like Lyon–Tours–Nantes and Rouen–Amiens under wires, the plan would eventually convert the one remaining diesel-worked main line out of Paris, to Clermont Ferrand. From a national viewpoint this electrification had the additional benefit of lifting off-peak demand for electricity closer to the average output of France's nuclear power stations. Nuclear plant is less easily adjusted to fluctuating demand than conventionally fuelled generators, and France has, since 1973, been the world's front-runner in crash programmes of nuclear power station construction, to the extent that 55 per cent of its electricity was already nuclear-generated by the end of the 1970s. By then nuclear power was an emergent factor in the railway decision-making of other countries besides France. Even in Switzerland the limit of hydro-electric resources had been breached and by the end of the 1970s the Swiss Federal was already drawing 15 per cent of its traction current from nuclear stations (as against 9 per cent from oil-fired plant).

Similar energy-led electrification programmes have been further planned by railways of Europe. Spain, as we have seen, is a major example, and Italy has recently budgeted £5billions to enlarge rail capacity through electrification and an upgrading of subsidiary lines. Equally, the Belgians and Austrians have launched an electrification attack on their secondary routes. And Denmark, the only West European country to be so far shy of any

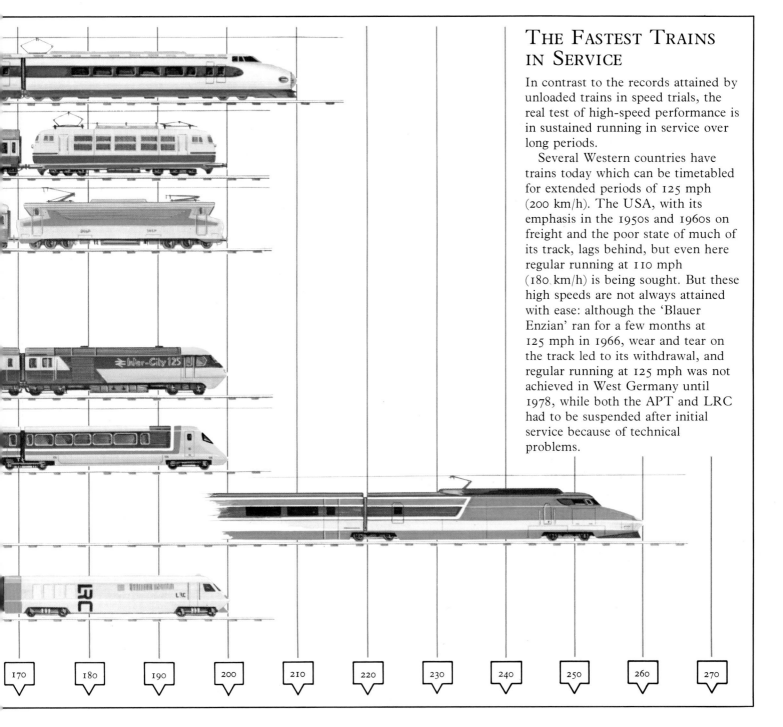

THE FASTEST TRAINS IN SERVICE

In contrast to the records attained by unloaded trains in speed trials, the real test of high-speed performance is in sustained running in service over long periods.

Several Western countries have trains today which can be timetabled for extended periods of 125 mph (200 km/h). The USA, with its emphasis in the 1950s and 1960s on freight and the poor state of much of its track, lags behind, but even here regular running at 110 mph (180 km/h) is being sought. But these high speeds are not always attained with ease: although the 'Blauer Enzian' ran for a few months at 125 mph in 1966, wear and tear on the track led to its withdrawal, and regular running at 125 mph was not achieved in West Germany until 1978, while both the APT and LRC had to be suspended after initial service because of technical problems.

170   180   190   200   210   220   230   240   250   260   270

Left: One of British Rail's latest diesel-electric locomotives, the Class 56, at the head of an MGR coal train. Weighing over 100 tons, it has half the output of some electric locomotives of the same weight or less.
Below left: The new DB Class 120 Bo-Bo electric locomotive has an output of 7,500hp for a weight of only 79.6 tons.
Right: A Soviet freight train on an electrified part of the Trans-Siberian railway.

of freight traffic thrust onto the railways in these countries.

Further east the Indians also dropped ideas of a transitionary diesel stage in the elimination of their residual steam power. At the beginning of the 1980s Indian Railways had 3,000 or so route-miles (5,000km) of electrified track, chiefly 25kV ac, which represented only 8 per cent of the system and bore no more than 25 per cent of all IR traffic. Those proportions would have to be increased if the national economy expanded – the railways were already moving two-thirds of the country's mechanically transported freight and private road haulage was anyway curbed by regulation on account of the inadequacy of India's roads. The prospects were that the Government, already committed to £1,750 millions of rail investment in its 1978–83 plan, would stump up more to permit an electrification rate of 300–350 miles (480–560km) annually, so as to have 60 per cent of all rail freight electrically powered by the end of the century.

The Chinese were gathering strength to electrify at a rate even faster than the USSR's. To the south of them the Australian Government decided in 1979 to back electrification of the key Sydney–Melbourne Interstate line; that was swiftly followed by main-line electrification commitments from the state administrations of Queensland and Western Australia, and by a similar decision in New Zealand.

With no more than 13 per cent of the world's railway route-mileage electrified and only 35 per cent of global rail tonnage electrically powered at the close of the 1970s, the main-line electrifiers would clearly be busy well into the twenty-first century. The intriguing question was whether they would at last be joined by the Americans. Thus far US railroads had been wedded to diesel traction, not only because it had become a staple of US

main-line electrification, has now voted to start conversion of its trunk system to 25kV 50Hz ac during the 1980s.

The most prolific electrifiers in the world, however, were the Soviet Railways, which were stringing up conductor wire at a rate of some 500 route-miles (800km) a year over track which included the new Trans-Siberian line. Other Eastern bloc countries were also desperate to step up their electrification pace but found themselves inhibited by the scarcity of capital resources. But the paramount concern to limit dependence on oil was epitomized by Poland, the world's fourth

largest coal producer, where the PKP was resigned to soldiering on with steam for 10 per cent of its traffic until the mid-1990s to avoid the purchase of more diesel traction. However, the PKP was one of the Eastern bloc's more energetic electrifiers, more than tripling its mileage of main-line catenary to cover 28 per cent of its network between 1965 and 1980. Hungary, which in 1965 had proclaimed an intention to add 700 (1,120km) to its previous 370 miles (576km) of electrified line, was still short of the objective in 1980. Behind the Iron Curtain electrification was more urgent in the 1970s and 1980s because of the weight railroading in the halycon era of cheap, plentiful oil, nor purely because of the daunting cost of putting up wires the length of US transcontinental routes, but also because the characteristic pattern of much US freight working – massive trains alternating direction over single line at infrequent intervals – did not exploit the economy of electric traction as well as the intensive operation of European trunk routes. But energy considerations outweighed that disadvantage to an increasing degree.

The crucial deterrent remained, however: no US railroad was generating enough cash – or could contemplate borrowing so much – to finance the first costs of electrification. Suddenly, in the autumn of 1980, the FRA revealed that it was drafting for discussion a $20 billion scheme to capitalize electrification of up to 25,000 route-miles (40,000 km) by the year 2010. The railroads would be asked only to buy their own traction and share resignalling and telecommunications costs, then to pay back the capital cost of the electrification itself in per-ton royalties on all traffic taking the converted routes. In effect, therefore, the railroads would rent the electrification. The four railroads which had previously been maintaining a continuously updated dossier on possible electrification – Southern, Union Pacific, Burlington Northern and Conrail – promptly expressed interest. But the scheme had been formulated in the twilight of the Carter administration (which had not formally endorsed it anyway). Whether President Reagan would smile on such Federal prodigality was another question as this chapter was written.

At the start of the 1980s British Rail's publicity machine proclaimed a new 'age of the train'. On its home ground that had a melancholy overtone of wish-fulfilment. Successive governments, the more recent ones wallowing in North Sea oil, had by comparison with neighbouring European administrations not only starved BR of investment funds but had steadily reduced upkeep support in real terms. As a result of this last parsimony, British Rail fares were substantially the dearest in Europe. But despite this deterrent, especially illogical when the rest of the world was increasingly concerned to discourage resort to personal transport, BR's Inter-City 125 services were nevertheless steadily increasing their business from year to year until the

recession hit rock-bottom in 1980. In 1979, in fact, BR recorded more passenger-mileage than it did at the start of the 1960s, when its systems had not been truncated under Beeching and its network was 30 per cent greater. Proof enough of a new age of the passenger train, at least.

As this chapter has shown, however, it is more specifically the age of the electric train. The French TGV is certain to prove that the electric train is not only much more energy efficient than a jet airliner, more comfortable and cheaper to run and ride, but its peer for speed, city centre to city centre, over all but transcontinental overland journeys. And North American experience demonstrates the same potential relation between train and road truck in the movement of merchandise by piggyback or container train, but in this case for all trips of more than 100–150 miles (160–240 km). If, as is quite probable, countries like the USA and Germany impose a reasonable share of its infrastructure costs on inland water transport, it will be no contest at all for bulk coal, mineral, chemical and oil transport. Important to remember, too, that the limits of electric rail traction's efficiency under any head are by no means established yet.

THE CHANNEL TUNNEL

A link between Britain and France has been a dream since it was suggested by Napoleon in 1802. Two schemes have been started and abandoned, the last as recently as 1975. But with modern engineering and interest in both countries the idea is alive again. Two proposals are for gigantic motorway bridges, which make for highly exciting engineering with giant spans, but their cost is enormous and the piers form a hazard to shipping. In contrast to the £3,245 millions (1981 prices) for a bridge, a single rail tunnel can be built for £800 millions. (Driver psychology and ventilation problems rule out a road tunnel.) British Rail anticipate an immediate 6 million passengers a year and a leap in its share of cross-Channel freight to 5.4 million tons annually from 885,600 tons. Passengers will be whisked from Paris to London without leaving the train in the same time as a centre-to-centre journey by air, the 31 miles in the tunnel taking only 35 minutes.

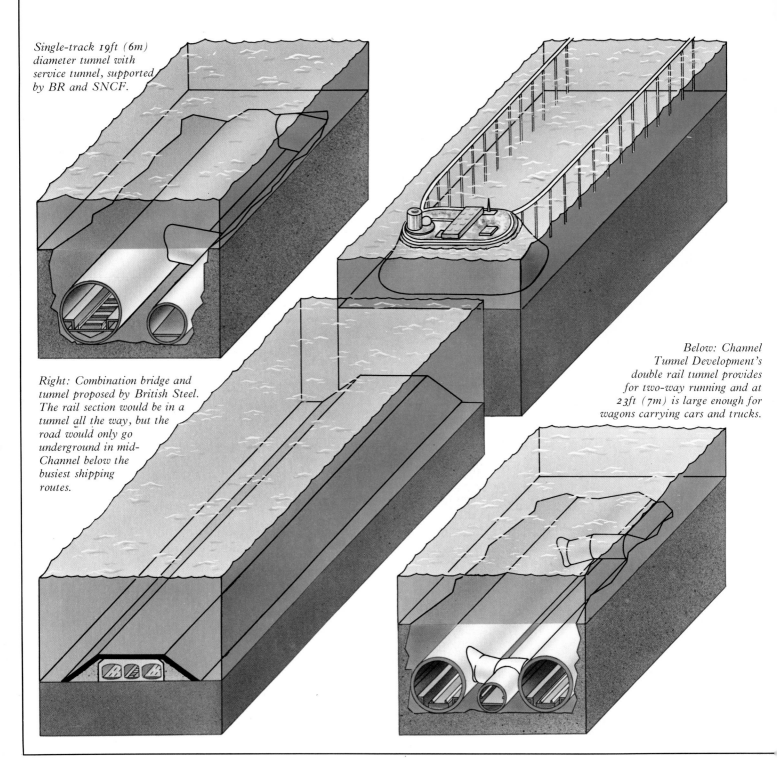

Single-track 19ft (6m) diameter tunnel with service tunnel, supported by BR and SNCF.

Right: Combination bridge and tunnel proposed by British Steel. The rail section would be in a tunnel all the way, but the road would only go underground in mid-Channel below the busiest shipping routes.

Below: Channel Tunnel Development's double rail tunnel provides for two-way running and at 23ft (7m) is large enough for wagons carrying cars and trucks.

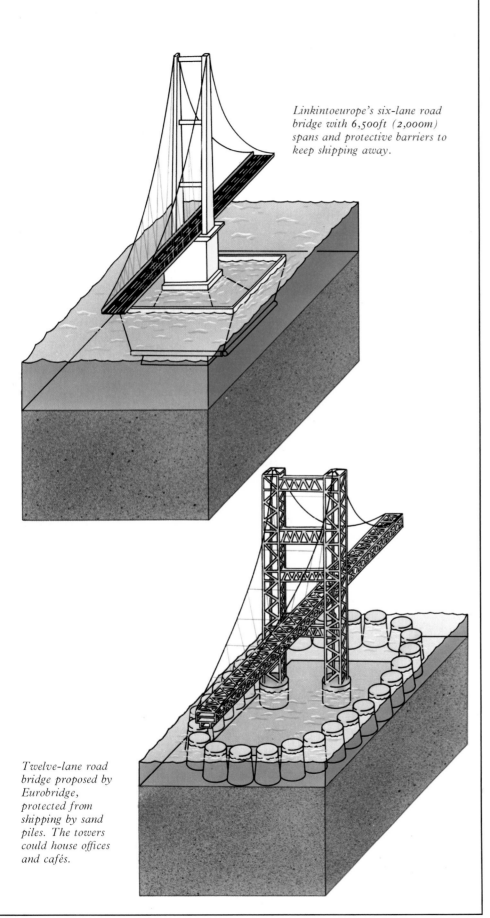

Linkintoeurope's six-lane road bridge with 6,500ft (2,000m) spans and protective barriers to keep shipping away.

Twelve-lane road bridge proposed by Eurobridge, protected from shipping by sand piles. The towers could house offices and cafés.

Even if oil were limitless and its price trailed instead of led inflation, two more factors would justify proclaiming a new age of the train. The world has become jealous of its environment. Even a diesel-powered 1,500-ton coal train creates far less pollution than the fifty juggernauts (seventy-five today in the UK) needed to shift its load by road. Just as important is the fifty juggernauts' need of more track space than the train to do the job. Ordinary citizens are more and more opposed to the surrender of their countryside to fresh ribbons of concrete, with its corollary of ugly service areas and consequent ribbon roadside development, when railway infrastructure that has been in place for a century has unused capacity – and fresh capacity to offer if electrified and properly operated. Railways can carry far more at competitive cost without any extra call on land space.

The other key factor in the railways' rediscovery is electronics. Because its trains run on fixed paths to a pre-planned and controlled discipline, the railway is the only transport mode able to maximize the potential of the micro-chip revolution. The fully automated metropolitan railway is already at hand. Full automation of all the interlocking functions of a national railway is much further away – not least because railwaymen cannot be discarded at the touch of a button – but the components of it are already operational, from automated signalling and train control to complex automated data processing systems that can within a few hours turn projected traffic inputs into an optimally efficient working plan for a hundred or more locomotives and their crews and thousands of wagons.

This is not, however, the new age of the train to the exclusion of other transport modes. It is also the inter-modal age. It is the age of the electrified COFC or TOFC trunk train married to local road haulage for distribution in the merchandise market. It is the age of the electric main-line passenger train that absorbs its rural passengers from precisely co-ordinated country bus services at convenient rail-heads. It is the age of the radial Metro that delivers its passenger comfortably to their cars or to buses at well-planned inter-changes for the last stage to their individual doorsteps. The railway must never again be corrupted from its prime role – a carrier of people and goods in bulk by the economic trainload.

BIBLIOGRAPHY

Allen, C.J. *Switzerland's Amazing Railways* London 1953

Allen, G.F. *Illustrated History of Railways in Britain* London 1979

Allen, G.F. *Luxury Trains of the World* London and New York 1979

Allen, G.F. *Modern Railways* London 1980

Allen, P.C. *On the Old Lines* London 1958

Allen, P.C. and Whitehouse, P.B. *Round the World on the Narrow Gauge* Shepperton 1966

Aubert, Marcel *Sur les Rails de France* Paris 1978

Bhandari, R.R. *Indian Railways* Delhi 1981

Bonavia, M.R. *The Organisation of British Railways* Shepperton 1971

Casserley, H.C. *Steam Locomotives of British Railways* Feltham 1973

Cookridge, E.H. *Orient Express* New York 1978

Cornwell, E.L. *Pictorial Story of Railways* London 1974

Cox, E.S. *Locomotive Panorama* (2 vols) Shepperton 1966

Croxton, A.H. *Railways of Rhodesia* Newton Abbot 1973

Dethier, Jean *All Stations* London 1981

Drummond, Dugald *Lectures on the Working of Locomotive Engines* London 1914

Durrant, A.E. *Garratt Locomotives of the World* Newton Abbot 1981

Ellis, C.H. *The Pictorial Encyclopedia of Railways* Feltham 1978; New York 1968

Ellis, C.H. *Railway Art* London and Boston 1977

Essex, R.J. and Jenkinson, D. *Locomotive Liveries of the LMS* Shepperton 1967

Fiennes, G.F. *I Tried to Run a Railway* Shepperton 1967

Garns, J.F. *Railways for All* London 1923

Haut, F.J.G. *The History of the Electric Locomotive* London 1969; San Diego 1980

Holland, D.F. *Steam Locomotives of South African Railways* (2 vols) Newton Abbot and North Pomfret 1975

Hollingsworth, J. B. *Atlas of Train Travel* London 1980

Hollingsworth, J. B. *Atlas of the World's Railways* New York 1980

Hughes, H. *Middle East Railways* London 1982

MacDermot, E.T. *History of the Great Western Railway* London 1927

Nock, O.S. (Ed.) *Encyclopedia of Railways* London 1977

Nock, O.S. *Railways Then and Now* London and New York 1975

Nock, O.S. (Gen. Ed.) *World Atlas of Railways* London and New York 1978

Semmens, P.W.B. *Stockton and Darlington* London 1975

Singer, Allen (Ed.) *Railroads of North America* London 1978

Small, C.J. *Rails to the Setting Sun* Tokyo 1971

Small, C.S. *Far Wheels* London 1959

Westwood, John *Trains: The Complete Book of Trains and Railways* London 1979

Whitehouse, P.B. *Great Trains of North America* London 1974

Whitehouse, P.B. *Great Trains of the World* London 1975

Whitehouse, P.B. *The Last Parade* London 1977

Whitehouse, P. B. *On the Narrow Gauge* London 1964

MAGAZINES:
The Railway Magazine; *Modern Railways*; *Trains Illustrated*; *Railway World*; *Trains Magazine*; *La Vie du Rail*; *Rhodesian Railways Magazine*; *Journal of the Stephenson Locomotive Society*; *Cecil J. Allen papers*; *Railway Wonders of the World*

INDEX

Acknowledgments

Special diagrams and drawings were done by Industrial Art Studio/David Lewis Artists, except for those on pages 130–31, 136–7 and 138 by Peter Nicholls/David Lewis Artists and on pages 278–9 by John Weal.

Photographs were kindly provided by the following sources (these abbreviations used – (t) = top, (c) = centre, (b) = bottom, (l) = left, (r) = right):

G.F. Allen 48(b), 73(tl & tr), 76(l), 77, 100, 101, 102, 104(t), 113, 114, 115, 124(r), 125(tl & tr), 128, 129, 132, 134(b), 141, 142(b), 148(b), 149(t & b), 157(b), 158(b), 164(t), 164(c), 164–5, 165(t), 172(t), 175, 176 (t & b), 184(b), 185, 186–7, 188(t & b), 192(tr), 193, 229, 256(b), 267(c), 268, 276(b), 285; American Antiquarian Society 36; Amtrak 208, 288; Association of American Railroads 17, 62(t); Atchison, Topeka & Santa Fe Railway 63, 110(t), 149(b), 176–7, 189, 207(t), 240; R. Bastin 90–91, 167(t); BBC Hulton Picture Library 57(b), 75, 80(t), 81, 86, 89, 94, 97(b), 120(b), 152–3, 184(t); Belgian State Railways 38(t); Bettman Archive 122(c), 124(l); Boeing Vertol Company 267; Bombardier Inc. 277; Bridgeman Art Library 10, 14–15, 15(t), 24, 30–31, 43(t); British Rail 145, 202, 237, 248, 253, 270–71, 280, 292(t); Brussels Metro 261(b); Budd Co. 289; Bundesarchiv 187(tr), 287(r); Burlington Northern 157(t), 239; Camera Press 259(tr); Canadian Pacific Railway 65, 246–7; Castello Sforzesco 98; J-L. Charmet 78, 187(tl); Chicago Historical Society 58(c), 122(b); Colour-Rail 159; Colourviews Lib. 11(t), 13, 22, 25, 40, 41, 42, 45(t), 51, 64, 67, 68–9, 72–3, 74(t), 84(t), 92(t & b), 93(b), 97(t), 104(b), 105, 116, 117, 118–19, 121(b), 123, 142(tr), 160(t), 168, 169(t), 170–71, 171(t), 173, 196, 198, 203, 212, 215, 218, 221(tl), 241, 265(l); Richard Cooke 270–71; Coverdale and Colpitts Collection/K. Young 47(t); D. Cross 94–5, 143, 166, 182, 224(t); Culver Pictures 52–3; Denver Public Library 60(b), 62(br); Deutsche Bundesbahn 31(t), 224(b), 225(tl), 225(b), 236, 244, 245(b), 252(t & b), 264(t), 292(b); J. Dunn 213; M.W. Earley 164(t); EBT Bahn 156; Robert Estall 251, 274–5; Mary Evans Picture Library 12, 18, 19, 20, 21, 26, 27, 32, 37(t), 48(t), 71(t), 103, 126, 127, 135(b); Fox Photos 258(c); Freightliners Limited 246; C. Gammell 106–7; C. Garratt 179(t); GEC 235; Thomas Gilcrease Institute 59; Grumman Aerospace 273; V. Hand endpapers, 167(b), 169(b), 172(b), 178–9, 190–91, 233, 250; Hamburger Hochbahn 257(b); Hawker Siddeley Canada 263; Archivio IGDA 33; Illinois Central Gulf Railroad 54, 110–11; Italian State Railways 38(b), 80(t), 121(t), 160(b); Japanese National Railways 231(t); Japanese National Tourist Office 259(br); J. Jarvis 2–3, 158(t), 162–3, 192(tl), 206; C. Kapolka 256(t); H. Kawai 205; G.M. Kitchenside 142(tl); Krauss-Maffei 272; C. Lamming 47; A. Le Garsmeur 208, 249; Library of Congress 55, 57(t), 60(t), 87(b), 125(b); London Transport Authority 153(t), 161, 248, 260; Mansell Collection 37(b), 72(t), 140; L.G. Marshall 197; Mechanical Archive & Research Services 16, 28(t & b), 43(b), 122(t), 288; Metro-Cammell Ltd 255; Montreal Metro 258; National Library of Australia 84(b); National Railway Museum 9, 11(b), 23, 49, 50, 74(b), 120(t), 133(t & b), 134(t), 183; Netherlands State Railways 222–3, 264(b); Peter Newark's Western Americana 44, 56(t), 62(bl), 66, 111(t); New Zealand Government Railways 109; Novatrans Ltd 245(t); Novosti Press Agency 259(bl), 293; Österreichische Bibliothek, Bild-Archiv 29; Österreichische Bundesbahnen 220(t); Österreichische Galerie 70–71; Photri 265(r); Popperfoto 1, 82, 85, 186(t), 257(t), 258(bl); B. Reeves 150; Rex Features 259(tl); J. van Riemsdijk 39, 45(b), 47(b), 61, 76(r), 108, 144(t); D.A. Robinson 278; P. Robinson 7, 280–81; Ann Ronan Picture Library 144(b), 148(t); Scala 34–5; Science Museum 14(t); SNCF 188(t), 196, 217, 220–21, 221, 225(tr), 228, 261(t), 274, 282, 282–3, 284; South African Railways 251(t); Spectrum 232, 258(br); B. Stephenson 78–9, 99, 107(t), 154, 174, 218(b); Swedish State Railways 214; Swiss Federal Railways 200, 276(t); Swiss National Tourist Office 96; John Topham Picture Library 88; N. Trotter 287(l); Tyne & Wear Metro 269; Union Pacific Railroad 58(l), 180–81, 191(t), 194–5, 238–9; Roger Viollet 93(t); Dr J. Westwood 112; J. Winkley 139, 151, 201, 207(b), 209, 219, 223, 262, 275; WMATA/Paul Myatt 266(l & r), 267(t & b); K. Yoshitani 87(t), 204; ZEFA 230–31.